Critical Survey of Poetry

Beat Poets

Editor

Rosemary M. Canfield Reisman
Charleston Southern University

Salem Press
A Division of EBSCO Publishing, Ipswich, Massachusetts

Cover photo:
Allen Ginsberg (© Lynn Goldsmith/Corbis)

ISBN: 978-1-42983-647-0

CONTENTS

Contributors iv

Beat Poets 1

Paul Blackburn 9
Richard Brautigan 21
Charles Bukowski 27
Gregory Corso 42
Diane di Prima 51
Robert Duncan 61
William Everson 73
Lawrence Ferlinghetti 89
Jack Gilbert 101
Allen Ginsberg 106
Thom Gunn 123
Anselm Hollo 136
Bob Kaufman 146
Philip Larkin 152
Michael McClure 165
Charles Olson 172
Kenneth Patchen 183
Marie Ponsot 191
Kenneth Rexroth 199
Gary Snyder 207
Gilbert Sorrentino 226
Jack Spicer 232
Diane Wakoski 238
Philip Whalen 251

Checklist for Explicating a Poem 257
Bibliography 260
Guide to Online Resources 265
Geographical Index 269
Category Index 270
Subject Index 272

CONTRIBUTORS

John Alspaugh
Richmond, Virginia

Franz G. Blaha
University of Nebraska-Lincoln

David Bromige
Sonoma State University

Susan Butterworth
Salem State College

Ann M. Cameron
Indiana University, Kokomo

David A. Carpenter
Eastern Illinois University

Richard Collins
Xavier University of Louisiana

Desiree Dreeuws
Sunland, California

Thomas L. Erskine
Salisbury University

Jack Ewing
Boise, Idaho

Thomas C. Foster
University of Michigan-Flint

Morgan Gibson
Urbana, Illinois

Sarah Hilbert
Pasadena, California

Tracy Irons-Georges
Glendale, California

Maura Ives
Texas A&M University

Philip K. Jason
United States Naval Academy

Lesley Jenike
Columbus College of Art and Design

Mark A. Johnson
Central Missouri State University

Sheila Golburgh Johnson
Santa Barbara, California

Leslie Ellen Jones
Pasadena, California

Rebecca Kuzins
Pasadena, California

William T. Lawlor
University of Wisconsin-Stevens Point

Leon Lewis
Appalachian State University

C. Lynn Munro
Belton, Missouri

David Peck
Laguna Beach, California

Mark Rich
Cashton, Wisconsin

William Skaff
Baltimore, Maryland

Martha Modena Vertreace-Doody
Kennedy-King College

Donald E. Winters, Jr.
Minneapolis Community College

BEAT POETS

The label "beat" designates a group of writers and their friends and affiliates who met at Columbia University in New York and gained fame and notoriety in the period between 1944 and 1961 as the Beat generation. The meaning and origin of the word "beat" are subject to some debate, and explanations range from "downtrodden" and "weary of the world" to "beatific" and "angelic." However, there is general agreement that Jack Kerouac (1922-1969) first used the term in 1948 to characterize himself and a small group of friends: Allen Ginsberg (1926-1997), William Burroughs (1914-1997), Neal Cassady (1926-1968), and Herbert Huncke (1915-1996), with Cassady and Huncke serving mainly as early literary models and muses for their writer friends. A little later, Gregory Corso (1930-2001) joined them. Closely associated with this pioneering group were Lucien Carr (1925-2005), who introduced Kerouac, Ginsberg, and Burroughs to one another, and John Clellon Holmes (1926-1998), whose novel *Go* (1952) is the first semifactual chronicle of the early life of the Beats.

The name "Beat generation" was designed not only to signify the downtrodden, renegade position the young men were proud to hold in an increasingly conformist, status-conscious, and materialistic society but also to hint at their affinity to the lost generation, a similarly disaffected group of American writers in the period after World War I. Like many artists and intellectuals of their time, the early Beat poets were disillusioned because the end of Word War II had not led to a spiritual and cultural reawakening. On the contrary, the Cold War and its threat of nuclear annihilation loomed over the nation, part of the expansion of American capitalist influence in the world with the help of an ever-more-powerful military-industrial complex. The main goal of McCarthyism—a campaign to drive out communist sympathizers led by Senator Joseph McCarthy in the mid-1950's—was to enlist Americans in the struggle against communism, and its hostility was not limited to communism and its sympathizers but extended to all individualists and those who deviated from the white Protestant norm. Therefore, it should come as no surprise that U.S. senator Joseph McCarthy once branded the Beat generation as one of the greatest dangers in the United States.

The early Beat poets were confronted by the problem faced by all individualists in repressive societies, namely, how to maintain their autonomy and integrity as individuals against the overwhelming pressure to conform and to fit in. The answer was an open flouting of accepted social, sexual, and literary norms; the confrontation of a cold, mechanistic world with unabashed romanticism; and a return to traditional American forms of literary expression in reaction to the prevailing modernist poetry and the New Criticism that supported it. Most Beat poets agreed with the assessment of William Carlos Williams (1883-1963) that T. S. Eliot's *The Waste Land* (1922) had set back American poetry by twenty years; they fully intended to correct this misstep by writing spontaneous, open-form Dionysian poetry in defiance of the prevailing structured Apollonian poetry of the formalists.

The Beat poets therefore saw themselves not only as a literary movement but also as a counterculture movement in which the abandonment of the literary forms and structures of formalist poetry was the obvious external parallel to their rejection of the values of American mainstream culture. Rather than using political activism as an agent for change, which would have meant the sacrifice of their individualism to a collective, they chose to remain an open, interactive collection of individuals, united only by their opposition to prevailing social conditions within very widely varying parameters: the subjugation of form to content; the rejection of traditional Christianity for more mystical, meditative religions, such as Buddhism and Hinduism; an attraction to and identification with oppressed minorities; the belief in spontaneous, unrevised expression (first thought/best thought); and the liberation of preconscious truth from centuries of rational and social brainwashing, with the aid of meditation or hallucinogens. Only when this spiritual liberation of the individual had been achieved would meaningful social change be possible.

LITERARY ANTECEDENTS

Despite their carefully cultivated image as "holy barbarians," the Beat poets were well read, and their work is full of intertextual references to past and contemporary writers whom they saw as their literary ancestors. Most of those mentioned are writers who saw themselves as being in conflict with their mainstream cultures. Of particular importance to the Beat poets were the British Romantic poets Percy Bysshe Shelley(1792-1822) and especiallyWilliam Blake (1757-1827), whom Ginsberg claims to have seen and heard in hallucinatory visions in 1948 and whom he considered a powerful influence on his early poetry. Blake's "dark Satanic mills" surely served as an inspiration for Ginsberg's figure of Moloch in his masterpiece "Howl" (1955). The works of American Romantic poet Henry David Thoreau (1817-1862), with their anticonformist, antitechnological message, were among the favorite books of many Beat poets, and the free-verse prophetic poetry of Walt Whitman (1819-1892) clearly inspired Ginsberg's best poems, including "Howl."

Beat poetry also contains frequent references to the French Symbolist poets. Arthur Rimbaud (1854-1891), in particular, fascinated many of them with his wild Bacchantic poetry and his dissolute lifestyle, including his homosexuality, which frightened the bourgeoisie of his time.

Closer to their own era, Dadaism and Surrealism directly influenced the works of the Beat poets, since a number of them had direct contact with Dadaist and Surrealist poets. Kenneth Rexroth (1905-1982) and Lawrence Ferlinghetti (born 1919) translated their poetry; Ginsberg and Corso are said to have met Marcel Duchamp (1887-1968), and Ginsberg allegedly kissed Duchamp's shoe at the occasion. What attracted the Beats to all of these earlier poets was their flouting of social and literary convention, as well their shocking the timid and conventional bourgeoisie with their abrasive and often vulgar attacks on middle-class morality.

THE BEAT MOVES WEST

During the formative years of the Beat poets, roughly between 1945 and 1955, the literary establishment took no notice of them at all. Only Kerouac and Holmes managed to publish substantial works (*The Town and the City*, 1950, and *Go*, respectively), while Corso languished in jail and Burroughs moved first to Texas and from there to Algiers and Mexico, writing novels that would be published much later. During these years, the original New York Beat poets were discussing and exchanging books while traveling across the United States and abroad, gathering material for their future publications, and exchanging their works-in-progress in manuscript form and debating their merit heatedly in coffeehouses and jazz clubs. While the Beat poets toiled in almost complete obscurity during these years, nearly all the works that brought them fame and notoriety were completed before 1956, including Kerouac's novels *On the Road* (1957), *The Dharma Bums* (1958), *Visions of Cody* (1960, 1972), and *The Subterraneans* (1958), as well as his long, epic poem, *Mexico City Blues* (1959). During the same period, Ginsberg attracted the attention of the poet Williams. He sent some of his poems to Williams, who became Ginsberg's mentor. Despite all this creative activity, none of the New York Beat poets managed to break into the very exclusive and snobbish New York literary establishment, firmly controlled by the academic formalist poets, and it became apparent to Ginsberg that a change of scenery was necessary.

Following Kerouac, who did some of his best writing while living with Cassady and his wife in San Francisco, Ginsberg moved in with the Cassadys for a while but then took a job with a marketing firm in downtown San Francisco in 1954. Armed with a letter of introduction by Williams, he discovered an already vibrant bohemian literary community presided over by Rexroth and consisting of a group of poets who were trying to revive earlier open forms of poetry and who emphasized spoken poetry, often accompanied by jazz, over the printed form. As a bonus, James Laughlin, the publisher of *New Directions* magazine, gave them an outlet for their avant-garde poetry that had not been available to the Beat poets in New York, where their West Coast counterparts were known as eccentric provincials. It is this fortuitous meeting of the youthful, iconoclastic East Coast Beat poets with the more established so-called First San Francisco Renaissance that led to the genesis of Beat literature as it is presently defined; indeed, this melding of East Coast and West Coast avant-garde poetry is sometimes and confusingly called the Second San Francisco Poetry Renaissance, although the label Beat generation is the more frequently used term. The New York Beat poets were now supplemented by the likes of Ginsberg's lover and life partner Peter Orlovsky (born 1933), Gary Snyder (born 1930), Michael McClure (born 1932), Ferlinghetti, Philip Whalen (1923-2002), and Lew Welch (1926-1971), as well as former members of the now defunct Black Mountain College, such as Charles Olson (1910-1970) and Robert Creeley (1926-2005). Apart from confirming the New York Beat poets in their formal innovations—in the direction of open-verse forms, as well as toward spontaneity and spoken poetry—the West Coast Beats instilled in them a greater awareness of Native American and Latino cultures and reinforced their incipient interest in Asian mysticism and ecological themes.

FROM ANONYMITY TO FAME

The breakthrough for the Beat poets that eventually catapulted them to national fame occurred on October 7, 1955, at the Six Gallery in San Francisco at a poetry reading that has become an integral part of the Beat legend. The reading was suggested by McClure to Ginsberg, who at first refused, claiming that he had nothing to contribute; he changed his mind after composing the first part of "Howl." The participants in the reading represent an interesting cross-section of all the elements of Beat literature. Rexroth, the elder statesman of the first poetry renaissance, was the moderator and introduced the poets. His friend and cohort, Philip Lamantia (1927-2005), read not his own surrealistic poems but the work of a recently deceased friend, and three members of the younger West Coast generation read poems that illustrated their ecological and mystical contribution to Beat literature. McClure recited "Point Lobos Animism" and "For the Death of One Hundred Whales," both of which have been frequently anthologized; Snyder read "A Berry Feast"; and Whalen recited "Plus Ça Change." Also present was an increasingly intoxicated Kerouac, who refused to read his own work but cheered the other poets on; he recounts the event in his novel *The Dharma Bums*.

The crowning point of the evening, however, was Ginsberg's first reading of "Howl," which produced a sensation and almost single-handedly catapulted the Beat poets to fame. Ferlinghetti, who had opened City Lights Bookstore in 1953, had recently expanded it into a publishing venture and asked Ginsberg for permission to publish the poem in a famous telegram modeled after the one Ralph Waldo Emerson (1803-1882) sent to Whitman at the occasion of the first appearance of *Leaves of Grass* (1855), exactly one century before. Having read what are now parts 1 and 3 of the final version, Ginsberg quickly completed parts 2 and 4 ("Footnote to Howl"), and the complete work was published by Ferlinghetti as number four of the Pocket Poets series in 1956, after considerable revision. This slim volume, *Howl, and Other Poems*, remains in print more than fifty years later and is without question the most famous and enduring work of Beat poetry.

"Howl" is a very cleverly structured work, amazingly so, since it was written in a drug-assisted frenzy and under the influence of Kerouac's theory of spontaneous, unrevised composition. The first part presents a nightmarish vision of modern America, in which the speaker prophetically envisions "the best minds of my generation" marginalized and driven to desperate acts or landing in mental institutions for their "deviant" lifestyles. The second part identifies those elements in contemporary society that are responsible for this dire state of affairs: materialism, conformity, and mechanization leading to a cataclysm. The metaphor for these forces is Moloch, the biblical idol to whom the Canaanites sacrificed children. The speaker claims that the characters portrayed in part 1 have been sacrificed to this idol. Moloch is also the name of an industrial, demoniac figure in Fritz Lang's film *Metropolis* (1927), which Ginsberg acknowledges as a direct influence. Part 3 uses a specific person, Ginsberg's friend Carl Solomon, with whom he spent some time in a New York mental hospital, as an illustration for the pernicious influence of Moloch. The hellish vision of the first three parts is finally mitigated by part 4, the "Footnote to Howl," that ends the poem on a note of redemption by declaring that even this nightmarish work is part of a divine plan and therefore "holy."

THE GOLDEN AGE

News of the events at the Six Gallery reading quickly reached the East Coast, despite the fact that "Howl" did not appear in print until a year later. For the first time, the Eastern establishment showed some interest in the West Coast poets, and *The New York Times* sent Richard Eberhart, an establishment poet and academic, to write a report on the San Francisco Renaissance. In "West Coast Rhythms," published in *The New York Times Book Review* (September 2, 1956), Eberhart noted that with regard to the Beat poets, "Ambiguity is despised, irony is considered weakness, the poem as a system of connotations is thrown out in favor of long-line denotative statements. . . . Rhyme is outlawed. Whitman is the only god worthy of emulation." About Ginsberg, he wrote:

> The most remarkable poem of the young group is "Howl" . . . a howl against everything in our mechanistic civilization which kills the spirit. . . . It is Biblical in its repetitive grammatical build-up. . . . It lays bare the nerves of suffering and spiritual struggle. Its positive force and energy come from a redemptive quality of love, although it destructively catalogues evils of our time from physical deprivation to madness.

While this was a considerable step forward, most Eastern reviewers and critics remained scathing in their condemnation of the West Coast "barbarians." What really attracted the attention of the public to the Beat poets was a series of highly publicized obscenity trials, most notably the one involving Ginsberg's "Howl" in 1957. The judge's decision that "Howl," despite many objectionable passages, was not obscene because it had "some redeeming social importance" created a sensation and forever changed pornography laws and prosecutions in the United States. Ferlinghetti, whose City Lights Publishers was a codefendant in the trial, facetiously recommended a medal for the prosecutor, because more than ten thousand copies of the book were sold during and immediately after the trial.

The "Howl" trial made instant celebrities of Ginsberg and his friends, particularly as the attacks on them by the literary establishment intensified. The years from the reading of "Howl" in 1955 until 1961 can be considered the golden age of Beat poetry, with Beat poets suddenly finding publishing outlets for their hitherto unpublished work, being hounded by the media, and even finding themselves in demand with advertising agencies. Ginsberg traveled the country, giving readings of "Howl" to enthusiastic audiences, and Corso published the collections still considered his best: *The Vestal Lady on Brattle, and Other Poems* (1955), *Gasoline* (1958), and *The Happy Birthday of Death* (1960). In 1958, Diane di Prima (born 1934) published her first collection of poems, *This Kind of Bird Flies Backward*, starting a long and prolific career, and Ferlinghetti's *A Coney Island of the Mind*, which many consider his best collection, appeared in print. Finally, Kerouac, known to many readers only for his autobiographical novels, published his poetic masterpiece, *Mexico City Blues*. Most of his other poems were published posthumously, collated and edited by his friends, particularly Ginsberg.

Mexico City Blues is a long epic poem, composed of 242 cantos, whose content parallels that of Kerouac's fourteen autobiographical novels dealing with what has become known as the Duluoz legend. Although Kerouac's novels are written in prose and thus use some conventions of narrative prose, *Mexico City Blues* abandons any pretense of a plot line. Indeed, Kerouac repeatedly insisted that he was a poet who happened to write long lines that looked like prose. *Mexico City Blues* is difficult to read, particularly without having read his novels first; it deals to a large extent with Kerouac's internal struggles while turning from Catholicism to Buddhism and his search for the truth through meditation. Therefore, the poem is laced with references to religious dogma, in addition to the intertextual references to philosophical and literary works. The casual reader can still enjoy the poem by approaching it as a piece of improvisational jazz music, as the title would suggest, and concentrate more on the rhythm and the sounds than on traditional literary interpretation.

THE BEGINNING OF THE END

Paradoxically, the rise to fame and notoriety of the Beat poets was at the same time the beginning of their decline as a literary movement, though individual members of the group continued to publish work of high quality well into the next century. The literary establishment, which saw the Beat poets as threatening intruders in "their" carefully guarded territory, continued to savage and disparage them in academic journals and other publications. However, since comparatively few people ever read these pieces, they had little or no impact on the public. More devastating was a switch in tactics to ridicule and parody, since it was conducted in the mass media, particularly film and television.

On April 2, 1958, the word "beatnik" appeared for the first time, in an article in the *San Francisco Chronicle*, six months after the launch of the Russian satellite Sputnik.

By adding the Russian suffix *-nik* to the word "Beat," the effect, if not the intent, was to depict the Beats as communistic and unpatriotic. This article, together with two feature articles in *Life* magazine, helped create the cartoon character of the Beatnik—in opposition to the middle-class squares—that became a staple of films and television programs in the years to follow. These cartoon characters reduced the serious social and poetic concerns of the Beat poets to a set of superficial, silly externals that have survived to this day: berets, goatees, sunglasses, poetry readings, coffeehouses, slouches, and "cool, man, cool" slang, as popularized by Maynard G. Krebs, the television character played by Bob Denver in *The Many Loves of Dobie Gillis* (1959-1963).

Adding to the detrimental effect of the Beatnik parody was the increasing absorption of the Beat legend into American mainstream commercial culture, which resulted in the slow disintegration of the Beat poets as a group, precipitated by some highly publicized squabbles and jockeying for position. Rexroth felt slighted by the media attention received by Kerouac, Ginsberg, and Burroughs, and he wrote a series of scathing articles and reviews of Kerouac's work. Corso felt equally neglected and expressed his discontent in several interviews. Kerouac himself became more and more distraught by his inability to reconcile his self-created public image as peripatetic rebel and loner with his yearning for stability and status and began drinking heavily. His appearances on talk shows added to the parodistic image of the stoned, dissolute Beatnik.

THE BEAT GOES ON

After the golden age (1955-1961), there was a noticeable diaspora in the Beat community, during which the individual members began to pursue their own interests and careers, many of them in academic positions. This diaspora was preceded by a flourish of important publications of Beat poetry in 1961 and 1962. Snyder, who had joined a Buddhist monastery in 1956, published *Myths and Texts* (1960), which contains some of his best poems. Burroughs, after experimenting with his "cut-up" technique, published *Naked Lunch* and *The Ticket That Exploded* in 1962, the former leading to another famous obscenity trial a few years later. Ginsberg's other masterpiece, his long confessional poem "Kaddish," was published in *Kaddish, and Other Poems, 1958-1960* (1961). Most notably, however, a substantial number of Beat poems were included in Donald Allen's anthology *The New American Poetry: 1945-1960* (1961), the first time a mainstream collection had considered the Beat poets part of the canon. Further evidence for the increasing absorption of the Beat poets into the mainstream can be seen in the awarding of a Guggenheim Fellowship to Ginsberg in 1963-1964, Snyder's accepting a faculty position at the University of California, Berkeley, in 1964, and Scribner's publishing the first critical study of the movement, *The Beat Generation: The Tumultuous '50s Movement and Its Impact on Today* (1969), by Bruce Cook.

The death of the triumvirate of Beat poetry—Kerouac in 1969, Ginsberg and Burroughs in 1997—gave rise to new scholarly interest in the Beat poets and produced a flood of biographies, memoirs, and critical studies. A number of English departments at colleges and universities have courses on the Beat generation, and most of the major work and collections of the Beat poets are still in print. Critics and scholars agree that while the creative period of the Beat poets as an identifiable movement with common goals and aspirations was relatively short, its influence is still felt in the twenty-first century. The trend toward performance-oriented, spontaneous, open-form poetry continues unabated, notably in the popular poetry slam, and there is consensus that the Beat poets directly affected political and social progress in the areas of ecology, gay and lesbian rights, and drug legislation.

BIBLIOGRAPHY

Charters, Ann, ed. *The Beats: Literary Bohemians in Postwar America*. 2 vols. Detroit: Gale Group, 1983. Very comprehensive documentary volume on the most important Beat poets. Good introductions, samples of critical articles, and correspondence.

Hemmer, Kurt, ed. *Encyclopedia of Beat Literature*. New York: Facts On File, 2007. Contains hundreds of entries on all the major figures and great works of the Beat movement, by distinguished Beat scholars and friends of the Beat generation.

Theado, Matt, ed. *The Beats: A Documentary Volume*. Detroit: Gale Group, 2001. An invaluable reference work for scholars and students. Contains copies and facsimiles of letters, articles, and essays by major and minor Beat poets.

Tytell, John. *Naked Angels: The Lives and Literature of the Beat Generation*. New York: McGraw-Hill, 1976. One of the earliest histories of the Beat movement, thorough but maybe a little too uncritically adoring.

Waldman, Anne, ed. *The Beat Book: Poems and Fiction of the Beat Generation*. Boston: Shambhala, 1996. A good introductory anthology of Beat literature by a former member of the group. Valuable introduction and bibliographical material.

Watson, Steven, ed. *The Birth of the Beat Generation: Visionaries, Rebels, and Hipsters, 1944-1960*. New York: Pantheon, 1995. A very good study of the beginnings and the heyday of the movement, with excellent layout and great pictorial material, and supporting marginal text.

Franz G. Blaha

PAUL BLACKBURN

Born: St. Albans, Vermont; November 24, 1926
Died: Cortland, New York; September 13, 1971

PRINCIPAL POETRY

The Dissolving Fabric, 1955
Brooklyn-Manhattan Transit: A Bouquet for Flatbush, 1960
The Nets, 1961
Sing-Song, 1966
Sixteen Sloppy Haiku and a Lyric for Robert Reardon, 1966
The Cities, 1967
The Reardon Poems, 1967
In. On. Or About the Premises: Being a Small Book of Poems, 1968
Two New Poems, 1969
The Assassination of President McKinley, 1970
Gin: Four Journal Pieces, 1970
Three Dreams and an Old Poem, 1970
The Journals: Blue Mounds Entries, 1971
Early Selected Y Mas: Poems, 1949-1966, 1972
Halfway Down the Coast: Poems and Snapshots, 1975
The Journals, 1975 (Robert Kelly, editor)
By Ear, 1978
Against the Silences, 1980
The Selection of Heaven, 1980
The Collected Poems of Paul Blackburn, 1985

OTHER LITERARY FORMS

Paul Blackburn was an ambitious translator, not only of such modern Spanish-language writers as Federico García Lorca, Julio Cortázar, and Octavio Paz but also of the medieval troubadours, who had some influence on his own verse. Although his work in the Provençal poets was primarily finished by the late 1950's, Blackburn continued to revise his translations for the rest of his life. The substantial manuscript was eventually edited by his friend, the scholar of medieval literature George Economou, and published posthumously as *Proensa: An Anthology of Troubadour Poetry* (1978).

ACHIEVEMENTS

Appreciated as a translator, Paul Blackburn limited his reputation as a poet during his lifetime by publishing only a small portion of his poetry and then in very limited editions. His position in literary history can be appreciated through the inevitable comparison with Frank O'Hara. Both poets were born and graduated from college in the same years; both were celebrators of the city, primarily New York, in verse that revealed their awareness of centuries of literary history at the same time that they were pursuing some of the more radical modernist innovations in poetic structure and idiom; and both bodies of work reveal warm, generous, witty sensibilities; unfortunately, both poets also died young. Blackburn and O'Hara were, in fact, simultaneously experimenting with the open-form poem, the poem that strives to convey the immediacy of life by presenting the poet's situation, observations, and responses as directly and precisely as possible, according to the chronology of the events themselves as they happened, thus giving the illusion of both inclusiveness and inconclusiveness. The mediating consciousness that shapes and judges experience, that yields a crafted, discursive, linearly logical development of images progressing to a closure that both evolves from and unifies them, is seemingly denied. O'Hara's affinities, however, are with the French: the post-Symbolists Pierre Reverdy and Guillaume Apollinaire, and the Surrealists. Consequently, his "lunch poems" retain a sense of a consciousness willing and directing, a gesture akin to that of the analogical subconscious managing the flow of his "automatic" texts. Blackburn, however, places the reader almost completely in reality, in the experience itself, perhaps because he is working within the more objectivist American tradition.

Blackburn readily acknowledged that Ezra Pound had the most influence on his work, along with William Carlos Williams, whom he first encountered through the poetry of Robert Creeley. Charles Olson's essay "Projective Verse" (1950) provided added incentive, as did the poetry of Louis Zukofsky. Blackburn worked in the modernist poetic technique pioneered by Pound and Williams, and E. E. Cummings and T. S. Eliot as well, and defined in 1945 by Joseph Frank in a seminal essay as "spatial form." This technique complements a nondiscursive content by replacing the linear conventions of typographically recorded language, appropriate to discursive content, with a two-dimensional, spatially oriented presentation. The unconventional spacing of words or phrases can establish rhythm by indicating length of pause between verbal elements, and calculated rather than conventional line endings can provide emphasis whenever strategically desirable. Blackburn consistently avails himself of both of these features of spatial form, as did his predecessors.

Blackburn's unique contribution to modernist poetics, however, is to use juxtaposition, the primary aspect of spatial form that yields thematic meaning, in the spontaneous, open-form poem of immediate experience to convey definite, if subtle, complex meanings within verse that appears simply to be recording random observations of the ongoing flow of life. The placing of material in different areas on the page according to subject not only isolates particular experiences, preserving their phenomenal integrity, but also facilitates a more profound kind of relationship between them. When Blackburn is at his best, he is shrewdly choosing for a given poem inherently related experiences that comment on one another, yet describing them with complete fidelity to their objective reality and presenting them nonchalantly, extemporaneously, as if they are insignificant coincidences. In this way, Blackburn creates in his poems a living world of joyous activity and sensuous appearance that is nevertheless intrinsically meaningful.

Blackburn was aware, however, that a poem is not merely a written, visual product, but also a spoken, aural event. What made Blackburn the complete poet, the virtuoso, was the other great influence on his poetic career besides Pound: the troubadours. Music in poetry was for Blackburn at once formal, the orchestration of material for thematic and emotional impact, and aural, the rhythm and sound of the language itself. To be sure, Blackburn, like his contemporaries, sought American speech rhythms and conversational diction, an aesthetic inaugurated by Walt Whitman. Blackburn had a fine ear for colloquialisms and slang, but that ear was also trained by Provençal. Consequently, the play of assonance, consonance, internal rhyme, off-rhyme, and rhythmic nuance inspired by troubadour lyric can be found at times alternating, or even blending, with modern idiom, for atmosphere, emphasis, or wit. Blackburn's range of diction, in fact, enables him to enliven his poetry with irony and humor, formal diction and slang clashing unexpectedly. Despite the minimalist tendencies of many of his contemporaries to strip poetry of all rhetorical beauty, Blackburn found ways to preserve the varied aural richness of language.

The troubadours may also be responsible, along with Blackburn's avowed Mediterranean sensibility, for the one quality of his poetry that is very rare in English verse: the comfortable ease, the relaxed poise, with which he treats the erotic. Cummings was, of course, always aware of the shock that he was creating with his references to sexual love. John Donne and even Robert Herrick are self-conscious by comparison. One would have to go back to Geoffrey Chaucer for a similar natural acceptance of sensuality. Certainly Blackburn's stature as an American poet is enhanced, not diminished, by such a foreign influence as Provençal poetry. A melting-pot culture remains vital by renewing component cultures latent in its native tradition, a program that Pound, as well as Eliot, followed. As Blackburn deliberately takes his place in the tradition of poetry from the Middle Ages on through his work with the troubadours, so he openly acknowledges a similar tradition of modern poetry by occasionally parodying or quoting poets of the immediate past, including Pound, Williams, Eliot, Robert Frost, Walt Whitman, William Butler Yeats, and Gerard Manley Hopkins.

This inclusive view of the modern poetic tradition is indicative of the richness of Blackburn's own poetry: its technical innovations with spatial form, sound and rhythm, and diction; its thematic and emotional range; and its ability to perceive, in the immediate and the personal, the general and the universal. Blackburn's verse is always grounded in private experience, yet it expresses the common concerns of humanity. He is able to structure the immediate without violating it, whereas others of his generation were only able, or simply content, to record. Thus, poetry for him is never therapy through confession, or a notebook of fragments from his reading, or a self-absorbed diary. When one speaks of significant postwar poets, one cannot with any justice mention any one of his contemporaries, no matter how well-respected at the present time, without mentioning Blackburn's name in the same breath.

BIOGRAPHY

Paul Blackburn was the son of the poet Frances Frost. Having been reared in Vermont, New Hampshire, South Carolina, and New York City, he attended New York University and the University of Wisconsin, where he received a B.A. degree in 1950. While at Wisconsin, Blackburn began corresponding with Ezra Pound, whose poetry he admired, and then occasionally visited Pound in St. Elizabeths Hospital, Washington, D.C. At Pound's suggestion, Blackburn began writing to Robert Creeley, who eventually published his poems in the *Black Mountain Review* and put him in touch with Cid Corman, who, in turn, published Blackburn's poems in *Origin* (a quarterly for the creative) and introduced him to Charles Olson, though Blackburn was never to study or teach at Black Mountain College. Pound also encouraged Blackburn's interest in the troubadours, which began when Blackburn encountered Pound's own quotations and imitations of Provençal verse in *Personae* (1909) and the *Cantos* (1925-1972). In 1953, Blackburn published a small volume of translations through Creeley's Divers Press, the early *Proensa*, that earned him a Fulbright scholarship in 1954 to do research in Provençal poetry at the University of Toulouse in southern France, and he returned as *lecteur américain* the following year. He remained in Europe, principally in Málaga, Spain, and Bañalbufar, Mallorca, with Winifred McCarthy, whom he married in 1954, until 1957, when they returned to New York.

For the next ten years in New York City, in addition to writing and translating, Blackburn worked to establish a sense of community among the poets centered on St. Mark's Church in the Bowery. As well as offering help and encouragement, he organized and tape-recorded weekly poetry readings at the church. His efforts eventually led to the funded Poetry Project at St. Mark's in 1967. He also conducted a "Poet's Hour" on radio station WBAI. In 1963, he was divorced from his first wife and married Sara Golden; that marriage also ended in divorce in 1967, around the time that he was poet-in-residence at the Aspen Writers' Workshop in Colorado. That year also saw the appearance of his most widely circulated collection of poems, *The Cities*, published by Grove Press. Toward the end of 1967, he returned to Europe on a Guggenheim Fellowship, where he met Joan Miller, whom he married in 1968, and with whom he had a son. In September, 1970, he assumed a teaching position at the state college in Cortland, New York, where he died of cancer the following year.

ANALYSIS

Because Paul Blackburn is a poet of immediate observation and spontaneous response, his poetry thrives on particular places. His work, however, is not rooted in a specific geographical location that is transformed into a frame of mind, as is Frost's New England, or that is elevated to a latter-day myth, as is Williams's Paterson. Blackburn's places are the environments in which he happens to be: a town plaza, a boat at sea, a wooded hill, a city street, a subway car, a tavern, a luncheonette, a kitchen, a bedroom. He would often generate a poem by immersing himself in his surroundings until man and place were one, the identification stirring in him a particular thought or emotion, a combination of his mood and the suggestion of that particular rush of outside activity. Although his thematic preoccupations and technical goals remain fairly uniform throughout the course of his work, he did tend to prefer certain themes and to express certain emotions through certain techniques when he was living in European cities, and others when he was living in New York. Perhaps because he could see sheep grazing in the town square in Málaga or burros passing through Bañalbufar, when Blackburn was living in Europe he often considered the relationship between humans and nature through such concepts as freedom, mutability, eternity, and religiosity; love is portrayed as sentiment. Perhaps because his mind was on the troubadours, living with his hands on their manuscripts near Provence, Blackburn's European poetry tends to be meditative and pensive, the soundplay more melodious, the language more metaphorical. When he was living in New York, in the densely populated modern city, where concrete substituted for grass, Blackburn focused on interpersonal relations, including friendship, complicity, estrangement, and anonymity; love becomes erotic energy. In a city whose traffic rushes and whose subway rumbles and roars, Blackburn's poetry becomes more immediate and involved, conversational and wtty; sound is orchestrated for dissonance; metaphor, if resorted to at all, is unexpected, shocking; but the occasional use of symbol is retained.

Early Selected y Mas

Blackburn is best read, then, chronologically, according to the place where he was living and writing. The dates given for the poems gathered in *Early Selected y Mas*, which includes the small, early books of limited circulation, makes such a reading possible for most of the first half of his work. In the poetry written or set in Europe between 1954 and 1958, Blackburn explores the existence of humans as creatures both fundamentally part of nature, with physicality and sensuousness, and separate through consciousness, will, and ephemerality.

In "A Permanence," Blackburn uses the seven-star constellation the bear to present nature as an eternal force separate from humanity: The bear "is there/ even in the day, when we do not see him." Nevertheless, humans cannot help responding to nature's perpetually changing life, being natural themselves. The lovers in "The Hour," for example, are "hungering" not only for food but also for the first sign of spring after a long winter: They sit "listening to the warm gnawing in their stomach/ the warm wind/ through the blossoms blowing." These lines exemplify the rich grammatical ambiguity made possible by spatial form: The appetites for food and for seasonal renewal are associated not only by repetition of the adjective "warm" but also by the possibility that "wind" as well as "gnawing" can be the object of the preposition "to," modifying "listening."

Separation from and unity with nature are confronted simultaneously in "Light." Initially, humanity and sea are only linguistically related through a simile; day moves inevitably into night, but an effort of the will is required for human action: "My thought drifts like the sea/ No grip between it and my act." By the end of the poem, however, the dark, drifting sea complements and then merges with the poet's gloomy mood. The assertion is metaphoric, but the poet's mind and his perceptual experience have indeed become one: "The sea flashes up in the night/ to touch and darken my sea."

"Mestrović and the Trees"

From this contemplation of the relationship between humans and nature, a religious sense develops, as expressed in "Mestrović and the Trees." For Blackburn, a feeling for the divine is unavoidable: "You never get passed the wood" where "The beginnings of things are shown." Religion for him is a matter of origins, and this poem is Blackburn's own version of the cosmological argument. From humanity's own existence, which cannot be denied—"Yes we are"—he moves back to origins—"Our mother and father," and by implication, Adam and Eve—to their origin, in nature, through God: "So these trees stand there, our/ image, the god's image." The trees "stand there/ naked" just as humans enter the world, their unity with nature now binding them also to the divine. By using the lower case for God and preceding his name with the definite article, Blackburn indicates that his religion is natural rather than orthodox. Although Blackburn is certain of the existence of the divine, its nature remains an enigma.

"How to Get Through Reality"

This mystery, essential to Blackburn's religious experience, is in itself sacred for him and not to be violated by forms and formulas that he considers to be ultimately human fabrications, at best mere approximations of the divine. In "How to Get Through Reality," Blackburn insists on the separation, epistemological despite a metaphysical complicity, between the temporal and the divine, that is, "Those who work with us . . . who create us from our stone." An impenetrable glass wall separates the two realms, and he celebrates the divine only in the most general of ways, aesthetically: "Our beauty under glass is your reality, unreachable/ sliding our gift to you." The insistence on the unintelligibility of the divine is portrayed grammatically with a sentence that ends incompletely just at the point God is to be named: "Beauty is the daily renewal in the eyes of." Feeling, the basis of his perception of beauty, provides his only sense of the divine: "One could kick the glass out, no?/ No./ Pass through." Breaking the glass, transcending the temporal, for direct communication with and precise knowledge of the supernatural is impossible; only intimations, illuminations, can pass through the transparency of the glass. A similar warning is sounded in "Suspension," where the poet's vision of the moon is obscured by tree branches: "—Shall I climb up and get it down?/ —No. Leave it alone."

"RITUAL I"

As a consequence, Blackburn's attitude toward orthodox religious forms—language, ceremony, observance—is ambivalent. "Ritual I" presents a religious "Procession," as it moves "with candles" from the church through the various streets of the Spanish town to the chant of "Ave Maria." Because the "fiesta" does not "celebrate," but rather "reenacts" the "event," "*time emerges*." Blackburn is observing that the religious ritual is "a timeless gesture" because its origin cannot be traced or dated, because it has been perpetuated throughout the course of history, and because it creates anew the event each time it is performed. Through this persistence of religion, this infinite renewal, this timelessness, human time is made possible: The participants too are renewed along with the ritual. Blackburn continues, however, to enlarge the concept of ritual to encompass secular as well as religious life. Midway through the poem a "lady tourist/ . . . joined the procession"; she appeared an "anomaly": "Instead of a rosary, carried/ a white pocketbook." After this secular irregularity in the religious ceremony, Blackburn immediately introduces what appear to be irregularities of subject in a poem describing a sacred ritual: He tells the reader that he rises everyday "in the dawn light"; he eats "Meat every Thursday/ when the calf/ is killed"; he gets "Mail from the bus at 4:30/ fresh milk at 5." What Blackburn is implying through these juxtapositions is that our everyday lives are composed of rituals that renew life on a daily basis, that make life itself possible. The "german anthropologist," then, "her poor self at the end of the line," is really not at a terminal point; for life, like this yearly ritual, is a perpetual process of renewal, a series of rebirths: "End of a timeless act of the peoples of the earth," hardly an end at all.

"RITUAL IV"

In poetry written after Blackburn's return to New York in 1957, the religious and the secular merge for him to the point where his rituals consist entirely of various activities repeated on a daily basis. Religion becomes the celebration of life, since the divine is immanent in the world itself. In "Ritual IV," for example, Blackburn juxtaposes a description of plants growing in his kitchen with a reenactment of a Saturday morning breakfast with his wife, in order to express the unity of all living things. "You sit here smiling at/ me and the young plants," as the "beams" of sunlight reveal the "dust" that "float[s]" from the plants to them. The poet concludes: "Everything/ grows,/ and rests."

"Lines, Trees, and Words"

Having united the sacred and profane to such a degree, Blackburn occasionally grows impatient with orthodox ceremony. In "Lines, Trees, and Words," walking through a park and overhearing children singing a hymn off-key, a friend observes how they are mutilating "it." Blackburn, however, willfully misunderstands the referent of the pronoun to be the divine and replies, "Don't we all." Any verbal attempt to embody the spiritual will result in such travesty: "Give the child words, give him/ words, he will use them." Characteristically, the poem ends with the preferred indefinite, natural, religious note: "How the trees hang down from the sky." At times, Blackburn will even imply that the more Puritanical strain in orthodox religion might very well obstruct his and others' more spontaneous celebration of the divine through joyous living, as in "Ash Wednesday, 1965."

"The Purse Seine"

Most of the poetry that Blackburn wrote between 1958 and 1967 had New York City for its setting and focused intimately on human psychology: the ways in which people relate to one another, how they react to the world in which they find themselves, and how they regard their own personalities and bodies. In Blackburn's love poems of this period, two symbols, fishing nets and the sea, continually recur, helping him to express his vision of love as unavoidable and overwhelming, as the persistent tide of the sea, and therefore frightening, threatening, as the confining fishing net, at first unnoticed. Love for Blackburn is a force that one can resist only for so long; then one gives in wholeheartedly, though with trepidation. "The Purse Seine" accumulates a number of aquatic images that express this ambivalence: what "gulls" "do that looks so beautiful, is/ hunt"; at once they are "crying freedom, crying carrion"; the eye of the gull, merging with that of his lover, "frightens," for both are the "beautiful killer"; "the net/ is tight," and then "The purse closes" and "we drown/ in sight of/ I love you and you love me." In "Park Poem," the poet reels from "the first shock of leaves their alliance with love"—the complicity of nature in romance. "How to Get up off It" is a contemporaneous poem that juxtaposes several random events ultimately related to the persistence of love in nature, and thus in human beings. The poet begins the poem by recalling a mountain climber's words: "Am I ready for this mountain?" As "they go up," so does the poet climb love's mountain, sitting with his second wife in front of the Public Library, next to a girl writing a letter to her boyfriend; they are passed by a couple holding hands who wave to them and then witness a mating dance: "The pigeons never seem to tire/ of the game," and neither do people, as the events recorded in the poem demonstrate.

"Call It the Net" and "The Net of Moon"

Depending on his mood, Blackburn can portray love as simply the drive of blind passion that results in a loss of freedom through its satisfaction. In such poems as "Call It the Net," love is a "silken trap . . . the net of lust." In "The Sea and the Shadow," that "damned sea" of sexuality will drive him back to his lover despite his anger at her; the waves become the rhythm of the sexual act: "I will come into your belly and make it a sea rolling against me." At other times, however, sexual love will be a joyous occasion, as in "lower case poem": "of that spring tide i sing/ clutched to one another." At such times, as Blackburn explains in "The Net of Moon," the lovers have achieved a union of the physical and the spiritual, "a just balance be-/ tween the emotion and the motion of the wave on the bay," lust being transformed into love. What Blackburn finds most striking, in the end, is the inevitable nature of both sexuality and love. On seeing a pretty girl on the street in "The Tides," the poet exclaims: "Terrible indeed is the house of heaven in the mind." After recalling the act of love, "its flood/ its ebb," the poet can only conclude: "What the man must do/ what the woman must do."

EROTIC POEMS

Blackburn accepts, as a natural dimension of human relations, this constant attraction between men and women, which exists as much on the physical as on the emotional level. Rather than trying to resist or repress the erotic impulse, Blackburn celebrates it in a series of erotic poems unique in the language. Never vulgar, tawdry, or exhibitionistic, they involve a drama of emotion as well as of desire, for Blackburn portrays the woman as well as the man being caught in the erotic moment and enjoying it with equal relish. This mutual, if often covert, complicity results in a sense of the erotic as all-pervasive and joyous rather than predatory or compromising. These poems are usually contemporaneous with the events and feelings they describe and involve witty shifts of tone through incongruous diction, ranging from colloquial ("all very chummy") to tabloid cliché ("the hotbed of assignation") to scientific jargon ("hypotenuse," "trajectory").

Two of his best erotic poems appear in *Brooklyn-Manhattan Transit*, for the subway is one of the more likely places to afford the modern troubadour an opportunity to admire the feminine. In "The Once-Over," a pretty blond woman is being appreciated by the poet and the other riders of the car. According to the poet, however, she is deliberately inviting their admiration: She is "standing/ tho there are seats"; "Only a stolid young man . . . does not know he is being assaulted"; "She has us and we her." In "Clickety-Clack," Blackburn is reading out loud a blatantly erotic passage from one of Lawrence Ferlinghetti's poems on the subway car, much to the amusement (and arousal) of a young lady, despite her frown, as the negative prefix split by the line ending from the rest of its root word indicates: She "began to stare dis-/ approvingly and wiggle." "The Slogan" records the provocative stroll of a "wellknit blonde in a blue knit dress" past a group of utility workers, Blackburn describing her walk with terms borrowed from physics. "Hands" portrays a girl entering her room and going to open a window with her boyfriend in pursuit, "bringing/ one thing up, & another down." Even in "The Assassination of President McKinley," the opportunistic proprietor of the drapery shop is not the only one who enjoys "the last rite/ for the assassinated Mr. McKinley."

Against the Silences

Blackburn's one long cycle of poems on love, published posthumously as *Against the Silences*, was written between 1963 and 1967, and deals with the dissolution of his second marriage. The cycle moves from uneasy marital contentment ("knowing we love one another/ sometime," from "The Second Message"), to the beginning of estrangement ("the thought dissolves & only/ fact remains," from "Slippers, Anyone?"), to argument resulting from a misunderstanding of the husband's deepest personal allegiances ("The Value"), to the wife's infidelity ("What Is It, Love?"), and finally to divorce ("Scenario for a Walk-On," in which the poet depicts the separation as the ending of a film). The sequence recalls George Meredith's *Modern Love* (1862), a series of fifty sixteen-line sonnets portraying the psychological dilemmas of an unhappy married couple through dramatic monologue or silent rumination, written the year after Meredith's divorce from his first wife. Because Blackburn's poems focus specifically on the intimate details of his own marriage, automatically recorded in the contemporaneous open-form poem of immediate experience, his cycle has somewhat greater emotional range and depth than Meredith's, which is a more conscious attempt to generalize from personal experience about the condition of romantic love in the modern world, as the title suggests.

In *Against the Silences*, the complexity of the beleaguered husband's feelings is captured in poems that often portray several conflicting emotions at once: confusion, frustration, pain, humiliation, anger, disgust, fear, loneliness. The subtle role that sexual passion assumes in the relationship is also treated. In the early "So Deep We Never Got," the poet wishes his wife to make love to him as a reassurance of her affection: Resorting to a favorite symbol, he needs to be with her "chest-deep in the surf/ and those waves coming and coming." In "Monday, Monday," however, the husband uses an offer of sex in an attempt to keep his wife from meeting her lover, but the response remains the same throughout the poem: "away,/ her body pushed me away." In this sequence, Blackburn's idea of love as a net to which one deliberately surrenders oneself attains its most explicit statement. Although staying with his wife was always an "act of will" ("The Second Message"), "reasons of choice" are "so obscure" that the process of choice can never ensure happiness; he can only "choose and fear and live it thru" ("Accident"). The result is equally ironic: The possessor of another in love becomes "possessed" by that very love ("The Price").

Elegies

If Blackburn adds a new genre to English-language verse, or revives one long defunct, through his erotic poems he contributes to an ongoing tradition with his elegies, which he composed throughout his career. In "The Mint Quality" (1961), the poet attempts to "Sing/ straight as I can" about the death of a vivacious young woman by first giving the details of her automobile accident in France and then presenting her monologue to her friends from the other side of death. The poem becomes ironic when Christiane assures them that "*next time*" she will "*wait til the middle of life/ know what you know/ just to understand*." The poem began with the poet, at middle age, professing his complete incomprehension of the cycle of life and death: "two friends' wives/ are near their term and large./ . . . One/ girl is dead. No choice."

THE REARDON POEMS

The Reardon Poems is a sequence of seven poems written in memory of Blackburn's friend Robert Reardon: "Bluegrass" presents the unsuccessful operation to save his life; "The Writer" tells of Reardon's vocation, novelist; "The Husband" treats his relationship with his wife and presents her disorientation and loneliness; "Sixteen Sloppy Haiku" are brief glimpses or thoughts of Reardon's last days of life; "The List" consists of Reardon's last rites, as specified by him before his death; and "St. Mark's-in-the-Bouwerie" is an elegy proper on death, its inexplicability amidst life ("When there's nothing anyone can do,/ reality/ comes on fast or slow"). "Seventeen Nights Later at McSorley's" is the epilogue, employing recorded conversation with great thematic effect; Blackburn is speaking to Reardon's former roommate in the hospital:

> You won't see him again, sez I
> "No?"
> No. You're well again? Mazeltov.
> "No?"
> No.

Perhaps Blackburn's finest elegy is "December Journal: 1968," on the death of his third wife's father, in which practically all his formal poetic resources come into play. The poem begins with the telephone call informing them of the death and moves through grief and tears to the wake and funeral in a passage in which breakfast and the Eucharist are superimposed; to a meditation on the mystery of life and death, creation and destruction, inspired by an open journal on alchemy lying before the poet; and finally to love-making and a renewal of domestic patterns ("'You have to get up and move the car.'/ I existed again, I/ was married to my wife!"). Inspired by his alchemical reading, the poet realizes that life mysteriously renews itself within materials that compose rock; that is, life dwells in and is sustained by essentially inanimate matter, a theme first heard in "How to Get Through Reality." This miracle, and the miracle of the living child in his wife's womb, has by the end of the poem put him at ease.

OTHER MAJOR WORKS

NONFICTION: "Das Kennerbuch," 1953; "Writing for the Ear," 1960; "The American Duende," 1962; "The Grinding Down," 1963.

TRANSLATIONS: *Proensa*, 1953; *Poem of the Cid*, 1966; *End of the Game, and Other*

Stories, 1967 (of Julio Cortázar); *Hunk of Skin*, 1968 (of Pablo Picasso); *Cronopios and Famas*, 1969 (of Cortázar); *Peire Vidal*, 1972; *The Treasure of the Muleteer, and Other Spanish Tales*, 1974 (of Antonio Jimenez-Landi); *Guillem De Poitu: His Eleven Extant Poems*, 1976; *Proensa: An Anthology of Troubadour Poetry*, 1978; *Lorca/Blackburn: Poems of Federico García Lorca Chosen and Translated by Paul Blackburn*, 1979.

BIBLIOGRAPHY

Malkoff, Karl. *Crowell's Handbook of Contemporary American Poetry*. New York: Thomas Y. Crowell, 1973. The entry on Blackburn lists him not only as a Black Mountain poet but also as a Projectivist, although like most Projectivists, his poetry is individualistic. Mentions his long sojourns abroad and discusses two of his works, *The Cities* and *The Nets*. Other than some insightful comments about Projectivist poetry—for example, that there is no real distinction between the inner and outer world—there is little noteworthy criticism here.

Marowski, Daniel G., and Roger Matuz, eds. *Contemporary Literary Criticism*. Vol. 43. Detroit: Gale Research, 1987. Lists Blackburn as a noted translator, scholar, and poet, whose poetry combines structural experimentation with colloquial forms. This combination creates a "visual, aural, and psychological reading experience." Gathers together some fine reviews of Blackburn's work, in particular critical commentary of his most widely acclaimed work, *The Journals*. Also notes that since the posthumous publication of *The Collected Poems of Paul Blackburn*, his verse has attracted a wider audience and has undergone critical reevaluation.

Rosenthal, M. L. Review of *The Cities*. *Poetry* 114 (May, 1969): 129-130. Comments on Blackburn's love of American lingo and his emphasis on the quality of movement, both of which lend his poems qualities of "humor and sensuality." Appreciates Blackburn's focus on the process of the poet's involvement in the poem as a "disciplining subject of the poem, as well as its range in action."

Stephens, Michael. "Common Speech and Complex Forms." *The Nation* 223 (September 4, 1976): 189-190. Reviews *The Cities*, *The Journals*, and *Halfway down the Coast*, which he considers a suitable introduction to Blackburn. Notes that the possibility of death that Blackburn explores in *Halfway* becomes the reality of dying in *The Journals*. Commends Blackburn for his ability to appreciate "overheard cadences in common speech," which he says is indicative of Blackburn's love of people.

William Skaff

RICHARD BRAUTIGAN

Born: Tacoma, Washington; January 30, 1935
Died: Bolinas, California; September, 1984

PRINCIPAL POETRY

The Return of the Rivers, 1957
The Galilee Hitch-Hiker, 1958
Lay the Marble Tea: Twenty-four Poems, 1959
The Octopus Frontier, 1960
All Watched over by Machines of Loving Grace, 1967
The Pill Versus the Springhill Mine Disaster, 1968
Please Plant This Book, 1968
Rommel Drives on Deep into Egypt, 1970
Loading Mercury with a Pitchfork, 1976
June 30th, June 30th, 1978

OTHER LITERARY FORMS

Richard Brautigan is best known for capturing the spirit of the 1960's counterculture. His earliest novels—*A Confederate General from Big Sur* (1964), *Trout Fishing in America* (1967), and *In Watermelon Sugar* (1967)—were extremely popular, especially among younger readers; *Trout Fishing in America* sold millions of copies worldwide. His later works (such as *The Abortion: An Historical Romance*, 1971, and *The Hawkline Monster: A Gothic Western*, 1974) continued the 1960's zeitgeist into the 1970's but were considerably less popular. Brautigan also published a collection of his short stories, *Revenge of the Lawn: Stories, 1962-1970* (1971).

ACHIEVEMENTS

Richard Brautigan can best be understood as providing the bridge from the writers of the Beat movement of the 1950's (Allen Ginsberg and Jack Kerouac) to those of the literary counterculture of the 1960's and early 1970's (Ken Kesey and Tom Robbins). Brautigan exploded onto the literary scene in the middle of the 1960's and became—like Hermann Hesse and J. R. R. Tolkien—a cult writer for younger readers. He was a poet-in-residence at the California Institute of Technology in 1967 and won a National Endowment for the Arts grant in 1968. It is hard to think of another writer whose rise was so meteoric, but Brautigan started out reading his own poetry on the streets of San Francisco and just a few years later was invited to read at Harvard University. His reputation has not lasted (in comparison to that of his contemporary, the California poet Gary Snyder), but for some years, he helped shape the dreams and attitudes of the younger generation.

Biography

Richard Gary Brautigan was born in Tacoma, Washington, and lived his early life in the Pacific Northwest. His father abandoned the family a few months after he was born, and Brautigan's childhood contained both poverty and abuse at the hands of a stepfather. He graduated from high school in Eugene, Oregon, but in a year had gravitated to the literary scene in San Francisco. He was a street poet in his first literary role, performing at coffeehouses and poetry clubs. Local presses published several collections of his poems in the late 1950's, but Brautigan was definitely viewed as a regional poet. He first won fame through his novels, especially after *Trout Fishing in America* and *A Confederate General in Big Sur* were reissued by the New York publisher Delacorte at the suggestion of the writer Kurt Vonnegut. Brautigan continued to publish both novels and poetry into the 1970's, but his popularity and his powers waned at the end of the 1960's.

Brautigan was twice married and had a daughter with his first wife, but he suffered from alcoholism, among other troubles, and he ended his life with a handgun in the fall of 1984. The exact date is unknown because his body was not discovered until some weeks after his death. He taught at Montana State University in 1982 and traveled extensively in Japan, but he lived mostly in the San Francisco area and died in his last home in Bolinas, just up the coast from the city.

Analysis

Richard Brautigan's poems are usually brief, often humorous, sometimes childlike in their innocence, and decidedly antipoetic. Much of his poetry sounds like prose, in the same way that the prose of his novels is often poetic. "January 17" (from *Rommel Drives on Deep into Egypt*) reads simply, "Drinking wine this afternoon/ I realize the days are getting/ longer." His best poems resemble brief haiku, and some have a Zen Buddhist quality to them. The short verse "Haiku Ambulance" (from his popular collection *The Pill Versus the Springhill Mine Disaster*) reads, in its entirety, "A piece of green pepper/ fell/ off the wooden salad bowl:/ so what?" His imagination is sometimes startling, and his images and metaphors often surprise the reader, although they rarely leave an aftertaste.

Many of his poems are nonsense verse; for example "The Amelia Earhart Pancake" (from *Loading Mercury with a Pitchfork*) tells readers that he is giving up trying to find a poem to fit this title, and in several cases, he prints titles with no poems beneath them, as in "A 48-Year-Old Burglar from San Diego" and "1891-1944" (both from *Rommel Drives on Deep into Egypt*). A good number of his poems are about love, love found and love lost (some in his first collection are dedicated "For Marcia" or simply "For M"), and some have explicit sexual images and language at their center.

His poetic voice is simple and direct, capturing the rhythms of the spoken word and providing easy access to his thoughts. A few of his poems are longer than a page, but most of his poems are only a few lines long. However, "The Galilee Hitch-Hiker" section of *The Pill Versus the Springhill Mine Disaster* contains nine linked poems, all but

Richard Brautigan
(Library of Congress)

the last featuring the nineteenth century French poet Charles Baudelaire in twentieth century America; the "Group Portrait Without the Lions" section of *Loading Mercury with a Pitchfork* has fourteen short poems (part 9, "Betty Makes Wonderful Waffles," reads simply, "Everybody agrees to/ that"); and the "Good Luck, Captain Martin" section of the same collection has seven poems. The last poem in the series, "Put the Coffee On, Bubbles, I'm Coming Home," consists of two lines, "Everybody's coming home/ except Captain Martin."

Brautigan's rise was sudden. He was known as a West Coast poet for about a decade, until the publication of his first major collection, *The Pill Versus the Springhill Mine Disaster*, in 1968, and for the next ten years—through his final three collections, *Rommel Drives on Deep into Egypt*, *Loading Mercury with a Pitchfork*, and *June 30th, June 30th*—he was a popular poet who was closely associated with the San Francisco cultural scene of rock bands, flower children, and drugs. Many of the poems in the first and second collections published during the peak of Brautigan's popularity first appeared in *Harper's*, *Mademoiselle*, *Poetry*, and *Rolling Stone* magazines. His later poetry collections, however, showed a falling off of poetic inspiration and imagination: More of the poems were flat or nonsense prose, with fewer startling images and metaphors than in his earlier collections.

The Pill Versus the Springhill Mine Disaster

Although Brautigan had been publishing in small presses and reading his own poetry in the late 1950's and early 1960's, his 1968 collection, *The Pill Versus the Springhill Mine Disaster*, was the first to gain wide popularity with young American readers. The ideas and images expressed in this work seemed to capture the magical, antiauthoritarian spirit of the late 1960's. Brautigan's novels, along with those of writers such as Peter S. Beagle (*The Last Unicorn*, 1968) and Kurt Vonnegut (*Slaughterhouse-Five: Or, The Children's Crusade, a Duty-Dance with Death*, 1969), were also vehicles of the counterculture.

The title poem of Brautigan's first major collection conveys its tone:

When you take your pill
it's like a mine disaster.
I think of all the people
lost inside of you.

The metaphor jolts readers with its juxtaposition of images, and the poem becomes a kind of ironic haiku on the birth control pill. It was the poetic language, particularly the images and metaphors, of this collection that struck readers most forcefully. Death was ". . . a beautiful car parked only/ to be stolen . . . ," a dish of ice cream looked "like Kafka's hat." The last three lines of "Your Departure Versus the Hindenburg" read, "When you leave the house, the/ shadow of the Hindenburg enters/ to take your place." Even in this collection, there were poems that fit the definition of poetry only by virtue of their linear spacing: "Widow's Lament" reads, "It's not quite cold enough/ to go borrow some firewood/ from the neighbors." Brautigan was drawing on William Carlos Williams and the Imagists, but often without a strong enough central image, and creating haiku without a sharp enough picture.

Rommel Drives on Deep into Egypt

Brautigan's second major poetry collection, *Rommel Drives on Deep into Egypt*, had many of the same qualities—the cryptic humor, the naïve tone, and the nonsense lyrics—but there seemed to be fewer fresh metaphors, and more poems seemed to be self-referential. "Critical Can Opener," for example, reads, "There is something wrong/ with this poem. Can you/ find it?" "Third Eye/ *For Gary Snyder*" reads simply, "There is a motorcycle/ in New Mexico," and "April 7, 1969" consists of the simple four-line lament: "I feel so bad today/ that I want to write a poem./ I don't care: any poem, this/ poem." Still, there were enough poems in which the images surprised and puzzled readers to maintain Brautigan's reputation, such as the two-line "Cellular Coyote": "He's howling in the pines/ at the edge of your fingerprints."

LOADING MERCURY WITH A PITCHFORK

Brautigan's third popular collection, *Loading Mercury with a Pitchfork*, continued the hip Brautigan poetic style, with images such as those in the title poem; jokes such as that in the one-line poem "Nine Crows: Two Out of Sequence," which reads, "1,2,3,4,5,7,6,8,9"; and the haiku-like brevity and irony of "Curiously Young Like a Freshly-Dug Grave":

> Curiously young like a freshly-dug grave
> the day parades in circles like a top
> with rain falling in its shadow.

Similarly, "Impasse" reads, "I talked a good hello/ but she talked an even/ better good-bye." He writes "the moon shines like a dead garage" in one poem and snowflakes in New York City appear ". . . like millions/ of transparent washing machines swirling/ through the dirty air of this city, washing/ it" in another. More poems, however, devolve into prose in this collection: "Ginger" reads simply, "She's glad/ that Bill/ likes her," and "Two Guys Get out of a Car," consists of three simple lines:

> Two guys get out of a car.
> They stand beside it. They
> don't know what else to do.

Other poems contain antipoetic gestures. In "Death Like a Needle," Brautigan writes, ". . . [I can't make/ the next two words out. I first/ wrote this poem in longhand]. . . ." Brautigan seems less imaginative and figurative in this collection and more inclined to write poems just to poke fun at the poetic process. As the spirit of the 1960's dissipated, so too did Brautigan's imaginative powers and popularity.

OTHER MAJOR WORKS

LONG FICTION: *A Confederate General from Big Sur*, 1964; *Trout Fishing in America*, 1967; *In Watermelon Sugar*, 1967; *The Abortion: An Historical Romance*, 1971; *The Hawkline Monster: A Gothic Western*, 1974; *Willard and His Bowling Trophies: A Perverse Mystery*, 1975; *Sombrero Fallout: A Japanese Novel*, 1976; *Dreaming of Babylon: A Private Eye Novel, 1942*, 1977; *The Tokyo-Montana Express*, 1980; *So the Wind Won't Blow It Away*, 1982; *An Unfortunate Woman*, 2000 (wr. 1982; first published in French as *Cahier d'un Retour de Troie*, 1994).

SHORT FICTION: *Revenge of the Lawn: Stories, 1962-1970*, 1971.

MISCELLANEOUS: *The Edna Webster Collection of Undiscovered Writings*, 1995.

BIBLIOGRAPHY

Abbott, Keith. *Downstream from "Trout Fishing in America."* Santa Barbara, Calif.: Capra Press, 1989. Abbott describes his friendship with Brautigan, from their meeting in 1966 through their parting in 1982 in San Francisco.

Barber, John F., ed. *Richard Brautigan: Essays on the Writings and Life*. Jefferson, N.C.: McFarland, 2007. The volume contains thirty-two memoirs and articles, many of them brief, including tributes by Michael McClure and Robert Creeley. A longer, more analytical piece is Steven Moore's "Paper Flowers: Richard Brautigan's Poetry," originally intended as the introduction to a volume of Brautigan's collected poetry that was never published.

Boyer, Jay. *Richard Brautigan*. Western Writers Series 79. Boise, Idaho: Boise State University Press, 1987. This early appraisal captures the Brautigan mystique in the 1960's, especially as readers discovered it in the novels.

Brautigan, Ianthe. *You Can't Catch Death: A Daughter's Memoir*. New York: St. Martin's Press, 2000. Brautigan's daughter, not satisfied with the portrayal of her father in his obituaries, writes of her childhood spent bouncing between the homes of her two bohemian parents.

Cutler, Edward. "Richard Brautigan." In *Twentieth Century American Western Writers, First Series*. Vol. 206 in *Dictionary of Literary Biography*. Detroit: Gale, 1999. Cutler approaches Brautigan both as a unique voice in Western literature and as an early postmodernist laying bare the relationships of language and representation.

Foster, Edward Halsey. *Richard Brautigan*. Boston: Twayne, 1983. Part of Twayne's United States Authors series. Foster includes an incisive analysis of the poetry as well as long discussions of the novels.

McDermott, James Dishon. *Austere Style in Twentieth-Century Literature: Literary Minimalism*. Lewiston: Edwin Mellen Press, 2006. This discussion of minimalism looks at Brautigan as well as Ludwig Wittgenstein, Raymond Carver, and David Mamet.

David Peck

CHARLES BUKOWSKI

Born: Andernach, Germany; August 16, 1920
Died: San Pedro, California; March 9, 1994

PRINCIPAL POETRY

Flower, Fist, and Bestial Wail, 1960
Longshot Poems for Broke Players, 1962
Poems and Drawings, 1962
Run with the Hunted, 1962
It Catches My Heart in Its Hand, 1963
Cold Dogs in the Courtyard, 1965
Crucifix in a Deathhand, 1965
The Genius of the Crowd, 1966
The Curtains Are Waving, 1967
At Terror Street and Agony Way, 1968
Poems Written Before Jumping out of an Eighth Story Window, 1968
A Bukowski Sampler, 1969
The Days Run Away Like Wild Horses over the Hills, 1969
Fire Station, 1970
Mockingbird Wish Me Luck, 1972
Me and Your Sometimes Love Poems, 1973 (with Linda King)
While the Music Played, 1973
Burning in Water, Drowning in Flame, 1974
Africa, Paris, Greece, 1975
Scarlet, 1976
Love Is a Dog from Hell, 1977
Maybe Tomorrow, 1977
Legs, Hips and Behind, 1978
We'll Take Them, 1978
Play the Piano Drunk Like a Percussion Instrument Until the Fingers Begin to Bleed a Bit, 1979
Dangling in the Tournefortia, 1981
The Last Generation, 1982
War All the Time: Poems, 1981-1984, 1984
The Roominghouse Madrigals: Early Selected Poems, 1946-1966, 1988
Last Night of the Earth Poems, 1992
Bone Palace Ballet: New Poems, 1997
What Matters Most Is How Well You Walk Through the Fire, 1999

Open All Night: New Poems, 2000
The Night Torn Mad with Footsteps, 2001
The Flash of Lightning Behind the Mountain: New Poems, 2003
Sifting Through the Madness for the Word, the Line, the Way: New Poems, 2003
Slouching Toward Nirvana: New Poems, 2005 (John Martin, editor)
Come on In! New Poems, 2006
The People Look Like Flowers at Last: New Poems, 2007
The Pleasures of the Damned: Poems, 1951-1993, 2007 (Martin, editor)

Other literary forms

In addition to poetry, Charles Bukowski (byew-KOW-skee) published stories and novels and first achieved recognition with *Notes of a Dirty Old Man* (1969). This volume brought him to the attention of many who were previously unfamiliar with his work. In conjunction with his first novel, *Post Office* (1971), and a volume titled *Erections, Ejaculations, Exhibitions, and General Tales of Ordinary Madness* (1972), about half of which was reissued in *Life and Death in the Charity Ward* (1973), *Notes of a Dirty Old Man* established his reputation as a no-holds-barred commentator, full of rage yet capable of surrealistic farce. In addition to subsequent novels, which include *Factotum* (1975), *Women* (1978), *Ham on Rye* (1982), and *Hollywood* (1989), there is *South of No North: Stories of the Buried Life* (1973), which reprints both *Confessions of a Man Insane Enough to Live with Beasts* (1965) and *All the Assholes of the World and Mine* (1966); a picture narrative of his trip abroad, *Shakespeare Never Did This* (1979); a screenplay, *Barfly* (1987); and assorted illustrations. His sketches underscore his farcical tone, especially in *You Kissed Lilly* (1978), a satire of the comics in which his Thurberesque style complements his prose.

Achievements

Charles Bukowski was awarded few honors during his lifetime. In 1974, he was given a National Endowment for the Arts grant, and he won a Loujon Press Award and the Silver Reel Award from the San Francisco Festival of the Arts for documentary film. Bukowski was always considered a maverick who was perceived by many academics and literary institutions to be hostile and antipoetic. His frank approach to life and writing is still too often considered simplistic or crude. Although Bukowski's literary achievements are still widely unrecognized and critically undervalued in the United States, he is already considered a classic American author in Europe. A new era of appreciation seemed to begin in the 1990's with the publication of several laudatory collections of critical analyses of his works. Few people familiar with Bukowski's work are indifferent to it. Although he neither won nor curried favor among academic or mainstream poets, he has attained an international reputation and has been widely translated. From the first, he sought to create a "living poetry of clarity," which defies the proprieties and "cages" established by academics and editors. He has been compared to Henry Miller, Jack London, Louis-Ferdinand Céline, Antonin Artaud, François Villon, and Arthur Rimbaud and had an acknowledged influence on Tom Waits, his musical heir.

Bukowski carried the Beat manifesto to its logical conclusion without compromising his vision or pandering to the idolatrous public. By incorporating the vantage point of the underclass, he artistically wrought the unfashionable voices of the streets, the factories, the racetracks, and other less seemly social enclaves. He fused the rawness of life with a personal sensitivity; he conveyed the horrors as well as the pathos of poverty, blue-collar jobs, hangovers, and jail yards. He was never a media personality, as the Beats were. Once it became financially feasible, he began refusing all invitations for readings to guard his private self, convinced that it was readings that had killed Dylan Thomas. This reticence, with his exclusive reliance on small publishers, made his international reputation all the more impressive.

Perhaps Bukowski's most significant achievement was his successful forging of a new American poetics characterized by its accessibility and its spontaneous narrative voice. Unlike T. S. Eliot's "vertical poetry," Bukowski's is a "horizontal poetry" that photographs the jagged surfaces of society and forces the reader to peer into the baser regions of human existence, to see humankind for what it is. His unique blend of powerful, physical imagery and sardonic wit allows the reader to grasp and yet transcend the essential absurdity of existence.

BIOGRAPHY

One cannot come to terms with the poetry of Henry Charles Bukowski, Jr., without acknowledging the fact that his is an extremely personal and autobiographical poetry; the terror and agony are not merely "felt-life" but life as Bukowski knew it. His survival was a thing of wonder. As Gerald Locklin notes, he "not only survived problems that would kill most men [but] survived with enough voice and talent left to write about it." He was a practicing alcoholic whose life revolved around the racetrack, women, and writing.

Born Heinrich Karl Bukowski to a German mother and an American soldier father on August 16, 1920, in Andernach, Germany, Bukowski came to the United States in 1922 with his family. They settled in Los Angeles, later the milieu for much of Bukowski's work. His father, a milkman, was a harsh and often violent man who struggled with his own powerlessness by wielding a razor strap. The resultant hostility and animosity is evident in many of the younger Bukowski's poems. Coupled with a blood disease that left his face badly pockmarked, Bukowski was predisposed to a life on the fringes of society.

At about the age of sixteen, partly to escape and partly because of a desire to become a writer, Bukowski began to haunt the public library, seeking literary models. His own self-directed reading was far more important in shaping his literary credo than the two years he spent at Los Angeles City College. He was drawn to the works of

Louis-Ferdinand Céline, John Fante, Fyodor Dostoevski, Ivan Turgenev, and the early Ernest Hemingway; in later years, he was attracted by Franz Kafka and Albert Camus. Just as the creative writing class in which he had enrolled seemed fraudulent and banal, however, so too did the voices of many of the "masters."

Bukowski's career as a writer had a rather fitful start. After receiving hundreds of rejections, "Aftermath of a Lengthy Rejection Slip" was accepted by *Story* in 1944 and *Portfolio* published "Twenty Tanks from Kasseldown." These publications were followed by ten years of virtual silence during which only four pieces were published. Toward the end of this literary hiatus, two important changes occurred. He began working sporadically at the post office, where he stayed fourteen years (until 1970, when John Martin of Black Sparrow Press convinced him to quit). This job provided the first steady source of income Bukowski had known. More important, however, was the shock of landing in the charity ward in 1955, near death from a bleeding ulcer. After receiving eleven pints of blood, he emerged "900 years older," promptly disregarded the warnings to quit drinking, and began publishing poetry in various little magazines. It was his appearance in *Outsider* and his friendship with editors Jon and Gypsy Lou Webb, who dubbed him "outsider of the year" in 1962, that launched his career. With their assistance, he began to develop an important reputation among editors and readers of the little magazines, ultimately establishing a friendship with John and Barbara Martin, who published the bulk of his work.

The barrage of women in his work revealed Bukowski's penchant for womanizing; he seemed to fall from one affair to another, yet his work revealed several significant pairings. Toward the beginning of his ten-year silence, he met Jane, "the first person who brought me any love," and began a relationship that was to continue until she finally died of alcoholism. Although their relationship, as *Factotum* demonstrates, was interrupted by intervening affairs, his cross-country meandering, and his two-and-a-half-year marriage to Barbara Fry, a Texas millionairess who edited *Harlequin*, it was a durable bond that inspired countless sensitive poems. Following Jane's death, Bukowski became involved with Frances, who bore his only child, Marina. Much later, both Linda King and Linda Lee Beighle were to play central roles in his life. The works dedicated to these women constitute a tribute of sorts and demonstrate that while his personal life was often tempestuous, he had the capacity and need for love. This is important to bear in mind to avoid misreading his oeuvre by exaggerating his sexism. Bukowski published prodigiously in his last decade and died from leukemia in 1994.

ANALYSIS

Living on the periphery of society, Charles Bukowski forged a brutally honest poetic voice. The futility and senselessness of most human endeavor conjoined with the desperation and essential solitude of the individual are constants reinforcing his "slavic nihilism." The trick, he suggested, is "carrying on when everything seems so terrible there is no use to go on. . . . You face the wall and just work it out. . . . Facing it right with yourself, alone." It is this kind of courage and stoicism that informs Bukowski's canon. He was neither a poet's poet nor a people's poet, but a personal poet who used his craft to ensure his own survival.

Bukowski's "tough guy" image was less posturing than self-protective. One senses that he was an idealist soured by the ravages of time, wearied by political betrayals, and rather appalled by the vacuity of the American left and contemporary American writers who seemed to be playing it safe and producing pallid prose and senselessly arcane poetry. Interestingly, in his best poems, the tough guy persona falls away and one discovers a sensitive poet who chose to adopt a savage bravado. Clearly, he knew the reality of the seamy side of life; his poetry teems with grotesque and sordid imagery; but unlike those who would write in order to reform, Bukowski was content to capture the pathos and rawness of the streets.

Bukowski's first four chapbooks properly acclimate the reader to his dual vision—his rawness and his compassion. They also reveal the risks inherent in this kind of personal, reportorial poetry. At his best, he blended seemingly incongruous elements to plunge the reader into a surreal landscape. At his worst, he succumbed to self-pity, mired in his own mundane reality.

FLOWER, FIST, AND BESTIAL WAIL

Flower, Fist, and Bestial Wail is the most consistently crafted of the four books and includes one of his best-known poems, "The Twins," which transforms his lingering animosity toward his father into a transcendent statement of shared humanity and mortality. The poem is replete with antithetical images: "We looked exactly alike, we could have been twins. . . . he had his bulbs on the screen ready for planting while I was laying with a whore from 3rd street." His own ambivalence is suggested by the scarecrow image he presented as he realized "I can't keep him alive no matter how much we hated each other." So, he stands, "waiting also to die." Read in conjunction with "All-Yellow Flowers," "The Twins" establishes one of the dominant motifs in Bukowski's work—the transient nature of life and the exaggerated import that human beings attach to ephemera.

These poems have the cadence of impending catastrophe. Beginning with "Ten Lions and the End of the World," Bukowski moved from the mundane to the apocalyptic without missing a beat; he forged a vantage point that is both ironic and sentimental as he pondered the cost of the pell-mell pace of modern life.

In Bukowski's world almost anything was possible. Although the potential for violence was ever present, it defied logic. His was the spirit of farce. He constantly challenged the contours of reality. He employed a farcical dialectic to conjoin the bizarre and the mundane; he used brutal undercutting, as in "Love Is a Piece of Paper Torn to Bits," in which a ship out of control and a wife being "serviced" by another are divested of significance while a worrisome cat is promoted to center stage. By focusing on the cat and the "dishes with flowers and vines painted on them," he effectively understated his angst. Similarly, in "I Cannot Stand Tears," a guard kills a wounded goose because "the bird was crying and I cannot stand tears."

Also evident in this first volume is Bukowski's justification for callous machismo as a defense against "the lie of love"; he established his argument by infusing his poems with countless oxymorons that rearranged the signposts of reality. In "Soiree," a bottle becomes a "dwarf waiting to scratch out my prayers," and in "His Wife, the Painter," a bus becomes "insanity sprung from a waving line"; he spoke of the sunlight as a lie and markets smelling of "shoes and naked boys clothed." "Soiree" also announces the impossibility of sustaining a relationship; "Did I Ever Tell You" captures the tragicomic element of love. The inescapable conclusion from this panoply is that love is futile, duplicitous, or, at best, based on mutual concessions. This explains the frequent crassness in Bukowski's work, which was already evident in "No Charge."

LONGSHOT POEMS FOR BROKE PLAYERS

Longshot Poems for Broke Players contains several poems that do justice to the existentialism and craftsmanship that Bukowski demonstrated in his first volume. "The State of World Affairs from a Third Floor Window," for example, melds an essentially voyeuristic point of view with reflections on a nuclear-infested world. Its tone is mellow and its counterpoint suggests the possibility of survival. Survival, it seems, is a matter of perspective, a point forcefully echoed in "The Tragedy of the Leaves," which embodies Bukowski's belief that what was needed was "a good comedian, ancient style, a jester with jokes upon absurd pain; pain as absurd because it exists." It concludes with an empathetic identification with his landlady "because the world had failed us both."

The surrealism of "What a Man I Was," which lampoons the legendary status of various Western heroes, is accelerated and refined in "The Best Way to Get Famous Is to Run Away," which revolves around the proverbial desire to live underground, away from the masses and the absurdity of explaining "why." Inherent in this piece, as well as in "Conversations in a Cheap Room" and "Poems for Personnel Managers," is the unattainability of resonance, the inability to comprehend the suffering of others: "Age was a crime . . . Pity picked up the marbles and . . . Hatred picked up the cash." A blend of the sensitive and ironic, an easy movement through cliché and culture dignifies these pieces. The result is a litany of sorts dedicated to those who have fallen through the cracks of the dream, unveiling a world of fraudulent promises that routinely casts aside those who do not conform to the dictates of propriety.

RUN WITH THE HUNTED AND IT CATCHES MY HEART IN ITS HAND

Run with the Hunted, the most uneven of Bukowski's early works, is more freewheeling than *Poems and Drawings*; it displays flashes of insight in "Old Man, Dead in a Room" and reaches innovative heights in "Vegas." Bukowski interwove the abstract and the concrete to capture the impossibility of communication and the essential insanity of social and artistic convention. The majority of the poems, however, seem self-indulgent and pointlessly crass.

Having gained recognition from the early chapbooks, Bukowski assumed a surer direction. *It Catches My Heart in Its Hand* culls some of the best from the early chapbooks and adds many new pieces. In this work, Bukowski mocked his own former self-pity and transforms it into a literary device with which to document the passage of time, as in "Old Poet" and "The Race." The danger of sanctifying art receives a lighter handling in "The Talkers," which is both a critique of art for art's sake and a renunciation of those who would hide behind abstraction and pretense.

CRUCIFIX IN A DEATHHAND AND THE GENIUS OF THE CROWD

Artistic distance is even more evident in *Crucifix in a Deathhand*, which centers around reawakened memories, senses deadened by the workaday world, and actual confrontations with death. In "Sunflower" and "Fuzz," for example, Bukowski muted his personal voice to universalize his own anguish; he often seemed, as in "Grass," to be observing himself. The workaday world, the province of "little men with luck and a headstart" emerges as deadening in "Machinegun Towers & Timeclocks" and "Something for the Touts, the Nuns, the Grocery Clerks and You. . . ." Bukowski was equally contemptuous of the bovine mentality of the masses and the group-think of the counterculture. In "This," he elevated himself above any prescriptions and became his own measuring rod. His is the stance of the loner, seeking pleasures where he finds them and deferring to no one. Survival, he suggested, demands egotism; otherwise, one can only await the fiery cleansing of the bomb contemplated in "A Report Upon the Consumption of Myself."

Bukowski's disdain for all that is average becomes more overt in a single-poem chapbook, *The Genius of the Crowd*, a jeremiad cautioning the poet to avoid the profane influence of culture. More boldly than any previous poem, it unmasks Bukowski's contempt for the masses and asserts that "There is enough treachery, hatred, violence, absurdity in the average human being to supply any given army on any given day." This is reinforced by the suggestion that most preaching is duplicitous, a game of mirrors.

COLD DOGS IN THE COURTYARD

A very different impression is gleaned from *Cold Dogs in the Courtyard*, over which Bukowski was given editorial control. In a prefatory note, he explained that he chose those poems that he felt had been unduly neglected. What emerges is a collection keynoted by an almost tender melancholia. "Imbecile Night," for example, establishes a delicate balance with which he endured the dreary cadence of darkness. Informing these poems is a sense of awe as he notes the consonance of nature's marvels and human invention, especially apparent in "It's Nothing to Laugh About." Compounding this is the poignant juxtaposition of the substantial and the ephemeral, as in "Existence," a poem built around the post office and the exaggerated importance attached to "dead letters." Like the roof in "2 Outside as Bones Break in My Kitchen," the letters maintain but fail to nurture the human spirit.

In "Layovers," the memories of lost love and the dreams of renewal serve as a reprieve from Bukowski's encounters with death. Serving a similar function are encounters with the unexpected, as in "Experience," and anarchistic protests such as the one depicted in "What Seems to Be the Trouble, Gentlemen?" These poems work, in part, because they lack the self-congratulatory tone of *The Genius of the Crowd* and the self-indulgence of *The Curtains Are Waving*, which reveals the limits of Bukowski's style; in an attempt to come to terms with his angst, he is left decrying his fate.

At Terror Street and Agony Way

By the time *At Terror Street and Agony Way* appeared, Bukowski had apparently regained artistic control; the volume substitutes self-mockery for self-pity. Although he continued to probe the plight of those caught under the technocratic juggernaut, he did so more emblematically and with greater levity. In "Red and Gold Paint," he conceives of luck and art as miracles against the cunning caprices of bosses, wars, and the weather. It is only playing against the odds, he repeatedly suggests, which ensures survival. Those who relinquish the good fight or never begin, he implied in "Reunion," may ingratiate themselves, but they never really live.

This volume is more thematically unified by the primacy of terror and agony in Bukowski's perspective. The lost innocence of "As I Lay Dying," the gratuitousness of "Beerbottle," and the resultant agony of blinding dreams in "K. O." quietly undergird the wanton destruction of "Sunday Before Noon" and the defeated dreams of "7th Race." Similarly, "I Wanted to Overthrow the Government" records Bukowski's suspicion of revolutionary schemes: "The weakness was not Government but Man, one at a time . . . men were never as strong as their ideas and . . . ideas were governments turned into men."

Poems Written Before Jumping out of an Eight Story Window and A Bukowski Sampler

Bukowski's next volume, *Poems Written Before Jumping out of an Eight Story Window*, constitutes a reversal. Absent are the literary allusions, the calm and urbanity of *At Terror Street and Agony Way*. The old shrillness is back as Bukowski donned the "beast" persona and vented his spleen, abandoning all finesse. Rapine, murder, and gothic elements dominate; an alcoholic fog blurs his vision. Even the best piece, "The Hairy Hairy Fist, and Love Will Die," despite its relentless "beat" and its examination of the individual turned back on himself, deafened by silence, is reduced in magnitude.

The publication of *A Bukowski Sampler* in 1969 signaled a change. In a little less than eighty pages, Doug Blazek assembled some of the best of Bukowski's work. His selection, a fairly representative one allowing the neophyte a full taste of Bukowski, also includes an editor's introduction, a letter from Bukowski, and several tributes from admirers of his work. Published about six months after *Notes of a Dirty Old Man*, the volume was directed at the growing Bukowski audience and the burgeoning counter-culture.

THE DAYS RUN AWAY LIKE WILD HORSES OVER THE HILLS

While *The Days Run Away Like Wild Horses over the Hills* again culls poems from the early chapbooks, the majority of the pieces are new and fresh. Since the book was dedicated to Jane, it is not surprising to find death as the leitmotiv. What is surprising is the almost sensual tone. In several poems to Jane, one can feel both the depth of Bukowski's love and the anguish which her death occasioned. While there are the obligatory accounts of womanizing, these pale before his elegies to Jane and his references to Frances and Marina. His attitude is encapsulated in "Birth," where the male dominion is muted by "small female things and jewels."

Allusions are multiplied without pretension; in "Ants Crawl My Drunken Arms," he criticized the banality of popular culture that prefers Willie Mays to Bach and the killing realities that essentially devoured Arthur Rimbaud, Ezra Pound, and Hart Crane. In "The Sharks" and "The Great One," the artist emerges as victim, and in "The Seminar" and "On a Grant" the pretense and incestuousness of the literary establishment are mocked through both the form and the content of the poems.

MOCKINGBIRD WISH ME LUCK

In *Mockingbird Wish Me Luck*, his next collection, Bukowski probed the culturally sanctioned disparities and skewed priorities which produce "shipping clerks who have read the Harvard Classics" and allow the powerful "a 15 percent take on the dream." "Hogs in the Sky" suggests that survival is a miracle, and yet, no more than a proper rehearsal for death "as old age arrives on schedule." The paraplegic who continues to play the longshots in "The World's Greatest Loser" is merely an extreme illustration of the fact that "nobody had any luck." Hence, the aspiring writer becomes a random assassin in "The Garbageman" and an ace crapshooter in "Moyamensing Prison."

Much of the humor in these poems is self-deprecatory, as in "The Last Days of the Suicide Kid," but subtler ironies emerge as well: the cost of success in "Making It" and the very real risk of becoming a noted writer in "The Poet's Muse." Bukowski recognized that often the skid row bums have more brains, more wit, and sometimes more satisfaction than those who have "won." Again it is a question of perspective—something which is a rare commodity in America, he notes in "Earthquake."

The second part of this volume is teeming with primordial images and energies.

Monkey feet, lions, and mockingbirds stalk and taunt the poet and reader while the mass media relentlessly promote diversions and distractions. The gullibility of the masses, not a new theme, is used to establish Bukowski's own superiority and contempt for platitudes. Recording his experiences with the draft board in "WW2," he compared himself to the draftees, concluding, "I was not as young as they." Not as young, perhaps, because he, like Robinson Jeffers, whom he eulogizes in "He Wrote in Lonely Blood," has solitary instincts and an understanding of what is essential. However, in both "The Hunt" and "The Shoelace," he realized that it is the little things which tip the scale and "sometimes create unemployed drunks . . . trying to grab for grunion."

The final section of *Mockingbird Wish Me Luck* is unified by the risks of love. Love, a tenuous miracle, endures for Bukowski only with Marina, who is the subject of several poems. "The Shower" suggests that others, like Linda King, will eventually pass out of his life despite the depth of their mutual feelings. At the other extreme are the large number of women who are sought because they are, by definition, "one-week stands." The only alternative to the ebb and flow is represented by the "old fashioned whore" and the "American matador" who opt out of conscriptive relationships.

Burning in Water, Drowning in Flame

These conversational poems are often riddled by the banter and banality which characterize the bulk of daily interactions, yet Bukowski insisted on the need for style—"a fresh way to approach a dull or dangerous thing." Herein lies the key to Bukowski's poetic credo—he did not seek new themes, but, rather, reworked the old from a new angle of vision. This approach is especially germane to *Burning in Water, Drowning in Flame*, which reprints many poems that had gone out of print and redirected his probing of such phenomena as love's impermanence. *Burning in Water, Drowning in Flame* constitutes a fitting conclusion to the third stage of Bukowski's career. Including sections of poems from *It Catches My Heart in Its Hand*, *Crucifix in a Deathhand*, and *At Terror Street and Agony Way* (to which *The Curtains Are Waving* has been added), it was a testimony to his growing reputation, and, having been published by one of the more prestigious small presses, accomplished the aim of *A Bukowski Sampler* with considerable finesse.

In addition to making selections from earlier volumes, this one includes a section of new poems. These are not gentle poems. Beginning with "Now," which compares writing poetry with lancing boils, Bukowski moved to "Zoo," which questions whether, in fact, humans have evolved significantly. "The Way" represents a brutal culmination, resembling the cascading cadence of Allen Ginsberg's "Howl" (1956, 1996) while managing not to fall away or to lose its sardonic tone.

The reportorial style which informs these poems is wryly explained in "Deathbed Blues" and panned in "My Friend, Andre," and while it is not always effective, at its best it gives testimony to the moral dignity which is attainable despite the depravity which threatens to consume the human spirit. "Death of an Idiot," which calls to mind "Conversations with a Lady Sipping a Straight Shot" in *The Days Run Away Like Wild Horses over the Hills*, displays compassion and achieves its impact by understatement.

Love Is a Dog from Hell

Bukowski's later poetry is more persistently autobiographical and more finely honed than his earlier work. Many of the poems, especially in *Love Is a Dog from Hell*, have fictional analogues in *Women*. A tendency already apparent in "Hell Hath No Fury . . ." in *Burning in Water, Drowning in Flame*, becomes more evident here; the poems often seem merely to have been transplanted into (or from) the novel. Similarly, several of the poems in *Dangling in the Tournefortia* correspond to *Shakespeare Never Did This*, and others clearly reveal the influence of Bukowski's move to San Pedro—a move which has not tempered his perspective.

Love Is a Dog from Hell, like the chapbook *Scarlet* which it incorporates, has loves and lusts as its primary focus. The proper context for viewing these poems is suggested by Bukowski's comment that "love is ridiculous because it can't last and sex is ridiculous because it doesn't last long enough." It was the tragicomedy which impelled him. Refusing to defer to feminist sensibilities, he related one sexual adventure after another, capturing both the eternal search and the predictable defeats which await everyone in "Another Bed."

Women are portrayed in a variety of stances; sometimes merely objects, they are at other times capable of turning the male into an object, as the black widow spider in "The Escape" and the teeth mother in "A Killer" are inclined to do. The women range from aspiring artists and reformers to whores, and the latter have the edge "because they lie about nothing." While some may take offense at the sexism in these pieces, it seems to cut both ways; the men are no less demeaned than the women. This is still the world of the streets where proprieties and pretense fall away. In poems such as "One for Old Snaggle-tooth," dedicated to Frances, Bukowski's sensitivity is economically and precisely conveyed.

The second section is concerned with the tragedies and inhumanities which transform artists into madmen or panderers. "What They Want" reads like a top ten list of artistic casualties. The artist emerges as vulnerable and damned in "There Once Was a Woman Who Put Her Head in an Oven," which calls to mind poet Sylvia Plath. However, in "The Crunch," Bukowski suggested that the artist is able to utilize the isolation and failure that drive others over the edge. Both survival and creativity seem to demand solitude, as long as it is not irreversible.

Play the Piano Drunk Like a Percussion Instrument Until the Fingers Begin to Bleed a Bit

Primarily a reissue of several chapbooks, *Play the Piano Drunk Like a Percussion Instrument Until the Fingers Begin to Bleed a Bit* lacks the thematic unity of the preceding volume, but it does demonstrate Bukowski's iconoclasm and his ability to revive old themes. The title deadpans the conception of the typewriter as a musical instrument, a theme first introduced in "Chopin Bukowski" in *Love Is a Dog from Hell.*

Beginning with "Tough Company," which turns poems into gunslingers waiting to receive their due, Bukowski unleashed his acerbic wit against ersatz holiday gaiety, feigned idealism, parental protocol, the notion of a limited nuclear war, and the pretense of civilization, which is compared to fool's gold in "Through the Streets of Anywhere." While there is a sense of absurdity and subterfuge rampaging through these poems, there is also a sense of durability and substance. Again the losers at the racetrack bars, in the bowels of the slaughterhouses, and in the sterile rooming houses are pummeled but maintain their dignity, accepting their exclusion and their inability to affect their fates: "We are finally tricked and slapped to death like lovers' vows, bargained out of any gain." They await the arrival of the urban renewal cranes in "2347 Duane," and while they occasionally master the bravado of Bogart, as in "Maybe Tomorrow," more often they simply await death, as in "The Proud Thin Dying." If one is careful, "Horse and Fist" implies, one may yet survive despite the open-endedness of the game. In the meantime, it is best to "play the piano drunk like a percussion instrument until the fingers begin to bleed a bit."

DANGLING IN THE TOURNEFORTIA

There is an interesting movement in *Dangling in the Tournefortia.* Several of the early poems are retrospective, establishing a counterpoint against which to view his status—something which is overt in poems such as "Guava Tree." It seems that he was suspicious of his newly won success, recognizing that he "can fail in many more ways now," as he said in "Fear and Madness," knowing that there are more "suckerfish" who will insist upon intruding and fretting about the state of his soul. However, "Notes Upon a Hot Streak" revealed the pleasure he took in the "lovable comedy" which "they are letting me win for this moment."

While success did not temper his perspective, it did temper his rage; even his references to his father's brutality were softened, and while death continued to loom, it no longer threatened to overwhelm him or his poetry. The more balanced tone is reinforced by his use of the tournefortia, a tropical tree with delicate flowers and a fleshy fruit, as a metaphor for the interplay of love and lust, being and nothingness. Again the tempestuous love affairs are paraded, sometimes callously but often with a quick parry, as in "The Descent of the Species" and "Snap Snap." In "The Lady in Red," he explores the compensatory function served by heroes such as Dillinger during the Depression; in "Fight On" and "Blue Collar Solitude," the needed respite offered by a good street brawl and/or several drinks; and in "Nothing," seeing a supervisor besotted somehow eases the pain and agony of the job.

The Last Generation

As one of the most prolific and well-known underground poets, Bukowski pinned his success on the authenticity of his voice. Even a casual encounter with his work reveals the lack of pretense and the refusal to kowtow to the critics. He refused to be beaten; as he suggested in *The Last Generation*, a single-poem broadside, it may be harder to be a genius with the proliferation of publishers and writers, but it is worth the attempt. There are too many unsung characters of the "unholy parade" and too many poems which demand to be written.

Bukowski's bawdiness no less than his free-form style constituted a manifesto of sorts. American poetry has long been cautious and unduly arcane, thereby excluding a large part of the potential poetry audience and a wide range of subjects and sentiments. Booze, hard loving, and horse racing, while not generally seen as poetic subjects, dominate Bukowski's oeuvre. His crassness, which weakened some of his pieces, was in his best work complemented by a sensitive understanding of the fringes of society. Beneath the veneer, one senses a man who was unaccustomed to and rather afraid of love; a man who simultaneously disdained and applauded the masses because of his own ambivalent self-concept.

Collections of the 1990's

In the 1990's Bukowski softened a bit and reflectively examined his feelings about aging and death. His last book of poems published in his lifetime was *Last Night of the Earth Poems*, his longest poetry collection. Like all his poetry, the poems here are rich in sarcasm and filled with antiauthoritarian diatribes, madness, satire, and death. However, while death has always been a facet of Bukowski's poetry, here it is not the death that stalked Bukowski through forty years of poetry, resulting from alcohol abuse or depravity. Rather, it is the end of a long-lived life. Bukowski reveals that he is and has been involved in the great seasonal cycles of life: birth, death, and rebirth; pain, sorrow, and love. The subtle sensitivity of the volume is also present in its obvious love poems, many seemingly addressed to Linda Lee Beighle.

Bone Pallace Ballet is divided into five sections that outline his life, from recollections that romanticize his drunken youth as a time when there was a "feeling of/ joy and gamble in/ the air" ("Beeting on the Muse") to the final section presenting poems that take stock of his life and square-off with death. *Open All Night*, like the collection of his poems titled *What Matters Most Is How Well You Walk Through the Fire*, is an expansive volume full of the grizzled mutterings that readers have come to expect from Bukowski: Former lovers, binge drinking, disillusioned souls, and the racetrack are well represented. Like other works of the 1990's, however, *Open All Night* reveals a more wistful Bukowski, an aging writer who was fearlessly confronting his mortality. Writing was never about praise or fame, he says, but "for myself/ to save what is left of/ myself." Bukowski is finally able to admit: "I've had a good run./ I can toss it in without regret."

OTHER MAJOR WORKS

LONG FICTION: *Post Office*, 1971; *Factotum*, 1975; *Women*, 1978; *Ham on Rye*, 1982; *You Get So Alone at Times That It Just Makes Sense*, 1986; *Hollywood*, 1989; *Pulp*, 1994.

SHORT FICTION: *Notes of a Dirty Old Man*, 1969; *Erections, Ejaculations, Exhibitions, and General Tales of Ordinary Madness*, 1972; *Life and Death in the Charity Ward*, 1973; *South of No North: Stories of the Buried Life*, 1973; *Bring Me Your Love*, 1983; *Hot Water Music*, 1983; *The Most Beautiful Woman in Town, and Other Stories*, 1983; *There's No Business*, 1984; *The Day It Snowed in L.A.*, 1986.

SCREENPLAY: *Barfly*, 1987.

NONFICTION: *Shakespeare Never Did This*, 1979 (photographs by Michael Montfort); *The Bukowski/Purdy Letters: A Decade of Dialogue, 1964-1974*, 1983; *Screams from the Balcony: Selected Letters, 1960-1970*, 1993; *Reach for the Sun: Selected Letters, 1978-1994*, 1999 (Seamus Cooney, editor); *Beerspit Night and Cursing: The Correspondence of Charles Bukowski and Sheri Martinelli, 1960-1967*, 2001 (Steven Moore, editor).

MISCELLANEOUS: *You Kissed Lilly*, 1978; *Septuagenarian Stew: Stories and Poems*, 1990; *Run with the Hunted: A Charles Bukowski Reader*, 1993; *Betting on the Muse: Poems and Stories*, 1996; *Charles Bukowski: Portions from a Wine-Stained Notebook—Uncollected Stories and Essays, 1944-1990*, 2008 (David Stephen Calonne, editor).

BIBLIOGRAPHY

Cain, Jimmie. "Bukowski's Imagist Roots." *West Georgia College Review* 19 (May, 1987): 10-17. Cain draws a parallel between Bukowski's poetry and the work of William Carlos Williams, America's premier Imagist poet. Cain claims that Bukowski's rough-and-tumble poetry shows palpable Imagist influences. For advanced students.

Cherkovski, Neeli. *Bukowski: A Life*. South Royalton, Vt.: Steerforth, 1997. This volume is "a slightly different version" of Cherkovski's *Hank: The Life of Charles Bukowski*, published in 1991. Its strength resides in the writer's close access to the subject during their early friendship and material from interviews with Bukowski. It purports to include the "wilder stories" which Bukowski regretted were previously omitted. The bibliography has been updated.

Harrison, Russell. *Against the American Dream: Essays on Charles Bukowski*. Santa Rosa, Calif.: Black Sparrow Press, 1994. An excellent study that examines Bukowski's critique of the work ethic in his poetry and prose.

McDonough, Tom. "Down and (Far) Out." *American Film* 13 (November, 1987): 26-30. McDonough discusses how Bukowski's real-life alcoholism was portrayed in the 1987 biographical film *Barfly*. In the film, the drunken Bukowski was played by actor Mickey Rourke, while Faye Dunaway played his drinking companion.

Gives an interesting popular insight into Bukowski's life.

Sounes, Howard. *Charles Bukowski: Locked in the Arms of a Crazy Life*. New York: Grove, 1999. Sounes indicates at the beginning of this book how Bukowski strived markedly to "improve upon" his life and make it even "more picaresque" than it was. Successfully conjures up the voice of this outrageous character and offers clear-eyed insight into his extraordinary life.

Wakoski, Diane. "Charles Bukowski." In *Contemporary Poets*, edited by James Vinson and D. L. Kirkpatrick. 4th ed. New York: St. Martin's Press, 1985. Wakoski traces Bukowski's rising popularity but laments the fact that though "Americans . . . honor truth," and Bukowski's poems are distinguished by their unself-pitying truthfulness, he has not received much serious criticism. Includes a list of his publications up to 1984.

Weizmann, Daniel, ed. *Drinking with Bukowski: Recollections of the Poet Laureate of Skid Row*. New York: Thunder's Mouth Press, 2000. Essays by friends of Bukowski such as Wanda Coleman, Raymond Carver, Karen Finley, Paul Trachtenberg, Fred Voss, and Sean Penn.

C. Lynn Munro
Updated by Sarah Hilbert

GREGORY CORSO

Born: New York, New York; March 26, 1930
Died: Robbinsdale, Minnesota; January 17, 2001

Principal poetry

The Vestal Lady on Brattle, and Other Poems, 1955
Gasoline, 1958
The Happy Birthday of Death, 1960
Minutes to Go, with Others, 1960
Long Live Man, 1962
Selected Poems, 1962
The Mutation of the Spirit, 1964
There Is Yet Time to Run Back Through Life and Expiate All That's Been Sadly Done, 1965
Ten Times a Poem, 1967
Elegiac Feelings American, 1970
Earth Egg, 1974
Herald of the Autochthonic Spirit, 1981
Mindfield: New and Selected Poems, 1989

Other literary forms

Although Gregory Corso published mainly poetry, he also wrote a short play, *In This Hung-up Age*, produced at Harvard University in 1955; a novel, *The American Express* (1961); and two film scripts: *Happy Death*, with Jay Socin, produced in New York in 1965, and *That Little Black Door on the Left*, included in a group of screenplays entitled *Pardon Me, Sir, But Is My Eye Hurting Your Elbow?* (1968). He also wrote, with Anselm Hollo and Tom Raworth, a series of parodies, *The Minicab War*, published in London by the Matrix Press in 1961.

Achievements

Perhaps Gregory Corso's greatest contribution to the Beat movement specifically and American poetry generally lies in his role as a literary paradigm for the "New Bohemianism" that appeared in the United States after World War II and through the 1950's. Although Corso never went beyond elementary school, he gained a reputation as one of the most talented of the Beat poets, a "poet's poet," a sort of *enfant terrible* of the Beats. He received teaching appointments on the basis of his reputation as a major figure in the Beat movement. He was awarded the Longview Foundation Award in 1959 for his poem "Marriage," the Poetry Foundation Award, and the Jean Stein Award in Poetry from the American Academy of Arts and Letters in 1986.

Biography

More than any of his contemporaries, Gregory Nunzio Corso lived the true Beat life. Brought up in the slums of New York City, with practically no formal education, Corso was, in the words of the poet-critic Kenneth Rexroth, "a genuine *naif.* A real wildman, with all the charm of a hoodlum . . . a wholesome Antonin Artaud."

He was born in New York City to poor Italian immigrant parents, Fortunato Samuel and Michelina (Colloni) Corso. His mother died when he was a child, and about this loss Corso wrote: "I do not know how to accept love when love is given me. I needed that love when I was motherless young and never had it." His unhappy childhood was marked by his being sent to an orphanage at eleven and to the Children's Observation Ward at Bellevue Hospital when he was thirteen. At that time, Corso later wrote, "I was alone in the world—no mother and my father was at war . . . to exist I stole minor things and to sleep I slept on the rooftops and in the subway." In summarizing his thirteenth year, however, Corso insists that although he went "through a strange hell that year" of 1943, it is "such hells that give birth to the poet."

After three years on the streets of New York, having lived with five different foster parents, Corso was arrested with two friends while attempting to rob a store. Instead of being sent to a boys' reformatory, Corso was sentenced to three years at Clinton Prison, where he began to write poetry. According to Corso, prison "proved to be one of the greatest things that ever happened to me." He even dedicated his second book of poems, *Gasoline*, to "the angels of Clinton Prison" who forced him to give up the often "silly consciousness of youth" to confront the world of men.

After his release from prison in 1950, Corso took on a number of short-term jobs, including manual labor from 1950 to 1951, reporting for the *Los Angeles Examiner* from 1951 to 1952, and sailing on Norwegian vessels as a merchant seaman from 1952 to 1953. He also spent some time in Mexico and in Cambridge, Massachusetts, where he was encouraged in his writing of poetry by an editor of the *Cambridge Review* and where, with the support of several Harvard students, he published his first book of poetry, *The Vestal Lady on Brattle, and Other Poems*, in 1955.

Between that time and his departure for Europe in 1959, Corso attracted widespread attention with a series of poetry readings he gave in the East and Midwest. Following the 1955 publication of *The Vestal Lady on Brattle, and Other Poems* and his meeting with Jack Kerouac, Allen Ginsberg, and Gary Snyder a year later, his poetry began to appear often in such publications as *Esquire*, *Partisan Review*, *Contact*, and the *Evergreen Review*. In 1958, Lawrence Ferlinghetti first published Corso's famous poem "Bomb" as a broadside at his City Lights Bookshop in San Francisco, as well as the book *Gasoline* in the same year. After an extended tour of England, France, Germany, Italy, and Greece,

Corso returned to the United States in 1961. During the following three years, he was hired to teach poetry for a term at New York State University at Buffalo. In November, 1963, he married Sally November.

For Corso, the 1960's were marked by a divorce and more travel in Europe. After the publication of *The Happy Birthday of Death* in 1960, which included such celebrated poems as "Bomb," "Power," "Army," and the award-winning "Marriage," the work that he did in the following decade was very uneven, frequently bordering on flippancy and sentimentality, such as some of the poems in *Long Live Man* and *The Mutation of the Spirit*. *Elegiac Feelings American* and *Herald of the Autochthonic Spirit* were published a decade apart, appearing in 1970 and 1981, respectively. The increased intervals between offerings indicate a shift in Corso's attitude toward the relationship between the poet and his poems. During the salad days of the Beat movement, Corso had taken his cue from his contemporaries (notably Kerouac) by rejecting any mode of writing except pure spontaneity, but his later poems are much more carefully revised and tightly crafted works. This can be seen in the newer poems that appear in *Mindfield*.

Corso traveled widely over the course of his lifetime, in Mexico and Eastern Europe as well as Western Europe, and in addition to teaching at the State University of New York at Buffalo, he taught in Boulder, Colorado. He was married three times and had five children. In his later years, he became somewhat reclusive, taking part in the occasional tribute or event and making an appearance at the funeral of Ginsberg in 1996. Ill health forced Corso to move from New York City to Minneapolis, where he lived with a daughter. He died in Robbinsdale, Minnesota, on January 17, 2001, at the age of seventy.

ANALYSIS

Two strains pervade the poetry of Gregory Corso: the Dionysian force of emotion and spontaneity, and a preoccupation with death. From Corso's early poems to his later work, one finds the recurring persona of the clown as an embodiment of the Dionysian force, as opposed to the Apollonian powers of order, clarity, and moderation. The clown's comedy, which has its root in the very fact of being "a poet in such a world as the world is today," ranges from the mischievous laughter of the child to the darker, often somber irony of the poet-in-the-world. This exuberance is bound up with the rebelliousness and political activism of the 1960's, as is evident in one of Corso's early and most widely anthologized poems, "Bomb." In this poem—typographically shaped like a bomb in its original 1958 publication by City Lights—Corso confronted the unalterable reality of the nuclear age and his inability "to hate what is necessary to love."

A large part of Corso's Dionysian spirit is romantic—and Corso is certainly in the tradition of Romantic poets John Keats and Percy Bysshe Shelley. He sees the child as a pure, spontaneous Dionysian being: always naturally perceptive, always instinctively aware of sham, pretense, and deception. Such perception runs throughout American literature, from the character of Pearl in Nathaniel Hawthorne's *The Scarlet Letter* (1850) to the child who "went forth" in Walt Whitman to Huckleberry Finn in Mark Twain's novel of 1884 to Holden Caulfield in J. D. Salinger's *The Catcher in the Rye* (1951). Similarly, in Corso's poetry, the child (particularly the self of the poet's recollection) stands for pure Dionysian perception without the intervening deceptions of rules and conventions.

The other strain in Corso's poetry is a passionate concern with the mystery of death, a theme that is more pervasive in his work than any other, with the exception of the pure experience of childhood. Indeed, the intermingling of these two motifs essentially characterizes the Dionysian spirit of Corso—as well as the art of the Beat generation in general. In a poem dedicated to one of his heroes, entitled "I Met This Guy Who Died" (*Mindfield*), Corso writes about a drunken outing with his friend Jack Kerouac. Taken home to see Corso's newborn child, Kerouac moans: "Oh Gregory, You brought up something to die." "How I love to probe life," Corso once wrote in an autobiographical essay. "That's what poetry is to me, a wondrous prober.... It's not the metre, or measure of a line, a breath; not 'law' music, but the assembly of great eye-sounds placed into an inspired measured idea."

Gasoline

In an early collection, *Gasoline*, Corso solidifies his poetic identity in a directly autobiographical poem, "In the Fleeting Hand of Time." Here the poet casts his lot not with the Apollonian academics, who "lay forth sheepskin plans," but with life in the "all too real mafia streets." In another poem from this early collection, entitled "Birthplace Revisited," the poet captures what Allen Ginsberg referred to as "the inside sound of language alone" by virtually overturning the expected or commonplace. This brief poem opens with a mysterious figure wandering the lonely, dark street, seeking out the place where he was born. The figure resembles a character from a detective story—"with raincoat, cigarette in mouth, hat over eye, hand on gat"—but when he reaches the top of the first flight of stairs, "Dirty Ears aims a knife at me . . . I pump him full of lost watches." This is not exactly the kind of image one would expect to find in the language of the standard-bearers of Corso's time, such as Allen Tate or John Crowe Ransom. In fact, in an act of Dionysian rebellion, Corso, in a poem entitled "I Am Twenty-five," bluntly proclaims "I HATE OLD POETMEN!"—especially those "who speak their youth in whispers." The poet-clown, in true Dionysian fashion, would like to gain the confidence of the "Old Poetman," insinuating himself into the sanctity of his home, and then "rip out their apology tongues/ and steal their poems."

The Happy Birthday of Death

The Happy Birthday of Death presents the best example of Corso as Dionysian clown. In the lengthy ten-part poem entitled simply "Clown," Corso presents this persona more explicitly than he does in any other place when he asserts, "I myself am my own happy fool." The fool or the clown is the personification of the "pure poetry" of Arthur Rimbaud or Walt Whitman, rejecting the academic Apollonian style of the formalists. "I am an always clown," writes Corso, "and need not make grammatic Death's diameter."

Several of the poems of *The Happy Birthday of Death*, notably the award-winning "Marriage," offer critiques of respected institutions of bourgeois society. This poem, perhaps Corso's most popular, is structured around the central questions: "Should I get married? Should I be good?" In a surrealistic feast of language-play, Corso contrasts the social ritual of marriage ("absurd rice and clanky cans and shoes," Niagara Falls honeymoons, cornball relatives) with the irrational and spontaneous phrases he inserts throughout the poem, such as "Flash Gordon soap," "Pie Glue," "Radio Belly! Cat Shovel!" and "Christmas Teeth." In opposition to the conformist regimentation of suburban life, the speaker contrives unconventional schemes, such as sneaking onto a neighbor's property late at night and "hanging pictures of Rimbaud on the lawnmower" or covering "his golf clubs with 1920 Norwegian books."

LONG LIVE MAN

In his later work *Long Live Man*, Corso continued his Dionysian assault on established literary conventions. The poem "After Reading 'In the Clearing,'" for example, finds the speaker admitting that he likes the "Old Poetman" Robert Frost better now that he knows he is "no Saturday Evening Post philosopher." Nevertheless, Frost is "old, old" like Rome, and, says the poet, "You undoubtedly think unwell of us/ but we are your natural children." What Corso intends is not to suggest that youth should respect age, but rather, as William Wordsworth wrote in "Ode: Intimations of Immortality from Recollections of Early Childhood," that "the child is father to the man." As Corso points out in his urban poem "A City Child's Day," the "Grownups do not go where children go/ At break of day their worlds split apart."

Two short poems in the earlier *Long Live Man*, viewed together, seem to foreshadow the approach Corso later used to criticize the institution of marriage and, still later, in *Elegiac Feelings American* and *Herald of the Autochthonic Spirit*, Corso maintains his Dionysian critique of Apollonian standards. The first poem is entitled "Suburban Mad Song"; the second, "The Love of Two Seasons." The first asks how the wife will look at the husband after "the horns are still," when the celebration is ended "and marriage drops its quiet shoe." In other words, when the Dionysian passions of the first experiences become the frozen form, the institution of marriage, the once-happy couple "freeze right in their chairs/ troubled by the table." The only solution for such stasis, Corso seems to be saying in the other short poem, "The Love of Two Seasons," is "the aerial laughter [of] mischief."

ELEGIAC FEELINGS AMERICAN

In "The American Way," a long poem from *Elegiac Feelings American*, Corso worries that the prophetic force of Christ is becoming frozen by American civil religion.

"They are frankensteining Christ," the poet says despairingly; "they are putting the fear of Christ in America" and "bringing their Christ to the stadiums." Christ, for Corso, is the pure force of reality, while religious institutions are merely perversions even as love between two people is a pure and sacred force, while marriage is profane. "If America falls," writes Corso, "it will be the blame of its educators preachers communicators alike."

HERALD OF THE AUTOCHTHONIC SPIRIT

Herald of the Autochthonic Spirit suggests not only that the poet has not withered with age but also that he has mastered an ironic voice while maintaining his comic, childlike energy. In a simple poem, "When a Boy," he remarks, first of all, how he "monitored the stairs/ alter'd the mass" in church, as opposed to the pleasure of summer camp, when he "kissed the moon in a barrel of rain." Similarly, in the poem "Youthful Religious Experience," he tells how he found a dead cat when he was six years old and compassionately prayed for it, placing a cross on the animal. When he told this to the Sunday school teacher, she pulled his ears and told him to remove the cross. The old, Corso maintains, can never comprehend the eternally young.

In another poem from this collection, "What the Child Sees," Corso depicts the child as "innocently contemptuous of the sight" of old age's foolishness. "There's rust on the old truths," Corso contends in "For Homer," and "New lies don't smell as nice as new shoes." What the poet, like the child, perceives as pleasurable is the immediate, sensual experience, such as the smell of new shoes, not the abstractions of dried-up old lies. The sadness at the root of this pleasure, however, is a sadness that appears in much of Corso's poetry, evoked by the perennial reality of death.

MINDFIELD

The 1989 collection *Mindfield* is a compilation of Corso's favorite poems throughout his career, along with new poems. Here, one can trace the maturation of the poet across three decades. Particularly revealing are the seven poems written after the appearance of *Herald of the Autochthonic Spirit* in 1981 but previously unpublished. These poems illustrate the growth of Corso as a poet who, at the half century point in his life, had broadened the range and scope of his poetry while maintaining some of the themes that have dominated his work from the early 1950's.

In the poem "Window," written in 1982, Corso confronts the painful reality of his own mortality. The horror of death, however, becomes merely an evil invention of the older generation that, asserts the man-child Corso, is notoriously "unreliable." Writes Corso:

> . . . your parents your priest your guru are people
> and it is they who tell you that you must die
> to believe them is to die . . .

As a romantic, Corso draws his lessons from nature. Proclaiming his "contempt for death" and asserting that "the spirit knows better than the body," Corso offers the reader lines of poetry as moving as many of Wordsworth's in his assertion of immortality:

> As the fish is animalized water
> so are we humanized spirit
> fish come and go   humans also
> the death of the fish
> is not the death of the water
> likewise the death of yr body
> is not the death of life
> So when I say I shall never know my death, I mean it . . .

To Corso, death is merely another limit or restraint that he challenges throughout his poetry. When he writes, at one point, "Death I unsalute you," Corso illustrates his resistance to all limits that restrict what he sees as the limitless strength of the human spirit.

In the longest of the previously unpublished poems, "Field Report," Corso confronts the inevitable approach of old age with words that are gentle and not fearful. That poem, like most of his other later works, seems to give support to the words of Corso's contemporary and friend, Allen Ginsberg, who writes in his introduction to *Mindfield* ("On Corso's Virtues") words that, while written about a single poem ("The Whole Mess . . . Almost" from *Herald of the Autochthonic Spirit*), could be said about most of Corso's later poetry: The poem is "a masterpiece of Experience, the grand poetic abstractions Truth, Love, God, Faith Hope Charity, Beauty, money, Death, & Humor are animated in a single poem with brilliant & intimate familiarity."

In others of his previously unpublished poems from the 1980's, particularly "Hi" and "Fire Report—No Alarm," Corso grapples with such large metaphysical issues as God, mortality, immortality, and the identity of Jesus. Without God, Corso concludes ironically, the Reverend Jerry Falwell (leader of the conservative Moral Majority and the Christian Right) might well be putting onions on hamburgers. Such pithy, concrete insights are what give humor and vividness to Corso's later poetry.

OTHER MAJOR WORKS

LONG FICTION: *The American Express*, 1961; *The Minicab War*, 1961 (with Anselm Hollo and Tom Raworth).

PLAYS: *In This Hung-up Age*, pr. 1955; *Standing on a Streetcorner*, pb. 1962; *That Little Black Door on the Left*, pb. 1967.

SCREENPLAYS: *Happy Death*, 1965 (with Jay Socin); *That Little Black Door on the Left*, 1968.

MISCELLANEOUS: *Writing from Unmuzzled Ox Magazine*, 1981.

Bibliography

Cook, Bruce. "An Urchin Shelley." In *The Beat Generation.* New York: Charles Scribner's Sons, 1971. Cook discusses the lives and works of key figures of the Beat generation. Corso, in a 1974 interview, charged Cook with lying about him in an interview that he conducted.

Corso, Gregory. *An Accidental Autobiography: The Selected Letters of Gregory Corso.* Edited by Bill Morgan. New York: New Directions, 2003. A collection that concentrates on Corso's critical years of 1962 to 1967.

Gifford, Barry, and Lawrence Lee. *Jack's Book: An Oral Biography of Jack Kerouac.* New York: St. Martin's Press, 1978. An extensive biography of Jack Kerouac and his relationships with others of the Beat generation, including Corso. Under the influence of Kerouac, Corso put words together in an extremely abstract, apparently accidental manner. According to Corso, Kerouac was a "strong, beautiful man."

Hamilton, Ian. *Against Oblivion: Some Lives of the Twentieth-Century Poets.* London: Viking, 2002. Contains a chapter on Corso, examining his life and works.

Knight, Arthur, and Kit Knight, eds. *The Beat Vision: A Primary Sourcebook.* New York: Paragon House, 1987. This fascinating collection includes an interview with Corso as well as a letter from Corso to Gary Snyder. The book includes vintage photographs, critical discussion of the Beat poets' place in American literature, and the impact of their controversial ideas in shaping and defining American society.

Masheck, Joseph, ed. *Beat Art.* New York: Columbia University Press, 1977. Some of Corso's drawings were included in an exhibition of work by writers associated with the Beats, and although the catalog is not illustrated, the comments on the drawings are interesting and instructive. Corso's drawings, which are also featured in *Mindfield*, are significant but often overlooked artifacts of the Beat generation.

Miles, Barry. *The Beat Hotel: Ginsberg, Burroughs, and Corso in Paris, 1958-1963.* New York: Grove Press, 2000. A narrative account of Beat poets in Paris, where some of their most important work was done. Based on firsthand accounts from diaries, letters, and interviews.

Olson, Kirby. *Gregory Corso: Doubting Thomist.* Carbondale: Southern Illinois University Press, 2002. Olson examines Corso's poetry from a philosophical point, painting him as ranging from a static Catholic Thomist viewpoint to that of a progressive surrealist.

Selerie, Gavin. *Gregory Corso.* New York: Binnacle Press, 1982. Selerie includes an interview with Corso that is particularly provocative because of Corso's comments on his books—such as *Gasoline*, *The Happy Birthday of Death*, and *Elegiac Feelings American*—as well as friends such as Jack Kerouac, Allen Ginsberg, and William S. Burroughs. Corso also provides information on his youthful crimes and time spent in prison.

Skau, Michael. *A Clown in a Grave: Complexities and Tensions in the Works of Greg-*

ory Corso. Carbondale: Southern Illinois University Press, 2000. An examination that covers the complete works of Corso and his complex imagination, his humor, and his poetic techniques in dealing with the United States, the Beat generation, and death. Includes a bibliography of Corso's work.

Stephenson, Gregory. *Exiled Angel: A Study of the Work of Gregory Corso*. London: Hearing Eye, 1989. A full-length study of Corso's poetry, offering individual chapters on principal collections of poetry.

Donald E. Winters, Jr.

DIANE DI PRIMA

Born: Brooklyn, New York; August 6, 1934

PRINCIPAL POETRY

This Kind of Bird Flies Backward, 1958
Dinners and Nightmares, 1961, 1974 (stories, poetry, prose)
The New Handbook of Heaven, 1963
Earthsong: Poems, 1957-1959, 1968
Hotel Albert: Poems, 1968
Revolutionary Letters, Etc., 1971, 2007
Freddie Poems, 1974
Selected Poems, 1956-1975, 1975
Loba, Parts I-VIII, 1978
Pieces of a Song: Selected Poems, 1990
Loba, 1998
Ones I Used to Laugh With: A Haibun Journal, 2003
TimeBomb, 2006

OTHER LITERARY FORMS

Although Diane di Prima (dee PREE-muh) is best known for her poetry, she has published more than twenty volumes of poetry and prose and has written and produced a substantial number of plays. She is the author of two prose memoirs, the highly erotic novel-memoir *Memoirs of a Beatnik* (1969, 1988), which contributed significantly to making her the most widely known woman poet of the Beat generation, and *Recollections of My Life as a Woman: The New York Years, a Memoir* (2001), a remembrance of her growing feminist consciousness in the 1950's and 1960's. Di Prima has also translated poems from Latin and written several treatises on Paracelsus, the sixteenth century alchemist and physician. She has expressed her opinions on poetics, politics, feminism, and the Beat generation in numerous interviews.

ACHIEVEMENTS

Diane di Prima has received grants from the National Endowment for the Arts (1973 and 1979) and an honorary degree from St. Lawrence University (1999). She was a finalist for poet laureate of San Francisco in 2002 and 2005 before becoming the city's fifth laureate in 2009, and she was a finalist for poet laureate of California in 2003. She has garnered such honors as the Secret Six Medal of Valor (1987), the National Poetry Association lifetime service award (1993), the Aniello Lauri Award for creative writing (1994), the Fred Cody Award for lifetime achievement (2006), and the Reginald

Lockett Lifetime Achievement Award (2008). As a female member of the Beat generation, she has had to labor under the stereotype of "Beat chick," characterized by Jack Kerouac as girls "who say nothing and wear black." The last decades of the twentieth century brought a gradual revision of this stereotype and greater recognition for her work. Although her poems have received little academic or critical attention, they have attracted a growing number of devoted readers.

George F. Butterick has argued that di Prima's greatest contribution to the poetry of her generation lies in her work as an organizer and editor/publisher, beginning with her collaboration on *The Floating Bear*, a monthly publication she published together with her occasional lover LeRoi Jones (who later changed his name to Amiri Baraka) in 1961 and for which she served as editor until 1969. Also in the 1960's, she founded Poets Press, which published some thirty books of poetry and prose of such well-known figures as Herbert Huncke and Timothy Leary, as well as the anti-Vietnam War anthology *War Poems* (1968), edited by di Prima herself.

Even though di Prima has often been described as a minor constellation next to stars of the Beat generation such as Kerouac, Allen Ginsberg, William S. Burroughs, and Gregory Corso, her mature work since the 1970's deserves critical attention. She is an important catalyst and chronicler of the bohemian counterculture of her generation. For more than half a century, despite sweeping changes that have transformed society, di Prima has remained true to many of the central tenets of radical thought as established by the Beats: rejection of government propaganda, exploration of mental and physical sensations, spirituality, spontaneity, and hope for a world free of constraints.

BIOGRAPHY

Diane di Prima was born in Brooklyn, New York, to first-generation Italian immigrants Francis di Prima and Emma Mallozzi di Prima. In interviews and in autobiographical writings, she emphasizes the strict, conservative upbringing to which a young girl of Italian ancestry was subjected during the 1930's, the years of the Great Depression. She credits her anarchist grandfather, Domenico Mallozzi, with sowing the seeds for her subsequent rebellion against this confinement by taking her to anarchist rallies and reading the works of Dante to her. She began writing when she was seven years old and, by the age of fourteen, had already decided to become a poet. She enrolled at Swarthmore College in 1951, intending to major in theoretical physics. In 1953, she abandoned her academic career and moved to New York's lower East Side, beginning her bohemian life as a poet and activist, and like her male counterparts, she freely experimented with sex and drugs. During this time, she met Ezra Pound, who—because of his public support for Italian dictator Benito Mussolini—had been institutionalized at St. Elizabeths Hospital, a mental institution in Washington, D.C., where she visited him several times. Pound found encouraging words for her fledgling attempts at poetry, and the two corresponded for some time.

A decisive factor in di Prima's career was her introduction in 1957 to the founding members of the Beat generation, a group with whom she remained closely connected for the next decade. Indeed, di Prima is considered the most important female writer of the Beat generation and features prominently in every anthology of that group. In 1958, Totem Press (founded by Jones) published her first collection of poetry, *This Kind of Bird Flies Backward*, the first of many works of poetry, prose, and drama.

During her years in Manhattan, di Prima published and edited several poetry magazines and newsletters and helped found the New York Poets Theatre in 1961. She married for the first time in 1962, to actor-director Alan Marlowe; they divorced in 1969. She married poet Grant Fisher in 1972, but they divorced in 1975. The two marriages resulted in five children (Jeanne, Dominique, Alexander, Tara, and Rudra), whom she raised, and her life as a single mother was strongly reflected in her poetry. In 1965, she moved to upstate New York and participated in Timothy Leary's psychedelic community at Millbrook. At other times, she traversed the continent in a Volkswagen bus, in the style of the male Beat writers and the Merry Pranksters, reading her poetry in churches, prisons, and schools.

In 1969, di Prima moved to the West Coast, a more hospitable place for female writers, and became involved with the Diggers, a radical community action and guerrilla theater group that supplied free food, medical care, housing, and musical concerts for street people. The move to the West Coast signaled the beginning of di Prima's gradual move away from the radical social-political emphasis of the Beat writers and toward a more contemplative life, including the study of Zen Buddhism, alchemy, and Sanskrit.

In the 1970's, di Prima became an instructor at the Jack Kerouac School of Disembodied Poetics at Naropa Institute in Boulder, Colorado; in the same decade, as part of the Poetry in the Schools programs, she held workshops and residencies in Wyoming, Arizona, Montana, Minnesota, and elsewhere. During the 1980's, she taught courses in the hermetic and esoteric traditions in poetry at the New College of California in San Francisco, and she has since taught at the California College of Arts and Crafts, the San Francisco Art Institute, the California Institute of Integral Studies, and Napa State Hospital. She was the cofounder of the San Francisco Institute of Magical and Healing Arts, where she also taught from 1983 to 1991. In 1971, she started work on *Loba*, a long, visionary serial poem; parts 1-8 were published in 1978 and an expanded and revised version was published in 1998.

The deaths of many of the best-known male writers of the Beat generation led to a renewed interest in the women associated with this movement, resulting in a substantial number of autobiographies and memoirs, including di Prima's *Recollections of My Life as a Woman*, which candidly chronicles her involvement with the Beat movement in the 1950's and 1960's, as well as her growing self-confidence and autonomy as a woman poet determined to shed the label of "Beat chick."

ANALYSIS

Diane di Prima's poetry falls into two clearly distinguished chronological and thematic categories. Her works from 1957 to 1975 are suffused with the idiom of the Beat generation, the language of the hipster and personal rebellion. Di Prima considers her association with the poets of the Beat generation and the San Francisco Renaissance as seminal for her work, as she explained in an interview:

> Don't forget, however great your visioning and your inspiration, you need the techniques of the craft and there's nowhere, really to get them . . . they are passed on person to person and back then the male naturally passed them to the male. I think maybe I was one of the first women to break through that in having deep conversations with Charles Olson and Frank O'Hara.

Further evidence of this mentoring process can be seen in the fact that Jones, through his Totem Press, published di Prima's first collection, *This Kind of Bird Flies Backward*, and Lawrence Ferlinghetti wrote a brief "non-introduction by way of an introduction" for it. The volume is full of Beat terminology, such as "hip," "cool," and "crazy." Although she saw herself, as did most of the female Beat writers, inhibited by the "eternal, tiresome rule of Cool," she also acknowledges that Ginsberg taught her to have confidence in her own spontaneity and emphasized the importance of technical writing skills. The best view of this phase of di Prima's work can be found in her collection *Selected Poems, 1956-1975*, which extracts her favorite poems from *This Kind of Bird Flies Backward* to *Freddie Poems*.

The second part of her work covers the period after she moved to Northern California in 1970. It is characterized by a less strident tone, a gradual decline in use of the Beat vocabulary, and a growing concern with spiritual and ecological matters, particularly her increasing involvement in Buddhism and her role as a woman and mother. Much of this changing perspective can be found in her collection *Pieces of a Song*. Many commentators consider the long serial poem *Loba* the most typical work of di Prima's mature creative period.

DINNERS AND NIGHTMARES

Di Prima's second poetry collection, *Dinners and Nightmares*, is dedicated to her "pads & the people who shared them with me." The first part consists of descriptions of meals she has shared with a variety of people in the bohemian milieu of New York, and there is good reason to believe that most of these sketches are in fact based on real people and events. The second part is a collection of poetic "nightmares," dark contrasts to the more pleasant dinners of the first section. The nightmares deal with the squalid living conditions on the lower East Side, with thwarted or hopeless love affairs, or with standing in unemployment lines:

Then I was standing in line unemployment green
 institution green room
green people slow shuffle. Then to the man ahead said
 clerk-behind-desk,
folding papers bored and sticking on seals
 Here are your twenty reasons for living sir.

Some of the "nightmares" are expressed in imagistic one-liners: "It hurts to be murdered" or "Get your cut throat off my knife."

The collection concludes with a section called "More or Less Love Poems," terse vignettes of love in the hipster pads, where "coolness" thinly disguises anguish and fear of loneliness:

Yeah that was
once in a lifetime
baby

you gotta be clean and
with new shoes
to love like I love you.

I think it won't happen again.

Or even more pithily:

You are not quite
the air I breathe
thank God.

so go.

It is possible to see rebellion and defiance in these lines, as well as an obstinate insistence on living life on her own terms, but while there is little self-pity (that would not have been "cool"), it is impossible to overlook her feelings of anguish and isolation.

EARTHSONG

The collection *Earthsong* was edited by Marlowe, di Prima's then-husband, and published by Poets Press. In the introduction, Marlowe writes, "these poems contain the hard line of the fifties, and the smell of New York winters, cold and grey, as well as Miles Davis' jazz and the search for new forms." Di Prima reveals her extensive classical reading in a lighthearted Beat parody of Elizabethan poet/dramatist Christopher Marlowe's pastoral "The Passionate Shepherd to His Love" (1599), which she turns into "The Passionate Hipster to His Chick." The collection also includes probably her best-known and most frequently anthologized poem. Untitled in *Earthsong*, the poem appears in *Selected Poems, 1956-1975* as "The Practice of Magical Evocation" and is a strident response to Gary Snyder's chauvinist poem "Praise for Sick Women" (from *Riprap*, 1959). In that poem, Snyder characterizes women as fertile and only confused by discipline. Di Prima's response is an unashamed acceptance of her femininity ("I am a woman and my poems/ are woman's: easy to say/ this"). She converts "fertile" into "ductile," emphasizing a woman's adaptability and strength in the face of male demands and expectations ("bring forth male children only"). Her final question, "what applause?" is rhetorical, indicating that women can expect no reward or even acknowledgment for their efforts. In *Recollections of My Life as a Woman*, di Prima sets the record straight when she writes:

> Disappointment or loss marked the men of that world. And silence; one simply didn't talk about it. Disappointment and silence marked the women too. But there the silence lay deeper. No tales were told about them. They did not turn from one career to another, "take up the law," but buried the work of their hearts in the basement, burned their poems and stories, lost the thread of their dreams.

LOBA

Di Prima began working on *Loba* in 1971, and part 1 of this long serial poem first appeared in the Capra Chapbooks series in 1973. Expanded over the next two decades, book 1 (parts 1-8) was published in 1978, and in 1998, Penguin published a full, though probably not final, version. The poem is characteristic of di Prima's post-Beat poetry: It is an attempt to emulate the mythical wanderings of the *Cantos* (1925-1972) of her first mentor, Pound. The title is a reference to the figure of the she-wolf (*loba* in Spanish), the symbol of fierce maternal love in many cultures and particularly in Native American lore. *Loba* is a long journey of exploration of the feminine consciousness, beginning in primeval myths and archetypes.

Book 1 concentrates on matters of the flesh, while book 2 focuses on the soul. Di Prima has indicated that a yet-to-be-written book 3 would concern itself with the spirit. The work exhibits the poet's vast literary background, with allusions to Iseult, Persephone, and Lilith, all contained in a loosely joined series of philosophical, humorous, and lyrical poems. In one section, di Prima invokes Ginsberg's "Howl" (1956) when she writes: "who walked across America behind gaunt violent yogis/ & died o-d'ing in methadone jail/ scarfing the evidence."

Loba is a difficult poem and should not be read with the intent of finding and recognizing all the references to literary characters and myths. The she-wolf is di Prima's fundamental female hero, whose mythical wanderings allow the poet to touch on all her favorite subjects—politics, religion, erotic love, and ecology—and to display her great versatility in manipulating a wide variety of poetic forms and themes.

Di Prima's poetry has been criticized as uneven and sometimes obscure. There can be no doubt, however, that most of her poems, particularly of the early period, are accessible to the average reader and live up to the definition of poetry and the role of the poet she expressed in a 1978 interview:

> The poet is the last person who is still speaking the truth when no one else dares to. . . . Pound once said, "Artists are the antennae of the race." . . . And we see very dramatically in our time how . . . the work of Allen [Ginsberg] and Kerouac in the 1950's and so on has informed the 1970's.

REVOLUTIONARY LETTERS

Originally published in 1971 and reissued several times before the 2007 edition produced by Last Gasp, *Revolutionary Letters* is one of the few significant literary efforts to emerge from the end of the hippie era. The new edition features re-edited earlier poems and is supplemented with later work.

Dedicated to her anarchist grandfather, *Revolutionary Letters* is di Prima's blank-verse chronicle of the cultural upheaval that began in the late 1940's and early 1950's with the Beats and metamorphosed into the counterculture of the 1960's before running out of steam in subsequent decades. Despite the apparent failure or suspension of the revolution, di Prima continues to be the standard-bearer, an army of one. She still proudly holds aloft the black, tie-dyed flag of utopian anarchy, the symbol for an idealized world in which individuals of all persuasions peacefully coexist without the necessity of government intervention or control, free to enjoy all the possibilities of mental, physical, and spiritual life to the fullest.

The earlier poems in the volume—some of them like haiku or epigrams in their brevity and impact—are upbeat and hopeful, in keeping with the ebullient, volatile nature of the late 1960's, when they were written. Drawing from a wealth of sources (alchemy, astrology, the history of the labor movement, Asian religions, and the female experience), di Prima keenly observes the flaws of society that detract from the ultimate freedom she espouses. She attacks obsolete traditions (such as the notion of feminine inferiority), beliefs (such as the public perception that the media always tell the unvarnished truth), and condemns meek compliance and the machinations of bureaucracy. She cajoles, warns, exhorts, and advises. In one early "letter," she confidently notes that it is not whether the revolution she envisions will happen, but simply a matter of when. In others, she reminds readers to wear shoes so they will not hurt their feet when they run away and to fill the bathtub with water in the event of government-manufactured crises. At the time of their writing, di Prima's letters were strong, powerful statements from a pioneering female spokesperson for radical change. With the passage of the years, however, their relevance to current events has been lost, and they now seem like antique moments preserved in amber.

Later letters, in which the poet seems to realize that the revolution has failed—or is at least on hiatus—are angrier in tone, less forgiving. "Revolutionary Letter #40," for example, paints a bleak picture of a devastated United States: burning oilfields, ruined cities, abandoned vehicles, and downed power lines. "Revolutionary Letter #51" maintains that those who submit to a system become slaves. "Revolutionary Letter: Memorial Day 2003" is essentially a listing of those di Prima contends gave their lives for some form of freedom, from Paracelsus to Ferdinando Nicola Sacco and Bartolomeo Vanzetti, from John Brown to Leo Trotsky, and from Socrates to Malcolm X. More contemporary letters dealing with di Prima's concept of utopia are less grounded in reality. Her idealized, anarchistic postrevolutionary world—where men, women and children love and live off nature's bounty without restrictions—is a wonderful concept, but in light of the human species' penchant for contention, seems impossible to attain.

"Notes Toward a Poem of Revolution"

"Notes Toward a Poem of Revolution" was published in a limited edition by di Prima's Eidolon Editions, as *Towers Down: Notes Toward a Poem of Revolution* (2002), and contained "Towers Down" by Clive Matson. Both poems also appeared in the antiwar anthology, *An Eye for an Eye Makes the Whole World Blind: Poets on 9/11* (2002). Matson's poem is a reaction to the traumatic terrorist attacks of September 11, 2001. Di Prima's poem, which was reprinted in the 2007 edition of *Revolutionary Letters*, is a series of fourteen short pieces—similar in tone and style to the more strident poems in that collection.

As might be expected, given the poet's lifelong anarchistic stance, di Prima, while sympathetic toward the victims of the tragedy, strongly condemns the behavior of the United States that resulted in the attacks. By aggressively seizing the role of the world's police officer and in broadening the gap between the haves and have-nots, she seems to be saying, the United States has made such atrocities inevitable. Although such suicidal acts as flying loaded passenger planes into populated buildings are inexcusable on a human scale, they are nonetheless understandable as gestures of frustration at the inability to change the way of the world through the normal channels of negotiation and compromise; collateral damage in the continuing war for the hearts and minds of the globe's citizens is part of modern reality. Poignantly, in a few brief lines, di Prima sums up the contemporary situation by comparing it to a child's game: ". . . nobody/ can hog the marbles & expect/ the others to play."

Other major works

LONG FICTION: *Memoirs of a Beatnik*, 1969, 1988; *The Calculus of Variation*, 1972.

PLAYS: *Paideuma*, pr. 1960; *The Discontent of a Russian Prince*, pr. 1961; *Murder Cake*, pr. 1963; *Like*, pr. 1964; *Poet's Vaudeville*, pr. 1964 (libretto); *Monuments*, pr. 1968; *The Discovery of America*, pr. 1972; *Whale Honey*, pr. 1975; *ZipCode: The Collected Plays of Diane di Prima*, 1992.

NONFICTION: "Light / and Keats," 1978; "Paracelsus: An Appreciation," 1979; *Recollections of My Life as a Woman: The New York Years, a Memoir*, 2001.

EDITED TEXT: *War Poems*, 1968.

BIBLIOGRAPHY

Charters, Ann. *The Portable Sixties Reader*. New York: Penguin Classics, 2003. An anthology featuring a collection of more than one hundred pieces: essays, poetry, and fiction from some of America's outstanding writers of the decade, including works by di Prima. Provides perspective on the times.

Di Prima, Diane. "Diane di Prima." http://dianediprima .com. Official Web site of di Prima lists her works, readings, reviews, and workshops. Also provides links to other informational sites.

_______. "Diane di Prima." Interview by David Meltzer and Marina Lazzara. In *San Francisco Beat: Talking with the Poets*, edited by Meltzer. San Francisco: City Lights, 2001. In 1999, di Prima discusses her development as a poet, including an early commitment to poetry; her meetings with Beat poets such as Allen Ginsberg and Robert Duncan; her connection to Millbrook and Timothy Leary; her years in the San Francisco area and her involvement with the Diggers; and her discovery of Buddhism.

_______. "Pieces of a Song: Diane di Prima." Interview by Tony Moffeit. In *Breaking the Rule of Cool: Interviewing and Reading Women Beat Writers*, edited by Nancy McCampbell Grace and Ronna Johnson. Jackson: University Press of Mississippi, 2004. Di Prima discusses the influences on her writing, as well as the community of the Beat movement.

Johnson, Ronna, and Nancy McCampbell Grace, eds. *Girls Who Wore Black: Women Writing the Beat Generation*. New Brunswick, N.J.: Rutgers University Press, 2002. Contains an essay on di Prima, as well as an overview on women in the Beat generation.

Knight, Brenda, ed. *Women of the Beat Generation: The Writers, Artists, and Muses at the Heart of a Revolution*. 1996. Reprint. San Francisco: Conari Press, 2000. A well-illustrated anthology containing essays, poems, and short autobiographical pieces from the long neglected women—including Denise Levertov, Joanna McClure, Carolyn Cassady, and di Prima—who associated with and worked alongside the men of the Beat generation. Includes a short biography of di Prima and a number of her poems.

Peabody, Richard, ed. *A Different Beat: Writing by Women of the Beat Generation*. London: Serpent's Tail, 1997. This anthology of writings by the women of the Beat generation places di Prima in context. Firsthand accounts of these women's experiences are provided by Jan Kerouac, Joyce Johnson, Hettie Jones, di Prima, and others, who attest to the decidedly sexist times. An introduction provides an overview of the social and cultural background.

Pekar, Harvey, et al. *The Beats: A Graphic History*. Art by Ed Piskor et al. New York: Hill and Wang, 2009. Comic legend Harvey Pekar provides a history of the Beat poets in this graphic book. Contains an entry on and references to di Prima.

Waldman, Anne, ed. *The Beat Book: Writings from the Beat Generation*. Rev. ed. Boston: Shambahla, 2007. This anthology contains an overview of the Beat generation and a short biography of di Prima, along with a selection of her poems.

Franz G. Blaha
Updated by Jack Ewing

ROBERT DUNCAN

Born: Oakland, California; January 7, 1919
Died: San Francisco, California; February 3, 1988
Also known as: Robert Edward Duncan; Robert Edward Symmes

PRINCIPAL POETRY

Early Poems, 1939
Heavenly City, Earthly City, 1947
Medieval Scenes, 1950 (reprinted as *Medieval Scenes 1950 and 1959*)
Poems, 1948-1949, 1950
Fragments of a Disordered Devotion, 1952
Caesar's Gate: Poems, 1948-1950, 1956
Letters: Poems, MCMLIII-MCMLVI, 1958
Selected Poems, 1959
The Opening of the Field, 1960
Roots and Branches, 1964
Writing, Writing: A Composition Book for Madison 1953, Stein Imitations, 1964
A Book of Resemblances: Poems, 1950-1953, 1966
Passages 22-27 of the War, 1966
Six Prose Pieces, 1966
The Years as Catches: First Poems, 1939-1946, 1966
Epilogos, 1967
Bending the Bow, 1968
Names of People, 1968
Achilles' Song, 1969
Derivations: Selected Poems, 1950-1956, 1969
The First Decade: Selected Poems, 1940-1950, 1969
Play Time: Pseudo Stein, 1969
Poetic Disturbances, 1970
Tribunals: Passages 31-35, 1970
Ground Work, 1971
Poems from the Margins of Thom Gunn's "Moly," 1972
A Seventeenth Century Suite in Homage to the Metaphysical Genius in English Poetry, 1590-1690, 1973
Dante, 1974
An Ode to Arcadia, 1974 (with Jack Spicer)
The Venice Poem, 1975
Veil, Turbine, Cord, and Bird, 1979

The Five Songs, 1981
Ground Work: Before the War, 1984
A Paris Visit, 1985
Ground Work II: In the Dark, 1987

OTHER LITERARY FORMS

Besides the poetic oeuvre, Robert Duncan produced a limited but essential corpus of essays concerning both his own work and life, and the work of those other writers important to him. Although *The Truth and Life of Myth: An Essay in Essential Autobiography* (1968) was published separately, it also opens the volume of his collected essays, *Fictive Certainties* (1985), and constitutes a major touchstone for an understanding of Duncan's work. "Towards an Open Universe" and "Man's Fulfillment in Order and Strife," also gathered in the same collection, are essential statements on poetics and politics. "The H. D. Book," first conceived as a study of the poetry of H. D. (Hilda Doolittle), became an encyclopedic investigation of mythopoesis and modernism, eighteen sections of which appeared in magazines during the late 1960's and 1970's. Other titles include *The Sweetness and Greatness of Dante's "Divine Comedy"* (1965) and *As Testimony: The Poem and The Scene* (1964). Duncan is also the author of two plays, *Faust Foutu: An Entertainment in Four Parts* (pb. 1959) and *Medea at Kolchis: The Maidenhead* (pb. 1965). Duncan was a spell-binding reader of his own work as well as a truly phenomenal raconteur: A multitude of tapes preserved either in private hands or in university archives bear witness to this, and future transcriptions of his talks and interviews will provide major additions to, and commentaries on, the oeuvre as it now stands.

ACHIEVEMENTS

Because of his erudition, his sense of poetic tradition, his mastery of a variety of poetic forms, and, most important, his profoundly metaphysical voice, Robert Duncan is a major contemporary poet. "Each age requires a new confession," Ralph Waldo Emerson declared, and Duncan presents his era with a voice it cannot afford to ignore. He was recognized with a Union League Civic and Arts Poetry Prize (1957), the Levinson Prize (1964) from *Poetry* magazine, and the Shelley Memorial Award (1984). *Ground Work: Before the War* was nominated for the National Book Critics Circle Award and won a National Book Award.

Although Duncan called himself a derivative poet, revealing his penetrating readings of Dante, Walt Whitman, Ralph Waldo Emerson, William Shakespeare, William Blake, and others, at the same time he generated contemporary visions, Emersonian prospects of discovery and renewal. An impressive collection of more than thirty volumes of poetry, drama, and prose constitutes Duncan's literary achievement. His serious notion of the role of the poet is evident in his many statements about his work, including the prefaces to such works as *The Truth and Life of Myth* and "The H. D. Book." Duncan wrote in a wide range of voices, including a bardic, visionary persona of high seriousness and metaphysical concerns, but he never lost his wit and joy in language-play. Not only was he a masterful lyricist, capable of penetrating epiphanies such as "Roots and Branches," but also he excelled in longer closed forms such as the serial poem ("Apprehensions," "The Continent") and the symphonic form of *The Venice Poem*. Finally, Duncan did some of his finest work in the form that is America's most distinctive contribution to world poetry in the twentieth century: the long, open-ended poem that can accommodate an encyclopedia if need be. Duncan's ongoing open poems, "The Structure of Rime" and "Passages," are in the tradition of Ezra Pound's *Cantos* (1925-1972), William Carlos Williams's *Paterson* (1946-1958), Louis Zukofsky's "*A*" (1927-1978), and Charles Olson's *The Maximus Poems* (1953-1983).

BIOGRAPHY

Robert Duncan was born Edward Howard Duncan in Oakland, California, on January 7, 1919, to Edward Howard and Marguerite Wesley Duncan. His mother died shortly after his birth, and his father was forced to put him up for adoption. His foster parents, "orthodox Theosophists," chose him on the basis of his astrological configuration. Duncan grew up as Robert Edward Symmes and published some two dozen poems under that name before resuming his original surname in 1942. The hermetic lore imparted by his family and the fables and nursery rhymes of his childhood constitute a major influence on his work.

He attended the University of California, Berkeley, from 1936 to 1938, publishing his first poems in the school's literary magazine, *The Occident*, and joining a circle of friends that included Mary and Lilli Fabilli, Virginia Admiral, and Pauline Kael. For several years he lived in the East, associating with the circle of Anaïs Nin in New York City and with a group of poets in Woodstock that included Sanders Russell and Jack Johnson. Receiving a psychiatric discharge from the army in 1941, he continued publishing poems and, with Virginia Admiral, edited *Ritual* (later *Experimental Review*). In 1944, he published his courageous essay, "The Homosexual in Society," in *Politics*.

Returning to Berkeley in 1946, he studied medieval and Renaissance culture and worked with Kenneth Rexroth, Jack Spicer, and Robin Blaser. In 1951, he began his continuing relationship with painter Jess Collins. Duncan directly addresses the significance of his sexuality to his art: "Perhaps the sexual irregularity underlay and led to the poetic; neither as homosexual nor as poet could one take over the accepted paradigms and conventions of the Protestant ethic."

In 1952, he began publishing in *Origin* and then in the *Black Mountain Review*. In the mid-1950's, he taught briefly at Black Mountain College, further developing his relationship with Olson, whose important essay, "Projective Verse," had been published in 1950. Duncan remains the strongest link between the Black Mountain poets and the

San Francisco Renaissance, although the name of such "schools" must be highly elastic to include such diverse poets as Olson, Robert Creeley, Edward Dorn, Allen Ginsberg, Lawrence Ferlinghetti, and Duncan.

The 1960's saw the publication of three major collections, the intense involvement with the poetry of H. D., and the writing of "The H. D. Book," as well as Duncan's strong commitment to antiwar politics, as evidenced in the "Passages" series of poems. By the early 1970's, his reputation had grown beyond the borders of the United States, and he often toured, giving poetry readings and publishing his works in Europe and elsewhere. In 1968, frustrated by his publishers' inability or unwillingness to print his work according to his own specifications, Duncan announced that he would let fifteen years elapse before publishing another major collection, although small, often private printings of work in progress would continue to appear throughout the 1970's and early 1980's. In 1984, New Directions published *Ground Work: Before the War*, typeset under the poet's direct supervision. *Ground Work II: In the Dark* followed in 1987, only a few months before the poet's death in February, 1988.

ANALYSIS

Of the many metaphors that Robert Duncan applied to his poetry—and very few poets have been so perceptive and articulate about their own practice—those dealing with limits, boundaries, and margins are numerous and permit a coherent if partial survey of his complex work. Such references are frequent in his poetry and are rooted in his life and his way of seeing. Living in San Francisco, at the edge of the North American continent, Duncan was acutely sensitive to the centrifugal pressures of his culture. Having been an adopted child, his identity and very name were under question during his early years. As a gay man, he felt distanced from "the accepted paradigms and conventions of the Protestant ethic." As a Theosophist, his way of thinking had been influenced by similarly unconventional assumptions. His very vision blurs distinctions and identities: He was cross-eyed, a way of seeing that he eloquently explored in such poems as "A Poem Slow Beginning" and "Crosses of Harmony and Disharmony," and that he relates to Alfred North Whitehead's "presentational immediacy."

Duncan referred to himself as "the artist of the margin," and the term is basic to an understanding of his vision and poetics. Although the concept can be traced to a number of eclectic and overlapping influences, William James's *Principles of Psychology* (1890), with its theme of the fluidity of consciousness, provides an instructive point of departure. For James, with his great interest in the "penumbra" of experience, "life is at the transitions." As he says in "A World of Pure Experience," "Our fields of experience have no more definite boundaries than have our fields of view. Both are fringed forever by a *more* that continuously develops and that continuously supersedes them as life proceeds." For Duncan as for James, life is at the edge, at the point of relationship, surprise, novelty—at the transgression of boundaries. Conceiving the universe as a constant rhythm between order and disorder, both writers (with Whitehead and John Dewey) maintained that order develops. Rejecting the extreme poles of a world of mere flux without any stability and a static world without crisis, such a worldview embraces the moment of passage as that of most intense life. Appropriately, Duncan's major ongoing poem is entitled the "Passages Poems." Primary here too is John Keats's notion of "negative capability," an acceptance of "uncertainties, mysteries, doubts, without any irritable reaching after fact and reason." Indeed, Duncan defines Romanticism as "the intellectual adventure of not knowing."

Duncan was fully cognizant of the implications that such ideas have for his poetics, scoffing in *The Truth and Life of Myth* at the "sensory debunkers" who "would protect our boundaries, the very shape of what we are, by closing our minds to the truth." The poet's charge is to challenge the boundaries of convention, with direct impact on his poetry's form: "Back of each poet's concept of the poem is his concept of the meaning of form itself; and his concept of form in turn where it is serious at all arises from his concept of the nature of the universe." Duncan's poetry challenges the boundaries of conventional ideas and conventional forms. He speaks of his poetry as a collage, an especially appropriate form for a poetry that incessantly interrogates boundaries, edges, identities. "The great art of our time," he says in "The H. D. Book," "is the collagist's art, to bring all things into new complexes of meaning."

The theme appears early in his work, developing in the poems of the 1940's and 1950's. From the first decade, in "Heavenly City, Earthly City," the poet as a "man in the solitude of his poetic form/ finds his self-consciousness defined/ by the boundaries of a non-committal sea." He apostrophizes the Pacific Ocean as an "Insistent questioner of our shores!" "A Congregation," similarly, sounds early poetic concerns of field, order, disorder, and fragmentation. In "The Festival," the fifth poem in *Medieval Scenes*, a strong early series, Duncan uses the motif of the dream to explore the unclear distinctions between wakefulness and sleep and, by extension, between ecstasy and madness, inspiration and inflated foolishness, the unicorn and the ass.

A pervasive concern with boundaries and limits is apparent in "The Venice Poem" (1948), Duncan's first indisputably major poem. In this work, based on Igor Stravinsky's *Symphony in Three Movements*, Duncan relates Berkeley to Venice and links his own lost love and self-questioning to the frustrations of Othello and Desdemona. The awareness of limits and edges crystallizes in a description of an image's coming into being: "She hesitates upon the verge of sound./ She waits upon a sounding impossibility,/ upon the edge of poetry." The final poem collected in *The First Decade*, "The Song of the Borderguard," announces by its very title Duncan's increasing awareness of transgressed boundaries: "The borderlines of sense in the morning light/ are naked as a line of poetry in a war."

The 1950's were productive years; poems written during that period include those published in *Derivations*; *Writing, Writing*; and *Letters*. Although many of these poems are all too explicitly derivative, Duncan reprints them as testimony to his roots and his past. In his 1972 preface to *Caesar's Gate*, Duncan does not use Ezra Pound's term *periplum*, but his description of the writing conveys something of the sense of a poetry "fearfully and with many errors making its way . . . seeking to regain a map in the actual." The first poem collected in *Derivations*, "An Essay at War," opens with a description of the poem "constantly/ under reconstruction," as "a proposition in movement." The poem contrasts the foolish ad hoc "design" of war itself with the imperfect pattern or design of a poem true to a changing experience. The preface to *Letters* argues that a poet's process is one of revision and disorganization, which takes place at the threshold. "I attempt the discontinuities of poetry," he announces, opening gaps that "introduce the peril of beauty." Although cynics assume that such poetry must be inflated or impossible and traditionalists abhor his assumption of a godlike role, Duncan answers both in deft lyrics such as "An Owl Is an Only Bird of Poetry," whose sure and witty inclusiveness articulates both design and disorder. Two poems near the end of *Letters*, "Changing Trains" and "The Language of Love," specifically employ the imagery of border crossing and entering new territory, clear harbingers of Duncan's major phase.

Although the early books are significant achievements, Duncan's reputation rests primarily on three major books of poetry published in the 1960's, *The Opening of the Field*, *Roots and Branches*, and *Bending the Bow*. Each is a unified whole rather than a collection of poems, and each manifests and extends Duncan's use of the theme of boundaries and margins.

THE OPENING OF THE FIELD

The terms of *The Opening of the Field* are proposed in the title, and the book's first and last poems reveal Duncan's awareness of beginnings and endings as they affect this book and much more. "Often I Am Permitted to Return to a Meadow" establishes the basic metaphor of the book, of poetry as an entry into a field of essences, "a scene made-up by the mind,/ that is not mine, but is a made place,/ that is mine." Granted entry into this field of poetic activity, the poet participates in the grand poem through his individual poems. Within this meadow, "the shadows that are forms fall," and in an act of faith ("as if"), the poet accepts it as a "given property of the mind/ that certain bounds hold against chaos." The poems seem to delineate boundaries or fields of order against chaos, but they only seem to do so because in the larger view that Duncan has of poetry and the universe, chaos or disorder are parts of a larger order. The real boundary of this poem, then, is between a state of awareness and its absence. Delineating that boundary, or more fundamentally recognizing the difference, is the responsibility of the poet. In the "disturbance of words within words," the poet's poems are constructs, architectures, flowers that turn into "flames lit to the lady." The limits and definitions of physical reality must give way before the reality of the visionary imagination.

Duncan returns to these images—indeed he never leaves them—in the final poem of this book, "Food for Fire, Food for Thought," in which he self-consciously comments on the paradox of a last poem in an open poetics: "This is what I wanted for the last poem,/ a loosening of conventions and a return to open form." The attempt to define or limit is frustrating and necessarily progressive rather than definitive. The activity, however, is the poet's preoccupation: "We trace faces in the clouds: they drift apart,/ palaces of air—the sun dying down/ sets them on fire." Fire is the concluding image, again transformed into a flower, as an "unlikely heat/ at the edge of our belief bud[s] forth." In these two poems and those in between, Duncan explores the shifting borderlines between essence and form, childhood and adulthood, flame and flower. Even as Leonardo da Vinci did, he sees "figures that were stains upon a wall" as he operates "at the edge of our belief."

The Opening of the Field includes "A Poem Beginning with a Line by Pindar," perhaps Duncan's best-known poem. Beginning with a misreading of a line from the third Pythian Ode, the poem then proclaims his recognition of a "god-step at the margins of thought." The poem is a mosaic or collage of images playing between light and dark, Cupid-sensuality and Psyche-spirituality, East and West, past and present, and it cannot be summarized here. The fourth section begins, "O yes! Bless the footfall where/ step by step the boundary walker," echoing the footstep of the poem's opening, and informs and clarifies the poet's memories and experiences. The poet, as a boundary walker, must be attuned to the elusive image or inspiration, even to a felicitous misreading of Pindar.

Other poems directly addressing the theme of boundaries include "After Reading *Barely and Widely*," a book by Louis Zukofsky, and the series "The Structure of Rime," in the second of which the poet interrogates the nature of poetry. "What is the Structure of Rime? I asked," and he is told, "*An absolute scale of resemblance and disresemblance establishes measures that are music in the actual world.*" Such a recognition of pervasive correspondences and rhymes inspires confidence in the face of difficulties and risks inherent in such poetry. In the eighth of the series, the poet is permitted to crawl through "interstices of Earth" in realizing the possible "from a nexus in the Impossible." The entire series, continuing in subsequent books and intersecting at times with other series, addresses major questions of poetry and reality.

ROOTS AND BRANCHES

Again, *Roots and Branches* enunciates in its title the basic metaphor of the book, "the ramifications below and above the trunk of vegetative life." The title lyric, one of Duncan's best, describes his delight in a monarch butterfly whose flight traces out an imaginary tree, "unseen roots and branches of sense/ I share in thought." The poet's epiphany, inspired by the correspondence between his spirit and the beauty of the common butterfly, denies yet another boundary respected by common sense, that between physical reality and a transcendent reality. Frank in its Romantic idealism, the poem evokes an Emersonian wonder at the harmony of physical and spiritual facts for a modern audience every bit as skeptical as Ralph Waldo Emerson's neighbors.

Roots and Branches closes with a more extended sequence of poems, the memorable series "The Continent," in which Duncan directly names and accepts his role as "the artist of the margin" who "works abundancies" and who recognizes that the scope of poetry "needs vast terms" because it is "out of earthly proportion to the page." On the literal level, Duncan calls for a long poem that will, like Whitman's, be creative and have "vista." Metaphorically and more significantly, he is calling for a poetry on the edge of consciousness, an expanding awareness of "marginal" realities, an openness to unusual or unconventional apprehensions. Unlike the coastal resident's awareness of the alien or the other, "The mid-Western mind differs in essentials." Without Buddhist temples or variant ways of seeing, midwesterners "stand with feet upon the ground/ against the/ run to the mythic sea, the fabulous." This is not praise for Antaeus.

The poem continues, describing a sparrow smashed on a sidewalk. More than an allusion to William Carlos Williams's famous poem, the passage illuminates the difference between having a perspective in space and time and being "too close/ for shadow,/ the immediate!" The central image of the poem, the continent, itself examines horizons, especially those between shore and land and night and day. The closing sections link such imagery with Easter (evidently the time of the actual writing of the poem) and its denial of any clear distinction even between life and death.

Far from fragmenting our beliefs and dissociating our sensibilities, such a vision asserts the oneness of things: one time, one god, one promise flaring forth from "the margins of the page." In the apparent chaos of flux and change—"moving in rifts, churning, enjambing"—both continent and poem testify to a dynamic unity. Again, at the border, at the edge of meaning, like Christopher Columbus one finds not the abyss but new worlds.

"Apprehensions" is a poem closely related to "The Continent." The central theme is again that which "defines the borderlines of the meaning." The opening chord, "To open Night's eye that sleeps in what we know by day," announces the familiar concern with overcoming common sense and sensory limitations, and with the assertion of paradoxical oneness. Quotidian preoccupations obstruct people's perspectives and limit their perceptions. In sharp contrast, the "Sage Architect" awakens "the proportions and scales of the soul's wonder" and lets light and shadow mix. The poem is a song to apprehension—both fearful and perceiving—of excavation of boundaries, resemblances, rhymes. The central apprehension is of concordances that overcome people's limited sense of shifting time, place, and boundaries in favor of an overriding order.

Bending the Bow

Continuing his development, Duncan followed four years later with yet another major book, *Bending the Bow*. In his introduction, he discusses his poetry with his accustomed insight, beginning by criticizing the Vietnam War, which, "as if to hold all China or the ancient sea at bay, breaks out at a boundary we name *ours*. It is a boundary beyond our understanding." Captured by a rigid form, by a fixed image of oneself, one is unable to adapt to new conditions and insights. In contrast, the pulse of the poet in moments of vision "beats before and beyond all proper bounds." The book's title establishes the contrasts of bow and lyre, war and music, Apollo and Hermes, whose tension generates this book's field. Duncan speaks of the poem not as a stream of consciousness but as an area of composition in which "the poet works with a sense of parts fitting in relation to a design that is larger than the poem" and which he knows "will never be completed."

The title lyric develops the bow and lyre analogy, articulating the central Heraclitean themes of design, connection, and unity in diversity: "At this extremity of this/ design/ there is a connexion working in both directions, as in/ the bow and the lyre." As Duncan explains in "Towards an Open Universe," the turn and return of prose and verses of poetry are phases of a dynamic unity, like the alternation of day and night or the systole and diastole of the heart. The focus of his poetry and poetics remains on the intensity of the point of transition.

While "The Structure of Rime" continues in this volume, a new series, the "Passages Poems," is also introduced, beginning with a telling epigraph: "For the even is bounded, but the uneven is without bounds and there is no way through or out of it." The first passage, "Tribal Memories," invokes "Her-Without-Bounds," and the importance of margins, borders, and boundaries continues. Describing "Passages Poems" in his introduction, Duncan states that "they belong to a series that extends in an area larger than my work in them. I enter the poem as I entered my own life, moving between an initiation and a terminus I cannot name. This is not a field of the irrational; but a field of ratios." Among the poem's many concerns are those ratios or correspondences, and some of the most provocative insights derive from the poetic theme of margins and transitions. "The Architecture, Passages 9" demands recesses so that "there is always something around the corner." In "Wine, Passages 12," the poet celebrates even as he is threatened by "the voice/ . . . the enormous/ sonority at the edge of the void." In "In the Place of a Passage 22," the poet prays for passage in "the vast universe/ showing only its boundaries we imagine."

Like "The Structure of Rime," "Passages Poems" is an exciting achievement. Like most long poems, it resists the sort of cursory treatment that consideration of space dictates here, and the project may well be victimized by the "magnificent failure" syndrome so characteristic of criticism of American literature. Certainly it is ambitious, as Duncan acknowledges in "Where It Appears, Passage 4": "Statistically insignificant as a locus of creation/ I have in this my own/ intense/ area of self creation." Even here, the telling conditionals of "as if I could cast a shadow/ to surround/ what is boundless" indicate Duncan's full, continuing, double-edged apprehension of his enterprise and its risks.

Ground Work: Before the War

Ground Work: Before the War, published fifteen years after *Bending the Bow*, carries on the concerns of the three major collections of the 1960's. If there had been fear of a possible waning of Duncan's powers, these were unjustified. The architectonics of this large volume are highly complex, though one can easily discern a moving back and forth between familiar modes: the large-scale "grand collage" manner of the ongoing "The Structure of Rime" and "Passages Poems," and sequences of smaller, more private and sentimental lyrics, such as the most delicately rhymed "Glimpse." Both kind of workings, however, involve Duncan's familiar subject matter: revelation, knowing, the "rimes" that the poet worries out of his sympathetic readings of the past masters ("A Seventeenth Century Suite" and "Dante Études"), as well as what George Butterick has called "protest against the violation of the natural order by systematic viciousness." The short lyrics seem a clear relief after the violent engagements with the political disasters of the time, as chronicled in the *Tribunals* section of "Passages Poems," and in what is Duncan's and, maybe, the age's best political poem: "Santa Cruz Propositions." The volume ends with "Circulations of the Song," a deeply moving love poem originating in the poet's reading of Jalāl al-Dīn Rūmī's work and celebrating the years spent with the painter Jess Collins, the "constant exchange" and the shared dance of the hearth-work: After the "Inferno" of the war poems, a kind of "Paradiso" has been achieved.

This delicate point of equilibrium, however, cannot last: It belongs to that specific book, that momentary configuration; the work, the oeuvre goes on, disrupting the gained *Paradiso*, as intimations of physical disease and death enter *Ground Work II*, the next and final volume of Duncan's late work, subtitled *In the Dark* and published just months before the poet's death. Even here, however, there is no weakening of Duncan's powers: The grand sweep of the late set of "Passages Poems" entitled "Regulators" is ample proof of the poet's unrelenting energy and vision. Duncan's long illness enters the preoccupations of the book—"my Death/ rearranged the date He has with me"—without ever being able to overcome that realm of the imagination from which the poet drew his breath and strength.

Duncan's art

It is another measure of Duncan's stature and complexity that all his work is of a piece and should be read entire. A single lyric, for example, can be read by itself, or as part of a longer series in many cases (several lyrics are parts of more than one series). It must also be seen as part of the book in which it appears, since Duncan has carefully ordered his collections, and as an integral part of Duncan's canon. Finally, as he says in his introduction to *The Years as Catches*, "Poems then are immediate presentations of the intention of the whole, the great poem of all poems, a unity." Appropriately, even the boundaries of his poems are fluid and dynamic.

In his pervasive border-crossing, Duncan brings his readers news of an other that is shut out by conventional boundaries. With his artful disclosures, his imaginative vision transcends false, self-imposed constrictions. His art ultimately dissolves the very restraints and boundaries he recognizes in the act of transgressing them, and it thus weds humans to nature and to other humans, a familiar but rarely realized ideal of art.

OTHER MAJOR WORKS

PLAYS: *Faust Foutu: An Entertainment in Four Parts*, pb. 1959; *Medea at Kolchis: The Maidenhead*, pb. 1965.

NONFICTION: *As Testimony: The Poem and the Scene*, 1964; *The Sweetness and Greatness of Dante's "Divine Comedy,"* 1965; *The Cat and the Blackbird*, 1967; *The Truth and Life of Myth: An Essay in Essential Autobiography*, 1968; *A Selection of Sixty-five Drawings from One Drawing-Book, 1952-1956*, 1970; *Fictive Certainties*, 1985; *The Last Letters*, 2000; *The Letters of Robert Duncan and Denise Levertov*, 2004 (Robert J. Bertholf and Albert Gelpi, editors).

BIBLIOGRAPHY

Bertholf, Robert J. *Robert Duncan: A Descriptive Bibliography*. Santa Rosa, Calif.: Black Sparrow Press, 1986. Contains photographs of many of Duncan's books, broadsides, illustrations, and drawings.

Bertholf, Robert J., and Ian W. Reid, eds. *Robert Duncan: Scales of the Marvelous*. New York: New Directions, 1979. Collects a variety of essays, including some by contemporary poets.

Davidson, Michael. *The San Francisco Renaissance: Poetics and Community at Mid-century*. New York: Cambridge University Press, 1989. Although only chapter 4 ("Cave of Resemblances, Cave of Rimes: Tradition and Repetition in Robert Duncan") of this study of poetics and community in the Bay Area is specifically centered on the poetics of Duncan, the book as a whole is an invaluable guide to the social, political, and literary environment in which Duncan lived and worked.

Duncan, Robert. Interview. In *Towards a New American Poetics: Essays and Interviews*, edited by Ekbert Faas. Santa Barbara, Calif.: Black Sparrow Press, 1978. One of the best of many interviews.

Ellingham, Lewis. *Poet Be Like God: Jack Spicer and the San Francisco Renaissance*. Hanover, N.H.: University Press of New England, 1998. Criticism and biographic material about Spicer and the San Francisco Renaissance group that included Robert Duncan. With bibliographic references.

Everson, William. *The Last Letters*. Berkeley, Calif.: Oyez, 2000. A collection of correspondence between Everson and Duncan.

Faas, Ekbert. *Young Robert Duncan: Portrait of the Poet as Homosexual in Society*. Santa Barbara, Calif.: Black Sparrow Press, 1983. A well-researched book about Duncan's early life, the complexity of being a foster child, the East Coast years so often neglected in Duncan studies, the early radical decision to assert his gay identity, and the effects this had on the development of Duncan as a writer.

Foster, Edward Halsey. *Understanding the Black Mountain Poets*. Columbia: University of South Carolina Press, 1995. This discussion of the Black Mountain poets contains valuable information on Duncan as well as on Charles Olson and Robert Creeley.

Johnson, Mark. *Robert Duncan*. Boston: Twayne, 1988. Provides a brief but intelligent overview of the poet's life and work.

O'Leary, Peter. *Gnostic Contagion: Robert Duncan and the Poetry of Illness*. Middletown, Conn.: Wesleyan University Press, 2002. Examines Gnosticism and illness in the poetry of Duncan. In addition to analyzing Duncan's work, O'Leary discusses his influence.

Sagetrieb 4 (Fall/Winter, 1985). This special issue includes critical essays on Duncan's work, poems dedicated to him, an excerpt from "The H. D. Book," a selection of letters from Duncan to the poet William Everson, and an interview.

Mark A. Johnson

WILLIAM EVERSON

Brother Antoninus

Born: Sacramento, California; September 10, 1912
Died: Davenport, California; June 3, 1994

PRINCIPAL POETRY

These Are the Ravens, 1935
San Joaquin, 1939
The Masculine Dead, 1942
X War Elegies, 1943
The Waldport Poems, 1944
War Elegies, 1944
Poems MCMXLII, 1945
The Residual Years: Poems, 1940-1941, 1945
The Residual Years, 1948
The Privacy of Speech: Ten Poems in Sequence, 1949
A Triptych for the Living, 1951
At the Edge, 1958 (as Brother Antoninus)
The Crooked Lines of God: Poems, 1949-1954, 1959 (as Brother Antoninus)
There Will Be Harvest, 1960
The Year's Declension, 1961
The Hazards of Holiness: Poems, 1957-1960, 1962 (as Brother Antoninus)
The Poet Is Dead: A Memorial for Robinson Jeffers, 1964 (as Brother Antoninus)
The Rose of Solitude, 1964 (as Brother Antoninus)
The Blowing of the Seed, 1966
Single Source, 1966
The Achievement of Brother Antoninus: A Comprehensive Selection of His Poems with a Critical Introduction, 1967
The Vision of Felicity, 1967 (as Brother Antoninus)
A Canticle to the Waterbirds, 1968 (as Brother Antoninus)
Poems of Nineteen Forty Seven, 1968
The Residual Years: Poems 1934-1948, 1968
The Springing of the Blade, 1968
Black Hills, 1973
Tendril in the Mesh, 1973
Man-Fate, 1974
River-Root: A Syzygy for the Bicentennial of These States, 1976
The Mate-Flight of Eagles, 1977

Blackbird Sundown, 1978
The Veritable Years: Poems, 1949-1966, 1978
Eastward the Armies: Selected War Poems, 1935-1942, 1980
The Masks of Drought, 1980
In Medias Res: Canto One of an Autobiographical Epic, Dust Shall Be the Serpent's Food, 1984
Renegade Christmas, 1984
The High Embrace, 1986
Mexican Standoff, 1989
The Engendering Flood: Book One of Dust Shall Be the Serpent's Food (Cantos I-IV), 1990
The Blood of the Poet, 1994
The Integral Years: Poems, 1966-1994, 2000

Other literary forms

Never hesitant about admitting his literary indebtedness to Robinson Jeffers, since it was the poetry of Jeffers that seized him as a youth and helped him realize his own vocation as a poet, William Everson wrote numerous introductions to reprinted editions of Jeffers's work, as well as a critical study, *Robinson Jeffers: Fragments of an Older Fury* (1968). Like his older mentor, Everson was intensely interested in the West as landscape and California as region, and he explored both of these concerns, as subject matter and sources for art, in *Archetype West: The Pacific Coast as a Literary Region* (1976). The importance of regional identity, as well as what he perceived to be the artist's responsibility in portraying as honestly as possible the disparity between the inner (human) and the outer (natural) landscapes, was the central focus of many of Everson's essays and lectures, many of which are contained in *Earth Poetry: Selected Essays and Interviews of William Everson, 1950-1977* (1980) and *Birth of a Poet* (1982).

Achievements

The most dramatic poet of the Western landscape since Jeffers, William Everson always provoked extreme responses from his audience—either intense admiration for his painful, self-probing, and self-revealing confessionalism, or intense dislike for the extremely visceral histrionics of his verse and his voice on the reading platform. In like manner, neither his poetry nor his life was ever lukewarm. Indeed, it is difficult to consider his art as separate from his life, since his poetry was personal from the beginning of his career; it was not until his third book of poems, *The Masculine Dead*, however, that he noticeably broke away from Jeffers and moving into the intensely confessional verse for which he became known. While Robert Lowell is usually acknowledged as the first American poet since Hart Crane to advance the art of the sequence and as the harbinger of the modern confessional mode of poetry, Everson had actually been developing the sequence form and the confessional voice since 1939, twenty years before Lowell's *Life Studies* (1959) was published. Using his literal self as a symbol of the modern predicament, Everson, as he says in *Birth of a Poet*, "spent the greater part of my life trying to probe down through the negative factors to find the living root which makes me what I am."

Probing down into himself to discover his "living root" meant, in a national sense, discovering the American character. During World War II, having taken his stand as a pacifist and having suffered the consequent about three years of incarceration in Oregon and California camps for conscientious objectors, Everson wrote some of the most incisive and forceful antiwar poetry ever to be produced in America or abroad. This did not go unnoticed, for it led to the national publication of an edition of his selected poems, *The Residual Years*, as well as a Guggenheim Fellowship in 1949.

Although Everson's entry into the Dominican Order in 1951, at which time he became Brother Antoninus, may have hurt his public following (for one poet had dropped out of sight nominally and thus publicly, and another one began to emerge), the confessional tenor of the poet's verse was intensified with his eventual entry into the "dark night of the soul" and Jungian psychoanalysis. Gradually, Brother Antoninus received greater public recognition than William Everson had: He was nominated for the Pulitzer Prize in 1959, awarded the Commonwealth Club of California Silver Medal in 1967 for *The Rose of Solitude*, and was sponsored to give public readings of his work not only throughout the United States but also in Dublin, London, Hamburg, Berlin, Munich, Rome, and Paris. He became, in short, world-renowned as the Dionysian monk who wrote dithyrambic and explicit poetry celebrating the sexual conjunction of man and woman and God. At the height of his career, however, Brother Antoninus confused his audience as Everson once had; in 1969, he abruptly left the Dominican Order and became William Everson once again.

Everson's hand-printed, limited edition of Jeffers's *Granite and Cypress* (1975) was chosen by Joseph Blumenthal, in his exhibition "The Printed Book in America" (1977), as one of the seventy best-made books in the history of American printing. Everson received the Shelley Memorial Award from the Poetry Society of America in 1978, a National Endowment for the Arts grant in 1981, a Body of Work Award from the PEN Center USA in 1989, the Fred Cody Award for lifetime achievement in 1991, and a Lannan Literary Fellowship in 1993.

BIOGRAPHY

William Oliver Everson, born September 10, 1912, in Sacramento, California, was the second of three children and the first son of Lewis Everson and Francelia Everson. It is noteworthy that Everson was the first son of his family because throughout his career he has stressed (in his poetry, in some autobiographical essays, and quite specifically in his autobiography, *Prodigious Thrust*, 1996) that an Oedipal complex is a key factor in his own psychology, in his strained relationship with his father, and in his relationship with the women in his life. Everson's mother, almost twenty years younger than his father, had been Roman Catholic but was forced to leave the Church to marry the man she loved (a fact of increasing importance to the poet later in his life when he converted to Catholicism). Everson's father was a Norwegian emigrant and had been an itinerant printer, musician, and bandmaster until, with a wife and children, he settled in Selma, California, in 1914, and there established the Everson Printery in 1920. As a boy, Everson looked to his mother for support, confidence, and emotional understanding, while growing increasingly intimidated, resentful, and—he has said—even hateful of his father, a taciturn and self-professed atheist who believed Christianity and faith in an afterlife were below the dignity of enlightened minds. In short, from infancy, Everson was exposed to—and often torn between—the extreme differences of his parents' dispositions and sensibilities.

Everson's first poetic attempts were love poems he wrote to his high school sweetheart, beginning in his junior year. In his senior year, he wrote topical poems for the Selma High School yearbook, *The Magnet*. After graduation (June, 1931), he enrolled in Fresno State College the following fall but remained there only one semester, during which time he had what might be called his first "literary" poem, "The Gypsy Dance" (blatantly derived from Edgar Allan Poe's "The Bells," with its strict trochaic meter and long lines), published in *The Caravan*, the Fresno State College literary magazine. Unable to find anything in college interesting enough to keep him, he returned to his parents' home (December, 1932) and remained there, while working at a local cannery, until June, 1933, when he entered the Civilian Conservation Corps (CCC). Except for short leaves of absence, Everson remained in the CCC camp for a year, but he felt intellectually deficient and painfully isolated, so he returned to Fresno State in the fall of 1934. This time, he remained enrolled for the entire academic year, and he found something that was not only interesting but also inspiring: the poetry of Robinson Jeffers. It was after this discovery that he decided to be the first poet of the San Joaquin Valley.

In 1935, again living in his parents' home, Everson had his first collection of poems, *These Are the Ravens*, published. Although the poems in the volume were not very remarkable, at twenty-three, he had begun a lifelong career that would encompass much more than the San Joaquin Valley. Everson married Edwa Poulson, the young woman to whom he had written the love poems in high school, in May, 1938; they settled on a small farm outside Selma, she teaching elementary school and he writing his poetry and tending the vineyard that surrounded their home. Although he was content with his domestic life, the threat of America's involvement in the war being waged in Europe set the tenor of much of the poetry contained in his next two published volumes, *San Joaquin* and *The Masculine Dead*. In 1940, Everson's mother died; in the same year, he was forced by the Selective Service Act to take a stand on the war, and he registered as a conscientious objector. Thus, in 1943, the poet was incarcerated in a Civilian Public Service (CPS) camp for conscientious objectors in Waldport, Oregon, where he would be instrumental in establishing the Waldport School of Fine Arts and the United Press, both precursors of the later San Francisco Renaissance.

Everson remained incarcerated, with the exception of short leaves of absence, for almost three years, during which time his father died, and he and his wife agreed to a divorce because she had fallen in love with another man; thus he lost all his familial connections with his home back in the valley. In August, 1946, two months after being released from a CPS camp in Weaverville, California, where he had been transferred earlier that year, Everson met and fell in love with Mary Fabilli, an artist and Catholic, recently divorced herself. They were married in the summer of 1948, a year that was also important for Everson because the first national publication of a volume of his selected poetry was issued (*The Residual Years*) and because he converted to Catholicism on Christmas Eve of that year. Paradoxically, the Roman Catholic Church refused to recognize the Eversons' marriage because both had been married previously and Mary had been married in a Catholic ceremony; in short, their marriage was annulled, they separated in May, 1949, and Everson was baptized in July. A month before his baptism, he was awarded a Guggenheim Fellowship that would enable him to write with financial support for a year; the stipend lasted only ten months, however, and shortly thereafter Everson entered a Catholic Worker House in Oakland, California, where he would remain for fourteen months. In June, 1951, he entered the Dominican Order at St. Albert's College in Oakland, as a *donatus*, and there he was given the name Brother Antoninus.

From *The Crooked Lines of God* through *The Hazards of Holiness*, the poems of Brother Antoninus emerge as a tortuous series of twists and turns as he struggles, because of his vows of celibacy, in the embrace of Thanatos (that is, the death-urge of the self). In 1960, however, he fell in love with Rose Tunnland, a Catholic divorcé and mother of three children; it was out of this intense love relationship and the breaking of his vows that *The Rose of Solitude* emerged. Partly out of guilt but mostly out of a difference in personalities, this relationship was ended in 1963, but in 1965, the poet fell in love with another woman, Susanna Rickson, again broke his vows, and this time made the painful decision to leave the Dominican Order. So, in December, 1969, Brother Antoninus concluded a poetry reading (at the University of California, Davis) by stripping off his monk's habit and walking off the platform as William Everson once again. He married Rickson six days later, and they lived at Stinson Beach until, in 1971, Everson became poet-in-residence at the University of California, Santa Cruz. He was diagnosed with Parkinson's disease in the 1970's, although he continued to give poetry readings. He died in Davenport, California, in 1994.

ANALYSIS

Always a poet of extremes, from the beginning of his career, William Everson expressed both need and fear, compulsion and revulsion, toward those things in his life most important to him. Much of the tension in his poetry seems to arise from his mind knowing what his heart would like to deny—that is, all is transitory, all is mutable, and there is no permanent security in life. Indeed, the major recurrent theme throughout his canon is that of thwarted love. While this is certainly not a unique theme, nor one limited to modern consciousness, Everson's attempt to understand the ongoing internal war that he suffers (between his heart and mind) leads him, in psychological terms, to his encounter with and ultimate victory over the personal shadow-side of consciousness, and to repeated sought-after encounters with the anima or feminine side. In fact, it is the feminine side in his own consciousness, as well as that embodied in woman, for which he expresses both the greatest need and, paradoxically, the greatest fear throughout his career.

THESE ARE THE RAVENS

In the 1930's, the world was a fearful place for young Everson, as he composed his first collection of poetry, *These Are the Ravens*; even nature, which he would consistently portray as feminine, seemed hostile and malignant. In his earliest poem, "First Winter Storm," the speaker is one who hunkers indoors, afraid of the unknown and ominous unpredictability of the elemental life force that moves outside his walls ("I felt the fear run down my back/ And grip me as I lay"). Humans, in this early volume, are rendered more or less passive in the face of nature's seemingly conscious enmity toward all life, and this human condition is indicative of the poet's own relation to the world of adulthood and experience. Everson was seventeen years old when the Great Depression began in 1929. He had no career plans when he graduated from high school in 1931; he had not prepared to go to college, so his first term there proved fruitless. He returned to his parents' home to live but realized that he had become a disappointment to his father. He worked in the Civilian Conservation Corps for a year, returned to Fresno State for a year, discovered the poetry of Jeffers, and made a lifelong decision to be a poet.

Unable to support himself while pursuing his chosen vocation, however, he had again moved in with his parents, and he would remain with them until his marriage, three months before his twenty-sixth birthday in 1938. However, because he had been unable to break away from his dependence on his parents, he grew, as he wrote in *Prodigious Thrust*, into "the full status of his ambivalence with the father-hunger and father-fear, the mother-hunger and mother-fear at war within him."

The "ambivalence" he suffered manifested itself in his inability to identify with the masculine or feminine in his own personality. The constant dark moodiness he experienced he attributed to his agnatic heritage (stemming, that is, from his masculine precursors), and this he eschewed because he believed it to be related to male savagery and patriarchal dominance. In "I Know It as the Sorrow," for example, Everson attempts to explain the "ache" in his blood, and his recurrent "waking as a child weeping in the dark for no reason," as a psychic condition he has inherited and for which he is not, therefore, responsible. This "sorrow," he says, lies in "the secret depths" of his soul; however, while he may not be responsible for his temperament, the "warriors" of the past which he calls up, as well as their "women/ Shivering in the cliff-wind," are integral to his own perspective of life. In short, at the a priori level, he views the masculine as dominant, savage, and strong, and the feminine as receptive, docile, and weak. Although he vehemently eschews his masculine heritage—stating, at the conclusion of "Fish-Eaters," that "I find no hunger for the sword"—what he implicitly praises in heroic terms is the very thing he denounces—that is, the assertiveness of the male libido.

"WHO SEES THROUGH THE LENS"

By consistently portraying women as weak and passive creatures, while at the same time portraying men pejoratively as the exact opposite, Everson leaves himself neither gender with which to identify; in other words, by dividing himself from both his father and his mother, from the patrilineal and matrilineal inheritances, he divides himself. He becomes, therefore, the "watcher" in "Who Sees Through the Lens" (from *San Joaquin*), a man who spends his nights staring through a telescope up at the stars, a man "fixed in the obsession of seeking, the dementia for knowing," and a man so determined to understand and explain the meaning of life that he intellectually vivisects his own being for understanding. Whereas his "cold mind needles the rock" of stars at night, during the day, he divides his mind from his body as he "fumbles the sleeping seed, pokes at the sperm." This seeker is reminiscent of Jeffers's Barclay, in *The Women at Point Sur* (1927), filled with a kind of self-loathing for the corruptibility of his flesh; thus he denies his body for the monomaniacal glorification of his intellect—until, that is, his alienation becomes too painful to bear and he then strives to submerge his consciousness in sexual ecstasy. Significantly, it is in "Who Sees Through the Lens" that Everson for the first time categorizes woman as receptacle and comforter for man's intellectual frustration—a role she will be forced to play often throughout the poet's career. After he describes the "watcher," therefore, the poet beseeches him to "give over;/ Come star-bruised and broken back to the need;/ Come seeking the merciful thighs of the lover." It is between the feminine thighs, in short, that surcease may be found for the intellectual man; indeed, she offers him a momentary, mindless oblivion that he both desires and fears.

"ABRASIVE"

Woman, like everything else in life for Everson, is not to be trusted with his heart, as she changes and thus forbids his dependency on her. He is, he says in "Abrasive" (from *San Joaquin*), "torn by the wars of perpetual change," and he finds that one side of his psyche longs "to slip yielding and drowned in an ocean of silence,/ Go down into some abstract and timeless norm of reality,/ Shadow the eyes, the uneasy heart, and be done." However, while woman can grant him the momentary oblivion of consciousness, as well as the anodyne for his "uneasy heart," another side of his nature scoffs at such a need and reminds his heart that "the sun makes a fool of you," for this symbol of the masculine principle flaunts life's transitions, "shocking with seasons" those individuals who search for stasis.

The Masculine Dead

Although Everson married Poulson in 1938 and in a sense fulfilled his emotional needs while suffering his own mental chiding for succumbing to the belief that a commitment such as marriage could last, he wrote no poems to or about his wife or his love for her; instead, he wrote such poems as "The Illusion" (from *The Masculine Dead*), wherein he denigrates those people who sit in the comfort of their homes, surrounding themselves with the security of a family, while all around them people are being destroyed by the unpredictable, as "they pitch and go down with the blood on their lips,/ With the blood on the broken curve of their throats,/ With their eyes begging." What he, in his heart, wanted desperately to believe possible (that, for example, emotional security could be sustained), he found himself unable to accept intellectually; therefore, he kept his wife at a distance, for she was part of "the illusion" that made him emotionally vulnerable.

In his life, Everson took definite steps to minimize his vulnerability. He had a vasectomy, which he explains in "The Sides of a Mind" (from *The Masculine Dead*) as his attempt to avoid guilt for the pain life would inflict on his children ("each shiver of pain they ever felt/ Would ripple in to the moment of my act,/ And I will not yield"). As he writes in *Earth Poetry*, another step he took was that of subordinating his marriage to his career:

> The mistake I made . . . in regard to being an artist . . . was when I married I sacrificed the inner viability of my marriage to my career . . . I denied the primacy of her person. By reducing her to an object and sacrificing that object even to a school of thought, I denied the reality of the situation.

When the Selective Service Act was instituted in 1940, and when the United States' involvement in World War II seemed imminent, Everson took yet another self-protective step by registering as a conscientious objector. Throughout *The Masculine Dead*, which was inspired by the moral revulsion he felt over the war being waged in Europe, Everson continued to denounce his father's world of masculine and militaristic aggression. In "The Sides of a Mind," he describes himself, a poet, sitting at a table and struggling to articulate some comprehensible explanation for the confusion and destruction in the world; suddenly a political activist bursts into his room and criticizes his physical passivity: "We have time no longer for the seeds of your doubt./ We have time only for man and man/ Facing together the brute confusion of the stubborn world." Because the poet is unable to embrace his father's ethics and values (as a young man, for instance, his father had been beaten and jailed for his efforts to establish a typographical union), he learns to embrace the old man's disappointment as a testament to his own, the son's, authenticity: "Father, whatever you hoped for," he says in the second section of the poem, "I am not what you wanted./ I sit hunched in a room."

"The Presence"

What Everson once viewed as weakness, consequently, he now views as virtue in the feminine; furthermore, in "The Presence" (from *The Residual Years*), he suggests that an individual and a nation are corrupted by such a thing as war only insofar as the feminine psychic principle is corrupt. What he views as "the presence" is primal, savage, and masculine, as it "stoops in the mind, hairy and thick," destroying "norms" and "modes of arrest" when it becomes actively motivating in the conscious mind. By this "presence," he maintains, women "will be used" if they relinquish their "precepts of will" ("Throwing their bellowing flesh on the tool/ That eases the rutting sow"). By taking the pacifistic stand against the war, therefore, Everson chose to accept for himself what he saw as the traditionally feminine response to life, as he states in "Now in These Days" (from *The Residual Years*): He will "wait in these rooms," he vows, accepting "the degradation of slavery and want" imposed on him in a camp for conscientious objectors.

"The Chronicle of Division"

In January, 1943, Everson was conscripted and sent to a camp in Waldport, Oregon. He would remain incarcerated for three years, during which time he composed his longest sequential and confessional poem, "The Chronicle of Division" (from *The Residual Years*). While this poem describes poignantly and incisively the human deprivation suffered by men locked up for their beliefs, the underpinning and gradually overriding focus is on the psychological condition of men without women. Paradoxically, while it had been the feminine temperament that Everson had espoused and embraced as a necessary response to what he perceived as a war caused by masculine aggression and warmongering, it was the feminine embodied in his wife that proved to be the most devastating to him. Because there had been no "primacy" in the relationship (and he gradually came to see his vasectomy as a testament to this), and because of the indefinite length of their separation, Everson's wife fell in love with another man and (in a letter) requested a divorce.

Although the poet deals with the consequent pain and feelings of rejection he experiences, throughout the poem, he discovers something within himself that is more awesome than the loss of his marriage and home: He discovers the capacity to kill, as he suddenly realizes that he desires to strangle his wife, "Till the plunging features/ Bulge and go black,/ And all his old hurt/ Lies healed on the bed." The disconcerting irony in this is immediately apparent to him, for he is locked up because he refuses to kill and yet finds within himself the desire to murder punitively; "the presence," then, "hairy and thick," hunkers in himself. Unable to accept this shadow-side of his consciousness, he attempts to purge himself of all his past familial and regional associations, believing that he might thereby conjoin his "divisible selves,/ Ill-eased with each other."

THE "WOMAN WITHIN"

With the war ended and his release from the CPS camp guaranteed in 1946, he began immediately to direct his attention, in "The Fictive Wish" (*The Residual Years*), to an introspective search for that "woman within," that woman "of his," whom he might learn to know well enough to recognize outside himself were he confronted by her. It is not surprising that Everson describes this woman in strictly physical and sexual terms, with "her breast" the "ease of his need,/ And the thigh a solace. . . ." Two months after being released from the camp, he met and fell in love with Mary Fabilli, a Catholic woman who had been recently betrayed by her husband and was also suffering the pain of rejection. In short, because of chance similarities in their respective pasts, and because he was actively searching for the woman "of his," Everson could truthfully feel about Fabilli, as he was to write in *Prodigious Thrust*, that "I knew her before I met her."

Three months after being released from his confinement in the CPS camp, Everson wrote "The Blowing of the Seed" to Fabilli and about the cathartic and rejuvenating power of their love. It is apparent that the woman had quickly become his "other self" and the nurturer of his "huge hope"; she "broke" his loneliness, he tells her, and she freed his "isolate heart." Not only has Fabilli allowed him to come "up out of darkness," allowed his courage to burst out of a "cold region" of "ash," but also her love for him has caused a new ascendancy of his masculine ego; consequently, Everson makes a 180-degree turn in attitude, abandons his "feminine," passive demeanor, and voices a traditional drive toward male primacy, wrenching their relationship into the age-old equation of strong male and weak female. This "new" attitude, voiced with a Dionysian and dithyrambic intensity, is Everson's way of compensating for the debilitating vulnerability and ultimate rejection he suffered with the breakup of his first marriage and with the treatment and alienation he suffered because of his moral position against the war. In other words, what he denied for almost ten years (that is, male aggression, libidinal masculinity, and male primacy), he affirms in *The Blowing of the Seed*; after all, the intellectual denial of the traditionally patriarchal world had involved an immense price and overwhelming nakedness emotionally, psychologically, and spiritually. While he attempts to continue writing with masculine bravado in his next poem, "The Springing of the Blade," trying to be a Whitmanesque singer of fecundity, he finds himself "strung" in "the iron dimension," his term for the past and its ineradicable cleavages and losses. Again he finds his capacity to love thwarted by his inability to live in face of the inevitable threats of infidelity that living entails—that is, the infidelity of time to life, of the real to the ideal, of the body to the spirit, and of the heart to the mind.

The Year's Declension

Although Everson and Fabilli were married, their love was thwarted by another factor as well: She was a Catholic and he was not. He felt, as he expresses in "The First Absence," increasingly fearful of her possible abandonment of him; and as she began to attend religious services more frequently than she had before their marriage, he began to accompany her. Believing, therefore, that by converting to Catholicism he could secure, as he says in "The Quarrel," the "necessary certitude to start anew," he decided to do what was necessary to be baptized a Catholic. What was necessary was not what he expected, for the Church refused to recognize their marriage because it had not granted the annulment of Fabilli's first marriage; in short, they were forced to separate. Left alone, Everson was again compelled to face his own incompleteness, was again forced to face life without the emotional security of his union with another; thus, in "In the Dream's Recess," he pleads to God: "Give me the cleansing power!/ . . . Make me clean!" He needed strength now, to face his own vulnerability, and to face the inferior shadow-side of his own personality: "The sullied presence crouches in my side,/ And all is fearful where I dare not wake or dream."

The Crooked Lines of God

Not surprisingly, after Everson decided to become Brother Antoninus, a *donatus* in the Dominican order, he set out with a convert's zealousness to denounce, in *The Crooked Lines of God*, all that he had been and believed secularly. In "The Screed of the Flesh," for example, he eschews the fleshly life he had lived with his two wives; in fact, he goes so far in his zealotry as to fictionalize his past persona as one who "gloried self,/ Singing the glory of myself." To anyone familiar with the poet's pre-Catholic verse, it is apparent that, to the contrary, Everson spent very little time "singing the glory" of himself or of his life, for his verse is tortured by self-analysis, doubt, and distrust. Obviously he intends for his conversion to purify his life and obliterate his past errors and losses, and because woman, with her tempting "merciful thighs," has hurt him the most, he claims, in "A Penitential Psalm," that his "corruptness" is his only through inheriting his mother's (and, before her, Eve's) "iniquities": "in sin did my mother conceive me!" Delegating the responsibility for his own shadow-side to another, however, could not last; thus, after his zealousness had been worn down by six years of celibacy and three years of almost total creative barrenness, in *The Hazards of Holiness*, Brother Antoninus's central poetic subject becomes his "dark night of the soul," as well as his contention with the shadow-side of his consciousness.

The Hazards of Holiness

The terse, almost truncated and imageless poetic lines throughout *The Hazards of Holiness* exemplify a period in Everson's life when, as expressed in "Saints," there is "No thing. Not anything," and the poet pleads to God: "Do something!/ Kiss or kill/ But move me!" Very similar to the pantheistical god in "Circumstance," a pre-Catholic poem in *San Joaquin*, who "hears not, nor sees," in "You, God," the supreme deity in this period of the poet's life is a "God of death,/ Great God of no-life." In "Jacob and the Angel," the man of the flesh and earth, Esau, becomes emblematic of Everson, and Jacob (Antoninus) must wrestle with his dark brother for supremacy—even in the face of the fact that God has apparently abandoned the celibate monk despite all his earlier confessions and self-denials. "But I?" the poet asks in "Sleep-Tossed I Lie," where he questions the value of his barrenness, bitterly imagining lovers locked in passion in the night beyond the walls of his monastery. As a result of his torturous introspection and out of the pain he suffers for the denial of the flesh, he laments: "Long have I lain,/ Long lain, and in the longing/ Fry." Again, in "Black Christ," he cries out of his barrenness, "Kill me./ . . . I beg thy kindness." Importantly, though, in the last poem of *The Hazards of Holiness*, "In Savage Wastes," a breakthrough is achieved, and the poet shows a lessening of his desire to retreat any longer into contemplation of a distant Celestial City. Instead, he affirms that "I [shall] go forth/ And return to the ways of man," no longer willing to deny his essential humanness, "And will find my God in the thwarted love that breaks between us!" With his new attitude, then, his quest for meaning and wholeness leads Brother Antoninus out of a ten-year period of celibacy and into a relationship with Rose Tunnland, to and about whom he wrote *The Rose of Solitude*.

THE ROSE OF SOLITUDE

After learning to embrace his fleshly, Esau-like nature, the poet begins to praise woman as the means through which the polarities of his psyche may be balanced and possibly synthesized, and through which he may be permitted to move closer to God. Brother Antoninus believes that, both emotionally and physically, he has been resurrected through the love for Tunnland ("I dream the dawn of the longest night: The one resurrection"); furthermore, all the poems in *The Rose of Solitude* attest to the victory of Eros (love directed toward self-realization) over Thanatos (the instinctual desire for death, as it was expressed throughout *The Hazards of Holiness*). The poet tells his reader, in "The Kiss of the Cross," that "She brought me back./ . . . I was brought back alive." Out of his desire for a sustained equipoise between the mind and the heart, the spirit and the flesh, while at the same time questioning the rightness of breaking his vows of celibacy, he pleads: "O Christ & Lady/ Save me from my law!" Ultimately, however, Brother Antoninus becomes with Tunnland like the proverbial tree that can reach heaven only if its roots have penetrated hell, as he indicates in "Immortal Strangeness":

When we fell—
  on the hard floor
  in the harsh dark,

on the bitter boards—,
When we fell
We rose.

In short, the conjunction of Christ with woman at the symbolic level, conjoined at the actual level by the act of love, reveals the *felix culpa*; furthermore, the poet has come to believe that, in spite of Catholic dogma and monastic strictures, Eros and the Christ-force are nonexclusive, and so the disparity between his human needs and the mode of his existence begins to dissolve.

The relationship with Tunnland ended in separation (she fell in love with another man, the poet said in several interviews), but in 1965, Brother Antoninus met and fell in love with Rickson, to whom he wrote and dedicated *Tendril in the Mesh*, the last poem he was to write as a monk. His love for her fuses mythologies: "Kore! Daughter of dawn! Persephone! Maiden of twilight!/ . . . In the node of your flesh you drip my flake of bestowal." Through her, furthermore, he witnesses the conjunction of Eros and Christ: "Dark God of Eros, Christ of the buried blood,/ Stone-channeled beast of ecstasy and fire. . . ." At the end of the first public reading of this poem, on December 7, 1969, the poet formally left the Dominican order.

MAN-FATE

A painful period of self-doubt followed for almost five years, chronicled in *Man-Fate*. In "The Gash," for instance, the poet says, "To covet and resist for years, and then/ To succumb, is a fearsome thing." To compensate for the vulnerability and alienation he feels, Everson sets out consciously to discover a masculine persona as powerful as that of Antoninus. While it is a slow birth back to what he calls, in "The Challenge," his "basic being," he makes a decision about the "garb" of his ethos and new identity in "The Scout." Reflecting on the fact that his monk's habit is being worn by someone else in the monastery, he says that now "I assume the regalia of the Old West:/ Beads, buckskin and bearclaws. . . ." This new persona, he believes, will be his "sentinel," as he states in "The Black Hills," just as his habit had been, standing between him and the outside world of chance and abrasion. While this may be true, the primal and stereotypically male "regalia" also noticeably prevents the integration of his anima or feminine side into his consciousness, as the reader witnesses in *The Masks of Drought*.

THE MASKS OF DROUGHT

After being hired in 1971 as poet-in-residence at the University of California, Santa Cruz, Everson began to experience a lessening of his poetic output, writing only one or two poems a year for eight years. While this "drought" was certainly one he was fighting, *The Masks of Drought* was inspired by two other droughts, the literal California drought in 1977 and 1978 and the poet's sexual impotence. Throughout the volume, the latter is not only objectified but also intensified by the former, as in "Kingfisher Flat," in which the poet, lying beside his wife at night, thinks of the creek outside their home as objectifying the blocked flow of his own sexuality: "The starved stream/ Edges its way through dead stones,/ Noiseless in the night." Like the rattlesnake, in "Rattlesnake August," who when "Fate accosts—/ Licks his lip and stabs back," Everson stabs back at his age, at his physical condition, and at nature (his symbol of the feminine and her power to cause his impotence). In "Cutting the Firebreak," the poet says he is "one" with his "mad scythe" when he cuts down weeds; furthermore, the reason he and his phallic instrument are "mad" is understood when he tells the reader, in the last two lines of the poem, that the wild flowers he cuts down are, to his mind, "All the women in my life/ Sprawled in the weeds—drunk in death." In "Chainsaw," Everson goes into the woods with his saw, "the annihilate god" (and, like the earlier scythe, another phallic symbol), intending to cut down three alders, symbols of the feminine, with "woman-smooth bark,/ . . . naked skin."

Everson is attempting to impose himself on nature, by enacting the old Western code of manhood that stressed participation insofar as it led to nature's submission, but what happens throws him into an acute awareness of his human condition and folly: the third tree bucks back, kicks the saw's chain against his leg, tears his pants, but misses his flesh entirely. Nevertheless, dazed by the near catastrophe, Everson imagines his leg's truncation, a "pitiful stump," for "Something is finished,/ Something cleanly done," and this imagined "absence" becomes distorted, transformed into a bitter reminder of the actual loss—his sexual virility. Gradually, however, he realizes the "folly" of the impulse that sent him to the woods in the first place: that is, his need to assert his maleness on the femaleness of nature to prove his virility. He acknowledges his foolishness and begins to accept his human limitations.

Although he says, in "Spotfire," that—between the extremes of his own nature—"I have seen my heart's fate/ Shaped in the balance,/ And know what I am," the last poem he composed for *The Masks of Drought*, "Moongate," indicates that he has still not realized a "balance" between his masculine and feminine sides. After staying up late one night and reflecting on all the losses in his life, Everson says that a "sudden yearn of unrealization" then "clutches" his heart, and this causes him to feel that "a dream awaits me, back in bed,/ And I turn to take it up." Significantly, in the dream he recounts in the poem, he finds himself with Poulson, back in the time before the first traumatic loss and betrayal he suffered for loving a woman. Suddenly a fox, clearly meant to represent Everson's vocation and the pursuit of success therein, darts into the poet's focus, and he abandons Poulson for his pursuit of "the illusive one." As he runs "urgently" up river, he hears the steps of someone behind him; when he turns he sees a "strange woman" who "cannot see" what it is that Everson pursues, but nevertheless, he says, "What I see she follows." After seeing her, he returns to his chase until "dusk draws down" and he can no longer follow the fox; importantly, it is only now, when he can go no farther, that he turns to face the anima image again: "And her eyes are shining, shining." Everson stated in an interview that he intended to write a sequel to this poem, and in the next poem, he would have the "strange woman" move out in front of him while the fox falls behind. It is noteworthy that the fox in "Moongate" is male.

The Integral Years

While Everson's pre-Catholic poetry was published in *The Residual Years* and the Catholic poetry he wrote as Brother Antoninus was published in *The Veritable Years*, the poetry written since his departure from the Dominican order appeared in one volume, *The Integral Years*. Smaller collections that are included in the trilogy's third volume had already been published: *Man-Fate*, *The Masks of Drought*, *Renegade Christmas*, and *Mexican Standoff*. Also included in *The Integral Years* are poems that had been published in limited editions: *In Medias Res* and "Skald" (1984), the first two cantos of an autobiographical epic titled *Dust Shall Be the Serpent's Food*.

Suffering for many years the increasingly debilitating effects of Parkinson's disease, Everson wrote poems much more slowly than he once did. However, throughout *The Residual Years*, *The Veritable Years*, and the early movements of *The Integral Years*, the poet ceaselessly affirmed and reaffirmed—by means of his own life and poetic witness—the human capacity for successful self-renewal and self-creation. Indeed, like most great artists, Everson created more than courageous life-affirming assertions; he created powerful and enduring testaments to the inexhaustible will of the human spirit to transcend mundane, gender-specific identities and to realize the integrated, whole, androgynous self.

Other major works

nonfiction: *Friar Among Savages: Father Luis Cáncer*, 1958 (as Brother Antoninus); *Robinson Jeffers: Fragments of an Older Fury*, 1968; *Archetype West: The Pacific Coast as a Literary Region*, 1976; *Earth Poetry: Selected Essays and Interviews of William Everson, 1950-1977*, 1980; *Birth of a Poet*, 1982; *William Everson, on Writing the Waterbirds and Other Presentations: Collected Forewords and Afterwords, 1935-1981*, 1983; *The Excesses of God: Robinson Jeffers as a Religious Figure*, 1988; *Naked Heart: Talking on Poetry, Mysticism, and the Erotic*, 1992; *Take Hold upon the Future: Letters on Writers and Writing, 1938-1946*, 1994; *Prodigious Thrust*, 1996.

miscellaneous: *William Everson: The Light the Shadow Casts, Five Interviews with William Everson Plus Corresponding Poems*, 1996 (Clifton Ross, editor); *Dark God of Eros: A William Everson Reader*, 2003 (Albert Gelpi, editor).

Bibliography

Bartlett, Lee. *William Everson*. Boise, Idaho: Boise State University Press, 1985. This brief monograph provides a useful introduction to the major phases of the poet's life, his movement from Everson to Antoninus and back to Everson. Strangely, however, Bartlett focuses more on Everson's accomplishments as a master printer than his achievements as a poet. Discussion of Everson's poems is minimal.

_______. *William Everson: The Life of Brother Antoninus*. New York: New Directions, 1988. Although informative about Everson's relationship with Kenneth Rexroth in the early 1950's, as well as about Everson's place in the San Francisco Renaissance, Bartlett's study provides only cursory readings of Everson's poems and no discussion at all of the poet's second marriage to Mary Fabilli, the relationship that served as a catalyst for Everson's conversion to Catholicism. Contains an excellent bibliography.

_______, ed. *Benchmark and Blaze: The Emergence of William Everson*. Metuchen, N.J.: Scarecrow Press, 1979. A collection of twenty-two critical appraisals of the poetry and printing of Everson, this work provides an excellent overview of the poet-printer's distinguished career and accomplishments. Presented here are appraisals by such writers as Robert Duncan, Ralph J. Mills, Jerome Mazzaro, William Stafford, Kenneth Rexroth, and Albert Gelpi.

Carpenter, David A. *The Rages of Excess: The Life and Poetry of William Everson*. Bristol, Ind.: Wyndham Hall Press, 1987. A critical biography that is also a Jungian study attempts to interpret the poet's complex psychology and life via close analysis of the poetic canon and vice versa. Noteworthy here are the close, detailed discussions of Everson's long poems, such as his "The Chronicle of Division" and *Tendril in the Mesh*. Good bibliography.

Everson, William. Interviews. *William Everson: The Light the Shadow Casts*. Edited by Clifton Ross. Berkeley, Calif.: New Earth, 1996. Five interviews with Everson with corresponding poems. Offers invaluable insight into the life and work of the poet.

Herrmann, Steven. *William Everson: The Shaman's Call—Interviews, Introduction, and Commentaries*. New York: Eloquent Books, 2009. Jungian psychotherapist Herrmann was asked by Everson to collaborate on a book in 1991. This work, which contains some interviews by Herrmann, examines shamanism in Everson's poetry.

Houston, James D., et al. *The Death of a Poet: Santa Cruz Writers, Poets, and Friends Remember William Everson*. Austin, Tex.: W. Thomas Taylor, 1994. A collection of biographical essays about Everson originally published in *Metro Santa Cruz* in 1994 following Everson's death.

David A. Carpenter

F

LAWRENCE FERLINGHETTI

Born: Yonkers, New York; March 24, 1919

PRINCIPAL POETRY

Pictures of the Gone World, 1955, 1995
A Coney Island of the Mind, 1958
Starting from San Francisco, 1961
An Eye on the World: Selected Poems, 1967
The Secret Meaning of Things, 1969
Tyrannus Nix?, 1969
Back Roads to Far Places, 1971
Open Eye, Open Heart, 1973
Who Are We Now?, 1976
Landscapes of Living and Dying, 1979
Endless Life: Selected Poems, 1981
A Trip to Italy and France, 1981
Over All the Obscene Boundaries: European Poems and Transitions, 1984
These Are My Rivers: New and Selected Poems, 1955-1993, 1993
A Far Rockaway of the Heart, 1997
San Francisco Poems, 1998
How to Paint Sunlight: Lyric Poems and Others, 1997-2000, 2001
Americus, Book I, 2004

OTHER LITERARY FORMS

Early in his career, Lawrence Ferlinghetti (fur-lihng-GEHT-ee) was very much interested in the French Symbolist poets, and in 1958, City Lights published his first and only translation of French poetry: *Selections from "Paroles" by Jacques Prévert*. His translations of pieces by an Italian poet, Pier Paolo Pasolini, appeared in 1986 as *Roman Poems*. He has also translated poetry by Nicanor Parra in *Antipoems: New and Selected* (1985) and by Homero Aridjis in *Eyes to See Otherwise* (2002). Ferlinghetti has primarily published poetry in book form, although, in addition to having written many critical and review articles that have appeared in both magazines and newspapers, he has produced a variety of works including novels, travel writing, political writing, drawings, and plays. Ferlinghetti's work crosses genre boundaries, and some of his prose works—like the novel *Her* (1960) and the travel journal *The Mexican Night* (1970)—sound so much like his poetry that it is questionable whether one should actually call them prose. He published another novel, *Love in the Days of Rage*, in 1988 and two commentaries on poetry, *What Is Poetry?* (2000) and *Poetry as Insurgent Art*

(2007), the latter consisting of thoughts on poetry written over more than fifty years.

Ferlinghetti's two plays, *Unfair Arguments with Existence* and *Routines*, were published by New Directions in 1963 and 1964, respectively. His interest in the theater and oral poetry led to various filmings and recordings of his readings. The two best-known performances of Ferlinghetti, "Tyrannus Nix?" and "Assassination Raga," are preserved in both film and audio recording. *Leaves of Life: Drawing from the Model* (1983) is a collection of his drawings, as is his *Life Studies, Life Stories: Eighty Works in Paper* (2003).

Achievements

In 1957, Lawrence Ferlinghetti first received national attention as a result of the "Howl" obscenity trial. At that time, Ferlinghetti was recognized not as a poet but as the publisher and distributor of Allen Ginsberg's *Howl, and Other Poems* (1956). After winning the controversial trial, Ferlinghetti received enough attention to boost his own collection of poems, *A Coney Island of the Mind*, into a best-seller position. His name became strongly associated with the new, or Beat, poetry being developed on the West Coast, and Ferlinghetti became recognized as a poet of movements and protests.

Often being antigovernment in his responses, Ferlinghetti has gone so far as refusing to accept government grants for either his own writing or the City Lights publishing house. Nevertheless, he received a National Book Award nomination in 1970 for *The Secret Meaning of Things*, the *Library Journal* Notable Book of 1979 citation for *Landscapes of Living and Dying* in 1980, and Silver Medals for poetry from the Commonwealth Club of California for *Over All the Obscene Boundaries* in 1984 and for *A Far Rockaway of the Heart* in 1997. In 1977, the city of San Francisco paid tribute to Ferlinghetti by honoring him at the Civic Art Festival—the first time a poet was so recognized. The City of Rome awarded him a poetry prize in 1993, and San Francisco not only named a street in his honor in 1994 but also named him the city's first poet laureate in 1998. The poet was presented the Fred Cody Award for lifetime achievement in 1996 and the Lifetime Achievement Award from the Before Columbus Foundation in 1999. In 2000, Ferlinghetti was a joint winner, with film critic Pauline Kael, of the National Book Critics Circle's Ivan Sandrof Award for Lifetime Achievement. Furthermore, in 2001, City Lights Bookseller and Publishers was designated an official landmark. He has continued to be recognized through a wide range of awards, including the Robert Kirsch Award for body of work from the *Los Angeles Times* (2000), the PEN Center West Literary Award for lifetime achievement (2002), the Frost Medal (2003), the Northern California Book Award in poetry (2004) for *Americus, Book I*, the Association of American Publishers Award for creative publishing (2005), and the Literarian Award from the National Book Foundation (2005) for outstanding service to the American literary community.

Ferlinghetti is noted for the many public readings he has given in support of free speech, nuclear disarmament, antiwhaling, and other causes. Often overlooked by critics, Ferlinghetti has remained an active voice speaking for the American people against many institutions and practices—government, corporate, and social alike—that limit individual freedom; he stands out as a poet and a true individual.

BIOGRAPHY

Lawrence Monsanto Ferlinghetti—born in Yonkers, New York, in 1919—was the youngest of five sons of Charles Ferlinghetti and Clemence Ferlinghetti. Several months before Lawrence's birth, his father died unexpectedly of a heart attack, and his mother suffered a breakdown as a result. She was unable to care for her son and was eventually institutionalized at the state hospital in Poughkeepsie, New York.

After these humble and tragic beginnings, it is ironic that Ferlinghetti was taken and cared for by his mother's well-to-do uncle, Ludwig Mendes-Monsanto, and his wife, Emily, in their Manhattan home. It is also ironic that American-born Ferlinghetti learned French as his first language. In fact, throughout his childhood, he actually believed himself to be French, having been taken in by his great-aunt Emily, who left her husband and returned to France, her homeland. Ferlinghetti spent the first five years of his life in Strasbourg with Mendes-Monsanto, whom he refers to as his "French mother." She was eventually persuaded to return to New York to rejoin her husband, but the reunion lasted only for a short time. Ferlinghetti—who knew himself only as Lawrence Ferling Monsanto—was placed in an orphanage for seven months. Eventually, Mendes-Monsanto reclaimed him and took him away, after leaving her husband again. This time they remained in New York.

Mendes-Monsanto took on work as a French tutor for the daughter of the very wealthy Presley Bisland and Anna Lawrence Bisland. She and Ferlinghetti lived in a small room in the third-floor servants' area until one day she mysteriously disappeared, whereupon Ferlinghetti was adopted by the Bislands.

The Bislands' son had died in early childhood. His name—and his mother's maiden name—was Lawrence, her father having founded Sarah Lawrence College near Bronxville. Presley Bisland was also a man of letters, with a profound interest in contemporary literature, although his experiences included being one of the last men to ride the Chisholm Trail on the last of the great cattle drives. The Bislands were aristocratic, adventuresome, and cosmopolitan, but also creative in spirit. In fact, Ferlinghetti maintains that Presley Bisland's writings gave him the idea that being an author was a dignified calling.

At the age of ten, Ferlinghetti was told about his natural mother, Clemence Ferlinghetti, whom he met one traumatic Sunday afternoon. He was given the choice to go with her, although he considered her a stranger, or to stay with the Bislands. He chose to stay. Unknown to Ferlinghetti, the Bislands had arranged to send him away to school. A few weeks later, he found himself boarding with a family named Wilson in one of New York City's rougher neighborhoods. Their son Bill, being older, became a hero to the young Ferlinghetti. Lawrence joined the Boy Scouts, went to baseball and football games, and was far less lonely than he had been at the Bisland mansion.

At the age of sixteen, Lawrence began to write poetry. His stepsister, Sally Bisland, gave him a book of Charles Baudelaire in translation. Ferlinghetti remembers it as the first collection of poems he read from cover to cover. He was then sent to a private high school, Mount Hernon, near Greenfield, Massachusetts. In his senior year, Anna Bisland took him for the first of a series of visits to see his natural mother and brothers at their home in Ossining.

Ferlinghetti attended college at the University of North Carolina at Chapel Hill and was graduated in 1941, after which he joined the U.S. Navy and served in World War II. It was while he was in the Navy that he received a telegram from Central Islip State Hospital saying that Emily Mendes-Monsanto, his "French mother," had died, having listed Ferlinghetti as her only living relative. This was the first he had heard of her since she had left him with the Bislands when he was ten.

In World War II, Ferlinghetti was on one of the primary naval submarine chasers coming in for the Normandy invasion. Later, in 1945, on the first day of the U.S. occupation of Japan, his ship landed there. Eventually, he was able to visit Nagasaki, where he witnessed the aftermath of the atomic bombing of that city. The devastation he witnessed left an indelible impression.

After his discharge from the U.S. Navy, Ferlinghetti returned to New York City and lived in Greenwich Village, taking on work as a mail clerk for *Time* magazine. His interest in poetry revived, and he returned to Columbia University under the G.I. Bill, receiving his M.A. degree in 1947. That summer Presley Bisland died. Soon afterward, Ferlinghetti left for Paris, where he met many literary figures. He completed work on a thesis and was awarded a degree from the Sorbonne. He also wrote a novel, which was rejected by Doubleday. In 1949, Ferlinghetti returned to the United States for a two-week visit with Anna Bisland. In 1951, both she and Ferlinghetti's natural mother died. In the same year, after several trips back and forth between Europe and the United States, Ferlinghetti married Selden Kirby-Smith, who was known as Kirby. They moved to San Francisco, where Ferlinghetti wrote articles for *Art Digest* and book reviews for the *San Francisco Chronicle*.

Influenced greatly by Kenneth Rexroth and Kenneth Patchen, who both lived in San Francisco, Ferlinghetti soon came to be considered a political poet. He was published in Peter Martin's magazine *City Lights*, and eventually the two men collaborated to open the City Lights Bookstore in 1953. In 1955, the same year that Ferlinghetti's first book of poetry, *Pictures of the Gone World*, was published under the City Lights imprint, Martin sold Ferlinghetti his interest in the store. At about that time, Ferlinghetti became acquainted with James Laughlin, president of the publishing house New Directions. It was through Laughlin that Ferlinghetti's second book of poems, *A Coney Island of the Mind*, became a best seller.

Ginsberg came into Ferlinghetti's life from the East, bringing a poem titled "Howl" with him. Ferlinghetti was impressed with Ginsberg and published *Howl, and Other Poems*. It was this book that caused Ferlinghetti to be arrested, the charge against him being that he printed and sold obscene writings. He was eventually cleared, and partly because of the publicity, City Lights flourished.

Although Ferlinghetti and his wife, Kirby, were divorced in the early 1970's, their marriage had been relatively stable; in 1962 a daughter, Julie, was born, and in 1963, a son, Lorenzo. During the 1960's, Ferlinghetti traveled to South and Central America, to Europe, and to the Soviet Union, giving poetry readings whenever possible. In 1974, he met Paula Lillevand; they moved in together in 1978, but they parted two years later.

Ferlinghetti first took lysergic acid diethylamide (LSD) in 1967, an experience that resulted in the poem "Mock Confessional." Throughout the 1970's and 1980's, Ferlinghetti remained actively interested in political and environmental matters, his poetry inevitably reflecting his political and social concerns. During these years, he traveled extensively in Europe and sometimes in Latin America, giving readings of his poems.

In 1977, Ferlinghetti took up drawing, an interest he had left behind some twenty years earlier, and soon he was painting as well. His expressionist-style works were displayed in a formal exhibition in the mid-1980's in the San Francisco Bay area, and another show was organized in Berlin in 1990. He continued to edit volumes of City Lights anthologies throughout the 1990's. Ferlinghetti also collaborated in a video, directed by Christopher Felver, called *The Coney Island of Lawrence Ferlinghetti*, released in 1996. In it, the poet acts in autobiographical vignettes, tours places of particular meaning to him, reads his poetry, and expounds on his artistic philosophy and political views.

Ferlinghetti has continued to play an active role in the cultural and literary life of San Francisco and has traveled frequently for poetry readings, interviews, and exhibitions of his art. A 2007 show of approximately twenty of his large canvases traveled to Woodstock, New York, under the title lit.paint. New volumes of poetry have included *How to Paint Sunlight* and the ambitious *Americus, Book I*, a poetic compendium of the historical, political, and cultural past of America through the early 1960's.

Analysis

Lawrence Ferlinghetti's poetry may be looked on as a kind of travelog in which he has subjectively recorded choice experiences or montages from experience, often in a jazzlike or free-associative manner. For Ferlinghetti, "reality" itself becomes metaphorical, something he endows with mythical import, although he is not a poet given to hidden meanings. Although his poetry is largely autobiographical, an adequate analysis of his poetry is possible without thorough biographical knowledge; Ferlinghetti's poetry is not excessively self-contained.

A CONEY ISLAND OF THE MIND

Whereas Ferlinghetti's poems are for the most part historical, or autobiographical, Ferlinghetti the man is a myth, appearing as a cult hero, one of the original Beats. Sometimes a martyr to a cause, Ferlinghetti will occasionally insert his political ideologies into a poem for no apparent reason other than that they seem to fit his role. Halfway through the sometimes absurd, sometimes delightful poem "Underwear," Ferlinghetti overextends his metaphor by becoming politically involved:

> You have seen the three-color pictures
> with crotches encircled
> to show the areas of extra strength
> and three-way stretch
> promising full freedom of action
> Don't be deceived
> It's all based on the two-party system
> which doesn't allow much freedom of choice

The reader is often seduced, but behind Ferlinghetti's speaking voice, full of American colloquialisms, is an intellect schooled in the classics, highly knowledgeable of literature, past and present—a voice full ofallusions. Rather surprisingly, Ferlinghetti makes many direct references to greater works of literature by borrowing lines to suit his own purposes. Even the title of Ferlinghetti's best-selling book *A Coney Island of the Mind* is taken from Henry Miller's *Into the Night Life* (1947). One repeatedly discovers lines and phrases such as T. S. Eliot's "Let us go then you and I" and "Hurry up please it's time" ironically enlisted for use in such poems as "Junkman's Obbligato." Ferlinghetti frequently employs fragments from literature without alerting his audience to his borrowing. In "Autobiography," he states, "I read the Want Ads daily/ looking for a stone a leaf/ an unfound door"—an oblique reference to Thomas Wolfe's opening in *Look Homeward, Angel* (1929). He makes even more esoteric references to William Butler Yeats's "horsemen" in poems such as "Reading Yeats I Do Not Think" and again in "Autobiography." In "Assassination Raga," one finds a variation on Dylan Thomas's "The force that through the green fuse drives the flower." In its stead, Ferlinghetti writes of "The force that through the red fuze/ drives the bullet"—the poem being in honor of Robert Kennedy and read in Nourse Auditorium, San Francisco, June 8, 1968, the day Kennedy was buried after having been assassinated during his presidential campaign in Los Angeles.

In his role as a subjective historian and political rebel, Ferlinghetti never orates with so much pomp as to raise himself above his audience. In his meager "Charlie Chaplin" manner—Chaplin being a persona to whom he continuously compares himself in poems such as "Constantly Risking Absurdity," "In a Time of Revolution for Instance," and "Director of Alienation"—Ferlinghetti is just as capable of making fun of himself as he is of satirizing various institutions and aspects of society.

"DOG"

Whereas some poets seek to find metaphorical reflections of themselves in nature, Ferlinghetti rarely looks there for inspiration. Furthermore, being more fond of philosophy than of drama, Ferlinghetti projects a sense of conflict mainly through his own personal quest—for his true self. His feelings of alienation and the quest for environmental constants that do not restrict one's freedom are depicted in the poem "Dog" (from *A Coney Island of the Mind*), which begins: "The dog trots freely in the street/ and sees reality/ and the things he sees/ are bigger than himself. . . ." As the poem progresses, the reader comes to understand that this is an ordinary stray dog—and also Ferlinghetti in a stray-dog suit. "And the things he sees/ are his reality/ Drunks in doorways/ Moons on trees. . . ." The dog keeps on going with a curiosity that demands diversity from experience.

Ferlinghetti goes deeper, allowing the reader also to don a dog suit, to see "Ants in holes/ Chickens in Chinatown windows/ their heads a block away." Thus the reader learns that he is roaming the streets of San Francisco. The dog trots past the carcasses that are hung up whole in Chinatown. At this point, the reader learns that he "would rather eat a tender cow/ than a tough policeman/ though either might do." The reader has already been told that the dog does not hate cops; he merely has no use for them.

Here the reader begins to wonder whether being stray is conditional on having no preferences. Is the dog a Democrat or a Republican? The reader later learns that this dog is at least "democratic." Ferlinghetti does deal with unusual specifics as the dog trots past the San Francisco Meat Market, and keeps going: "past the Romeo Ravioli Factory/ and past Coit's Tower/ and past Congressman Doyle of the Unamerican Committee. . . ." Here Ferlinghetti manages to make a political statement that is alien to a dog's perspective. This "Unamerican Committee" is obviously something that Ferlinghetti the Beat poet—not the Ferlinghetti in the dog suit—has recognized. The Ferlinghetti in the dog suit says that ultimately "Congressman Doyle is just another/ fire hydrant/ to him." A few lines earlier, Ferlinghetti alludes to the poet Thomas by labeling the dog "a sad young dog" (see Thomas's *Portrait of the Artist as a Young Dog*, 1940): The dog appears to be metaphorical of all poets and artists, especially Ferlinghetti himself.

Ferlinghetti proceeds to declare that a dog's knowledge is only of the senses. His curiosity already quite obvious, the day becomes:

a real live
        barking
            democratic dog
engaged in real
            free enterprise
with something to say
                about ontology
something to say
            about reality.

In this segment, a major change can be noted: Ferlinghetti has abandoned flush left margins. Beginning with the line "barking," Ferlinghetti demonstrates a newfound freedom through his staggered, free-form typography. The poem continues, and the dog trots more freely, cocking his head sideways at street corners "as if he is just about to have/ his picture taken/ for Victor Records." His ear is raised, and it is suggested that he embodies a question mark as he looks into the "great gramophone of puzzling existence," waiting and looking, just like Ferlinghetti, for an answer to everything—and it all sounds like poetry.

A Far Rockaway of the Heart

In 1997, nearly forty years after the publication of *A Coney Island of the Mind*, Ferlinghetti published a volume whose title insists that it be taken as a companion piece to the earlier work: *A Far Rockaway of the Heart*. Its 101 poems revealed that both the poet's strengths and his weaknesses were in full force as he approached his eightieth birthday. The colloquial diction is as easy as ever, but its novelty is somewhat tarnished; the wide-ranging quotation from and reference to the words of other poets is as masterful as ever, and all the more impressive as the common literary canon has all but disappeared from the cultural landscape. A number of critics noted that Ferlinghetti's styles, themes, and techniques seemed barely to have changed over the long course of his career, yet the poet himself begins the volume acknowledging this fact:

> Everything changes and nothing changes
> Centuries end
>
> and all goes on
> as if nothing
> ever ends
> As clouds still stop in mid-flight
> like dirigibles caught in cross-winds
>
> And the fever of savage city life
> still grips the streets. . . .
>
> It's as if those forty years just vanish.

Perhaps it is presumptuous of the poet to proclaim his own timelessness. However, perhaps his ongoing social and political concerns are timeless because in forty years, little has occurred to remedy the ills he sees around him, and the world goes on as absurd—and as beautiful—as ever.

How to Paint Sunlight

In the introductory note to *How to Paint Sunlight*, Ferlinghetti paraphrases American painter Edward Hopper by saying that "all I ever wanted to do was paint light on the walls of life." The thirty-four poems of this volume, subdivided into four sections, each headed by a note or an epigraph, signal varying concerns with images of light and darkness. Ferlinghetti sees the world as art and light as its paint. The poet's job is to "paint" the world with authenticity and innocence and in all its various hues. Ferlinghetti also suggests that the poet is the medium, the source of the tempera and the gesso. The poet thus creates the world anew on a canvas of former "paintings" and is astonished by each new creation.

Ferlinghetti relies on techniques familiar from earlier work: wide-ranging allusion, an oral quality, free-form lines, and humor. The first section explores varieties of light and darkness in such California landscapes as San Francisco and Big Sur. The introductory poem, "Instructions to Painters & Poets," theorizes about the connections between creating poetry and creating paintings. Subsequent poems begin with images of bright light and end with darker meditations. "Yachts in Sun" begins with the image of bright light catching the sails of the yachts on the bay and ends with the image of the dead lying drowned in the bay beneath the hulls of the boats. The second section, "Surreal Migrations," traverses world and time in search of transcendent light, incorporating allusions to Eliot, Adolf Hitler, Wolfgang Amadeus Mozart, Marcel Proust, Walt Whitman, and the Beatles. The poem ends with images of the creation of song arising from the sounds of leaves and birds. "New York, New York," the more political and sarcastic third section, focuses on urban settings and explores images of New York and personal memories of the narrator's past.

The fourth section, "Into the Interior," combines poems set in midwestern venues and transitions to meditations on the death of Beat poet Ginsberg, including one of the few prose poems of the volume, "Allen Still." Early poems in the section treat the interior of the country (the Midwest) and transition to poems that explore the human interior. "Blind Poet," a poem meant to be performed blindfolded, alludes to the poet's interior vision and to blind bards such as Homer and John Milton. The final poems of this section turn increasingly introspective as the narrator of one poem ("Mouth") laments his inability to express himself and another ("A Tourist of Revolutions") describes the superficiality of his political activism and foreshadows his own death with a wry comment: "And when I die without a sound/ I'll surely join I'll surely join/ the permanent Underground." The final poem of the section, in keeping with the overall tenor of the entire volume, is a paean to the god of light.

AMERICUS, BOOK I

Ferlinghetti's ambitious *Americus, Book I* combines both epic and palimpsest. Its title suggests that it is only the first part of Ferlinghetti's epic of the United States. The volume traces American history from the first European encounters with the natives through the death of President John F. Kennedy in 1963. Ferlinghetti's work combines political and cultural history with the individual story of its titular bardic character,

Americus.

The work alludes to a variety of events, including the European colonization of North America, the French Revolution, westward expansion, and the two world wars. Much of this history takes the form of a collage of newspaper headlines, letters, and stream-of-consciousness prose poems.

Ferlinghetti sets his work firmly in the epic tradition, particularly in the third of the book's twelve sections, where the long monologue by the epic poet Homer situates the poem in the context not only of Homeric epic and Dante's *La divina commedia* (c. 1320; *The Divine Comedy*, 1802) but also of the epic works of American poets Whitman (*Leaves of Grass*, 1855), Ezra Pound (*Cantos*, 1925-1972), William Carlos Williams (*Paterson*, 1946-1958), and Charles Olson (*The Maximus Poems*, 1953-1983). Homer defines poetry in an extended catalog of inventive aphorisms that serve as an index to the themes of Ferlinghetti's poetry. Ferlinghetti alternately presents his compendium of American history and pieces together its larger cultural and artistic history, alluding to influential writers and artists.

In addition to delineating the national history and character of the United States, *Americus* also describes the personal, semi-autobiographical journey of Americus, the central character. Americus begins his journey to America in the womb of his European mother and grows up in the East with all the hopefulness and opportunity contained in the stereotypical immigrant vision of the American Dream. He experiences the horrors, the deaths, and the disillusion of World War II and, following the war, moves west. This central singer of Ferlinghetti's epic is reminiscent of Whitman's central voice in *Leaves of Grass*.

Americus is also a palimpsest, as suggested by the use of the term in the second line of the poem. A palimpsest is a painting or a manuscript that has been created over a previously existing work, so that sometimes the previous work shows through the new work like a ghost. Ferlinghetti layers his work over previous works by making allusions to them, a technique accentuated by the existence of the notes section at the end of the poem. In the notes, Ferlinghetti lists the numerous sources for the various quotations and references that serve as the basis for his poem, quotations that are often elided, parodied, and reworked in much the same manner as the allusions in modernist poet Eliot's *The Waste Land* (1922) or *The Four Quartets* (1943). Ferlinghetti also uses lists and catalogs in much the same manner as Whitman, trying to express the vastness and variability of America in a cornucopia of references to people, events, and impressions that help capture the American experience.

Americus provides a compendium of poetic techniques from Ferlinghetti's work. He uses free-form verse, dialogue, an oral quality, the stream-of-consciousness prose poem, humor, puns, and satire to capture the face and the sights and sounds of America and its past. Ferlinghetti notably ends this volume with a prose poem that portrays a hopeful and celebratory view of the "splendid life of the world." This final prose poem is especially striking when contrasted with the descriptions of the horrors of war and the assassination of Kennedy that precede it. The final three pages of the poem celebrate the joys of the world in all its vitality and beauty.

Other major works

LONG FICTION: *Her*, 1960; *Love in the Days of Rage*, 1988.

PLAYS: *Unfair Arguments with Existence*, pb. 1963; *Routines*, pb. 1964.

NONFICTION: *The Mexican Night*, 1970; *Literary San Francisco: A Pictorial History from Its Beginnings to the Present Day*, 1980 (with Nancy J. Peters); *Leaves of Life: Drawing from the Model*, 1983; *What Is Poetry?*, 2000; *Life Studies, Life Stories: Eighty Works on Paper*, 2003.

TRANSLATIONS: *Selections from "Paroles" by Jacques Prévert*, 1958; *Roman Poems*, 1988 (of Pier Paolo Pasolini).

MISCELLANEOUS: *Poetry as Insurgent Art*, 2007.

Bibliography

Cherkovski, Neeli. *Ferlinghetti: A Biography*. Garden City, N.Y.: Doubleday, 1979. Reviews the wrenching dislocations of Ferlinghetti's childhood, his stint in the U.S. Navy, his studies at Columbia and in Paris, and the development of his artistic and political commitments, always emphasizing the theme of the poet's search for a self. Illustrated with photographs. Provides a primary and a secondary bibliography; indexed.

Ferlinghetti, Lawrence. "Ferlinghetti." Interview by David Meltzer and Jack Shoemaker (1969) and by Meltzer, Marina Lazzara, and James Brook (1999). In *San Francisco Beat: Talking with the Poets*, edited by Meltzer. San Francisco: City Lights, 2001. Ferlinghetti discusses politics, his bookstore, his poetry, and the Beat movement and poets. The contrast between the early interview, conducted during a very active time for San Francisco, and the later interview, thirty years later, sheds light on Ferlinghetti and other Beat poets.

Fontane, Marilyn Ann. "Ferlinghetti's 'Constantly Risking Absurdity.'" *Explicator* 59, no. 2 (Winter, 2001): 106-108. This short article argues that Ferlinghetti's "drop-line" form and stanza divisions provide the structure of a visual staircase for a poem that initially seems unstructured.

Pekar, Harvey, et al. *The Beats: A Graphic History*. Art by Ed Piskor et al. New York: Hill and Wang, 2009. Comic legend Harvey Pekar provides a history of the Beat poets in this graphic book. Contains an entry on and references to Ferlinghetti.

Silesky, Barry. *Ferlinghetti: The Artist in His Time*. New York: Warner Books, 1990. A chatty biography, written with the informality and punchiness of a popular-magazine article. Based on extensive interviews with Ferlinghetti and his associates. Silesky leaves critical appraisal of the poetry to numerous poets and critics interviewed in the book's final chapter; they include Ginsberg, Robert Creeley, Paul Carroll, Ralph Mills, Diane Wakoski, and Gary Snyder. Features a selected bibliography, an index, and photographs.

Skau, Michael. *"Constantly Risking Absurdity": Essays on the Writings of Lawrence Ferlinghetti*. Troy, N.Y.: Whitston, 1989. A brief monograph, illustrated, on Ferlinghetti's works.

Smith, Larry R. *Lawrence Ferlinghetti, Poet-at-Large*. Carbondale: Southern Illinois University Press, 1983. This well-written book has one particularly interesting feature: a multicolumned chronology that parallels events in Ferlinghetti's personal life, his writing achievements, and City Lights publishing history. After presenting a "biographic portrait," Smith argues that Ferlinghetti is best placed within a European rather than American literary tradition. Smith provides a thoughtful treatment of Ferlinghetti's poetic themes and devices and surveys the prose writings and drama as well. Contains photographs, notes, a selected bibliography, and an index.

Stephenson, Gregory. *The Daybreak Boys: Essays on the Literature of the Beat Generation*. Carbondale: Southern Illinois University Press, 1990. Contains the chapter "The 'Spiritual Optics' of Lawrence Ferlinghetti," which offers a general view of Ferlinghetti's writings.

John Alspaugh; Leslie Ellen Jones
Updated by Ann M. Cameron

JACK GILBERT

Born: Pittsburgh, Pennsylvania; February 17, 1925

PRINCIPAL POETRY

Views of Jeopardy, 1962
Monolithos: Poems, 1962 and 1982, 1982
Kochan, 1984
The Great Fires: Poems, 1982-1992, 1994
Refusing Heaven, 2005
Tough Heaven: Poems of Pittsburgh, 2006
Transgressions: Selected Poems, 2006
The Dance Most of All, 2009

OTHER LITERARY FORMS

Jack Gilbert is known primarily for his poetry. He has taught literature and writing and given public readings of his own work.

ACHIEVEMENTS

Jack Gilbert's *Views of Jeopardy* won the Yale Series of Younger Poets competition in 1962 and was nominated for a Pulitzer Prize. *Monolithos* was a finalist for the Pulitzer Prize and won the Stanley Kunitz Prize and American Poetry Review Prize among others. Gilbert earned the Lannan Literary Award for Poetry and the PEN Center USA West Poetry Award, both in 1995 for *The Great Fires*, and the Lila Wallace-*Reader's Digest* Writers' Award in 1998. *Refusing Heaven* won the National Book Critics Circle Award (2005) and a Los Angeles Times Book Prize (2005). Gilbert's career has been spent largely outside the literary world, living abroad or in near-solitude, giving weight to his primary subjects of loneliness and loss and his ultimate message of pleasure in living. The gaps in time between published volumes are because of his insistence on careful attention to craft. For Gilbert, good poetry takes time, experience, and focus.

BIOGRAPHY

Jack Gilbert was born in Pittsburgh on February 17, 1925, the son of James Gilbert and Della Gilbert. His father died when he was ten years old. Gilbert failed high school and was forced to leave, so he found work fumigating houses, in the steel mills, and as a door-to-door salesperson. He served in the U.S. Army during World War II. He was always a voracious reader, and when he was admitted to the University of Pittsburgh through a clerical error, he began writing poetry. He earned a B.A. in 1947 and spent the next few years traveling in France and Italy, where he fell in love with Gianna Gelmetti, one of the great loves of his life and the subject of some of his poems.

By the early 1950's, Gilbert was in San Francisco, studying and writing at San Francisco State University (where he earned an M.A. in 1962) and playing a part in the thriving Beat poetry scene, befriending such poets as Kenneth Rexroth and Allen Ginsberg. In 1962, Gilbert's first collection, *Views of Jeopardy*, won the Yale Series of Younger Poets competition, and at the age of thirty-seven, he became a celebrity poet, a rising star giving readings and being honored at dinners and photographed by *Vogue* and *Glamour* magazines.

Gilbert enjoyed the limelight for a short time, but he felt that his real work was living and writing poetry. He would not publish again for twenty years. In 1964, he won a Guggenheim Fellowship and left for Greece with his former student, the poet Linda Gregg, to whom he was married for six years. After six years in Greece, London, and Denmark, the couple returned to San Francisco and were separated and divorced. Gilbert met and married Michiko Nogami, a sculptor and language instructor based in San Francisco.

Between 1971 and 1982, Gilbert taught at various institutions and traveled widely. He lived with Nogami in Japan, teaching at Rikkyo University in 1974 and 1975 until beginning a fifteen-country tour as lecturer in American literature for the U.S. State Department. In 1982, the same year that his second book, *Monolithos*, was published, Nogami died of cancer at the age of thirty-six. Gilbert published *Kochan*, a limited-edition volume of elegiac poems for Nogami, in 1984. Many of his best love poems, inspired by Nogami, were written through the early 1990's and were published in *The Great Fires* in 1994.

Refusing Heaven appeared eleven years later in 2005, the year that Gilbert became eighty years old. The collection was critically reviewed as the culmination of a lifetime of poetry, but Gilbert was still writing and publishing. *Tough Heaven* and *Transgressions* were published in 2006 and *The Dance Most of All* in 2009.

Gilbert made his home in Northampton, Massachusetts, living quietly and writing poetry. His later years have been marked by a close friendship with Gregg, a recognized poet and teacher at Princeton University. Gilbert has struggled with dementia and has been aided by a small circle of friends, especially Gregg, to whom he dedicated his last two books.

ANALYSIS

Jack Gilbert lived outside literary circles, often abroad, in solitude or in the company of a woman whom he loved. He found these conditions necessary to be able to concentrate on being alive and to discover the fresh perceptions that would become the subjects of his poems. The subject matter of his poetry is simply being alive and being in love, accompanied by an awareness that life ends in death and love ends in loss. Gilbert's personae include the bard Orpheus, the lover of women Don Giovanni, and the aging magician and poet Prospero. The poems are personal and introspective, yet the themes and insights are universal.

Gilbert's poetry is distinguished by its clarity, simplicity, and straightforward language and tone. Classical images, extended metaphors, precise language, and pacing characterize a style that is influenced by the modernists of the early twentieth century. Many of the poems are constructions of declarative sentences, often with endline enjambment and midline caesura for movement and emphasis. While seclusion, loneliness, loss, and mortality are significant themes, Gilbert's final message is one of joy in being alive.

VIEWS OF JEOPARDY

Views of Jeopardy introduces Gilbert's clean, spare style and insights. Some of the poems are set in San Francisco; many are set in Italy and refer to his parting from Gelmetti. In his foreword to the volume, poet and critic Dudley Fitts writes that the subject of the book is "the art of poetry itself, and the problem is the tormenting one of communication." The opening poem, "In Dispraise of Poetry," introduces the idea of poetry as a difficult gift, but one that cannot be refused. Gilbert uses the symbol of the Greek bard Orpheus to represent the serious artist in an indifferent or hostile society. In "Orpheus in Greenwich Village," Gilbert writes of the poet "confident in the hard-/ found mastery," who descends into Hell, readies his lyre, and suddenly notices that his listeners have no ears. The poet in *Views of Jeopardy* is struggling against fashion: "the important made trivial." San Francisco is "this city of easy fame." It is apparent from Gilbert's tone and subject matter that revision, time, care, and craft are Gilbert's tools and that his influences are the classics and the modernists of the first half of the twentieth century; it is no surprise to the reader of Gilbert's poems that he would leave the modern literary world to seek a more compatible place to write.

MONOLITHOS

After twenty years of silence, Gilbert published *Monolithos* at the insistence of his friend and editor Gordon Lish. The volume, dedicated to Gregg, is divided in two parts. The first part, "1962," consists of poems reprinted from *Views of Jeopardy*. However, the opening poem is not "In Dispraise of Poetry," but rather "The Abnormal Is Not Courage," in which Gilbert refers to his assertion that art and craft take time to polish. The poet speaks of ". . . the beauty/ that is of many days. . . ." The second part, "1982," which takes up two-thirds of the collection, documents Gilbert's life since his departure from the literary scene. In the opening poem, "All the Way from There to Here," the poet speaks of dying, of grace, of the end of his marriage to Linda and of Monolithos, their home in the Greek islands. Themes of leaving and loss and the beauty of life's everyday details permeate the poems. Don Giovanni is in trouble, he tells the reader in one poem's title. The poet begins to look back to Pittsburgh, that tough steel-mill town. Even though the city is more temporal, gritty, and solid than any image in Gilbert's work, the poet notes ". . . Even Pittsburgh will/ vanish. . . ." In *Monolithos*, mortality emerges as one of Gilbert's great themes.

The Great Fires

The Great Fires is dedicated to Nogami. In this volume, the poet speaks as Prospero, the aging magician and poet. The volume includes many elegies for Nogami, unsentimental and powerful statements of grief, and speaks of the reality of pain. To be in pain is to be alive; to be in pain is to be a poet. In "Measuring the Tyger," the poet writes: "I want to go back to that time after Michiko's death/ when I cried every day among the trees. To the real/ To the magnitude of pain, of being that much alive." The volume also includes many poems celebrating solitude and distance from society. In "Prospero Without His Magic," Prospero ". . . knows/ that loneliness is our craft. . . ." All three lost loves—Gelmetti, Gregg, and Nogami—appear, as do Orpheus and Don Giovanni. His themes are love, loneliness, and mortality, but never regret. "Michiko Dead" speaks of grief as a box that is too heavy to carry, yet the poet makes the effort to "go on without ever putting the box down." In addition, poetry has always been a heavy burden, the gift that cannot be refused. Although Orpheus in "Finding Eurydice" may be ". . . too old for it now. His famous voice is gone/ and his career is past. . . ." Although "nobody listens," Orpheus ". . . sings because/ that is what he does. . . ."

Refusing Heaven

Refusing Heaven was hailed by critics as Gilbert's greatest poem and his final gift. The volume is infused with the recurring themes of loneliness and happiness, struggle and delight as the poet transmits the clarity and understanding gained from a lifetime spent endeavoring to render his insights into precise language. The places and women he has known are all here: Pittsburgh, San Francisco, Greece, Manhattan, the New England woods, Gelmetti, Gregg, and Nogami. In "A Brief for the Defense," the first poem in the collection, Gilbert sums up his philosophy of life: "We must have/ the stubbornness to accept our gladness in the ruthless/ furnace of this world. . . ." He continues with his philosophy of death: "If the locomotive of the Lord runs us down,/we should give thanks that the end had magnitude." Gilbert's classical imagery and personae as Prospero and the writer who struggles to "do poetry" and get it right are in the volume as well. Mortality is a concern for the aging poet, but he will not give up life yet. He writes in the title poem "Refusing Heaven": ". . . But he chooses/ against the Lord. He will not abandon his life." In "Michiko Dead," the poet had carried the heavy box of his grief in his arms. Ten years later, in "Bring in the Gods," he is "carrying the past in my arms."

The Dance Most of All

Refusing Heaven turned out not to be Gilbert's final gift, despite the critics' predictions. In *The Dance Most of All*, the poet continues to look backward and inward. Mortality, loneliness, and silence are among the aging poet's themes. In "Prospero Goes Home," the old magician is happy to return to the bare solitude of his island. In "Waiting and Finding," he admits that he is "Beginning to like the silence maybe too much." In "The Spell Cast Over," set in Pittsburgh, he reveals the difficulty of aging: "The old men came from their one room/ . . . To remember what used/ to be . . ." and ". . . To see/ their young hearts just one more time." However, it is the beauty of life, imperfect as it is—the dance most of all—that poet Gilbert celebrates above all.

BIBLIOGRAPHY

Dow, Philip, ed. *Nineteen New American Poets of the Golden Gate*. San Diego, Calif.: Harcourt Brace Jovanovich, 1984. In an essay Gilbert wrote to introduce a selection of his poems, Gilbert discusses his poetic style. This manifesto contrasts his concrete style and themes of knowing and understanding with rhetorical poetry's ornamentation and symbolic language.

Freeman, John. "*Refusing Heaven*: A Profile of Jack Gilbert." *Poets and Writers*. (March/April, 2005). This profile based on an interview of the elusive poet on the eve of the publication of *Refusing Heaven* discusses Gilbert's views on aging, mortality, and a life dedicated to poetry.

Genesis West. "Genesis West Celebrates the Excellence of Jack Gilbert." 1, no. 1 (Fall, 1962): 66-94. This feature article in the first issue of *Genesis West* is devoted to the winner of the Yale Series of Younger Poets competition. Several major poets, including Denise Levertov, Theodore Roethke, Stephen Spender, Muriel Rukeyser, and Stanley Kunitz, praise, analyze, and discuss Gilbert's first book. This issue contains an interview with Gilbert and a selection of his poems.

Gilbert, Jack. "An Interview with Jack Gilbert." Interview by Chard deNiord. *American Poetry Review* 38, no. 1 (January/February, 2009): 26-30. Gilbert discusses his views on poetry, saying that he wants a poem to make a person feel something. He talks about love and the process of creating a poem.

_______. "Jack Gilbert." Interview by Sarah Fay. In *"Paris Review" Interviews*, edited by Philip Gourevitch. Vol. 1. New York: Picador, 2006. In this interview of the poet at his home in Northhampton, conducted in January and July, 2005, by *Paris Review* interviewer Fay, he discusses his life and poetry.

Susan Butterworth

ALLEN GINSBERG

Born: Newark, New Jersey; June 3, 1926
Died: New York, New York; April 5, 1997

PRINCIPAL POETRY

Howl, and Other Poems, 1956, 1996
Empty Mirror: Early Poems, 1961
Kaddish, and Other Poems, 1958-1960, 1961
The Change, 1963
Reality Sandwiches, 1963
Kral Majales, 1965
Wichita Vortex Sutra, 1966
T.V. Baby Poems, 1967
Airplane Dreams: Compositions from Journals, 1968
Ankor Wat, 1968
Planet News, 1961-1967, 1968
The Moments Return, 1970
Ginsberg's Improvised Poetics, 1971
Bixby Canyon Ocean Path Word Breeze, 1972
The Fall of America: Poems of These States, 1965-1971, 1972
The Gates of Wrath: Rhymed Poems, 1948-1952, 1972
Iron Horse, 1972
Open Head, 1972
First Blues: Rags, Ballads, and Harmonium Songs, 1971-1974, 1975
Sad Dust Glories: Poems During Work Summer in Woods, 1975
Mind Breaths: Poems, 1972-1977, 1977
Mostly Sitting Haiku, 1978
Poems All over the Place: Mostly Seventies, 1978
Plutonian Ode: Poems, 1977-1980, 1982
Collected Poems, 1947-1980, 1984
White Shroud: Poems, 1980-1985, 1986
Hydrogen Jukebox, 1990 (music by Philip Glass)
Collected Poems, 1992
Cosmopolitan Greetings: Poems, 1986-1992, 1994
Making It Up: Poetry Composed at St. Marks Church on May 9, 1979, 1994 (with Kenneth Koch)
Selected Poems, 1947-1995, 1996
Death and Fame: Poems, 1993-1997, 1999
Collected Poems, 1947-1997, 2006

OTHER LITERARY FORMS

Allen Ginsberg recognized early in his career that he would have to explain his intentions, because most critics and reviewers of the time did not have the interest or experience to understand what he was trying to accomplish. Consequently, he published books that include interviews, lectures, essays, photographs, and letters to friends as means of conveying his theories about composition and poetics.

ACHIEVEMENTS

The publication of "Howl" in 1956 drew such enthusiastic comments from Allen Ginsberg's supporters, and such vituperative condemnation from conservative cultural commentators, that a rift of immense proportions developed, which has made a balanced critical assessment very difficult. Nevertheless, partisan response has gradually given way to an acknowledgment by most critics that Ginsberg's work is significant, if not always entirely successful by familiar standards of literary excellence. Such recognition was underscored in 1974, when *The Fall of America* shared the National Book Award in Poetry. Ginsberg was awarded a Los Angeles Times Book Prize (1982) and the Frost Medal by the Poetry Society of America (1986). Included among the many honors he garnered during his lifetime were an Academy Award in Literature from the American Academy of Arts and Letters in 1969, the Woodbury Poetry Prize, Guggenheim fellowships, the National Arts Club Medal of Honor, the Before Columbus Foundation award for lifetime achievement, the University of Chicago's Harriet Monroe Poetry Award, an American Academy of Arts and Sciences fellowship, and the Medal of Chevalier de l'Ordre des Arts et Letters.

The voice Ginsberg employed in "Howl" not only has influenced the style of several generations of poets, but also has combined the rhythms and language of common speech with some of the deepest, most enduring traditions in American literature. In both his life and his work, Ginsberg set an example of moral seriousness, artistic commitment, and humane decency that made him one of the most popular figures in American culture. The best of his visionary and innovative creations earned for him recognition as one of the major figures of the twentieth century.

BIOGRAPHY

Allen Ginsberg was born Irwin Allen Ginsberg, the second son of Naomi Levy Ginsberg, a Russian-born political activist and communist sympathizer, and Louis Ginsberg, a traditional lyric poet and high school English teacher. He attended primary school in the middle-class town of Paterson, New Jersey. He grew up in a conventional and uneventful household, with the exception of his mother's repeated hospitalizations for mental stress. He entered Columbia University in 1943, intending to pursue a career in labor law, but the influence of such well-known literary scholars as Lionel Trilling and Mark Van Doren, combined with the excitement of the Columbia community, which included fellow student Jack Kerouac and such singular people as William Burroughs and Neal Cassady, led him toward literature as a vocation. He was temporarily suspended from Columbia in 1945 and worked as a welder and apprentice seaman before finishing his degree in 1948. Living a "subterranean" life (to use Kerouac's term) that incorporated drug use, a bohemian lifestyle, and occasional antisocial acts of youthful ebullience, Ginsberg was counseled to commit himself for several months to Columbia Presbyterian Psychiatric Institute to avoid criminal charges associated with the possession of stolen goods; there, in 1949, he met Carl W. Solomon, to whom "Howl" is dedicated. During the early 1950's, he began a correspondence with William Carlos Williams, who guided and encouraged his early writing, and Ginsberg traveled in Mexico and Europe.

In 1954, Ginsberg moved to San Francisco to be at the center of the burgeoning Beat movement. He was living there when he wrote "Howl," and he read the poem for the first time at a landmark Six Gallery performance that included Gary Snyder, Philip Whalen, and Michael McClure. His mother died in 1956, the year *Howl, and Other Poems* was published, and he spent the next few years traveling, defending *Howl* against charges of obscenity, working on "Kaddish"—his celebration of his mother's life, based on a Hebrew prayer for the dead—and reading on college campuses and in Beatnik venues on both coasts.

The growing notoriety of the Beat generation drew Ginsberg into the media spotlight in the early 1960's, and he was active in the promotion of work by his friends. He continued to travel extensively, visiting Europe, India, and Japan; he read in bars and coffeehouses, and published widely in many of the prominent literary journals of the counterculture. His involvement with various hallucinatory substances led to the formation of LeMar (Organization to Legalize Marijuana) in 1964 with the poet, songwriter, and publisher Ed Sanders, and his continuing disaffection with governmental policies took him toward active political protest. In 1965, he was invited to Cuba and Czechoslovakia by Communist officials, who mistakenly assumed that his criticism of American society would make him sympathetic to their regimes, but Ginsberg's outspoken criticism of all forms of tyranny and suppression led to his expulsion from both countries.

His political activism—particularly in reaction to the Vietnam War—and close association with the counterculture continued throughout the 1960's and 1970's. During the 1960's, he invented the nonviolent concept of "flower power" in an attempt to neutralize martial aggression. In 1967, he was one of the organizers of the first "Human Be-In." The following year, he was arrested in Chicago at the Democratic National Convention with many other demonstrators, and in 1969, he testified at the Chicago Seven trials; that same year, he was at the center of a semi-serious effort to exorcise the Pentagon. In the early 1970's, he spent some time on a farm in rural New York, formally accepted the teachings of Buddhism from Chögyam Trungpa, who initiated him with the name "Lion of Dharma," and afterward cofounded, with Anne Waldman, a school of literary inquiry, the Jack Kerouac School of Disembodied Poetics at the Naropa Institute in Colorado. He was inducted into the American Institute of Arts and Letters in 1974, an indication of recognition as an artist in the mainstream of American culture, and he further confirmed this status by traveling with Bob Dylan's Rolling Thunder Review as a "poet-percussionist" in 1975. Continuing to combine artistic endeavor with a commitment to social justice, Ginsberg took part—with longtime lover Peter Orlovsky—in protests at the Rocky Flats Nuclear Facility in 1978 and wrote the "Plutonium Ode," which expressed his concern about the destructive forces humans had unleashed.

During the 1980's, Ginsberg continued to travel, teach, write, and perform his work. The publication of his *Collected Poems, 1947-1980* in 1984 was received with wide attention and respect, and he was appointed distinguished professor at Brooklyn College in 1986, the year he published *White Shroud*, which includes an epilogue to "Kaddish" along with other poems from the 1980's. His ability as a teacher was clearly demonstrated in his appearance on the Public Broadcasting Service series *Voices and Visions* in 1987. As the decade drew to a close, he was involved in collaboration with composer Philip Glass on a chamber opera called *Hydrogen Jukebox* (a phrase from "Howl"), which was performed in 1990. Continuing to write with energy while teaching a graduate-level course on the Beats at the City University of New York Graduate Center, Ginsberg described his goals in the 1990's, in a poem called "Personals Ad," as similar to the ones he had always pursued: "help inspire mankind conquer world anger & guilt." It was an appropriate task for a "poet professor in his autumn years." Afflicted with diabetes, hepatitis, and liver cancer, he died at age seventy following a stroke on April 5, 1997, in New York City.

ANALYSIS

"Howl," the poem that carried Allen Ginsberg into public consciousness as a symbol of the avant-garde artist and as the designer of a verse style for a postwar generation seeking its own voice, was initially regarded as primarily a social document. As Ginsberg's notes make clear, however, it was also the latest specimen in a continuing experiment in form and structure. Several factors in Ginsberg's life were particularly important in this breakthrough poem, written as the poet was approaching thirty and still drifting through a series of jobs, countries, and social occasions. Ginsberg's father had exerted more influence than was immediately apparent. Louis Ginsberg's very traditional, metrical verse was of little use to his son, but his father's interest in literary history was part of Ginsberg's solid grounding in prosody. Then, a succession of other mentors—including Williams, whose use of the American vernacular and local material had inspired him, and great scholars such as art historian Meyer Shapiro at Columbia, who had introduced him to the tenets of modernism from an analytic perspective—had enabled the young poet to form a substantial intellectual foundation.

In addition, Ginsberg was dramatically affected by his friendships with Kerouac,

Cassady, Burroughs, Herbert Hunke, and other noteworthy denizens of a vibrant underground community of dropouts, revolutionaries, drug addicts, jazz musicians, and serious but unconventional artists of all sorts. Ginsberg felt an immediate kinship with these "angelheaded hipsters," who accepted and celebrated eccentricity and regarded Ginsberg's homosexuality as an attribute, not a blemish. Although Ginsberg enthusiastically entered into the drug culture that was a flourishing part of this community, he was not nearly as routed toward self-destruction as Burroughs or Hunke; he was more interested in the possibilities of visionary experience. His oft-noted "illuminative audition of William Blake's voice simultaneous with Eternity-vision" in 1948 was his first ecstatic experience of transcendence, and he continued to pursue spiritual insight through serious studies of various religions—including Judaism and Buddhism—as well as through chemical experimentation.

His experiments with mind-altering agents (including marijuana, peyote, amphetamines, mescaline, and lysergic acid diethylamide, or LSD) and his casual friendship with some quasi-criminals led to his eight-month stay in a psychiatric institute. He had already experienced an unsettling series of encounters with mental instability in his mother, who had been hospitalized for the first time when he was three. Her struggles with the torments of psychic uncertainty were seriously disruptive events in Ginsberg's otherwise unremarkable boyhood, but Ginsberg felt deep sympathy for his mother's agony and also was touched by her warmth, love, and social conscience. Although not exactly a "red diaper baby," Ginsberg had adopted a radical political conscience early enough to decide to pursue labor law as a college student, and he never wavered from his initial convictions concerning the excesses of capitalism. His passionate call for tolerance and fairness had roots as much in his mother's ideas as in his contacts with the "lamblike youths" who were "slaughtered" by the demon Moloch: his symbol for the greed and materialism of the United States in the 1950's. In conjunction with his displeasure with what he saw as the failure of the government to correct these abuses, he carried an idealized conception of "the lost America of love" based on his readings in nineteenth century American literature, Walt Whitman and Henry David Thoreau in particular, and reinforced by the political and social idealism of contemporaries such as Kerouac, Snyder, and McClure.

Ginsberg brought all these concerns together when he began to compose "Howl." However, while the social and political elements of the poem were immediately apparent, the careful structural arrangements were not. Ginsberg found it necessary to explain his intentions in a series of notes and letters, emphasizing his desire to use Whitman's long line "to *build up* large organic structures" and his realization that he did not have to satisfy anyone's concept of what a poem should be, but could follow his "romantic inspiration" and simply write as he wished, "without fear." Using what he called his "Hebraic-Melvillian bardic breath"—a rhythmic pattern similar to the cadences of the Old Testament as employed by Herman Melville—Ginsberg wrote a three-part prophetic elegy, which he described as a "huge sad comedy of wild phrasing."

"Howl"

The first part of "Howl" is a long catalog of the activities of the "angelheaded hipsters" who were his contemporaries. Calling the bohemian underground of outcasts, outlaws, rebels, mystics, sexual deviants, junkies, and other misfits "the best minds of my generation"—a judgment that still rankles many social critics—Ginsberg produced image after image of the antics of "remarkable lamblike youths" in pursuit of cosmic enlightenment, "the ancient heavenly connection to the starry dynamo in the machinery of night." Because the larger American society had offered them little support, Ginsberg summarized their efforts by declaring that these people had been "destroyed by madness." The long lines, most beginning with the word "who" (which was used "as a base to keep measure, return to and take off from again"), create a composite portrait that pulses with energy and excitement. Ginsberg is not only lamenting the destruction—or self-destruction—of his friends and acquaintances, but also celebrating their wild flights of imagination, their ecstatic illuminations, and their rapturous adventures. His typical line, or breath unit, communicates the awesome power of the experiences he describes along with their potential for danger. Ginsberg believed that by the end of the first section he had expressed what he believed "true to eternity" and had reconstituted "the data of celestial experience."

Part 2 of the poem "names the monster of mental consciousness that preys" on the people he admires. The fear and tension of the Cold War, stirred by materialistic greed and what Ginsberg later called "lacklove," are symbolized by a demon he calls Moloch, after the Canaanite god that required human sacrifice. With the name Moloch as a kind of "base repetition" and destructive attributes described in a string of lines beginning with "whose," the second part of the poem reaches a kind of crescendo of chaos in which an anarchic vision of frenzy and disruption engulfs the world.

In part 3, "a litany of affirmation," Ginsberg addresses himself to Solomon, a poet he knew from the Psychiatric Institute; he holds up Solomon as a kind of emblem of the victim-heroes he has been describing. The pattern here is based on the statement-counterstatement form of Christopher Smart's *Jubilate Agno* (1939; as *Rejoice in the Lamb*, 1954), and Ginsberg envisioned it as pyramidal, "with a graduated longer response to the fixed base." Affirming his allegiance to Solomon (and everyone like him), Ginsberg begins each breath unit with the phrase "I'm with you in Rockland" followed by "where . . ." and an exposition of strange or unorthodox behavior that has been labeled "madness" but that to the poet is actually a form of creative sanity. The poem concludes with a vision of Ginsberg and Solomon together on a journey to an America that transcends Moloch and madness and offers utopian possibilities of love and "true mental regularity."

During the year that "Howl" was written, Ginsberg wondered whether he might use the same long line in a "short quiet lyrical poem." The result was a poignant tribute to his "old courage teacher," Whitman, which he called "A Supermarket in California," and a meditation on the bounty of nature, "A Strange New Cottage in Berkeley." He continued to work with his long-breath line in larger compositions as well, most notably the poem "America," which has been accurately described by Charles Molesworth as "a gem of polyvocal satire and miscreant complaint." This poem gave Ginsberg the opportunity to exercise his exuberant sense of humor and good-natured view of himself in a mock-ironic address to his country. The claim "It occurs to me that I am America" is meant to be taken as a whimsical wish made in self-deprecating modesty, but Ginsberg's growing popularity through the last decades of the century cast it as prophetic as well.

"KADDISH"

Naomi Ginsberg died in 1956 after several harrowing episodes at home and in mental institutions, and she was not accorded a traditional orthodox funeral because a *minyan* (a complement of ten men to serve as witnesses) could not be found. Ginsberg was troubled by thoughts of his mother's suffering and tormented by uncertainty concerning his own role as sometime caregiver for her. Brooding over his tangled feelings, he spent a night listening to jazz, ingesting marijuana and methamphetamine, and reading passages from an old bar mitzvah book. Then, at dawn, he walked the streets of the lower East Side in Manhattan, where many Jewish immigrant families had settled. A tangle of images and emotions rushed through his mind, organized now by the rhythms of ancient Hebrew prayers and chants. The poem that took shape in his mind was his own version of the Kaddish, the traditional Jewish service for the dead that had been denied to his mother. As it was formed in an initial burst of energy, he saw its goal as a celebration of her memory and a prayer for her soul's serenity, an attempt to confront his own fears about death, and ultimately, an attempt to come to terms with his relationship to his mother.

"Kaddish" begins in an elegiac mood, "Strange now to think of you gone," and proceeds as both an elegy and a kind of dual biography. Details from Ginsberg's childhood begin to take on a sinister aspect when viewed from the perspective of an adult with a tragic sense of existence. The course of his life's journey from early youth and full parental love to the threshold of middle age is paralleled by Naomi's life as it advances from late youth toward a decline into paranoia and madness. Ginsberg recalls his mother "teaching school, laughing with idiots, the backward classes—her Russian speciality," then sees her in agony "one night, sudden attack . . . left retching on the tile floor." The juxtaposition of images ranging over many years reminds him of his own mortality, compelling him to probe his subconscious mind to face some of the fears that he has suppressed about his mother's madness. The first part of the poem concludes as the poet realizes that he will never find any peace until he is able to "cut through—to talk to you—" and finally to write her true history.

The central incident of the second section is a bus trip the twelve-year-old Ginsberg took with his mother to a clinic. The confusion and unpredictability of his mother's behavior forced him to assume an adult's role, for which he was not prepared. For the first time, he realizes that this moment marked the real end of childhood and introduced him to a universe of chaos and absurdity. As the narrative develops, the emergence of a nascent artistic consciousness, poetic perception, and political idealism is presented against a panorama of life in the United States in the late 1930's. Realizing that his growth into the poet who is revealing this psychic history is closely intertwined with his mother's decline, Ginsberg faces his fear that he was drawing his newfound strength from her as she failed. As the section concludes, he squarely confronts his mother's illness, rendering her madness in disjointed scraps of conversation while using blunt physical detail as a means of showing the body's collapse: an effective analogue for her simultaneous mental disorder. There is a daunting authenticity to these details, as Ginsberg speaks with utter candor about the most intimate and unpleasant subjects (a method he also employs in later poems about sexual contacts), confirming his determination to bury nothing in memory.

This frankness fuses Ginsberg's recollections into a mood of great sympathy; he is moved to prayer, asking divine intervention to ease his mother's suffering. Here he introduces the actual Hebrew words of the Kaddish, the formal service that had been denied his mother because of a technicality. The poet's contribution is not only to create an appropriate setting for the ancient ritual but also to offer a testament to his mother's most admirable qualities. As the second section ends, Ginsberg sets the power of poetic language to celebrate beauty against the pain of his mother's last days. Returning to the elegiac mode (after Percy Bysshe Shelley's "Adonais"), Ginsberg has a last vision of his mother days before her final stroke, associated with sunlight and giving her son advice that concludes, "Love,/ your mother," which he acknowledges with his own tribute, "which is Naomi."

The last part of the poem, "Hymmnn," is divided into four sections. The first is a prayer for God's blessing for his mother (and for all people); the second is a recitation of some of the circumstances of her life; the third is a catalog of characteristics that seem surreal and random but coalesce toward the portrait he is producing by composite images; and the last part is "another variation of the litany form," ending the poem in a flow of "pure emotive sound" in which the words "Lord lord lord," as if beseeching, alternate with the words "caw caw caw," as if exclaiming in ecstasy.

By resisting almost all the conventional approaches to the loaded subject of motherhood, Ginsberg has avoided sentimentality and reached a depth of feeling that is overwhelming, even if the reader's experience is nothing like the poet's. The universality of the relationship is established by its particulars, the sublimity of the relationship by the revelation of the poet's enduring love and empathy.

The publication of "Kaddish" ended the initial phase of Ginsberg's writing life. "Howl" is a declaration of poetic intention, while "Kaddish" is a confession of personal necessity. With these two long, powerful works, Ginsberg completed the educational process of his youth and was ready to use his craft as a confident, mature artist. His range in the early 1960's included the hilarious "I Am a Victim of Telephone," which debunked his increasing celebrity, the gleeful jeremiad "Television Was a Baby Crawling Toward That Deathchamber," the generously compassionate "Who Be Kind To," and the effusive lyric "Why Is God Love, Jack?" A tribute to his mentor, "Death News," describes his thoughts on learning of Williams's demise.

"Kral Majales"

In 1965, after he had been invited to Cuba and Czechoslovakia, Ginsberg was expelled from each country for his bold condemnation of each nation's policies. In Prague, he had been selected by students (including young Václav Havel) as Kral Majales (king of May), an ancient European honor that has lasted through centuries of upheaval. In the poem "Kral Majales"—published accompanied by positive and negative silhouettes of the smiling poet, naked except for tennis shoes and sporting three hands bearing finger cymbals, against a phallic symbol—he juxtaposed communist and capitalist societies at their most dreary and destructive to the life-enhancing properties of the symbolic May King: a figure of life, love, art, and enlightenment. The first part of the poem is marked by discouragement, anger, and sorrow mixed with comic resignation to show the dead end reached by governments run by a small clique of rulers. However, the heart of the poem, a list of all the attributes that he brings to the position of Kral Majales, is an exuberant explosion of joy, mirth, and confidence in the rising generation of the mid-1960's. Written before the full weight of the debacle in Vietnam had been felt and before the string of assassinations that rocked the United States took place, Ginsberg reveled in the growth of what he thought was a revolutionary movement toward a utopian society. His chant of praise for the foundations of a counterculture celebrates "the power of sexual youth," productive, fulfilling work ("industry in eloquence"), honest acceptance of the body ("long hair of Adam"), the vitality of art ("old Human poesy"), and the ecumenical spirit of religious pluralism that he incarnates: "I am of Slavic parentage and Buddhist Jew/ who worships the Sacred Heart of Christ the blue body of Krishna the straight back of Ram the beads of Chango." In a demonstration of rhythmic power, the poem builds until it tells of the poet's literal descent to earth from the airplane he took to London after his expulsion. Arriving at "Albion's airfield" with the exultation of creative energy still vibrating through his mind and body, he proudly presents (to the reader or listener) the poem he has just written "on a jet seat in mid Heaven." The immediacy of the ending keeps the occasion fresh in the poet's memory and alive forever in the rhythms and images of his art.

"Witchita Vortex Sutra"

The Prague Spring that was to flourish temporarily in events such as the 1965 May Festival was crushed by Soviet tanks in 1968. By then, the United States had become fully involved in the war in Southeast Asia, and Ginsberg had replaced some of his optimism about change with an anger that recalled the mood of the Moloch section of "Howl." In 1966, he was in Kansas to read poetry, and this trip to the heartland of the United States became the occasion for a poem that is close to an epic of American life as the country was being torn apart. "Witchita Vortex Sutra," one of Ginsberg's longest poems, combines elements of American mythological history, personal psychic exploration, multicultural interaction, and prophetic incantation. The poem is sustained by a twin vision of the United States: the submerged but still vital American spirit that inspired Whitman and the contemporary American realities by which "many another has suffered death and madness/ in the Vortex." A sense of a betrayal informs the narrative, and the poet is involved in a search for the cause and the cure, ultimately (and typically) discovering that only art can rescue the blighted land.

The first part of the poem depicts Kansas as the seat of American innocence, where the spirit of transcendental idealism is still relatively untouched by American actions in Vietnam. Whitman's dream of an open country and worthy citizens seems to remain alive, but events from the outside have begun to reach even this sheltered place. The land of Abraham Lincoln, Vachel Lindsay, William Jennings Bryan, and other American idealists is being ruined by the actions of a rogue "government" out of touch with the spirit of the nation. The poet attempts to understand why this is happening and what consequences it has for him, for any artist. After this entrance into the poem's geopolitical and psychic space, the second part presents, in a collage form akin to Ezra Pound's *Cantos* (1925-1972), figures, numbers, names, and snatches of propaganda about the conflict in Vietnam. Following Pound's proposal that a bad government corrupts a people by its misuse of language, Ginsberg begins an examination of the nature of language itself to try to determine how the lies and deceptions in "black language/ writ by machine" can be overcome by a "lonesome man in Kansas" who is "not afraid" and who can speak "with ecstatic language": that is, the true language of human need, essential human reality. Calling on "all Powers of imagination," Ginsberg acts as an artist in service to moral being, using all the poetic power, or versions of speech, that he has worked to master.

Ginsberg's "ecstatic language" includes the lingo of the Far Eastern religions he has learned in his travels. To assist in exorcising the demons of the West, he implores the gods of the East to merge their forces with those of the new deities of the West, whose incarnation he finds in such American mavericks as the musician Dylan. He summons them as allies against the Puritan death-wish he locates in the fanaticism of unbending, self-righteous zealots such as Kansas's Carrie Nation, whose "angry smashing ax" began "a vortex of hatred" that eventually "defoliated the Mekong Delta." Ginsberg has cast the language artist as the rescuer and visionary who can restore the heartland to its primal state as a land of promise and justice. In a testament to his faith in his craft, Ginsberg declares, "The war is over now"—which, in a poem that examines language in "its deceits, its degeneration" (as Charles Molesworth says), "is especially poignant being only language."

THE FALL OF AMERICA

Other poems, such as "Bayonne Entering NYC," further contributed to the mood of a collection titled *The Fall of America*, but Ginsberg was also turning again toward the personal. In poems such as "Wales Visitation," a nature ode written in the spirit of the English Romantics, and "Bixby Canyon," which is an American West Coast parallel, Ginsberg explores the possibilities of a personal pantheism, attempting to achieve a degree of cosmic transcendence to compensate for the disagreeable situation on earth. His loving remembrance for Beat poet Cassady, "On Neal's Ashes," is another expression of this elegiac inclination, which reaches a culmination in *Mind Breaths*.

MIND BREATHS

"Mind Breaths," the title poem of the collection *Mind Breaths*, is a meditation that gathers the long lines of what Ginsberg has called "a chain of strong-breath'd poems" into a series of modulations on the theme of the poet's breath as an aspect of the wind-spirit of life. As he has often pointed out, Ginsberg believes that one of his most basic principles of organization is his ability to control the rhythms of a long line ("My breath is long"). In "Mind Breaths," he develops the idea that the voice of the poet is a part of the "voice" of the cosmos—a variant on the ancient belief that the gods spoke directly through the poet. Ranging over the entire planet, Ginsberg gradually includes details from many of the world's cultures, uniting nations in motive and design to achieve an encompassing ethos of universality. Beneath the fragmentation and strife of the world's governments, the poet sees "a calm breath, a silent breath, a slow breath," part of the fundamentally human universe that the artist wishes to inhabit.

PLUTONIAN ODE

In the title poem of *Plutonian Ode*, Ginsberg offers another persuasive poetic argument to strengthen the "Mind-guard spirit" against the death wish that leads some to embrace "Radioactive Nemesis." Recalling, once again, "Howl," in which Moloch stands for the death-driven impulses of humankind gone mad with greed, Ginsberg surveys the history of nuclear experimentation. The poem is designed as a guide for "spiritual friends and teachers," and the "mountain of Plutonian" is presented as the dark shadow-image of the life force that has energized the universe since "the beginning." Addressing himself, as well, to the "heavy heavy Element awakened," Ginsberg describes a force of "vaunted Mystery" against which he brings, as always, the "verse prophetic" to "wake space" itself. The poem is written to restore the power of mind (which is founded on spiritual enlightenment) to a civilization addicted to "horrific arm'd, Satanic industries"—an echo of Blake's injunctions at the dawn of an era in which machinery has threatened human well-being.

"Birdbrain"

The tranquility of such reveries in poems such as "Mind Breaths" did not replace Ginsberg's anger at the social system but operated more as a condition of recovery or place of restoration, so that the poet could venture back into the political arena and chant, "Birdbrain is the ultimate product of Capitalism/ Birdbrain chief bureaucrat of Russia." In the poem "Birdbrain," published in *Collected Poems, 1947-1980*, Ginsberg castigates the idiocy of organizations everywhere. His humor balances his anger, but there is an implication that neither humor nor anger will be sufficient against the forces of "Birdbrain [who] is Pope, Premier, President, Commissar, Chairman, Senator!" In spite of his decades of experience as a political activist, Ginsberg never let his discouragement overcome his sense of civic responsibility. The publication of *Collected Poems, 1947-1980* secured Ginsberg's reputation as one of the leading writers of late twentieth century American literature.

White Shroud

The appearance in 1986 of *White Shroud* revived Ginsberg's political orations; in this work, he identifies the demons of contemporary American life as he sees them: "yes I glimpse CIA's spooky dope deal vanity." There is a discernible sense of time's passage in "White Shroud," which is a kind of postscript to "Kaddish." Once again, Ginsberg recollects the pain of his family relationships: His difficulties in dealing with aging, irascible relatives merges with his responsibility to care for those who have loved him, and his feeling for modern America fuse with his memories of the Old Left past of his immigrant family. The poem tells how Ginsberg, in search of an apartment, finds himself in the Bronx neighborhood where his family once lived. There he meets the shade of his mother, still berating him for having abandoned her, but now offering him a home as well. There is a form of comfort for the poet in his dream of returning to an older New York to live with his family, a return to the "lost America," the mythic America that has inspired millions of American dreams.

Cosmopolitan Greetings

Ginsberg in the 1990's expressed his introspective side with lyric sadness in such poems as "Personals Ad" (from *Cosmopolitan Greetings*), in which he communicates his quest for a ". . . companion protector friend/ young lover w/empty compassionate soul" to help him live "in New York alone with the Alone." With the advent of his seventh decade, he might have settled for a kind of comfortable celebrity, offering the substance of his literary and social experiences to students at the Graduate Center of the City University of New York and to countless admirers on reading tours throughout the nation. Instead, he accepted his position as the primary proponent and spokesperson for his fellow artists of the Beat generation, and he continued to write with the invention and vigor that had marked his work from its inception. Acknowledging his perspective as a "poet professor in autumn years" in "Personals Ad," Ginsberg remains highly conscious of ". . . the body/ where I was born" (from "Song," in *Howl, and Other Poems*), but his focus is now on the inescapable consequences of time's passage on that body in poems that register the anxieties of an aging man trying to assess his own role in the cultural and historical patterns of his era.

The exuberance and the antic humor that have always been a feature of Ginsberg's poetry of sexual candor remain, but there is a modulation in tone and mood toward the rueful and contemplative. Similarly, poems presenting strong positions about social and governmental policies often refer to earlier works on related subjects, as if adding links to a chain of historical commentaries. Although few of Ginsberg's poems are as individually distinctive as the "strong-breath'd poems" such as "Howl," "Kaddish," or "Witchita Vortex Sutra," which Ginsberg calls "peaks of inspiration," Ginsberg's utilization of a characteristic powerful rhythmic base figure drives poems such as "Improvisation in Beijing." "On Cremation of Chogyam Trungpa, Vidadhara," "Get It," and "Graphic Winces" offer statements that are reflections of fundamental positions that Ginsberg has been developing throughout his work.

"Improvisation in Beijing," the opening poem, is a poetic credo in the form of an expression of artistic ambition. Using the phrase "I write poetry . . ." to launch each line, Ginsberg juxtaposes ideas, images, data, and assertion in a flux of energetic intent, his life's experiences revealing the desire and urgency of his calling. Ginsberg has gathered his responses to requests for his sources of inspiration: from the explicitly personal "I write poetry to make accurate picture my own mind" to the overtly political ". . . Wild West destroys new grass & erosion creates deserts" to the culturally connected "I write poetry because I listened to black Blues on 1939 radio, Leadbelly and Ma Rainey" to the aesthetically ambitious in the concluding line, "I write poetry because it's the best way to say everything in mind with 6 minutes or a lifetime."

"On Cremation of Chogyam Trungpa, Vidadhara," a tribute to a spiritual guide, reverses the structural thrust of "Improvisation in Beijing" so that the lines beginning "I noticed the . . ." spiral inward toward a composite portrait built by "minute particulars," Ginsberg's term for Williams's injunction "No ideas but in things." Ginsberg concentrates on specifics in tightly wound lines that present observations of an extremely aware, actively thoughtful participant: "I noticed the grass, I noticed the hills, I noticed the highways,/ I noticed the dirt road, I noticed the cars in the parking lot." Eventually, the poet's inclusion of more personal details reveals his deep involvement in the occasion, demonstrating his ability to internalize his guide's teaching. The poem concludes with a summation of the event's impact, a fusion of awe, delight, and wonder joining the mundane with the cosmic. Typically at this time in his life, Ginsberg acts from a classic poetic position, speaking as the recorder who sees, understands, and appreciates the significance of important events and who can find language adequate for their expression.

The collection, like Ginsberg's other major volumes, contains many poems that are not meant to be either especially serious or particularly profound. These works include poems written to a musical notation ("C.I.A. Dope Calypso"), poetic lines cast in speech bubbles in a "Deadline Dragon Comix" strip, three pages of what are called "American Sentences" (which are, in effect, a version of haiku), and a new set of verses to the old political anthem, "The Internationale," in which Ginsberg pays homage to the dreams of a social republic of justice while parodying various manifestations of self-important propagandists and salvationists.

The poems in the volume that show Ginsberg at his most effective, however, occur in two modes. Ever since his tribute to Whitman, "A Supermarket in California," Ginsberg has used the lyric mode as a means of conveying his deeply romantic vision of an idealized existence set in opposition to the social disasters he has resisted. These are poems of appreciation and gratitude, celebrating the things of the world that bring delight. "To Jacob Rabinowitz" is a letter of thanks for a translation of Catullus. "Fun House Antique Store" conveys the poet's astonishment at finding a "country antique store, an/ oldfashioned house" on the road to "see our lawyer in D.C." The lovingly evoked intricate furnishings of the store suggest something human that is absent in "the postmodern Capital." Both of these poems sustain a mood of exultation crucial to a lyric.

The other mode that Ginsberg employs is a familiar one. Even since he described himself as "Rotting Ginsberg" in "Mescaline" (1959), Ginsberg has emphasized physical sensation and the extremes of sensory response as means for understanding artistic consciousness, a mind-body linkage. Some of the most despairing lines Ginsberg has written appear in these poems— understandable considering the poet's ailments, including the first manifestations of liver cancer, which Ginsberg endured for years before his death. Nonetheless, the bright spirit that animates Ginsberg's work throughout is present as a counterthrust.

"In the Benjo," which has been placed at the close of the collection, expresses Ginsberg's appreciation for Snyder's lessons in transcendent wisdom and epitomizes a pattern of affirmation that is present in poems that resist the ravages of physical decline ("Return to Kral Majales"), the loss of friends ("Visiting Father & Friends"), the sorry state of the world ("You Don't Know It"), and the fraudulent nature of so-called leaders ("Elephant in the Meditation Hall"). In these poems, as in many in earlier collections, Ginsberg is conveying the spirit of an artistic age that he helped shape and that his work exemplifies. As Snyder said in tribute, "Allen Ginsberg showed that poetry could speak to our moment, our political concerns, our hopes and fears, and in the grandest style. He broke that open for all of us."

Collected Poems, 1947-1997

Collected Poems, 1947-1997 is a massive chronological compilation—combining *Collected Poems, 1947-1980*, *White Shroud*, *Cosmopolitan Greetings*, and *Death and Fame*—that gathers virtually every poem Ginsberg ever wrote, from his first published effort, "In Society" (1947), to his last written work, "Things I'll Not Do (Nostalgia)," finished just days before he died. The volume incorporates drawings, photographs, sheet music, calligraphy, notes, acknowledgments, introductions, appendixes, and all the other addenda included in the previous publications that collectively reveal Ginsberg's far-reaching interests and his enormous skill. Ginsberg's entire body of work portrays the poet's growth as a craftsperson, a seeker of truth, a spokesperson for his generation, and ultimately as a human being.

Even in his earliest work, "In Society"—which alludes to his homosexuality and includes epithets that polite society would deem vulgar—Ginsberg demonstrated that no subject was unworthy of consideration, no phrase taboo. Though his topics from the beginning were sometimes controversial, the format of his poems was still restrained and formal because he had not yet rejected his father's traditionalist ways. Such poems as "Two Sonnets" (1948), with their conventional fourteen-line structures and rhyme schemes, would not look out of place in collections of William Shakespeare or Edmund Spenser. Indeed, much of Ginsberg's early work (in the first section, "Empty Mirror: Gates of Wrath, 1947-1952") constitutes rhyming verse as the poet experimented with meter, line length, and language in his fledgling efforts to find a unique voice. Subject matter, too, is fairly traditional: love poems, contemplation of nature, and musings on life, death and religion. With few exceptions, the titles of these poems—"A Very Dove," "Vision 1948," "Refrain," "A Western Ballad," "The Shrouded Stranger," "This Is About Death," "Sunset," "Ode to the Setting Sun"— give little indication of Ginsberg's pixie-like humor or his coming break with literary convention.

Part 2 of the collection ("The Green Automobile, 1953-1954") provides the first inkling that Ginsberg was beginning to discover the appropriate form of expression for ideas too large to be otherwise contained. The long poem "Siesta in Xbalba and Return to the States," an impressionistic work based on Ginsberg's travels in Mexico, sets the stage for the angry, dynamic, no-holds-barred compositions that would follow and characterize the bulk of his poetic career. The main part of Ginsberg's career is collected in eleven sections: "Howl, Before and After: San Francisco Bay Area (1955-1956)," "Reality Sandwiches: Europe! Europe!" (1957-1959)," "Kaddish and Related Poems (1959-1960)," "Planet News: To Europe and Asia (1961-1963)," "King of May: America to Europe (1963-1965)," "The Fall of America (1965-1971)," "Mind Breaths All over the Place (1972-1977)," "Plutonian Ode (1977-1980)," "White Shroud: Poems, 1980-1985," "Cosmopolitan Greetings: Poems, 1986-1992," and "Death and Fame: Poems, 1993-1997."

At the very end of his life, as he lay dying, Ginsberg, like someone reviewing the span of his existence in clarifying flashes, seemed to return full circle to where he had begun. Brief bursts of inspiration, such as "American Sentences," are whimsical, epigram-like in nature. Other final thoughts, including "Sky Words," "Scatological Observations," "My Team Is Red Hot," "Starry Rhymes," "Thirty State Bummers," and "Bop

Sh'bam," are almost childlike ditties in conventional verse forms such as rhyming couplets and quatrains.

Collected Poems, 1947-1997 captures the essence of an artist who, like Whitman before him, exploded the notion of what poetry could or should be. Mostly, though, it lays bare the mind and soul of an individual of consummate craft, a person of fierce intelligence and insatiable curiosity, a human blessed with playful wit, undying optimism, all-encompassing compassion and unstinting generosity for other people.

Other major works

NONFICTION: *Indian Journals*, 1963; *The Yage Letters*, 1963 (with William Burroughs); *Indian Journals, March 1962-May 1963: Notebooks, Diary, Blank Pages, Writings*, 1970; *Allen Verbatim: Lectures on Poetry, Politics, Consciousness*, 1974; *Gay Sunshine Interview*, 1974; *Visions of the Great Rememberer*, 1974; *To Eberhart from Ginsberg*, 1976; *As Ever: The Collected Correspondence of Allen Ginsberg and Neal Cassady*, 1977; *Journals: Early Fifties, Early Sixties*, 1977, 1992; *Composed on the Tongue: Literary Conversations, 1967-1977*, 1980; *Allen Ginsberg Photographs*, 1990; *Snapshot Poetics: A Photographic Memoir of the Beat Era*, 1993; *Journals Mid-Fifties, 1954-1958*, 1995; *Deliberate Prose: Selected Essays, 1952-1995*, 2000; *Family Business: Selected Letters Between a Father and Son*, 2001 (with Louis Ginsberg); *Spontaneous Mind: Selected Interviews, 1958-1996*, 2001; *The Letters of Allen Ginsberg*, 2008 (Bill Morgan, editor); *The Selected Letters of Allen Ginsberg and Gary Snyder*, 2009 (Morgan, editor).

EDITED TEXT: *Poems for the Nation: A Collection of Contemporary Political Poems*, 2000.

MISCELLANEOUS: *Beat Legacy, Connections, Influences: Poems and Letters by Allen Ginsberg*, 1994; *The Book of Matyrdom and Artifice: First Journals and Poems, 1937-1952*, 2006.

Bibliography

Baker, Deborah. *A Blue Hand: The Tragicomic, Mind-Altering Odyssey of Allen Ginsberg, a Holy Fool, a Lost Muse, a Dharma Bum, and His Prickly Bride in India*. New York: Penguin, 2009. A well-researched study of the life-changing travels in India undertaken by Ginsberg and various companions in search of enlightenment, and the aftereffects of the journeys on the poet's work and attitudes.

Edwards, Susan. *The Wild West Wind: Remembering Allen Ginsberg*. Boulder, Colo.: Baksun Books, 2001. A fond and enlightening reminiscence from an author, teacher, artist, and metaphysician who worked for twenty years alongside Ginsberg at Naropa University.

Felver, Christopher, Lawrence Ferlinghetti, and David Shapiro. *The Late Great Allen Ginsberg: A Photo Biography*. New York: Running Press, 2003. A compendium of images and impressions of the poet from all stages of his life, with contributions from many of those who knew him and worked or performed alongside him, including Philip Glass, Ray Manzarek, Ed Sanders, Norman Mailer, Peter Orlovsky, Gary Snyder, Gregory Corso, William Burroughs, and Lawrence Ferlinghetti.

Ginsberg, Allen. *Howl: Original Draft Facsimile, Transcript, and Variant Versions, Fully Annotated by Author, with Contemporaneous Correspondence, Account of First Public Presentation*. New York: Harper Perennial Modern Classics, 2006. An in-depth examination of Ginsberg's first important work, which resulted in charges of obscenity—eventually dismissed—and which made the poet a household name.

Landas, John. *The Bop Apocalypse*. Champaign: University of Illinois Press, 2001. An illuminating account of the religious aspects and elements of the work of Ginsberg, Jack Kerouac, and William Burroughs. Particularly good on the historical dynamics operating in the writers' lives.

Miles, Barry. *The Beat Hotel: Ginsberg, Burroughs, and Corso in Paris, 1958-1963*. New York: Grove Press, 2000. A narrative chronicle of the Beats in Paris from the "Howl" obscenity trial to the invention of the cut-up technique. Based on firsthand accounts from diaries, letters, and many original interviews.

Morgan, Bill. *I Celebrate Myself: The Somewhat Private Life of Allen Ginsberg*. New York: Viking Press, 2006. Morgan drew on unpublished letters and journals to create an extensive, full-length biography, the first to be published after Ginsberg's death. Morgan veers away from lending his own opinion and chronicles rather than interprets Ginsberg's life; however, he manages to highlight the events that inspired Ginsberg to write his unique brand of poetry.

Podhoretz, Norman. *Ex-Friends: Falling Out with Allen Ginsberg, Lionel and Diana Trilling, Lillian Hellman, Hannah Arendt, and Norman Mailer*. New York: Encounter Books, 2000. Podhoretz, the conservative editor of *Commentary*, presents a different and highly entertaining perspective on the infighting that went on among the New York intellectual community of which Ginsberg was a part during the 1950's and 1960's.

Raskin, Jonah. *American Scream: Allen Ginsberg's "Howl" and the Making of the Beat Generation*. Berkeley: University of California Press, 2006. Describes Ginsberg's composition and presentation of his groundbreaking poem against the twin backdrops of the poet's personal life and the era in which it was created.

Trigillo, Tony. *Allen Ginsberg's Buddhist Poetics*. Carbondale: Southern Illinois University Press, 2007. This scholarly study focuses on the poet's adoption of Buddhism and its effect on Ginsberg's work, in terms of form, content, and spirituality.

Leon Lewis
Updated by Jack Ewing

THOM GUNN

Born: Gravesend, Kent, England; August 29, 1929
Died: San Francisco, California; April 25, 2004

PRINCIPAL POETRY

Fighting Terms, 1954, 1962
The Sense of Movement, 1957
My Sad Captains, and Other Poems, 1961
Selected Poems, 1962 (with Ted Hughes)
A Geography, 1966
Positives, 1966 (with photographs by Ander Gunn)
Touch, 1967
The Garden of the Gods, 1968
The Explorers, 1969
The Fair in the Woods, 1969
Poems, 1950-1966: A Selection, 1969
Sunlight, 1969
Last Days at Teddington, 1971
Moly, 1971
Moly and My Sad Captains, 1971
Poems After Chaucer, 1971
Mandrakes, 1973
Songbook, 1973
To the Air, 1974
Jack Straw's Castle, 1975
Jack Straw's Castle, and Other Poems, 1976
The Missed Beat, 1976
Bally Power Play, 1979
Games of Chance, 1979
Selected Poems, 1950-1975, 1979
Talbot Road, 1981
The Menace, 1982
The Passages of Joy, 1982
Undesirables, 1988
The Man with Night Sweats, 1992
Collected Poems, 1993
In the Twilight Slot, 1995
Boss Cupid, 2000
Site Specific: Seventeen "Neighborhood" Poems, 2000

OTHER LITERARY FORMS

Thom Gunn was best known for his poetry as well as his essays that present criticism and autobiographical information. *The Occasions of Poetry: Essays in Criticism and Autobiography* (1982) collects Gunn's reviews and essays on poets from Fulke Greville and Ben Jonson to Robert Creeley and Robert Duncan. It also contains four valuable essays on the composition and inspiration of Gunn's own poetry, including the autobiographical sketch "My Life up to Now" (1977).

ACHIEVEMENTS

Thom Gunn was richly honored for his work during his lifetime. He won the Levinson Prize in 1955, the Somerset Maugham Award in 1959, the Arts Council of Great Britain Award in 1959, a National Institute of Arts and Letters Award in 1964, and a Rockefeller Foundation award in 1966. He won a Gold Medal in poetry from the Commonwealth Club of California in 1976 for *Jack Straw's Castle*. *The Passages of Joy* earned the W. H. Smith Award (1980), two Northern California Book Awards in poetry (1982, 1992), and the PEN/Los Angeles Prize for poetry (1983). In 1988, he won the Robert Kirsch Award for body of work from the *Los Angeles Times* as well as the Sara Teasdale prize. He was honored with the Shelley Memorial Award of the Poetry Society of America and the Lila Wallace-*Reader's Digest* Writers' Award in 1990. *The Man with Night Sweats* earned him the Lenore Marshall Poetry Prize and the PEN Center USA West Poetry Award, both in 1993. He received a Lambda Literary Award in 1994 and the Award of Merit from the American Academy of Arts and Letters in 1998. He held a Guggenheim Fellowship in 1971 and a MacArthur Fellowship in 1993. In 2001, he received the Thom Gunn Award for Gay Poetry for *Boss Cupid*.

BIOGRAPHY

Born Thomson William Gunn, Thom Gunn grew up in the London suburb of Hampstead Heath, "forever grateful" that he was "raised in no religion at all." During the Blitz, he read John Keats, Alfred, Lord Tennyson, and George Meredith, who have all influenced his verse in various ways. His parents—both journalists, although his mother had stopped working before his birth—were divorced when he was eight or nine. After two years in the British army, Gunn went to Paris to work in the offices of the Metro. He attended Trinity College, University of Cambridge, during the early 1950's; there he attended the lectures of F. R. Leavis and began to write poetry in earnest, publishing his first book, *Fighting Terms*, in 1954, while still an undergraduate. He worked briefly on the magazine *Granta* and, as president of the English Club, met and introduced Angus Wilson, Henry Green, Dylan Thomas, and William Empson, among others. Here he also became a pacifist, flirted with socialism, hitchhiked through France during a summer vacation, and met Mike Kitay, his American companion, who influenced his decision to move to the United States.

After graduation, Gunn spent a brief period in Rome and Paris. At the suggestion of the American poet Donald Hall, Gunn applied for and won a creative writing fellowship to Stanford University, where he studied with the formalist poet and critic Yvor Winters. After a short teaching stint in San Antonio, Texas, where he first rode a motorcycle ("for about a month"), heard Elvis Presley's songs, and saw James Dean's movies, Gunn accepted an offer to teach at the University of California, Berkeley, in 1958.

Gunn returned to London for a year (1964-1965) just as the Beatles burst on the scene. Back in San Francisco, he gave up tenure in 1966, only a year after it was granted, and immersed himself in the psychedelic and sexual revolution of the late 1960's. While teaching at Princeton University in 1970, Gunn lived in Greenwich Village when the first art galleries began to appear in SoHo. He moved to San Francisco and began his tenure at University of California, Berkeley, first as a lecturer and then, beginning in 1973, as an associate professor of English. He continued to teach on a part-time basis to allow him, as he says, to write relatively unfettered by academic demands. Gunn died in San Francisco on April 25, 2004.

Analysis

Thom Gunn first achieved notoriety in England, as part of what was called the Movement, an unofficial tag applied to some poets of the 1950's who were, in Gunn's words, "eschewing Modernism, and turning back, though not very thoroughgoingly, to traditional resources in structure and method." Poets of the Movement included Philip Larkin, Kingsley Amis, and Donald Davie, among others. Gunn continued to achieve critical acclaim by approaching a diverse number of subjects previously excluded from poetry, with a similar regard for structure and meter.

Having moved to the United States in the late 1950's, Gunn is somewhat of an amphibious poet. One might say that while his poetry has its formal roots in the English tradition, his subject matter has been taken largely from his American experience. He is known particularly for his exploration of certain counterculture movements from the 1950's to the 1980's. He is comfortable on the fringes of society, where popular culture thrives; rock music, motorcycle gangs, leather bars, and orgies have been his milieu. He is also considered one of the poets who deal most frankly with gay subject matter and themes. What distinguishes Gunn from other poets working with the same material is that he has refused to abandon structure and meter, preferring to impose form on chaotic subjects. Since the mid-1960's, however, Gunn has been increasingly influenced by American poets, notably William Carlos Williams; he turned first to the flexible meters of syllabic verse and subsequently to free verse, without sacrificing his demanding sense of form.

A poet interested in the possibilities of identity, Gunn is best known for his explorations into the existential hero, who takes many guises in his poetry, including the soldier and the motorcyclist. The greatest influence on his thought in these matters has been the existentialism espoused by Jean-Paul Sartre in his philosophical treatise *L'Être et le néant* (1943; *Being and Nothingness*, 1956). For Sartre, humanity is condemned to freedom to make its own meaning in an absurd universe. For Gunn, poetry has been the vehicle of this creation.

Fighting Terms

Gunn began his poetic career while still at Cambridge, with the publication of *Fighting Terms*. The image of the soldier is first of all, Gunn has written, "myself, the national serviceman, the 'clumsy brute in uniform,' the soldier who never goes to war, whose role has no function, whose battledress is a joke," but it is also the "attractive and repellant" real soldier, who kills but also quests, like Achilles and Odysseus. Above all, the soldier is the poet, "an existential conqueror, excited and aggressive," trying to make sense of his absurd situation.

These poems show Gunn's propensity to try, not always successfully, to make meaning of action in the intervals between action. "The Wound" is a good example. While recuperating, a soldier remembers the engagement of battle. As "the huge wound in my head began to heal," he remembers the Trojan War, but it is unclear whether this was his actual experience or only a hallucination. It could be that he is a contemporary soldier reverting to myth in the damaged and "darkened" valleys of his mind. When he rises to act again, his wound "breaks open wide," and he must again wait for "those storm-lit valleys to heal." His identity is thus never resolved.

Similarly, in "Looking Glass," the narrator is a kind of gardener who observes his life under glass. He compares it to a Garden of Eden in which "a fine callous fickleness" sent him in search of pleasure, "gratification being all." Yet there is no God present in this world to give the world an a priori meaning: "I am the gardener now myself. . . . I am responsible for order here." In the absence of God, "risks are authorized"—a theme that imbues Gunn's later poems of experience. He is also alienated from society and does not "care if villagers suspect" that his life is going "to seed." He takes a kind of pride in his status as outsider: "How well it goes to seed." The act of observing the wild garden of his life is a pleasure in itself, even though he is an outcast, "damp-booted, unemployed."

In "The Beach Head," the narrator is a would-be conqueror planning a campaign into his own society: "I seek a pathway to the country's heart." Again the alienated outsider ("I, hare-brained stranger") is heard making sense of his life, wondering whether to enter history through a fine gesture, "With little object other than panache/ And showing what great odds may be defied." His alternative to action is to watch and "wait and calculate my chances/ Consolidating this my inch-square base." This conflict is at the heart of Gunn's poetry, early and late: whether to risk the heroic act or succumb to the passivity of contemplation. Yet the latter too has its risk—namely, that his failure to act may cause society's "mild liking to turn to loathing."

The Sense of Movement

The Sense of Movement continues Gunn's exploration of the active versus the contemplative existential hero. Here the pose, poise, or panache of the hero is more important than the goal of the action, the movement constituting its own meaning. The volume introduces Gunn's idealized "American myth of the motorcyclist, then in its infancy, of the wild man part free spirit and part hoodlum"; his motorcyclist series is based on Andrew Marvell's mower poems. Gunn admits that the book is largely derivative ("a second work of apprenticeship"), partaking of Yvor Winters's formalism, William Butler Yeats's theory of the mask, and Jean-Paul Sartre's existentialist philosophy of engaged action.

The opening poem of the volume, "On the Move," explores the conflict between "instinct" and "poise." This is a key dichotomy in Gunn's work. The natural world of instinct is largely unavailable to thinking human beings, who, unlike birds, must create a kind of surrogate impetus for the meaningful movement. The motorcyclists become the focus for this conflict because of their assumed pose of wildness; yet it is a pose, a posture that is only "a part solution, after all," to the problem. Riding "astride the created will," they appear "robust" only because they "strap in doubt . . . hiding it." The doubt has to do with their destination, as they "dare a future from the taken routes." The absurdity of action (a notion central to existential thought) is emphasized in that the person can appeal neither to natural instinct nor to metaphysics for the meaning he must himself create: "Men manufacture both machine and soul." Unlike "birds and saints," the motorcyclists do not "complete their purposes" by reaching a destination. The movement is its own excuse: "Reaching no absolute, in which to rest,/ One is always nearer by not keeping still."

"In Praise of Cities" affirms the disorderly evolution of human attempts to create meaning in the cityscape, which is personified as a woman, "indifferent to the indifference which conceived her." She withholds and offers herself to the one who wants to discover her secrets. "She wanders lewdly, whispering her given name,/ Charing Cross Road, or Forty-Second Street." Yet the city is really a mirror in which the narrator sees his "own designs, peeling and unachieved" on her walls, for she is, finally, "extreme, material, and the work of man." As in "On the Move," however, the narrator does not so much comprehend as simply embrace the city, with "a passion without understanding." His movement is its own excuse, but the communion with humankind, through his created cityscape, is real.

My Sad Captains, and Other Poems

My Sad Captains, and Other Poems marks a turning point in Gunn's career, a border crossing that is evident in the book's two-part structure. The first half is concerned with the conflict between the "infinite" will and the "confined" execution, and the meter is suitably traditional. The epigraph from William Shakespeare's *Troilus and Cressida* (pr. c. 1601-1602) suggests that while "desire is boundless," "the act is a slave to limit."

Limit is represented by the formalist quality of the poems in this first part of the book.

The second half of the book is much less theoretical, more concerned with direct experience, as its epigraph from F. Scott Fitzgerald suggests: "It's startling to you sometimes—just air, unobstructed, uncomplicated air." This thematic quality is reflected in the breathy technique of syllabic verse, in which the line is determined by the number of syllables rather than accents; the rhymes are random or, when regular, slant. The syllabic form is well suited to the direct apprehension of experience in such poems as "Light Among Redwoods," where "we stand/ and stare—mindless, diminished—/ at their rosy immanence."

Thematically, the volume continues to develop Gunn's "existential conqueror" motif in poems such as "The Book of the Dead" and "The Byrnies," while expanding his poetic repertoire to include snails and trucks as well as some more exotic familiars: tattoo parlors in "Blackie, the Electric Rembrandt" and gay and leather bars in "Modes of Pleasure" (two poems, one title) and "Black Jackets."

"A Map of the City" is perhaps even more successful than "In Praise of Cities" in affirming the human chaos of the city by its treatment of the theme within a traditional form. The speaker stands on a hill at night, looking at the "luminous" city like a map below. Like William Blake's "London," Gunn's city is a maze of drunks, transients, and sailors. From this vantage point, he can "watch a malady's advance," while recognizing his "love of chance." He sees the city's concrete boredom and suffering but also its abstract "potential" for both satisfaction and danger. From this perspective, he can, if only for a moment, get his bearings in relation to the city as a whole, as a map, so that when he descends into the maze again, he will be able to navigate his way through its dangers and flaws. He embraces the "crowded, broken, and unfinished" as the natural concomitants to the riches of city life, as he concludes: "I would not have the risk diminished."

The title poem, "My Sad Captains," is a tribute to all those friends who have inspired the poet, "a few with historical/ names." These men who were immersed in experience once seemed to him to have lived only to "renew the wasteful force they/ spent with each hot convulsion"; yet now they exist "apart" from life, "winnowed from failures," and indeed above life, "and turn with disinterested/ hard energy, like the stars."

Though this poem closes the volume, it can be profitably read together with any number of poems from the book, but especially the opening poem, "In Santa Maria del Popolo," which describes a painting of the "one convulsion" of "Saul becoming Paul" by the sixteenth century artist Caravaggio (Michelangelo Merisi). Here Paul becomes "the solitary man," "resisting, while embracing, nothingness." Yet it is to Caravaggio that Gunn looks for this revelation, the artist being one of his "sad captains."

Although Gunn did not do much more with syllabic verse after *My Sad Captains, and Other Poems*, it was, he said, a way of teaching himself about "unpatterned rhythms," or free verse. From this point onward, he worked in both traditional and "open" forms.

POSITIVES

Positives is written entirely in open forms. These poems were written to accompany his brother Ander's photographs of life in London. Poems about other works of art are common, especially in modern poetry. W. H. Auden's "Musée des Beaux Arts" (1939) and John Ashbery's "Portrait in a Convex Mirror" (1964) are examples of poems that interpret paintings from a distant time and place, as is Gunn's own "In Santa Maria del Popolo." In *Positives*, however, the collaboration is very much contemporary. The poems are written with the photographs, which seem to have taught Gunn to pay attention to the details of street life, pubs, construction sites, abandoned houses, and bridges in a way he never had before. As a result, Gunn gives up the symbolism of Yeats for luminous realities: "It is not a symbolic/ bridge but a real bridge;/ nor is the bundle/ a symbol." This quality makes *Positives* the least philosophical of his early works, even though the theme is large: the progress from birth and "doing things for the first time" to old age and "the terror of full repose." Written to face the photographs, the poems are freed of the burden of description, so that they have a transparent quality, a light touch, and, on the whole, a positive tone.

The poems and photographs depict the "memoirs of the body" in the lines of a face or a stance or gesture. In most cases, "an ambiguous story" can be read there: either as "the ability to resist/ annihilation, or as the small/ but constant losses endured/ but between the lines/ life itself!" These moments of activity in the present—human beings absorbed in the space between past and future—are Gunn's subjects: a child bathing, boys waiting to grow up, motorcyclists riding, a bride overwhelmed by the weight of lace, an old woman balancing a bundle on her head. Each has a history and a destiny, but these are components of their present hopes and fears.

TOUCH

Touch similarly reaches out to a real humanity. By making choices one may cut off other possibilities, but one also affirms a commitment to the individual experience. In "Confessions of the Life Artist," the narrator is "buoyant with the sense of choice." Having chosen, one finds that the death of possibilities unchosen only fortifies "one's own identity."

The opening poem addresses the "Goddess" of loneliness—Proserpine, the fruitful goddess confined away from human touch in the underworld. When she arises in a park, one of Gunn's ever-present soldiers is waiting for "a woman, any woman/ her dress tight across her ass/ as bark in moonlight." The final line seems to reject the idea that myth can enrich human lives; rather, it is persons, "vulnerable, quivering," who lend to myth their own "abundance."

The movement explored in previous volumes here becomes not linear motion through time but the spatial, encircling movement of the imagination wedded to emotion. In the "turbulence" of "The Kiss at Bayreuth," there is a paradoxical moment in which two "may then/ be said to both move and be still." The egotism of the "inhuman eye" of contemplation is overcome in the moment that two are able to "not think of themselves."

Similarly, in the title poem, touch is what Gunn's narrators seem to have been gravitating toward all along. As the narrator slips into the familiar space of a shared bed, he discovers an "enclosing cocoon . . . where we walk with everyone." This personal communion implies a larger community of sleepers who partake in the "continuous creation" of humanity.

There is not room here for a full discussion of the long poem "Misanthropos," but it is in this poem of seventeen sections that the theme of *Touch* is most fully explored. The protagonist is the last man on Earth after a great holocaust, or at least he seems to be. The problem of identity in the absence of others to validate one's existence is explored as the man sheds old values, memories, and emotions as he sheds his former clothes. When he at last loses the distinctions of language, he encounters other survivors, and direct sensation, experienced anew, is shocking.

MOLY

The background informing *Moly* is Gunn's experience with lysergic acid diethylamide (LSD), which, he said, "has been of the utmost importance to me, both as a man and as a poet." Although he recognized the acid trip to be "essentially non-verbal," it was important and "possible to write poetry about any subject that was of importance to you." Unlike other drug-induced poetry, which tends to mimic the diffusion and chaos of the raw experience in free verse, the poems in *Moly* attempt to present "the infinite through the finite, the unstructured through the structured." These poems are highly controlled by structure and meter, while dealing with strange transformations.

The title poem, "Moly," is a dramatic monologue in the voice of one of Odysseus's men who has been turned into a pig by the witch Circe. Its rhymed couplets underscore the dual nature of man, part human and part beast, in search of the essential and magical "root" that will restore his humanity: "From this fat dungeon I could rise to skin/ And human title, putting pig within." The herb he is seeking is moly ("From milk flower to the black forked root"), which rhymes with "holy." The influence of Yeats's "Leda and the Swan" (1924) is evident, yet the swine-man of Gunn's poem is a typically contemporary twist on the mythological theme of the beast-god of Yeats's modernist poem.

Gunn's 1973 essay "Writing a Poem" discusses the conception and composition of "Three," but it is illuminating as a more general discussion of how a poem comes to be. Gunn says that he encountered a naked family on the beach and wanted to preserve them on paper as a kind of "supersnapshot," to find "an embodiment for my haunting cluster of concepts" about them. He calls his desire to perserve this feeling a sense of "decorum"—that is, a description that would be true to his direct experience of them, not the "pat" theme of "innocence and repossession."

JACK STRAW'S CASTLE, AND OTHER POEMS

This idea of decorum seems to dominate the poems in *Jack Straw's Castle, and Other Poems*. Here there is a kind of easy humor and simplicity of emotion only glimpsed in the earlier poems. In "Autobiography," perhaps influenced by Robert Creeley, the speaker desires (and achieves) "the sniff of the real." "Last Days at Teddington" tells of a return to a house that "smelt of hot dust through the day," and all sensation is clear and complete, like the garden that "fell back on itself."

The title poem, however, is a nightmarish version of a fairy tale, in which Gunn confronts his own worst enemy, himself: "I am the man on the rack/ I am the man who puts the man on the rack/ I am the man who watches the man who puts the man on the rack." Yet by confronting the demons of the imagination in this way, he seems to clear the air for a renewed apprehension of experience, to recognize that the "beauty's in what is, not what may seem." In this way, "Jack's ready for the world."

THE PASSAGES OF JOY

The Passages of Joy is the world the poet of "Jack Straw's Castle" has readied himself for. In "The Menace," the speaker discovers "the stifling passages" of the mind, where "the opposition lurks" not outside himself, but within: "I am, am I,/ the one-who-wants-to-get-me." The joys seem less simple, more problematic after the decades of easy sex and drugs. This volume, in fact, contains Gunn's frankest expression of gay concerns in the era of acquired immunodeficiency syndrome (AIDS), although its focus shifts away from leather bars and orgies to long-standing relationships of shared domesticity.

The title is taken from Samuel Johnson's *The Vanity of Human Wishes* (1749), a satire on the tragic and comic elements of human hopes and errors. One of the poems ("Transients and Residents") bears an epigraph from Johnson's poem:

> Time hovers o'er, impatient to destroy,
> And shuts up all the Passages of Joy.

The very personal poems of this volume show Gunn, now past fifty, dealing with the effects of age—in a person, in a generation, and perhaps in the race.

The three parts of the book show Gunn in a range of moods, from what might be called the meditative poems of the first and third parts to the hip pop-culture poems of part 2. Part 2 begins with a poem for Robert Mapplethorpe, the controversial photographer of the more dangerous elements of the gay scene. Another poem features a "dead punk lady," the murdered girlfriend of Sid Vicious of Sex Pistols fame.

The poet of "A Map of the City" still "would not have the risk diminished," for in the risks are to be found certain "passages of joy." In addition to the literal underground passages of "Another All Night Party," in which orgies occur, there are also the symbolic rites of passage of "Adultery" and "Talbot Road."

"Talbot Road" is a poetic treatment of Gunn's "year of great happiness" in London during the Beatles era, when, according to his almost-identical prose account in "My Life up to Now" (1977), "barriers seemed to be coming down all over." One of these barriers had to do with Gunn's own sexuality. The centerpiece of the five-part poem is a return to Hampstead Heath, where he meets "my past self" in the form of a nineteen-year-old. "This was the year," he says, "the year of reconciliation," but it is unclear whether he means his own nineteenth year of 1964-1965; the ambiguity is intentional, for he means both. Hampstead Heath had been for him the scene of childish play and vague adolescent longings, where by day he "had played hide and seek/ with neighbor children"; in 1964, however, he could see the dark side that had always been there, since by night the Heath had long been a notorious venue for promiscuous sexual encounters, and there he now "played as an adult/ with troops of men whose rounds intersected/ at the Orgy Tree."

The central poem of the volume, however, is "Transients and Residents," in which these literal and figurative passages give way to the real passage of time. The four poems that make up this sequence stand in their own right as powerful and timely meditations on the passage of joy in the age of AIDS. Subtitled "An Interrupted Sequence," these four portraits of gay men in different roles explore the passing of a time of carefree sexual awakening and put the reader in the midst of sickness and death. The last portrait is of the poet himself at his desk, catching a glimpse of himself writing—which interrupts the sequence. This interruption perhaps provides a clue into the poet's view of the other portraits he has been drawing, for like the drug dealer in "Crystal," "he puts his soul/ Into each role in turn, where he survives/ Till it is incarnation more than role."

On the streets of "Night Taxi," a cabdriver takes his "fares like affairs/ — no, more like tricks to turn:/ quick, lively, ending up/ with a cash payment." As in the earlier motorcycle poems, Gunn remains obsessed with movement. The cabdriver is intent on maneuvering his way gracefully through the maze of the city, one with his machine. There is still a sense of independence, yet there is also a sense of community; the driver's movement depends on others, even is subservient to the wishes of others: "It's all on my terms but/ I let them think it's on theirs." It is an appropriate poem to end this book that focuses mostly on the importance of other people.

UNDESIRABLES

Gunn's later poems, such as those in *Undesirables*, return to the gritty side of city life in the 1980's, observing characters and situations with an edge of black humor, like scenes reflected in a switchblade. He has not given up his preoccupation with Yeats—"Old Meg" is an incarnation of Yeats's Crazy Jane—but all sense of imitation is gone. Gunn has renounced the Yeatsian pronouncement for the rabbit punch and the belly laugh. "Punch Rubicundus," for example, is a ribald poem about an aging gay man, in which the satire is all self-directed. The host, Mr. Punch, enters one of his "vaudeville of the sexual itch" parties, riding on a donkey, and says, "But this *can't* be Byzantium. (Though/ they do say Uncle Willie's ghost got an invite)." The irreverent reference to Yeats's "Sailing to Byzantium" (1927) and "Byzantium" (1932) is clear: Uncle Willie is William Butler Yeats, whose spirits were supposed to ride "astraddle on the dolphin's mire and blood" to "the holy city of Byzantium."

The poetry of Gunn continued to develop as an up-to-the-minute report on the contemporary scene. Yet his roots in the tradition of poetry were deep, and his dialogue with the poets and forms of the past was as much a part of his evolution as a poet as was his keen eye for the realities of his time.

THE MAN WITH NIGHT SWEATS

Gunn received critical acclaim for *The Man with Night Sweats*, recognized for its unsentimental examination of AIDS, death, and neglected members of contemporary American society. He wrote the poems during 1982 to 1988, a period when the AIDS epidemic was devastating the gay community and the global community shared widespread homophobia and concerns over its transmission. Here the topic of AIDS seemed a theme to which Gunn could attach a particular passion and poetic craft, a place to offer heartbreaking poems of young men struggling with a disease that consumes them with fear and its cruelty. The skepticism of his past poetry here gives way to elegy and lament, lyrical meditation, and a form of rage that is finely tooled with his poetic balance.

In this collection, Gunn acts as both a witness to the devastation of AIDS as well as one deeply involved with it. He writes in "The Renaissance," "You came back in a dream./ I'm all right now you said." His witnessing of the suffering also takes on a ferocity, a compulsion to attest to the wreckage of AIDS, almost as a way to provide a kind of defense:

> I shall not soon forget
> . . . .
> The angle of his head,
> Arrested and reared back
> On the crisp field of bed, . . .

One of the strongest poems of the collection is "Lament," an elegy of more than one hundred lines in which the speaker describes in great detail the slow dying of a close friend in a hospital ward. Rather than elevate the dying friend with praise and abstraction as does traditional elegy, this piece repeats that death is a "difficult enterprise" and chronicles the tedium and pain experienced by his friend—the "clumsy stealth" that has "distanced" him "from the habits of health." "Lament" is a perfect example of Gunn's tightly channeled, yet deeply felt elegies that form this collection.

BOSS CUPID

Boss Cupid echoes the elegiac style of *The Man with Night Sweats*, its three sections examining the loss of friends, lovers, and even, in one case, a lifestyle. Rather than focusing entirely on loss, however, the collection also explores the sexual allure of youth, and renewal and recovery. Frank references to "the sexual New Jerusalem" of Gunn's younger years are here, and in "Saturday Night," he writes a genuinely affecting lament for the sex and drugs scene of the mid-1970's. It moves beyond the endpoints referenced in *The Man with Night Sweats* and his subsequent *Collected Poems* by pushing the boundaries of his poetry to include, in one loose whole, the makings of legend, myth, phantasmagoria, and autobiography. Historic, mythic figures such as Arachne and King David make appearances here, as well as the homeless, college students, and social deviants (as in his five "songs for Jeffrey Dahmer" grouped under the title "Troubadour"). His edgy wit, lyric versatility, and adept caricatures of personas help make this collection a powerful reminder that every life is "dense/ with fine compacted difference."

OTHER MAJOR WORKS

NONFICTION: "My Life up to Now," 1977; *The Occasions of Poetry: Essays in Criticism and Autobiography*, 1982, 1985 (Clive Wilmer, editor); *Shelf Life: Essays, Memoirs, and an Interview*, 1993; *Thom Gunn in Conversation with James Campbell*, 2000.

EDITED TEXTS: *Poetry from Cambridge 1951-52: A Selection of Verse by Members of the University*, 1952; *Five American Poets*, 1963 (with Ted Hughes); *Selected Poems of Fulke Greville*, 1968; *Ben Jonson*, 1974; *Ezra Pound*, 2000; *Selected Poems*, 2003 (by Yvor Winters).

MISCELLANEOUS: *Thom Gunn at Seventy*, 1999.

BIBLIOGRAPHY

Brown, Merle E. *Double Lyric: Divisiveness and Communal Creativity in Recent English Poetry*. New York: Columbia University Press, 1980. Brown argues that poetry is the result of the dialectic between the poet's thinking and speaking selves, the poem being a communal expression of that double consciousness. The theory bears fruit in the two chapters devoted to Gunn's work. The first explores the idea of "inner community" in the long poem "Misanthropos," the second the idea of "authentic duplicity" in Gunn's poetry up to *Jack Straw's Castle, and Other Poems*.

Gunn, Thom. "Thom Gunn." Interview by Christopher Hennessy. In *Outside the Lines: Talking with Contemporary Gay Poets*, edited by Hennessy. Ann Arbor: University of Michigan Press, 2005. Gunn explores his works, technical and emotional development, and the links between his sexuality and verse.

Guthmann, Edward. "A Poet's Life, Part 1: Reserved but Raw, Modest but Gaudy, Thom Gunn Covered an Enormous Amount of Ground in His Exquisite Work and His Raucous Life." *San Francisco Chronicle*, April 25, 2005, p. C1. On the one-year anniversary of Gunn's death, Guthmann wrote a two-part profile of the poet that described his life largely through conversations with friends and colleagues.

_______. "A Poet's Life, Part 2: As Friends Died of AIDS, Thom Gunn Stayed Healthy—Until His Need to Play Hard Finally Killed Him." *San Francisco Chronicle* April 26, 2005, p. E1. The second installment in a profile of the deceased Gunn reveals much about his life in San Francisco with partner Mike Kitay.

King, P. R. *Nine Contemporary Poets: A Critical Introduction*. London: Methuen, 1979. The chapter devoted to Gunn, "A Courier After Identity," discusses five distinct personas in Gunn's poetic development: the "embattled" stance of *Fighting Terms*, "a life of action and of pose" in *The Sense of Movement*, the "divided self" of *My Sad Captains, and Other Poems*, the striving for "contact" with humankind and nature in *Touch*, and the "widening sympathies" of *Moly* and *Jack Straw's Castle, and Other Poems*. An excellent overview.

Leader, Zachary, ed. *The Movement Reconsidered: Essays on Larkin, Amis, Gunn, Davie, and Their Contemporaries*. New York: Oxford University Press, 2009. A collection of essays on the Movement poets, including one on Gunn and one discussing Gunn and Donald Davie.

Michelucci, Stefania. *The Poetry of Thom Gunn: A Critical Study*. Jefferson, N.C.: McFarland, 2009. Michelucci finds a desire for freedom in Gunn's early poetry that leads to his vindication of his closeted sexuality.

Weiner, Joshua, ed. *At the Barriers: On the Poetry of Thom Gunn*. Chicago: University of Chicago Press, 2009. A collection of critical essays examine Gunn's poetry, including "Meat," "Considering the Snail," and "Duncan."

Richard Collins
Updated by Sarah Hilbert

ANSELM HOLLO

Born: Helsinki, Finland; April 12, 1934

PRINCIPAL POETRY

Sateiden Valilla, 1956
& It Is a Song, 1965
Faces and Forms, 1965
The Coherences, 1968
Tumbleweed, 1968
Waiting for a Beautiful Bather: Ten Poems, 1969
Gee Apollinaire, 1970
Maya: Works, 1959-1969, 1970
Message, 1970
Alembic, 1972
Sensation 27, 1972
Smoke Writing, 1973
Spring Cleaning Greens, from Notebooks, 1967-1973, 1973
Some Worlds, 1974
Black Book 1, 1975
Heavy Jars, 1977
Lingering Tangos, 1977
Sojourner Microcosms: New and Selected Poems, 1959-1977, 1977
Curious Data, 1978
Lunch in Fur, 1978
With Ruth in Mind, 1979
Finite Continued: New Poems, 1977-1980, 1980
No Complaints, 1983
Pick Up the House: New and Selected Poems, 1986
Near Miss Haiku: Praises, Laments, Aphorisms, Reports, 1990
Outlying Districts, 1990
Space Baltic: The Science Fiction Poems, 1962-1987, 1991
Blue Ceiling, 1992
High Beam, 1993
West Is Left on the Map, 1993
Corvus, 1995
Survival Dancing, 1995
AHOE (And How on Earth), 1997
AHOE 2 (Johnny Cash Writes a Letter to Santa Claus), 1998

Rue Wilson Monday, 2000
Notes on the Possibilities and Attractions of Existence: New and Selected Poems, 1965-2000, 2001
Braided River: New and Selected Poems 1965-2005, 2005
Guests of Space, 2007

Other literary forms

Anselm Hollo (HAH-low) early established himself as an important literary translator, bringing into English the works of Russian, Finnish, and Swedish poets in the 1960's and 1970's. Authors he translated included Andrei Voznesensky, Aleksandr Blok, and Paul Klee. The genres he has translated range the gamut from poetry and fiction to nonfiction, plays, and screenplays. In his translations from Russian, he collaborated with his mother, Iris Walden-Hollo. He also has translated into Finnish and German the works of such varied authors as Allen Ginsberg, Gregory Corso, William Carlos Williams, and John Lennon. In his translations into German, he several times collaborated with Josephine Clare.

In collaboration with Corso and Tom Raworth, he wrote parodies collected in *The Minicab War* (1961). His critical and autobiographical essays appeared in *Caws and Causeries: Around Poetry and Poets* (1999). Hollo's editing work has included a guest stint with London magazine *Horde* (1964) and the anthology *Modern Swedish Poetry in Translation* (1979), with Gunnar Harding.

Achievements

Anselm Hollo has repeatedly received the praise of such notable poets as Ted Berrigan and Andrei Codrescu, with the latter calling him "indispensable." While often identified with Language poetry, a movement sometimes seen to have antiacademic and antiauthoritarian leanings, Hollo has nevertheless earned notable awards from both academia and formal poetry and arts organizations. In 1976, he was awarded the New York State Creative Artists' Public Service Award. This was followed in 1979 with a National Endowment for the Arts Fellowship in poetry, in 1989 and 1991 with the Fund for Poetry Award for Contributions to Contemporary Poetry, and in 1996 with the Gertrude Stein Award in Innovative American Poetry. For *Notes on the Possibilities and Attractions of Existence*, he was awarded the 2001 San Francisco State University Poetry Center Award.

His work as a translator has garnered him considerable attention. In 1981 and 1989, he received the American-Scandinavian Foundation Award for Poetry in Translation, and, in 1996, the Finnish Government Prize for Translation of Finnish Literature. In 2004, he received the Harold Morton Landon Translation Award for his translation of *Trilogy* by Pentti Saarikoski. His own poetry has been translated into Finnish, French, German, Hungarian, and Swedish.

Biography

Anselm Hollo received his early education in Finland and first spent time in the United States on an exchange scholarship during his senior year, attending a high school in Cedar Rapids, Iowa. He subsequently attended Helsinki University in Finland and the University of Tübingen in Germany. His early employment in the 1950's included working as a commercial correspondent for a lumber export company in Finland and as an interpreter for the United Nations Atomic Energy Agency in Vienna, Austria. By the mid-1950's, he was acting as a translator and book reviewer for both German and Finnish periodicals, while also serving as secretary to his grandfather, Professor Paul Walden of the University of Tübingen. In 1958, he accepted employment with the British Broadcasting Corporation's European Services in London. He became a program assistant and coordinator, remaining through 1966.

Beginning in 1967, Hollo accepted a series of positions as a visiting lecturer, visiting professor, and visiting poet at universities in the United States, including, in the late 1960's and 1970's, the State University of New York, Buffalo; Bowling Green University, Ohio; Hobart and William Smith Colleges, Geneva, New York; Michigan State University, East Lansing; the University of Maryland, Baltimore; Southwest State University, Marshall, Minnesota; and Sweet Briar College, Virginia. This period included his serving as head of the translation workshop at the University of Iowa in Iowa City, in 1971-1972. In 1981, Hollo began a long association with the Naropa Institute at Naropa University in Boulder, Colorado, which would lead to his being named associate professor in the graduate department of writing and poetics in 1989. From 1981 through 1983, he also served as a lecturer at the New College of California, San Francisco.

Throughout much of his career, Hollo has been associated with literary movements often seen in opposition to academe, including the Beat, New York, and Language schools of American poetry. Simultaneously, he has held academic positions, initially as lecturer and later as professor. That Hollo felt the tension inherent in this pairing of professions may be indicated by his long tenure at Naropa, a Buddhist-inspired yet nonsectarian alternative college. He married Josephine Wirkus in 1957, with whom he had one son and two daughters. In 1985, he married the artist Jane Dalrymple. She has provided artwork for several of Hollo's books.

Analysis

Anselm Hollo's poetry has a light and airy appearance, with short and sometimes abrupt lines of verse arranged sparingly on the page. While spare, the poems often demonstrate remarkable depth, and while often short, they are richly endowed with humor, intelligence, and imagination.

Against the tradition in which poets become best known for their longest works, Hollo first established and then maintained a reputation for short poems. This emphasis is a conscious one, reflected in the way he has presented individual poems in more than the usual number of retrospective and summary collections. The appearance of the poem "bouzouki music" in successive books, including the major early compilations *Maya* and *Sojourner Microcosms*, for example, helped give the short poem a prominence it might have lacked if Hollo had not actively kept it before his readers.

Hollo has also used the context of the different compilations to give new perspective on his poems. He offered his collection *Space Baltic*, for example, as a collection of his "science-fiction" works. The inclusion of many poems within this book broadened the ways in which they could be read. A poem such as "old space cadet speaking," which earlier might have been taken as a purely metaphorical exploration of unrealistic ambitions, lent itself to a more literal, narrative reading within this new context.

As might be expected of a poet involved in translation work and whose own career carried him far beyond the borders of his native country, Hollo has demonstrated a deep concern with European literary traditions. At the same time, as a longtime U.S. resident, his poems have become deeply interwoven with the literature of his adopted country. In his frequent dedications of poems to contemporary writers and in his frequent allusions to writers of other times, however, he reveals his true allegiance, which is to a literary world whose borders transcend political lines.

While the seriousness of his poetry has never been in question, neither has Hollo's sense of humor, much of which is based on his observations of modern life. On occasion, his poems take a turn toward black humor, as in "manifest destiny." Others draw their humor from his observations of the literary world. Whether using situational humor or wordplay, Hollo has managed to steer clear of the coy and artificial.

"MANIFEST DESTINY"

Anselm Hollo's shorter poems often have a more distinctively assertive character than his longer poems. Some of this distinctiveness may arise from the pointed emphasis on the intersection of the personal and political worlds. The short "manifest destiny," first published in *No Complaints*, ranks alongside such other poems as "t.v. (1)," "t.v. (2)," and "the terrorist smiles," from *Finite Continued*. In "manifest destiny," Hollo initially creates a vision of a comfortable middle- or upper-class life, "in pleasantly air-conditioned home with big duck pond in back,/ some nice soft drinks by elbow, some good american snacks as well." Hollo explicitly evokes the wealth of the privileged: "at least four hundred grand in the bank, & that's for checking." The evocations of comfort and wealth ground the reader in a reality that becomes unreality by the end of the poem, when the meaning of the poem's title becomes clear. The unspecified people who "arrive in front of a large video screen" in the poem's first line spend "a copacetic evening" at the end of the poem,

> watching the latest military *techné*
> wipe out poverty everywhere in the world
> in its most obvious form, the poor.

The poem is notable not only for its concision and effectiveness but also for its prescience in making a point that would remain undiminished in its accuracy during succeeding decades.

"BOUZOUKI MUSIC"

Originally written and published in the late 1960's, "bouzouki music" is a poem that demonstrates the poet's ease at handling classical or mythological subject matter. Introducing the figure of Odysseus in its first line, the poem can be read as an incantatory exploration of this particular character, or of the type of character Odysseus represents. Written in five brief sections, the poem includes some of Hollo's finest lines:

> a man's legs grow
> straight out of his soul
>
> who knows where they take him

A light touch and glancing vision, as opposed to a possessive grip and direct stare, give the poem expansive force. Other poems, such as "on the occasion of becoming an echo," which invokes Gaia, and even "the new style western," which draws on a modern, media-created mythology, give similar demonstrations of Hollo's approach.

"OLD SPACE CADET SPEAKING"

One of Hollo's "science-fiction," or speculative, poems, "old space cadet speaking" explores notions of reality and unreality. While a poem without the political dimension of "manifest destiny," it similarly begins by presenting an unreal world in terms to establish it as real and similarly concludes by exposing its empty underpinnings. After beginning with a storyteller's opening phrase, "let me tell you," Hollo introduces the character of a spaceship captain possessed by the sensual vision of union with his lover. Although his physical destination goes unmentioned, the Captain dwells on

> exactly what he would do
> soon as he reached the destination
> he would fuse with her plumulous essence
> & they would become a fine furry plant.

The adventure of space travel is reduced to the entirely personal dimensions of an erotic dream, the "ultimate consummation of long ethereal affair." Above and beyond the erotic episode, moreover, the Captain envisions a kind of transcendence, in which "he would miss/ certain things small addictions/ acquired in the colonies." This dream of transcendence seems his destination: "he was flying high/ he was almost there." Hollo then dissolves the image, in the manner of someone turning away from an entertaining show or absorbing story:

> & that is where
> we leave him to go on hurtling through the great warp
> & at our own ineffable goals.

In its final few words, the poem expands to include the reader. Like the goals of the Captain, those of the reader also may be "ineffable." The reader longs for that "ultimate consummation of long ethereal affair" and participates in the same fantasy of "hurtling through the great warp."

rue Wilson Monday

A major work, *rue Wilson Monday* presents the daybook in verse of a period of time Hollo spent in France. His ruminations on events and personalities past and present, enriched by an ironically conscious Surrealist approach, combine with sensory passages to make *rue Wilson Monday* among Hollo's most rewarding efforts. "When I was invited to spend five months in France, in an old hotel long frequented by artists and writers, I decided to write something that would NOT be your typical 'sabbatical poem,'" he writes in a prefatory note. He calls the work a "hybrid of day book, informal sonnet sequence (though more 'simultaneist' than chronological), and extended, 'laminated' essay-poem." He credits the influence of Guillaume Apollinaire's 1913 poem "Lundi rue Christine," "a Cubist work composed almost entirely out of verbatim speech from various conversations in a café."

Hollo's work draws not on actual conversations he overhears at the Hotel Chevillon but instead on conversations "in and around my head during that stay." For longtime readers of Hollo, many participants in the "conversations" are decidedly familiar to the territory, while some, such as Robert Louis Stevenson, appear as figures specially connected to the French hotel. The familiar figures, who help make these informal sonnets resonate with Hollo's earlier work, include such diverse individuals as Berrigan, Gertrude Stein, Lennon, Oscar Wilde, Heraclitus of Ephesus, Robert Bly, and "Archy the Vers Libre Cockroach." In a move some readers might regard as overly self-conscious, Hollo includes footnotes to help the reader participate in the "conversations" of the poems. While the poems themselves are lucid, these notes distinctly augment the reader's pleasure.

Early in the sonnet sequence, in poem number 2, Hollo positions himself as poet, by issuing the warning "beware of those who write to write beautiful thoughts." He then establishes parameters: "upper limit: poet as brain in jar/ lower limit: poet as hectoring moralistic asshole." His preference for "gamesome pasquinade" suggests that Hollo's playfulness will come to the fore, in the course of the sequence of poems, even against the influence of "Mister Intellectual Rigor."

Many of the poems reflect Hollo's own experience in the world of poetry and serve occasionally as poetic defenses. In poem number 9, he answers the charge "thou art too elliptical" with a response appropriately elliptical: "but what's not foible anymore?" In poem number 15, he makes an even more pointed statement of his position:

> give up your ampersands & lowercase i's
> they still won't like you
> the bosses of official verse culture
> (U.S. branch) but kidding aside
> I motored off that map a long time ago.

The imaginary conversations pervade these poems in unexpected ways. In poem number 56, Hollo quotes from a Kerouac School workshop led by Berrigan in 1978 and then notes,

> yes Ted yes it is very much like it
> but you are the master of intelligent conversation
> and no emotional slither.

In his footnote, Hollo notes how his interior conversation with Berrigan also includes Ezra Pound, whose words he appropriates.

While the inspirational Apollinaire poem is directly quoted within the numbered sonnets, perhaps its most striking echo appears in poem number 21, which is literally cobbled together out of the words of other poets, as if overheard in Apollinaire's café. In his footnote, Hollo states that he composed the poem out of lines drawn from Sir Philip Sidney; Alfred, Lord Tennyson;Michael Drayton; and Sir Thomas Wyatt, among others.

NOTES ON THE POSSIBILITIES AND ATTRACTIONS OF EXISTENCE

The major collection *Notes on the Possibilities and Attractions of Existence* includes poems from collections up through *AHOE 2*. With its 317 selections heavily favoring Hollo's two *AHOE* volumes, the collection offers a revisionary presentation of the poet's career and shows him at the height of his powers as a writer in his sixth decade. The selections, according to Hollo, are works "that have retained a modicum of resonance for me through all that time and up to the year 2000." The book's title is a borrowing from Louis Zukofsky's 1950 "A Statement for Poetry," which argued that verse is not "free," "if its rhythms inevitably carry the words in contexts that do not falsify the function of words as speech probing the possibilities and attractions of existence." The choice of title gives a focal point for Hollo's selections from across four decades of writing.

In his selections for this volume, Hollo emphasizes poems that best exhibit his wry, witty sensibility. The chronological arrangement helps clarify the direction he has been taking in his practice of poetry, as he increasingly finds the means to seize the present moment not of the senses but of the mind, which moves in ways that are sometimes coherent and rational and at other times unpredictable. The effort seems to be, as in "Script Mist," to "hang on to moment, naked, fair/ frail as a butterfly—." In his poem written as a memorial to Ginsberg, "A Hundred Mule Deer in the Back Yard," Hollo poses the question that may prompt his continuing Zukofskian effort to probe "the possibilities and attractions": "why did we say what we just seem to have said/ not a thought in our heads/ is the thought in my head."

Some spirit of retrospection animates these poems, as Hollo makes clear by constant reference to writers, musicians, and painters of past times, and by several poems written as memorials to other poets. The reflective spirit even moves through entire poems, as is made clear by the title of one that spins dizzily back to the time of Hollo's first publications in English: "Hey, Dr. Who, Let's Dial 1965." In "Hi, Haunting," Hollo even steps back to the youth of a writer, who may or may not be Hollo himself. Its lines "back then it seemed he had more to say/ than could be said in a lifetime" are followed by another that expresses the satisfaction of one who has lived a rewarding life: "but there was time enough." Hollo makes reference to Raymond Chandler and Stein and adds, "the grand narratives are dead," a statement he then reverses in such a way as to present Chandler and Stein as being among "the dead," as ". . . our grand narratives/ the dreadful great." In contrast to this seriousness, Hollo often adopts a tone of irreverence for the past, combining it with a playful embrace of the mind's present moment. The attitude is cleverly expressed in the title "Tempus? Fuggit!" for one such poem that follows the "idle swoop and dazzle" of immediacy.

GUESTS OF SPACE

The directness and candor of *rue Wilson Monday* comes to the fore again in Hollo's collection *Guests of Space*. Containing many poems that may ultimately rank among Hollo's most successful works, *Guests of Space* is divided into the subsections "Guests of Space I," "Guests of Space II," "So the Ants Made It to the Cat Food," "The Guy in the Little Room," and "Such an Expensive Dream." The book's title derives from the answer given to a question once posed by Pippin, son of Charlemagne: "'What is man?' asked the King/ Alcuin's reply: 'A guest of space.'" The section title "The Guy in the Little Room" refers to an image conceived by Berrigan in describing the unconscious mental processes of the poet.

These poems continue Hollo's exploration of the meaning of writing, speech, and poetry, with a new sense of summation and self-evaluation intermixing with his continuing questioning of self and world: An untitled poem begins: "here have I summed my sighs, playing cards with the dead/ in a broke-down shack on the old memory banks/ e'en though my thoughts like hounds/ pursue me through swift speedy time." Another untitled poem begins with lines that seem to simultaneously deny and embrace the sense of regret. Hollo writes, "Once you've said something, you can't unsay it/ Once you haven't said anything, it remains unsaid/ and anything you can't say, well, it's unsayable."

Hollo gives his most sustained consideration of the writing of poetry in "It Was All Right," which has the subtitle, "What I Learned from Kenneth Koch." The poem begins "It was all right to be funny . . ." and continues with a litany of "all right" approaches to the art that Koch and Hollo share. Using bald statements and apparent contradictions and balancing the "all right" approaches with "But never all right to be pompous," the poem is a free expression of the limits that have been pushed by both poets. Perhaps, too, it offers a description of the "larger logic to defy/ The dumbly trembling unities" which is mentioned in the poem that begins "Against meaning, lunatic, real."

Although that latter poem suggests that it is when "you work a line" that the poet works "Against meaning, lunatic, real,/ Possible in appearance . . . ," in *Guests of Space*, Hollo offers poems laden with what he considers meaningful politics, in which he is clearly seeking to communicate his puzzlement and outrage about "one of the stupidest cultures/ ever constructed on this planet" (from "this is not the bear this is a picture of the bear" In the poems of the section "Such an Expensive Dream," Hollo confronts many of the uncomfortable realities of the world in the twenty-first century, railing against a government he sees as being ruled by thieves, and struggling to understand the "expensive dream" itself, which is America.

OTHER MAJOR WORKS

NONFICTION: *Caws and Causeries: Around Poetry and Poets*, 1999.

TRANSLATIONS: *Kaddisch*, 1962 (of Allen Ginsberg's poem); *Red Cats: Selections from the Russian Poets*, 1962; *Some Poems*, 1962 (of Paul Klee); *In der flüchtigen Hand der Zeit*, 1963 (of Gregory Corso's poetry); *Selected Poems*, 1964 (of Andrei Voznesensky's poetry); *Querelle*, 1966 (of Jean Genet's novel); *Helsinki: Selected Poems of Pentti Saarikoski*, 1967; *Selected Poems*, 1968 (of Paavo Haavikko's poetry); *Paterson*, 1970 (with Josephine Clare; of William Carlos Williams's poem); *The Twelve, and Other Poems*, 1971 (of Aleksandr Blok's poetry); *Beautiful Days*, 1976 (of Franz Innerhofer's novel); *Modern Swedish Poetry in Translation*, 1979 (with Gunnar Harding); *Strindberg*, 1984 (of Olof Lagercrantz's biography); *Au revoir les enfants*, 1989 (of Louis Malle's play); *The Czar's Madman*, 1992 (of Jaan Kross's novel); *And Still Drink More! A Kayankaya Mystery*, 1994 (of Jakob Arjouni's novel); *Jungle of Cities, and Other Plays*, 1994 (of Bertolt Brecht's plays); *Starfall: A Triptych*, 1998 (of Lars Kleberg's philosophic dialogues); *Serious Poems*, 2000 (of Kai Nieminen's poetry); *Small Change: A Film Novel by François Truffaut*, 2000; *Trilogy*, 2003 (of Saarikoski's verse trilogy).

EDITED TEXTS: *Jazz Poems*, 1963; *Negro Verse*, 1964.

MISCELLANEOUS: *The Minicab War*, 1961 (parodies; with Gregory Corso and Tom Raworth).

BIBLIOGRAPHY

Cline, Lynn. "Anselm Hollo's Poetry Speaks Volumes." *Santa Fe New Mexican*, May 13, 2001. Cline writes about the poet's views on "life outside the box," based on Hollo's lectures.

Hegnauer, Lilah. Review of *Guests of Space*. *Virginia Quarterly Review* 83, no. 3 (Summer, 2007): 266. Hegnauer praises the risks that Hollo takes by using experimental and varied forms in this collection. She finds that the collection reads like a conversation among Hollo, metaphysicians, other poets, and friends.

Hollo, Anselm. "Anselm Hollo." Interview by Edward Halsey Foster. In *Postmodern Poetry: The Talisman Interviews*, edited by Foster. Hoboken, N.J.: Talisman House, 1994. The poet discusses his work and influences. Foster places Hollo alongside such figures as Alice Notley, Ron Padgett, and Rosemarie Waldrop.

Waldman, Anne. *Nice to See You: Homage to Ted Berrigan*. Minneapolis, Minn.: Coffee House Press, 1991. Presents a valuable picture of New York's Lower East Side poetry community of the 1960's and 1970's, in which Hollo was deeply involved.

Weatherhead, A. Kingsley. *The British Dissonance: Essays on Ten Contemporary Poets*. Columbia: University of Missouri Press, 1983. Kingsley discusses Hollo in terms of his status as a poet once active in England, alongside such British poets as Basil Bunting, Charles Tomlinson, and Tom Raworth.

Mark Rich
Updated by Rich

BOB KAUFMAN

Born: New Orleans, Louisiana; April 18, 1925
Died: San Francisco, California; January 12, 1986

PRINCIPAL POETRY
Solitudes Crowded with Loneliness, 1965
Golden Sardine, 1967
The Ancient Rain: Poems, 1956-1978, 1981
Cranial Guitar: Selected Poems, 1996

OTHER LITERARY FORMS

Bob Kaufman is known primarily for his poetry, but he was a contributing editor for *Beatitude*, a mimeographed literary magazine first published in San Francisco in 1959. Kaufman's poetry, which began as a form of oral literature, crosses over into theater because he was a San Francisco poet known for his spontaneous performances on the streets of the city and at the Co-existence Bagel Shop.

ACHIEVEMENTS

Bob Kaufman's "Bagel Shop Jazz" was nominated for the Guinness Prize for Poetry in 1961 and appeared in Volume 4 of *The Guinness Book of Poetry, 1959-1960* (1961). In 1979, Kaufman received a fellowship from the National Endowment for the Arts. His *Cranial Guitar* won a PEN Center USA West Poetry Award in 1997.

Because Kaufman applied the improvisational jazz style of saxophonist and composer Charlie Parker to poetry, Kaufman became known as the Original Bebop Man. In addition, because Kaufman followed the examples of Surrealism and Dadaism, creating extraordinarily imagistic combinations of words that eluded explication, some critics refer to Kaufman as the Black American Rimbaud. Although Kaufman made little effort to collect his writings, his poems still appear in major anthologies of African American and Beat generation writing. Both National Public Radio and the Public Broadcasting Service have produced programs on Kaufman.

BIOGRAPHY

Separating the legend of Robert Garnell Kaufman from the verifiable details of his life is a difficult task. Kaufman himself contributed to the development of his legend, and various biographical sources have recorded unverifiable information that has been reproduced in other sources.

The legend indicates that Kaufman's father was an orthodox Jew of German ancestry and his mother was a Catholic from Martinique who had some acquaintance with voodoo. Perhaps Kaufman's grandfather was partly Jewish, but Kaufman's siblings report that the New Orleans family was middle class and Catholic. His father, Joseph Kaufman, was a Pullman porter who worked on trains running between New Orleans and Chicago; his mother, Lillian, was a schoolteacher who made her book collection and piano important parts of the family home. The couple had thirteen children.

The legend suggests that Kaufman joined the United States Merchant Marine at age thirteen, traveled around the world numerous times, and developed his interest in literature when a shipmate influenced him and loaned him books. However, Kaufman probably did not enter the merchant marine until he was eighteen, and thereafter, he became an active member of the National Maritime Union. This union of merchant sailors faced federal review because it reputedly had ties to communist organizations, and Kaufman was one of two thousand sailors driven from the merchant marine because of his political views.

Kaufman moved to New York, where he studied for a time at the New School of Social Research and lived on the lower East Side. It was in New York that he met Allen Ginsberg and William Burroughs. Kaufman returned to San Francisco in 1958. Later that year, he married Eileen Singe.

Kaufman emerged as a literary artist in San Francisco in the late 1950's. *Abomunist Manifesto* was published as a broadside in 1959 by City Lights, and Kaufman's witty and innovative poem made him famous in the North Beach section of San Francisco. *Life* magazine (November 30, 1959) published Paul O'Neil's scathing report on the Beat generation, and a posed photo mocking Beatniks in their "pad" included Kaufman's broadside as an example of standard Beatnik reading. City Lights published two additional broadsides by Kaufman, *Does the Secret Mind Whisper?* and *Second April.* In 1960, Kenneth Tynan's *We Dissent*, a ninety-minute British television program included Kaufman among the featured Beatnik writers. Kaufman also was shown in Ron Rice's underground film *The Flower Thief* (1960), which dealt with the Beat generation in North Beach. As Kaufman became more flamboyant as a street poet in San Francisco, he came into conflict with the police and was often arrested and sometimes beaten. To be free of such treatment, he briefly went to New York, where he read poetry in Greenwich Village. He returned to San Francisco in 1963.

In 1965, New Directions published *Solitudes Crowded with Loneliness*, which included the broadsides and a selection of other poems. In 1967, City Lights published *Golden Sardine*, and in 1981, New Directions published *The Ancient Rain.*

The legend says that Kaufman took a vow of silence when John F. Kennedy was assassinated and maintained it until after the war in Vietnam ended. At a local gathering place, Kaufman is reported to have ended his silence in 1975 by reciting from T. S. Eliot's *Murder in the Cathedral* (pr., pb. 1935) and performing his own composition, "All Those Ships That Never Sailed."

Weakened by drug dependency and emphysema, Kaufman died in San Francisco in

1986. In tribute, a procession of artists, family members, and friends followed a New Orleans jazz band through the North Beach section of San Francisco to view the sites that Kaufman frequented during his career in poetry.

Through the collaboration of Eileen Kaufman (Kaufman's wife), Gerald Nicosia, and David Henderson, *Cranial Guitar*, a selection of poems by Kaufman, was published in 1996. Critical attention to Kaufman grew after its publication, and slowly critics began recognizing that categories such as Beat poet, jazz poet, and Surrealist poet only partially describe Kaufman.

ANALYSIS

As presented in Bob Kaufman's *Solitudes Crowded with Loneliness*, "Abomunist Manifesto" is a sequence of eleven parts. The title plays on *Manifest der Kommunistischen Partei* (1848; *The Communist Manifesto*, 1850) by Karl Marx and Friedrich Engels, but in the conversion of "com" to "abom," Kaufman calls attention to the world's focus on the A-bomb, or atomic bomb. The Abomunists contrast with communists and capitalists and have a modified language and special world perspective that Kaufman's manifesto humorously and provocatively discloses. For example, the Abomunists "vote against everyone by not voting for anyone." Never accepting candidacy, the Abomunists insist, "The only office Abomunists run for is the unemployment office." The worldview of the Abomunists is suggested in apparent contradictions: "Abomunists do not feel pain, no matter how much it hurts." Kaufman adds, "Laughter sounds orange at night, because/ reality is unrealizable while it exists."

Kaufman lends the sequence dramatic proportions when he indicates that the author is "Bomkauf," apparently a fusion of "Bomb" and "Kaufman" that humorously suggests the atomic bomb and the author's name, but also supplies a variation on *dummkopf*, a German word meaning idiot. Bomkauf extends the dramatic proportions of the poem when he indicates that "Further Notes," the third part in the sequence, is "taken from 'Abomunismus und Religion' by Tom Man," apparently a reference to Thomas Mann, and, for some readers, Tom Paine.

"Excerpts from the Lexicon Abomunon," the fifth part of the sequence, is a brief comical dictionary of Abomunist terms "compiled by BIMGO," or Bill Margolis, who, among others, collaborated with Kaufman on the editing of *Beatitude*, the mimeographed magazine in which "Abomunist Manifesto" first appeared. Kaufman's lexical game is shown in entries such as "Abomunize," which means "to carefully disorganize." An "Abomunasium" is a "place in which abomunastics occur, such as bars, coffee shops, USO's, juvenile homes, pads, etc."

The speakers in "Still Further Notes Dis- and Re-Garding Abomunism" include Bomkauf (with his associates, since he says "We"), who provides an introductory passage for five diary entries by Jesus from "the Live Sea Scrolls." The entries comically chronicle the last days of Jesus, who speaks in hipster language, complaining, "Barabbas gets suspended sentence and I make the hill. What a drag. Well, that's poetry, and I've got to split now."

For "Abominist Rational Anthem," a sound poem that defies logical interpretation, Schroeder, the child pianist from the comic strip Peanuts, is cited as the composer of the music. "Abomunist Documents," which includes two pieces of eighteenth century correspondence, one written by Hancock (founding father John Hancock) and the other by Benedict (traitor Benedict Arnold), is material that, according to Bomkauf, was "*discovered during ceremonies at the Tomb of the Unknown Draftdodger*."

The final entry in "Abomunist Manifesto" is "Abomnewscast . . . on the Hour . . . ," in which an unnamed newscaster presents comical headlines that refer to people, current events, and history. The newscast is "sponsored by your friendly neighborhood Abomunist." Kaufman satirizes society's quest for material gratification even as society stands on the brink of a nuclear apocalypse. The newscaster refers to a bomb shelter available in "decorator colors" with a "barbecue unit that runs on radioactivity." In a cemetery, one can acquire "split-level tombs." Norman Rockwell's charming interpretation of American life in "The Spelling Bee" becomes "The Lynching Bee" in the newscast, and the image is so American that the Daughters of the American Revolution give the work an award. The world spins forward with its population explosion, Cold War, arms race, and television programs, and the newscaster warns that the pending "emergency signal" will not be a drill. He advises, ". . . turn the TV off and get under it."

BAGEL SHOP JAZZ

Kaufman frequented the Co-existence Bagel Shop in San Francisco, and the shop became a forum for his presentations. In "Bagel Shop Jazz," Kaufman analyzes and describes the "shadow people" and the "nightfall creatures" who populate the bagel shop and give it a special atmosphere. Among the people at the shop are "mulberry-eyed girls in black stockings." The girls are "love tinted" and "doomed," yet ". . . they fling their arrow legs/ To the heavens,/ Losing their doubts in the beat." There are also "angel guys" who have "synagogue eyes." These men are "world travelers on the forty-one bus" and they blend "jazz with paint talk." They are "lost in a dream world,/ Where time is told with a beat." In contrast to the guys and girls are "coffee-faced Ivy Leaguers, in Cambridge jackets." These men discuss "Bird and Diz and Miles" (jazz musicians Charlie "Bird" Parker, Dizzie Gillespie, and Miles Davis) and flash "cool hipster smiles" even as they hope that "the beat is really the truth."

Though the community of bagel-shop patrons poses no apparent threat, these people become "brief, beautiful shadows, burned on walls of night" because "the Guilty police arrive" and end the interaction the bagel shop encourages. The patrons are probably Abomunistic in their attitude, and society, as represented by the police, cannot tolerate their individuality and edginess.

THE ANCIENT RAIN

The title poem of *The Ancient Rain* is topical and prophetic, satirical and tender, as well as symbolic and surreal. A prose poem set in stanzas that often begin with the refrain "The Ancient Rain . . . ," Kaufman's "The Ancient Rain" honors the history of the United States and decries social injustice. The falling of the Ancient Rain is an apocalyptic event that strikes down evil and honors the righteous. The Ancient Rain has godlike powers: "The Ancient Rain is supreme and is aware of all things that have ever happened." Kaufman adds, "The Ancient Rain is the source of all things, the Ancient Rain knows all secrets, the Ancient Rain illuminates America." Kaufman foresees a destructive world war, but he also sees that the Ancient Rain will prevail over the war, giving righteous triumph to those who are just.

Among the heroes Kaufman names in the poem are Abraham Lincoln, George Washington, John F. Kennedy, Franklin Delano Roosevelt, Nathan Hale, Crispus Attucks, Hart Crane, Federico García Lorca, Ulysses S. Grant, John Brown, and Martin Luther King, Jr. Among the villains are George Custer, D. W. Griffith, the members of the Ku Klux Klan, Julius Caesar, Robert E. Lee, warmongers, and bigoted and hypocritical immigrants. Kaufman draws his greatest inspiration from Attucks, the black man who was the first to die in the American Revolution, and García Lorca, whose poetry lifted Kaufman into "crackling blueness" and led him to "seek out the great Sun of the Center."

BIBLIOGRAPHY

Anderson, T. J. *Notes to Make the Sound Come Right: Four Innovators of Jazz Poetry*. Fayetteville: University of Arkansas Press, 2004. Examines the jazz poetry of Bob Kaufman, as well as of Nathaniel Mackey, Stephen Jonas, and Jayne Cortez. Anderson provides overviews on jazz poetry as well as chapters on each of the poets. He studies Kaufman's appropriation of the rhythms and tones of jazz.

Christian, Barbara. "Whatever Happened to Bob Kaufman?" In *The Beats: Essays in Criticism*, edited by Lee Bartlett. Jefferson, N.C.: McFarland, 1981. Christian calls attention to social protest and jazz in Kaufman's work.

Damon, Maria. "'Unmeaning Jargon'/Uncanonized Beatitude: Bob Kaufman, Poet." In *The Dark End of the Street: Margins in American Vanguard Poetry*. Minneapolis: University of Minnesota Press, 1993. Examines the poetic works of Kaufman and the language he used.

_______, ed. "Bob Kaufman: Poet A Special Section." *Callaloo: A Journal of African American and African Arts and Letters* 25, no. 1 (Winter, 2002): 105-231. This special section in *Callaloo* presents articles on Kaufman by Aldon Lynn Nielsen, James Smethurst, Amor Kohli, Jeffrey Falla, Rod Hernandez, and Horace Coleman.

Henderson, David. Introduction to *Cranial Guitar*, by Bob Kaufman. Minneapolis: Coffee House Press, 1996. Henderson explains Kaufman's career and quotes extensively from a radio documentary on Kaufman.

Kohli, Amor. "Black Skins, Beat Masks: Bob Kaufman and the Blackness of Jazz." In *Reconstructing the Beats*. New York: Palgrave Macmillan, 2004. Kohli sees jazz performance as a means of protest.

Lawlor, William T. "*Cranial Guitar*." In *Masterplots II: African American Literature*, edited by Tyrone Williams. Rev. ed. Pasadena, Calif.: Salem Press, 2009. Provides in-depth analysis of *Cranial Guitar*, paying attention to themes and meanings. Also contains brief biography of Kaufman.

Thomas, Lorenzo. "'Communicating by Horns': Jazz and Redemption in the Poetry of the Beats and the Black Arts Movement." *African American Review* 26, no. 2 (1992): 291-299. Thomas draws a connection between jazz artists and rebellion against conformity.

Winans, A. D. "Bob Kaufman." *American Poetry Review* 29, no. 3 (May-June, 2000): 19-20. Winans offers a compact review of Kaufman's life.

William T. Lawlor

PHILIP LARKIN

Born: Coventry, England; August 9, 1922
Died: Hull, England; December 2, 1985

PRINCIPAL POETRY

The North Ship, 1945, 1966
The Less Deceived, 1955
The Whitsun Weddings, 1964
High Windows, 1974
Collected Poems, 1988
Early Poems and Juvenilia, 2005 (A. T. Tolley, editor)

OTHER LITERARY FORMS

Although Philip Larkin is thought of today primarily as a poet, his first literary successes were novels: *Jill* (1946, 1964) and *A Girl in Winter* (1947). The two were widely acclaimed for their accomplished style, accurate dialogue, and subtle characterization. *Jill* was valued highly for its intimate look at wartime Oxford. The protagonist in each is an outsider who encounters great difficulty in attempting to fit into society, and the two novels explore themes of loneliness and alienation to which Larkin returns time and again in his later poetry. Larkin wrote comparatively little about literature and granted few interviews. His literary essays were collected into *Required Writings: Miscellaneous Pieces, 1955-1982* (1984). He also wrote extensively on jazz, chiefly in his reviews for the *Daily Telegraph*, and a number of those pieces appear in the volume *All What Jazz: A Record Diary, 1961-1968* (1970). His opinions of jazz works are frequently instructive for the reader who wishes to understand his views on poetry, particularly his comments on what he saw as the "modernist" jazz of Charlie Parker, which, like all modernism, concentrates on technique while violating the truth of human existence. True to his precepts, Larkin eschewed, throughout his career, technical fireworks in favor of a poetic that reflects the language of the people. He edited *New Poems*, 1958, with Louis MacNeice and Bonamy Dobrée, and he was chosen to compile *The Oxford Book of Twentieth-Century English Verse* (1973).

ACHIEVEMENTS

Few poets succeeded as Philip Larkin did in winning a large audience and critical respect for such a small body of poetry, and indeed his success may be attributable in part to the rate at which he wrote poems. Because he brought out, according to his own estimate, only three to five poems a year, he could give each one the meticulous attention required to build extremely tight, masterful verse. As a result, each of his slim volumes

Philip Larkin

contains numerous poems that immediately catch the reader's attention for their precise yet colloquial diction.

His chief contribution to British poetry may well be his sustained determination to work in conventional forms and colloquial, even vulgar and coarse, language. In this attempt, as in his ironic self-deprecation and his gloomy outlook, he resembles Robert Frost. Also like Frost, he worked consciously against the modernist poetics of Wallace Stevens, T. S. Eliot, Ezra Pound, and their heirs, the poetics of disjunction and image. Most of Larkin's poetry demonstrates a distrust of symbolic and metaphorical language, and a reliance instead on discursive verse. His insistence on plain language reflects a belief in the importance of tradition, a faith in the people who remain in touch with the land, and a suspicion of modern society, urban development, and technological advancement. Larkin stands as the chief example among his contemporaries of the line of counter-modernist poetry running not from William Butler Yeats and the Symbolists but from Thomas Hardy and Rudyard Kipling, for both of whom he had great admiration.

Larkin's popularity also results, in part, from his speaking not only as one of the people but for them as well. For all its bleakness and irony, or perhaps because of it, his poetry represents the attitudes of a segment of the British population that found itself with greatly diminished expectations following World War II; institutions were losing their traditional value and function, and the problems of empire (the crowning achievements of those institutions) were rushing home to roost. His poetry represents a search for meaning within the bewildering complexity of the twentieth century. His awards include the Queen's Gold Medal for Poetry (1965), the Russell Loines Award (1974), and the W. H. Smith Literary Award (1984).

BIOGRAPHY

The Englishness of Philip Arthur Larkin's poetry is decidedly provincial; his England does not revolve around London, and in fact, there is a marked suspicion of the capital and the cosmopolitan urbanity it represents. From his diction to the frequency with which his speakers are seated in cars or trains traveling through the countryside, his poems reflect the provincialism of his life. Larkin was born August 9, 1922, in Coventry, where his father served as city treasurer throughout his childhood. He described his childhood as a bore and not worth mentioning, suggesting that no biography of him need begin before he turned twenty-one. Although he was not a particularly good student at the King Henry VII School in Coventry, he matriculated at St. John's College, Oxford, in 1940, hoping to get in a year of school before he was called into the military. As it eventually turned out, he failed his army physical and stayed in college, graduating with first-class honors in 1943. His time at Oxford had a profound effect on the youthful Larkin; in the introduction to *Jill*, he suggests that the war radically diminished the students' grand view of themselves, and this sense of reduced importance stuck with him in his poetry. Perhaps even more crucial to his development, though, were his friendships with budding writers Bruce Montgomery (Edmund Crispin) and Kingsley Amis. The Amis-Larkin friendship seems to have influenced both men, and their early writings share many attitudes and themes.

While at the university, Larkin published poems in the undergraduate magazines and in the anthology *Poetry in Wartime* (1942). (He had had one poem published in the *Listener* in 1940.) Fortune Press took notice and asked him to submit a collection; he did, and *The North Ship* was published in 1945. The poetry in that collection is heavily influenced by Yeats's work, to which he was introduced by the poet Vernon Watkins, who read and lectured at the English Club at Oxford and with whom Larkin subsequently developed a friendship.

After graduation, Larkin took a post as librarian in Wellington, Shropshire. While there he began to read Thomas Hardy's poetry seriously, which allowed him to throw off the Yeatsian influence. He subsequently worked as a librarian in Leicester, in Belfast, and, after 1955, as head librarian at the University of Hull. His attitudes toward his work vacillated, and that ambivalence is displayed in his poems, particularly in "Toads" and "Toads Revisited." Nevertheless, he remained at his position as librarian and eschewed the life of poet-celebrity. He died in Hull of cancer on December 2, 1985.

ANALYSIS

If Rudyard Kipling's is the poetry of empire, then Philip Larkin's is the poetry of the aftermath of empire. Having lived through the divestiture of England's various colonial holdings, the economic impact of empire building having finally come home, together with the ultimate travesty of imperial pretensions and the nightmare of Nazi and Soviet colonization in Europe, Larkin was wary of the expansiveness, the acquisitiveness, and the grandeur implicit in the imperial mentality. Many features of his poetry can be traced to that wariness: from the skepticism and irony, to the colloquial diction, to the formal precision of his poems.

Indeed, of all the writers who shared those ideals and techniques and who came to be known in the 1950's as the Movement, Larkin most faithfully retained his original attitude and style. Those writers—Kingsley Amis, Donald Davie, John Wain, Elizabeth Jennings, and Thom Gunn, among others—diverse though they were, shared attitudes that were essentially empirical, antimodernist, skeptical, and ironic. Most of those views can be understood as outgrowths of an elemental alienation from society and its traditional institutions. Amis's Jim Dixon is the outstanding fictional embodiment of these attitudes; although he desperately wants and needs to be accepted into university society and the traditional power structure it represents, his contempt for the institution and those in it, bred of his alienation, carries him into situations that border on both hilarity and disaster. *Lucky Jim* (1954) is *the* Movement novel.

Isolation and alienation figure prominently in both of Larkin's novels, as well; yet it is in his poems that they receive their fullest development. The speakers of his poems—and in the great majority of cases the speaker is the poet himself—seem alienated from their surroundings, cut off from both people and institutions. While that alienation normally shows itself as distance, as irony and wry humor, it can sometimes appear as smugness, complacence, even sneering judgment. Larkin turns his sense of isolation, of being an outsider or fringe observer, into a position of centrality, in which the world from which he is alienated seems to be moving tangentially to his own sphere. In his best poems, that distance works two ways, allowing the poet to observe the world in perspective, as if viewing it through the wrong end of a pair of binoculars, so that weighty matters seem less momentous, while at the same time reminding the poet that he, too, is a figure of little consequence. When his poems fail, the poet risks very little of his own ego as he sits back in safety, judging others across the frosty distance.

Larkin gains his perspective in large measure through his belief that nothing lies beyond this world, that this existence, however muddled it may be, is probably the only one. His skepticism is thoroughgoing and merciless; he rarely softens his tone. In some writers such belief might provoke terror or a compulsion to reform the world. In Larkin, it gives rise to irony. He examines the feeble inhabitants of this tiny planet surrounded by the void and asks if it can all be so important.

The resulting sense of human insignificance, including his own, leads him to several of the characteristic features of his work. He rejects "poetic" devices in favor of simpler, more mundane vehicles. His diction, for example, is nearly always colloquial, often coarse, vulgar, or profane. His distrust of a specialized diction or syntax for poetry reflects his distrust of institutions generally. Similarly, he shies away from the intense poetic moment—image, symbol, metaphor—in favor of a discursive, argumentative verse. Although he will occasionally resolve a poem through use of an image or a metaphor, particularly in *High Windows*, he more commonly talks his way through the poem, relying on intellect rather than emotion or intuition.

This rejection of the stuff of poetry leads him to a problem: If overtly poetic language and poetic devices are eschewed, what can the poet use to identify his poems as poems? For Larkin the answer lies in the external form of the poems: scansion, rhyme schemes, stanzaic patterns. The tension and the power of a Larkin poem often result from the interplay of common, unexceptional language with rigorously formal precision. "The Building," from *High Windows*, is an example of such tension. The poet meditates on the function of the hospital in modern society and the way in which it takes over some of the duties traditionally performed by the Church, all in very ordinary language. The poem, however, is stretched taut over not one but two sophisticated units: a seven-line stanza and an eight-line rhyme scheme (*abcbdad*). Rhyme pattern and stanzaic pattern come together at the end of the eighth stanza, but the poem does not end there; rather, the poet employs another rhyme unit, a stanza plus a line, as a means of resolving the poem. Even here Larkin's shrewd distrust of the intellectual viability of poetic forms displays itself: Ending neatly on the fifty-sixth line would be too neat, too pat, and would violate the poem's ambivalence toward the place. Similarly, although his rhyme schemes are often very regular, the same cannot be said for the rhymes themselves: speech/touch, faint/went, home/welcome. If Larkin recognizes his need for traditional forms in his poems, he recognizes also the necessity of altering those forms into viable elements of his poetry.

Finally, there is in Larkin a sense of an ending, of oblivion. For all his distrust of the "new apocalypse crowd," many of his poems suggest something similar, although with a characteristic difference. Where the "crowd" may prophesy the end of the world and everything in it, he, working out of his alienation, more commonly seems to be watching the string run out, as if he were a spectator at the edge of oblivion.

THE NORTH SHIP

Larkin's first volume of poetry, *The North Ship*, went virtually unnoticed at the time of its original publication and would be unnoticed still were it made to stand on its own merits. (It has few.) The poems are almost uniformly derivative Yeatsian juvenilia, laden with William Butler Yeats's imagery but shorn of its power or meaning; this is the verse of a young man who wants to become a poet by sounding like a known poet. No one has been more critical, moreover, of the volume than the poet himself, characterizing it as an anomaly, a mistake that happened when he did not know his own voice and thought, under the tutelage of Vernon Watkins, that he was someone else. That he allowed the republication of the work in 1966, with an introduction that is more than anything else a disclaimer, suggests a desire to distance the "real" poet from the confused adolescent.

Despite his objections, the book can be seen as representative of certain tendencies in his later verse, and it is enlightening to discern how many features of his mature work show themselves even when buried under someone else's style. A major difference between Larkin's poems and Yeats's lies in the use of objects: While the younger poet borrows Yeats's dancers, horses, candles, and moons, they remain dancers, horses, candles, and moons. They lack transcendent, symbolic value; objects remain mere objects.

There is also in these early poems a vagueness in the description of the phenomenal world. Perhaps that generality, that vagueness, could be explained as the result of the Yeatsian influence, but it is also a tendency of Larkin's later work. One often has the impression that a scene, particularly a human scene, is typical rather than specific.

One of the things clearly missing from this first work is a suspicion of the Yeatsian symbols, attitudes, and gestures, almost none of which the mature Larkin can abide. His assertion that it was his intense reading of Hardy's poetry that rescued him from the pernicious influence of Yeats may have validity; more probably, time heals youthful excess, and during the period when he was outgrowing the poetry of *The North Ship*, he began a salutary reading of Hardy.

The Less Deceived

A striking development in Larkin's second book of poems, *The Less Deceived*, is his insistence on the mundane, the unexceptional, the commonplace. In "Born Yesterday," a poem on the occasion of Sally Amis's birth, for example, he counters the usual wishes for beauty or brilliance with the attractive (for him) possibility of being utterly unextraordinary, of fitting in wholly by having nothing stand out. This wish he offers, he says, in case the others do not come true, but one almost has the sense that he wishes also that the others will not come true, that being average is much preferable to being exceptional.

Larkin makes a similar case for the ordinary in the wickedly funny "I Remember, I Remember," which attacks the Romantic notions of the writer's childhood as exemplified in D. H. Lawrence's *Sons and Lovers* (1913). In other places, he has described his childhood as boring, not worthy of comment, and in this poem, he pursues that idea vigorously. In the first two stanzas, he comes to the realization that he does not recognize the Coventry station into which the train has pulled, although he used it often as a child. When his traveling companion asks if Coventry is where he "has his roots," the poet responds in his mind with a catalog of all the things that never happened to him that supposedly happen to writers in their youth, "the splendid family/ I never ran to," "The bracken where I never sat trembling." Through the course of that list, he recognizes that the place looks so foreign now because it never gave him anything distinctive, that there is nothing that he carries with him that he can attribute to it. Then, in a remarkable about-face, he realizes that the location has very little to do with how his childhood was spent or misspent, that life is largely independent of place, that the alienation that he senses is something he carries with him, not a product of Coventry.

The poem at first seems to be an honest appraisal of his youth in contradistinction to all those romanticized accounts in biographies and novels, but the reader is forced finally to conclude that the poet protests too much. There is no childhood in which nothing happens, and in insisting so strongly on the vacuum in which he grew up, Larkin develops something like the inverse of nostalgia. He turns his present disillusionment and alienation back against the past and views it from his ironic perspective. Larkin is often the victim of his own ironies, and in this poem, his victim is memory.

His irony, in this poem as in so many, is used defensively; he wards off criticism by beating everyone to the punch. Irony is in some respects safer than laying oneself open for inspection. In many of his finest poems, however, he drops his guard and allows himself to think seriously about serious subjects. The foremost example in *The Less Deceived* is "Church Going." The title turns out to be marvelously ambiguous, appearing at first blush to be a mere reference to attending church, but then becoming, as the poem progresses, an elliptical, punning reference to churches going out of fashion.

The first two stanzas are curtly dismissive in a manner often encountered in Larkin, as he describes his stop from a bicycle trip at a church that is apparently Ulster Protestant. Neither he (since he stops for a reason he cannot name and acts guilty as he looks around) nor the church (since it is not at all out of the ordinary) seems worthy of attention. He leaves, thinking the church "not worth stopping for." In the third stanza, however, the poem shifts gears in a way typical of Larkin's finest work: the dismissive attitude toward mundane existence, the wry observations give way to serious contemplation. "Church Going," in fact, contains two such shifts.

In stanzas 3 through 7, Larkin reflects on the fate of churches when people stop going altogether—whether they will become places that people will avoid or seek out because of superstition, or become museums, or be turned to some profane use—and wonders, as well, who will be the last person to come to the church and what his reasons will be. Larkin has a sense, conveyed in a number of poems, that he and his generation of skeptics will be the end of religion in England, and in this poem he wonders about the results of that doubting. The final stanza contains yet another shift, this one rather more subtle. As if the "serious house on serious earth" were forcing the poet to be more serious, he shifts away from his musings about its fate, which are after all only another kind of dismissal, and recognizes instead the importance of the place. He suggests, finally, that the shallowness and disbelief of modern people cannot eradicate the impulse to think seriously and seek wisdom that the Church, however outmoded its rituals, represents.

The Whitsun Weddings

The two finest poems in Larkin's succeeding volume display similar movements of thought. In the title poem, "The Whitsun Weddings," the movement takes on further embellishment; not only does the poem move from dismissiveness to contemplation, but also the language of the poem moves from specificity toward generality in a way that mirrors the theme. The poem also contains one of Larkin's favorite devices: the use of a train ride (occasionally a car ride) to depict the movement of thought.

The poem opens with the concern for specificity of someone who, like the speaker, is late; when the train leaves the station at "one-twenty," it is "three-quarters-empty." He catches glimpses of scenery along the way, none of it very interesting, much of it squalid and polluted. Not until the third stanza (suggesting the incompleteness of his detailed observation) does he notice the wedding parties at each station. Even then, it is with the dismissive attitude of someone who, as a professional bachelor and alienated outsider, rather scorns the tackiness of the families gathered on the platforms to see the couples off, as well as that of the unreflective couples with whom he shares the coach. His ironical, detailed description takes up most of the next five stanzas.

Toward the end of stanza 7, however, he undergoes a change, has a moment of vision in which the postal districts of London appear as "squares of wheat." That image leads him, in the final stanza, to see the couples as symbols of fertility, so that finally the slowing train inspires in him an image of arrows beyond the scope of his vision, "somewhere becoming rain." That he loosens the reins of his vision, so that he can describe not merely what he sees but also what he can only envision, is a major development in his attitude from the beginning of the poem. It demonstrates a breaking down, however slight or momentary, of his alienation from the common run of existence and of his resistance to recognizing his own relationship with these others. The poem may ultimately be judged a failure because of the brevity of that breaking down, but the image it spawns of fertility and life just beginning is magnificent.

"Dockery and Son" displays a similar movement and is a stronger poem because the poet is forced to lower his defenses much earlier and reveal himself more fully during the course of his meditation. An offhand comment by the Dean that a fellow student now has a son at school sets the speaker's mind in motion. His first musings on the train home are again mundane, dismissive, of the "you-never-know-do-you" sort, and so boring that he falls asleep. On reconsideration, though, the poet experiences the shock of being brought up hard against the reality of having missed, irrevocably, what is for most men a major part of life—familial relations. Even this reflection remains thin and unsatisfactory, and he moves on to explore the nature of unquestioned and unquestioning belief and its source, deciding that it results not from wisdom or truth but from habit and style grown sclerotic. Yet those beliefs are what a man's life turns on, producing a son for Dockery and nothing for the poet.

At this point, very late in the poem, Larkin develops one of his marvelous reversals on the word "nothing." For most, it connotes an absence, a negation, a nonentity, but for Larkin "nothing" is a positive entity, a thing or force to be reckoned with, "Nothing with all a son's harsh patronage." The line suggests that the poet has had to wrestle with this "nothing" he has created even as a father, such as Dockery, has had to wrestle with the problems brought on by having a son. The similarity, however, does not stop there; the poet goes on to recognize the common fate that awaits not only Dockery and himself but everyone as well. Most commentators read the final phrase, "the only end of age," as meaning death, and certainly that meaning is there. Nevertheless, to understand it as merely meaning death is to lose some of the force it holds for the speaker. Rather, it must be read back through the stanza and the poem as a whole, so that the emphasis on nothingness informs that certain knowledge of death. That the poet not only knows he will die but also has already tasted the nothingness he knows, as an unbeliever, that death entails, makes the experience of that knowledge the more poignant. As is so often true in Larkin's work, that poignancy, which could border on self-pity, is tempered by the understanding that he at least comprehends, and there lies behind the poem's ending an unstated irony aimed at those such as Dockery who engage life so fully as to obscure that reality.

Again, that constant strain of alienation insinuates its way into poem after poem. Throughout *The Whitsun Weddings*, the poet feels himself cut off from his fellow humans, often struggling to retrieve a spirit of community with them, sometimes simply wondering why it is so. The volume, while it represents little change from its predecessor, renders a picture of a man in middle age who feels life passing him by, and who sees more and more clearly the inevitable. Settings are close, small; lives are petty, insignificant; society is filled with graffiti and pollution. In "The Importance of Elsewhere," he finds comfort in being a foreigner in Ireland, since at least he can explain his estrangement from his fellow inhabitants there. In England, ostensibly at home, he has no such excuse.

HIGH WINDOWS

A number of the poems in *High Windows* display that estrangement, often in unsettlingly smug tones. "Afternoons," in the previous book, shows Larkin at his judgmental worst, picking out nasty little details of petty lives and common tastes. In this volume, "The Old Fools," a poem that is often praised for its unexpected ending, displays a similar attitude. After railing against the infirmity and senility of the elderly throughout the poem, the tag line of "Well, we shall find out" rings false, sounding too much like an attempt to dodge inevitable criticism.

"Going, Going" presents some of the same problems, yet it implicates the poet in his critique in a way that "The Old Fools" does not. What is going is England itself, and that entity, it turns out, is place, not people. People have ruined the landscape and the architecture, reducing everything to rubbish. The poem redeems itself through its linguistic implication of its creator. The piece remains polemical throughout, avoiding the impulse to resolve through metaphor, as if the misanthropic, gloomy sensibility demands a crabbed style distrustful of the richness of figurative language and, perhaps, mirroring the destruction of English literature: If "carved choirs," echoing as they do William Shakespeare's "bare ruined choirs where late the sweet birds sang," are ruined and replaced with "concrete and tyres," then this poem's language is the replacement for Shakespeare's. Everywhere the poet turns, he finds traditional institutions, including poetry, degraded into mundane modern forms.

A much finer expression of that discovery is to be found in "The Building," which brings together numerous themes and ideas from throughout Larkin's canon. Like "Dockery and Son," it is a meditation on the foretaste of death; like "Going, Going," a consideration of the degradation of institutions in the modern world; like "Church Going," a questioning of what people shall do without churches.

The first two stanzas examine the ways the building in which the speaker sits resembles so many other modern buildings—high-rise hotels, airport lounges—although there is something disturbingly unlike them, as well. Not until the end of the second stanza does he reveal that it is a hospital. What unites people here is the common knowledge of their own mortality; even if they are not to die immediately, they are forced by the place to confront the fact that they will die eventually. The inescapability of that knowledge tames and calms the people in the building, as once the knowledge of death and its aftermath quieted them in church.

The recognition of this similarity grows slowly but steadily throughout the poem. The words keep insinuating a connection: "confess," "congregations," a "locked church" outside. The reaction people have in the hospital also suggests a function similar to that of the Church; outside they can hide behind ignorance or refusal to face facts, while inside the hospital those illusions are stripped away and reality is brought into the clear, sharp light, the unambiguous clarity of hospital corridors. This growing realization culminates in a final understanding that unless the modern hospital is more powerful than the traditional cathedral (and Larkin, suspicious of all institutions, does not think it is), then nothing can stop the ineluctable fate that awaits humanity, although (and now the similarities are overwhelming) every night people bring offerings, in the form of flowers, as they would to church.

A remarkable poem such as "The Building" can overcome a score of "Afternoons," and what is more remarkable about it is the way Larkin overcomes his initial alienation to speak not only at, but also to, and even for, his fellow humans and their very real suffering. His finest poems end, like this one, in benedictions that border on the "Shantih" of T. S. Eliot's *The Waste Land* (1922), giving the reader the sense that a troubling journey has reached a satisfying end.

Collected Poems

The publication of his *Collected Poems* in 1988 brought to light scores of poems previously uncollected, long out of print, or unavailable to the general reading public. These poems will not significantly alter Larkin's reputation, other than to expand the base on which it rests. For fans of his work, however, the additions prove quite valuable, showing as they do the movement from juvenilia to maturity. The early work displays even more clearly than, say, *The North Ship* the various influences on the young poet: Yeats and W. H. Auden. A work such as "New Year Poem" demonstrates a remarkable prescience, dated as it is the day before (and written an ocean away from) Auden's famous "New Year Letter" of 1941; both poems look at the future and consider the social and spiritual needs in a time of crisis.

Larkin, ever parsimonious, wrote very few poems during the last decade of his life: *Collected Poems* reveals a mere seventeen. Many of those concern themselves with his standard topics—the ravages of age, the sense of not being in step with the rest of society, the approach of death. In "The Mower," for example, he ruminates on having run over a hedgehog in the tall grass, killing it. From this experience, he takes away a feeling of responsibility for the death, a sense of the loss of this fellow creature, and the reflection that, given our limited time, we should be kind to one another. This slight poem (eleven lines) sums up much of Larkin's thought in his later years: Death is a complete cessation of experience, not a transmutation but a blankness, an end, while life itself is a vale of unhappiness, and people therefore owe it to themselves and one another to make the way as pleasant as possible.

In "Aubade," perhaps the most substantial of the late poems, Larkin writes of the approach of death, now another day closer because it is a new morning. He declares that we have never been able to accept death, yet are also unable to defeat it. Once religion offered the consolation of afterlife; for Larkin, that promise is no longer valid. What people fear most, he asserts, is the absence of sensation, of affect, that is death, as well as the absolute certainty of its coming. His "morning poem" is really a poem of the dark night of the soul. The fifth, and final, ten-line stanza brings the light of day and the unmindful routine of the workaday world, the routine that acts as a balm by taking our minds off our ultimate problem. Indeed, the poem's closing image presents those representatives of the mundane, postal carriers, going among houses like doctors, their daily rounds offering temporary solace.

These two poems present Larkin's typically ironic approach to the literary tradition. "The Mower" is a highly unconventional garden song. Although its title recalls Andrew Marvell's poems "The Garden" and "The Mower, Against Gardens," it shares none of their pastoral innocence or coyness. It finds death, not life, in the world of nature. Similarly, he subverts the traditional use of the aubade form to discuss not the coming day but also a coming night. In both cases, he undermines traditionally upbeat forms. Yet these poems also point to the playfulness of which Larkin was capable even in his bleakest moments, finding amusement in poems of abject despair. That may prove to be his great gift, the ability to face darkness fully, to take it in, and still to laugh, to be ironic even about last things.

Other major works

long fiction: *Jill*, 1946, 1964; *A Girl in Winter*, 1947.

nonfiction: *Selected Letters of Philip Larkin, 1940-1985*, 1992 (Anthony Thwaite, editor); *Further Requirements: Interviews, Broadcasts, Statements, and Book Reviews, 1952-1985*, 2001 (Anthony Thwaite, editor); *Larkin's Jazz: Essays and Reviews, 1940-1984*, 2001 (Richard Palmer and John White, editors).

edited texts: *New Poems*, 1958 (with Louis MacNeice and Bonamy Dobrée); *The Oxford Book of Twentieth-Century English Verse*, 1973.

miscellaneous: *All What Jazz: A Record Diary, 1961-1968*, 1970; *Required Writings: Miscellaneous Pieces, 1955-1982*, 1984.

Bibliography

Booth, James. *Philip Larkin: The Poet's Plight*. New York: Palgrave Macmillan, 2005. Offers readers insight into the themes of Larkin's poetry and the histories behind them.

_______, ed. *New Larkins for Old: Critical Essays*. New York: St. Martin's Press, 2000. A collection of essays on Larkin's work by established commentators and younger critics. Individual essays examine Larkin's novels and poetry in the light of psychoanalytical, postmodern, and postcolonial theories.

Bradford, Richard. *First Boredom, Then Fear: The Life of Philip Larkin*. Chester Springs, Pa.: Dufour Editions, 2005. A biography of Larkin that delves into his youth, romances, and career as a poet.

Castronovo, David. *Blokes: The Bad Boys of English Literature*. New York: Continuum, 2009. Discusses the poets Larkin, Kinsley Amis, John Osborne, and Kenneth Tynan. Examines socialism and radicalism in their works.

Leader, Zachary, ed. *The Movement Reconsidered: Essays on Larkin, Amis, Gunn, Davie, and Their Contemporaries*. New York: Oxford University Press, 2009. This work on the Movement poets sheds light on their views and poetry. Contains three essays on Larkin.

Motion, Andrew. *Philip Larkin: A Writer's Life*. New York: Farrar, Straus and Giroux, 1993. This short work provides an introduction to the man and his work. The book offers thematic and literary-historical overviews, although only one chapter on the poems themselves.

Osborne, John. *Larkin, Ideology and Critical Violence: A Case of Wrongful Conviction*. New York: Palgrave Macmillan, 2007. Osborne sees Larkin as a poet of undecidability, part of the transition to postmodernist indeterminacy.

Palmer, Richard. *Such Deliberate Disguises: The Art of Philip Larkin*. New York: Continuum, 2008. Palmer examines the poetry of Larkin at length.

Rossen, Janice. *Philip Larkin: His Life's Work*. New York: Simon & Schuster, 1989. This intelligent and highly readable overview traces Larkin's development through the first two books, then looks at his lyric impulse, his firmly rooted Englishness, his sexual ambivalence, his use of vulgarity, and his struggle with mortality. The study ties in the poetry with the novels, jazz criticism, and literary criticism to develop a total view of the context of the poetry.

Stojkovic, Tijana. *Unnoticed in the Casual Light of Day: Philip Larkin and the Plain Style*. New York: Routledge, 2006. This comprehensive linguistic and historical study of plain style poetry examines Larkin's poetry from that framework.

Thomas C. Foster

MICHAEL MCCLURE

Born: Marysville, Kansas; October 20, 1932

PRINCIPAL POETRY

Passage, 1956
Peyote Poem, 1958
For Artaud, 1959
Hymns to St. Geryon, and Other Poems, 1959
Dark Brown, 1961
The New Book/A Book of Torture, 1961
Ghost Tantras, 1964
Thirteen Mad Sonnets, 1964
Two for Bruce Conner, 1964
Dream Table, 1965
Mandalas, 1965
Poisoned Wheat, 1965
Unto Caesar, 1965
Love Lion Book, 1966
Hail Thee Who Play, 1968, 1974
The Sermons of Jean Harlow and the Curses of Billy the Kid, 1968
Hymns to St. Geryon/Dark Brown, 1969
"Little Odes," and "The Raptors," 1969
The Surge, 1969
Star, 1970
The Book of Joanna, 1973
Solstice Blossom, 1973
A Fist Full, 1956-1957, 1974
Fleas 189-195, 1974
An Organism, 1974
Rare Angel (writ with raven's blood), 1974
September Blackberries, 1974
Jaguar Skies, 1975
Man of Moderation, 1975
Antechamber, and Other Poems, 1978
Fragments of Perseus, 1983
Selected Poems, 1986
Rebel Lions, 1991
Simple Eyes, and Other Poems, 1994

Three Poems: "Dolphin Skull," "Rare Angel," and "Dark Brown," 1995
Huge Dreams, 1999
Rain Mirror: New Poems, 1999
Touching the Edge: Dharma Devotions from the Hummingbird Sangha, 1999
The Masked Choir: A Masque in the Shape of an Enquiry into the Treena and Sheena Myth, 2000

OTHER LITERARY FORMS

Michael McClure is the author of more than twenty plays. A production in New York of *The Beard* (pr., pb. 1965) won Obie Awards for best play and best director. In 1978, McClure's *Josephine, the Mouse Singer* was produced at the WPA Theatre in New York and won the Obie Award for Best Play of the Year. His autobiographical novel *The Mad Cub* (1970) set many of the central themes, moods, and goals for his writing. *Meat Science Essays* (1963) provides scientific and ecological background for McClure's other writings. *Scratching the Beat Surface* (1982) and *Lighting the Corners* (1993) offer theories of art, memoirs of the Beat generation, and interviews.

McClure's work as an editor is revealed in *Ark II, Moby I* (1957) and *Journal for the Protection of All Beings* (1961). Performances by McClure have been recorded on video in *Love Lion* (1991) and in the audio recording *Howls, Raps, and Roars* (1993). He may also be seen in the film *The Source* (2000).

ACHIEVEMENTS

Michael McClure has been committed to full and open exploration of consciousness, perception, sexual fulfillment, and artistic action. To this end, McClure pursued an interdisciplinary approach to his work. He argues against environmental destruction and seeks to protect and enhance the planet. In all, he stands as a positive and unifying force in art, science, literature, and ecology. Often published through small presses dedicated to artistry in the making of books, his work reflects a combination of spontaneous creativity and enduring, specialized publication.

McClure has been the recipient of grants from the National Endowment for the Arts, the Guggenheim Foundation, and the Rockefeller Foundation, and has won the Alfred Jarry Award (1973), several Obie Awards for his theater work, and a Pushcart Prize (1991). The National Poetry Association honored McClure for distinguished lifetime achievement in poetry in 1993, and he received the Northern California Book Award in poetry in 1999 for *Touching the Edge*.

BIOGRAPHY

Michael Thomas McClure was born to Thomas and Marian Dixie Johnston McClure in Marysville, Kansas, and he soon gained a sense of the immensity of the plains. Following the divorce of his parents, he lived in Seattle, Washington, with his maternal grandfather, whose interests included medicine, ornithology, and horticulture. In Seattle, the rich forests and stunning beaches excited McClure's young imagination. At age twelve, McClure returned to Kansas, where he lived with his mother and her new husband.

In high school, McClure and his friend Bruce Conner developed an interest in abstract expressionist painters, including Clyfford Still, Mark Rothko, and Jackson Pollock. As a writer, McClure pursued traditional forms and patterns, composing a collection of villanelles as his project for a creative writing course at Wichita University. At the University of Arizona, he studied anthropology and painting, but after meeting Joanna Kinnison, McClure fell in love, married, and traveled with her to San Francisco. Though disappointed not to find Mark Rothko and Clyfford Still teaching in San Francisco, McClure took delight in the Bay Area's natural splendor. After meeting the poet Robert Duncan, McClure reaffirmed his focus on poetry, exploring the tension between Duncan's advice to experiment and McClure's own need to work with traditional forms.

In 1956, McClure's first publication of his poems—two villanelles dedicated to Theodore Roethke—appeared in *Poetry*. In the same year, McClure coedited *Ark II, Moby I*, in which he brought together San Francisco writers with Black Mountain writers, including Charles Olson and Robert Creeley. The maturation of McClure's poetics followed, in large part, from an extended correspondence with Olson. In 1956, *Passage*, McClure's first book of poetry, was published.

A production of McClure's play *The Beard* was offered at the Actor's Workshop in San Francisco in 1965; the play's sexual frankness resulted in the arrest of several of the actors and producers. With support from the American Civil Liberties Union, *The Beard* survived efforts to stifle its production.

With these varied accomplishments behind him, McClure settled into a diverse and prolific artistic career. He is an avant-garde figure whose participation in and commentaries about spontaneity, music, art, and the environment are central to understanding his artistic generation. In addition to sustaining academic positions or fellowships at institutions such as the California College of Arts and Crafts (Oakland), State University of New York, Buffalo, and Yale University's Pierson College, he has edited literary and ecology journals, has lectured widely, and has continued to publish.

ANALYSIS

Michael McClure's first published poems were two villanelles dedicated to Theodore Roethke published in the January, 1956, issue of *Poetry*. The works reveal McClure grounded in the requirements of the villanelle, but in "Premonition," he expresses his need to soar and fly. "Beginning in the heart," writes McClure, "I work towards light." He insists, "My eyes are spiralled up"; he adds, "Feet burn to walk the mackerel sky at night," and "Ears are aching for the Great Bird's bite." Nevertheless, the poem concludes with the idea that McClure's earthly "skin and wingless skull . . . grow tight." He longs for ascent, but his longing is not yet fulfilled.

The second villanelle reinforces and intensifies the sense of confinement and limitation. McClure is mindful of "Elysium" but finds that it "is dwindled." His body is likened to a "corpse," his hands are his "defeat," and his eyes are "dumb." The "ouzel" (a thrush) and the "undine" (a water spirit) represent the loftiness that McClure longs for, but the poem declares that they are "past and future sense, not circumstance." In these poems, McClure reveals the heavy thought and meticulous craftsmanship of Roethke, but McClure outlines the aim at transcendence that marks all his subsequent writings.

The historic second issue of *Evergreen Review* includes poems also found in *Passage* and *Hymns to St. Geryon, and Other Poems*. "Night Words: The Ravishing" expresses calm and satisfaction as McClure declares, "How beautiful things are in a beautiful room." He enjoys "ambrosial insomnia," finds that the "room is softened," and repeatedly states pleasure about the fact that the features of the room are "without proportion."

"The Rug"

In "The Rug," McClure draws a contrast between experience and the poem as a record of the experience. Describing intimacy, McClure writes, "I put my hands// to you—like cool jazz coming." Yet even in the act of describing the intimacy, words are insufficient, and McClure insists, "THIS IS NOT IT." The poem may be colorful and elegant but ultimately "is failure, no trick, no end/ but speech for those who'll listen." Nevertheless, the insufficiency of language does not prevent experience from rising to special excitement.

"The Robe"

In "The Robe," McClure returns to the subject of intimacy, telling his lover that they "float about each other—// bare feet not touching the floor." McClure writes, "Aloof as miracles. Hearing/ jazz in the air. We are passing—//our shapes like nasturtiums." Although "HEROIC ACTS/ won't free" the lovers, they do find blissful sleep. The poems in this issue of *Evergreen Review* present McClure alongside Jack Kerouac, Allen Ginsberg, Lawrence Ferlinghetti, and other major writers of the so-called San Francisco scene, marking McClure as a major contributor to the San Francisco poetry renaissance.

"Hymn to St. Geryon, I"

Donald Allen's *The New American Poetry, 1945-1960* (1960) presents poems from *Hymns to St. Geryon, and Other Poems* and *For Artaud* and places McClure in the context of a broad national awakening in poetry marked by multiple and interacting schools of poetry. The poems in the anthology fully demonstrate McClure's attempt to liberate himself and the form of poetry through experimentation in language and sensory experience. The lines are not aligned but are freely distributed on the page. Rhyme and metrics have no place in the record of the action of the mind and body.

"Hymn to St. Geryon, I" is a statement of poetic philosophy and method. At the outset, McClure cites abstract expressionist Clyfford Still, who commits himself to "an unqualified act" and states, "Demands for communication are presumptuous and irrelevant." McClure insists, "But the thing I say!! Is to see." He wants to turn "THE GESTURE" into "fists" so that he can "hit with the thing" and "make a robe of it/ TO WEAR" and thereby "clothe" him and his readers "in the action." McClure asserts, "I am the body, the animal, the poem/ is a gesture of mine."

"PEYOTE POEM, PART I"

In "Peyote Poem, Part I," McClure explores hallucinogenic experience, aware that he and his belly "are two individuals/ joined together/ in life." His mind rides high "on a mesa of time and space," yet his body exerts its authority with "STOMACHE." The effect of the peyote is intense, but McClure is calm in his intensity, saying, "I smile to myself. I know/ all that there is to know. I see all there/ is to feel." In sum, peyote provides a transcendent experience.

"FOR ARTAUD"

Like "Peyote Poem," "For Artaud" describes the effects of hallucinogens, including heroin and peyote. McClure writes, "I am free and open from the blackness." He asks, "Let me feel great pain and strength of suffering." In the spirit of French writer Antonin Artaud, McClure seeks heightened awareness through derangement of his ordinary sensory impressions.

SELECTED POEMS

In 1986, McClure published *Selected Poems*, which gathered material from nine of his previous books. From *The New Book/A Book of Torture*, McClure selects "Ode to Jackson Pollock," a tribute to the abstract expressionist who rendered "the lovely shape of chaos," found "the secret/ spread in clouds of color," and pressed experience through himself "onto the canvas." From *"Little Odes" and "The Raptors"* appears "Hummingbird Ode," in which McClure addresses a dead hummingbird. McClure speaks to this "spike of desire" that met its end by smashing into a plate-glass window. McClure asks the hummingbird, "WHAT'S/ ON YOUR SIDE OF THE VEIL??/ DO YOU DIP YOUR BEAK/ in the vast black lily/ of space?"

From *Star*, McClure selected "The Surge," an exclamatory poem that McClure, in a prefatory note, describes as "the failure of an attempt to write a beautiful poem." McClure insists that there is "a more total view!" asserting, "The Surge of Life may not be seen by male or female/ for both are halves." He asks, "Is all life a vast chromosome stretched in Time?" From *September Blackberries*, McClure includes "Gray Fox at Solstice," a poem in honor of the fox that savors "the beat of starlight/ on his brow, and ocean/ on his eardrums." At home in his "garden," the fox "dance-runs through/ the Indian paintbrush." A similar appreciation of wildlife occurs in "To a Golden Lion Marmoset," which is selected from *Jaguar Skies*. The animal is an endangered species, and McClure declares, "Your life is all I find/ to prove ours are worthwhile."

A selection from the long poem "Rare Angel" (1974) concludes *Selected Poems*. This poem "tracks vertically on the page" and seeks "luck—swinging out in every direction." Testing the limits of perception, consciousness, and reality, McClure writes, "We swirl out what we are and watch for its return."

McClure notes that he does not include any sampling of *Ghost Tantras* in *Selected Poems* because "beast language" does not coordinate with his other verse. *Ghost Tantras* is dominated by phrases such as "GOOOOOOR! GOOOOOOOOOO!" mixed with a few intelligible phrases, creating poetry based on sound rather than meaning, aiming at "the Human Spirit & all Mammals."

LATER POEMS

McClure's later poetry looks to both the past and present. *Huge Dreams* regathers the work of the early Beat period, and *Three Poems* presents anew Rare Angel and "Dark Brown," McClure's long and boldly erotic "ROMANTIC CRY." New in *Three Poems* is "Dolphin Skull," a long poem revealing subconscious and conscious artistic production. McClure writes, "Never say: Hold, let this moment never cease," then reverses himself, declaring, "HOLD, LET THIS MOMENT never cease. Drag it out/ of context look at the roots of it in quarks/ and primal hydrogen. It's the sound/ of Shelley's laugh in my ears." Both *Rain Mirror* and *Touching the Edge* are intended as vertical poems that scroll down. In *Rain Mirror*, the first series of poems is titled "Haiku Edge," and McClure writes, "HEY, IT'S ALL CON/ SCIOUSNESS—thumps/of assault/ rifles/ and/ the/ stars," pitting "con" against "consciousness" and violence against nature's serenity. The haiku often focus on such dualities. The second series of poems is "Crisis Blossoms," a sequence of "graftings." The poet explores memories and contemplates death: "BYE/ BYE/ SWEET/ OLD/ STORY/ HELLO/ FUTURE/ MAYBE/ UH/ WITH/ GHOST SMILE." *Touching the Edge* is a set of dharma devotions divided into three sequences: "RICE ROARING," "OVAL MUDRA," and "WET PLANK." McClure asks to be "cheerful/ and modest" as he reflects on the diversity around him, noticing not only fruit, flowers, and wildlife, but also chain saws, airplanes, and asphalt. He is calmly aware of both destruction and creation, and ultimately concludes that these forces are one and the same.

OTHER MAJOR WORKS

LONG FICTION: *The Mad Cub*, 1970.

PLAYS: *The Beard*, pr., pb. 1965; *The Growl*, pr. 1971; *Minnie Mouse and the Tap-Dancing Buddha*, pr. 1978; *Josephine, the Mouse Singer*, pr. 1978.

nonfiction: *Meat Science Essays*, 1963; *Scratching the Beat Surface*, 1982; *Lighting the Corners*, 1993; *A Fierce God and a Fierce War: An Interview with Michael McClure*, 2007 (with Rod Phillips).

edited texts: *Ark II, Moby I*, 1957 (with James Harmon); *Journal for the Protection of All Beings*, 1961.

Bibliography

Jacob, John, ed. "Symposium on Michael McClure." *Margins* 18 (1975). This special issue is entirely devoted to analysis and discussion of McClure.

Pekar, Harvey, et al. *The Beats: A Graphic History*. Art by Ed Piskor et al. New York: Hill and Wang, 2009. Comic legend Harvey Pekar provides a history of the Beat poets in this graphic book. Contains an entry on and references to McClure.

Phillips, Rod. "Let Us Throw Out the Word Man: Michael McClure's Mammalian Poetics." In *"Forest Beatniks" and "Urban Thoreaus": Gary Snyder, Jack Kerouac, Lew Welch, and Michael McClure*. New York: Peter Lang, 2000. Philips emphasizes McClure's fascination with nature and his combining of poetry with ideas in biology and ecology.

_______. *Michael McClure*. Boise, Idaho: Boise State University Press, 2003. A biography of McClure that looks at his place in the Beat generation and in the poetry scene in California.

Stephenson, Gregory. "From the Substrate: Notes on the Work of Michael McClure." In *The Daybreak Boys: Essays on the Literature of the Beat Generation*. Carbondale: Southern Illinois University Press, 1990. Stephenson provides a clear and thorough survey of McClure's writings, appreciating McClure's effort to heal humankind, to reconcile body and spirit, and to develop harmonious coexistence with the environment.

Thurley, Geoffrey. "The Development of the New Language: Michael McClure, Philip Whalen, and Gregory Corso." In *The Beats: Essays in Criticism*, edited by Lee Bartlett. Jefferson, N.C.: McFarland, 1981. Thurley examines McClure as a poet experimenting with hallucinogens, especially in "Peyote Poem," but expresses reservations about the validity of McClure's triumphs in perception while under the influence of narcotic substances.

Watson, Steven. "Michael McClure." In *The Birth of the Beat Generation*. New York: Pantheon, 1995. Watson provides a sketch of McClure's youth, education, and career, with recognition for McClure's interdisciplinary role among the Beats and his dedication to science and the environment.

William T. Lawlor

CHARLES OLSON

Born: Worcester, Massachusetts; December 27, 1910
Died: New York, New York; January 10, 1970

PRINCIPAL POETRY

Y & X, 1948
Letter for Melville 1951, 1951
This, 1952
In Cold Hell, in Thicket, 1953
The Maximus Poems 1-10, 1953
The Maximus Poems 11-22, 1956
O'Ryan 2 4 6 8 10, 1958 (expanded 1965, as *O'Ryan 12345678910*)
The Distances, 1960
The Maximus Poems, 1960
Charles Olson: Reading at Berkeley, 1966 (transcription)
The Maximus Poems, IV, V, VI, 1968
Archaeologist of Morning: The Collected Poems Outside the Maximus Series, 1970
The Maximus Poems, Volume 3, 1975
The Horses of the Sea, 1976
The Maximus Poems, 1983
The Collected Poems of Charles Olson: Excluding "The Maximus Poems," 1987
A Nation of Nothing but Poetry: Supplementary Poems, 1989
Selected Poems, 1993 (Robert Creeley, editor)

OTHER LITERARY FORMS

Charles Olson was a prolific essayist, espousing the essay form to advance his poetic concerns to a wider audience. His prose style can present as many difficulties as his poetry; however, difficulties to a large extent were deliberately sought by Olson, who was concerned that his literary production not be consumed too easily in an era of speed-reading. With *Call Me Ishmael: A Study of Melville*, a book-length study of Herman Melville, published in 1947, Olson announced his intention to define the United States for his day, even as he believed that Melville had defined the nation for his day in *Moby-Dick* (1851). Key essays published within four years of *Call Me Ishmael* include "The Human Universe" and the celebrated "Projective Verse," which, together with many others, may be found in one of several collections, namely *Human Universe, and Other Essays* (1965), *Selected Writings of Charles Olson* (1966), *Pleistocene Man* (1968), *Causal Mythology* (1969), *The Special View of History* (1970), *Poetry and*

Truth: The Beloit Lectures and Poems (1971), and *Additional Prose: A Bibliography on America, Proprioception, and Other Notes and Essays* (1974).

Olson's letters have also proved of much interest, and many are collected in *Mayan Letters* (1953), *Letters for "Origin," 1950-1956* (1969), and the series of volumes issuing from Black Sparrow Press of his correspondence with the poet Robert Creeley.

ACHIEVEMENTS

With his first poems and essays, Charles Olson caught the attention of readers ready, like himself, for a profound renaming of a present grown extremely ambiguous with the destruction of traditional values during World War II. This audience continued to grow, and with the publication of Donald Allen's anthology *The New American Poetry, 1945-1960* in 1960, a year that also saw the publication in one book of the first volume of *The Maximus Poems* and another book of poems, *The Distances*, he was widely hailed as a leader of a revolution in poetry. Olson's section in the Allen anthology came first and was the largest; the poetry conference held at the University of British Columbia in 1963, and another, held at the University of California, Berkeley, in 1965, were dominated by his presence. He remained center-stage until his death in 1970, and since then, his contribution has continued to receive attention from the scholarly community, and his influence is still evident in younger poets.

Olson spoke through his art to a historical moment that had come unhinged, and the cogency with which he advocated "screwing the hinges back on the door of civilization" inspired a fervor of response. Poets, editors, teachers, and lay readers formed a kind of "Olson underground," a network that disseminated the kinds of information which Olson's project favored, and these were various indeed: the founding and the decline of early civilizations (Sumer, Egypt, Greece, the Maya), the pre-Socratics, the Tarot, psychedelic drugs, non-Euclidean geometry, the philosophy of Alfred North Whitehead, and documents of the European settlement of New England—a far from exhaustive list. For the most part, Olson shunned publicity and was therefore less known to the counterculture of the 1960's than was his fellow poet Allen Ginsberg, but there can be no doubt that Olson, both in his own person and through this network, helped instigate and name the cultural revolution then attempted.

Olson's poetry instructs, deliberately, as do his essays. In this respect, it is noteworthy that his career as a teacher spanned four decades, starting at Clark University in the 1930's and resuming (after an interim during which he worked first for the American Civil Liberties Union and then in the Office of War Information) at Black Mountain College in the late 1940's. Olson continued to teach at Black Mountain until the college closed in 1956; he moved on to the State University of New York at Buffalo in 1963, where he worked for three years, and concluded his teaching career at the University of Connecticut. A partial list of his distinguished students includes John Wieners, Edward Dorn, Michael Rumaker, Fielding Dawson, Joel Oppenheimer, and Jonathan Williams.

While serving as rector of Black Mountain College, from 1951 to 1956, Olson turned it into a center of the literary arts and was responsible for the publication of the *Black Mountain Review* (edited by Creeley), which gave its name to the group of writers most often published therein.

Olson was the recipient of two Guggenheim grants, in 1939 to continue his work on his dissertation on Herman Melville and in 1948 to write about the interaction of racial groups during the settling of the American West. In 1952, he received a grant from the Wenner-Gren Foundation to study Mayan hieroglyphics in the Yucatan. (It is characteristic of Olson that he completed none of these projects within the guidelines proposed but instead transmuted them into poetic essays and poetry.) In 1965, he was awarded the Oscar Blumenthal-Charles Leviton Prize by *Poetry* magazine, possibly the most prestigious award he received for his poetry. His poetry was too radical, and his life too short, for further such acknowledgment to come his way during his lifetime. In 1984, his *The Maximus Poems* received the *Los Angeles Times* Book Prize. In 1988, *The Collected Poems of Charles Olson* received the American Book Award from the Before Columbus Foundation.

BIOGRAPHY

Charles John Olson was born on December 27, 1910, in the central Massachusetts town of Worcester. His mother, Mary Hines, was of Irish immigrant stock; his father, also named Charles, was of Swedish origin. Olson's giant proportions (fully grown, he was to stand six feet, nine inches) obviously came from his father's side, the elder Olson having stood well over six feet tall himself, whereas the poet's mother was barely above five feet tall. Olson's father worked as a letter carrier, a career the poet was to take up at one point in his life. From 1915 until he left home, Olson spent part of each summer with his family in Gloucester, a small seaport of Massachusetts north of Boston; he would later live there and anchor his Maximus poems in this, to him, "root city." In 1928, he entered Wesleyan University, being graduated in 1932 and receiving his M.A. there the following year; his thesis, "The Growth of Herman Melville, Prose Writer and Poetic Thinker," led him to discover hitherto unknown portions of Melville's library, and this, in turn, led to his paper "Lear and Moby-Dick," written in the course of his doctoral studies at Harvard and published in *Twice-a-Year* in 1938. Between 1932 and 1939, Olson supported himself either by grants or by teaching: at Clark University from 1934 to 1936 and at Harvard from 1936 to 1939.

In 1939, awarded a Guggenheim Fellowship, Olson lived with his widowed mother in Gloucester, laying the groundwork for what was to become *Call Me Ishmael*. In 1940, he moved to New York City, working first as publicity director for the American Civil Liberties Union and then as chief of the Foreign Language Information Service of the Common Council for American Unity. During this period, Olson met and married Constance Wilcock. From 1942 to 1944, Olson served as associate chief of the Foreign

Language Division of the Office of War Information, in Washington, D.C., and during Franklin D. Roosevelt's campaign for a fourth term in 1944, he served on the Democratic National Committee. The following year, he was offered high office in the new Democratic administration but chose instead to devote himself to writing, and with the help of Ezra Pound, whom Olson often visited at St. Elizabeths Hospital, he published *Call Me Ishmael* in 1947.

For the next ten years, Olson's life was to be closely associated with Black Mountain College, an experiment in education being carried on near Asheville, North Carolina, where he worked first as a lecturer and subsequently, starting in 1951, as rector. Olson during this period wrote his landmark essays on poetics and the poems that made up his book *The Distances*. Through Vincent Ferrini, a Gloucester poet, Olson met Robert Creeley, and a correspondence ensued that was to prove seminal to the movement in poetry known as Black Mountain poetry or projective verse (the latter from the Olson essay so titled). In 1954, Creeley came to teach at the college and edited the *Black Mountain Review*. Another poet, Robert Duncan—association with whom was to prove vital to Olson—also taught at Black Mountain during this time. Olson, meanwhile, had ended his first marriage (which produced one child, Katherine, born in 1951) and embarked on a second, to Elizabeth Kaiser, whom he met and married in 1954; their son, Charles Peter, was born in May of the following year.

As Black Mountain College was no longer proving fiscally viable, Olson closed it in 1956, the year that saw the publication of *The Maximus Poems 11-22* (*The Maximus Poems 1-10* had been issued in 1953). In 1957, Olson journeyed to San Francisco to read at the Museum of Art and The Poetry Center and to deliver in five lectures his "special view of history." Olson then settled with his wife and son in Gloucester, working on another volume of Maximus poems. The year 1960 was his *annus mirabilis*: He was included in the anthology *The New American Poetry, 1945-1960*, his Maximus poems were reissued as a single book, and his other poems were collected into the volume *The Distances*. Thenceforth Olson's star, in the ascendant throughout the previous decade, was much more visibly so, and he met his quickly growing audience at a number of venues, among these the Vancouver Poetry Conference (1963), the Festival of the Two Worlds in Spoleto, Italy (1965), the Berkeley Poetry Conference (1965), the Literary Colloquium of the Academy of Art in Berlin (1966), the International Poetry Festival in London (1967), and Beloit College (1968), where he delivered the lectures subsequently published as *Poetry and Truth*. Several collections of his essays were also issued during this decade. From 1963 to 1965, Olson served as visiting professor of English at the State University of New York at Buffalo; in 1969, he accepted a similar post at the University of Connecticut.

These years were marked, however, by dissipation and heartbreak. His wife died in an automobile accident in 1964; Olson's health began to fail, and in 1969, cancer of the liver was diagnosed; he died in a New York City hospital on January 10, 1970.

Analysis

Charles Olson's poetry is political in a profound, not superficial, sense; it does not spend time naming "current events," but rather devotes itself to defining "the dodges of discourse" that have enabled humanity (especially in the West) to withdraw from reality into increasingly abstract fictions of life. Olson came of age during the Great Depression and admired Roosevelt's New Deal, but with the death of the president in 1945 and the bombing of Hiroshima and Nagasaki, Olson lost faith in the possibilities for liberal democracy. Olson believed that it did not go wide enough or deep enough in the attempt to restore humanity's lost meaning—nor did it provide enough checks and balances against the corporate takeover of the world.

Resistance

Olson encouraged a resistance based on knowledge from a range of sources which he endeavored, through his essays and his poems, to bring to common attention. "Resistance," in fact, is a key word here: One of his first essays bears that title, and often, Olson's stance reminds one of the Maquis and other "underground" pockets of resistance to the fascists during World War II. His is a sort of intellectual commando operation bent on destroying, marshaling not yards or military arsenals but modes of thought (and therefore of action) that are out of kilter with current realities and "fascistic" in their ability to crush individual senses of value that would struggle toward a coherence—where the merely subjective might transcend itself and establish a vital community.

However sweeping Olson's proposals, in effect his program is reactive; such a reaction against the status quo was, as he saw it, the essential first step toward building a civilization that put people before profits. "When man is reduced to so much fat for soap, superphosphate for soil, fillings and shoes for sale," Olson wrote, the news of the Nazi death camps fresh in the minds of his audience as in his own, "he has, to begin again, one answer, one point of resistance only to such fragmentation, one organized ground. . . . It is his physiology he is forced to arrive at. . . . It is his body that is his answer."

This answer led Olson to ground his poetics in the physical breathing of the poet, the vital activity that registers the smallest fluctuations of thought and feeling. Language had become separated from being over the centuries of Western civilization, so that, for example, it became more important to carry out orders than to consider their often terrible consequences. In the words of Paul Christensen, "The denotational core of words must be rescued from neglect; logical classification and the principles of syntax must be suppressed and a new, unruly seizure of phenomena put in their place." Civilization, to the extent that it alienates one from one's experience of the actual earth and the life that arises therefrom, has failed, and it supplants with "slick pictures" the actual conditions of human lives.

Deconstructing authority

Therefore, it has become necessary, Olson argues, to deconstruct the accepted authorities of Western thought, while seeking to preserve the thought of such persons who, throughout history, have warned against systems of ideation that debase human beings. In Olson's vision, one of the great villains is Aristotle; one of the heroes, Apollonius of Tyana. With Aristotle, "the two great means appear: logic and classification. And it is they," Olson continues in the essay "Human Universe," "that have so fastened themselves on habits of thought that action is interfered with, absolutely interfered with, I should say." Olson in this same passage points out: "The harmony of the universe, and I include man, is not logical, or better, is post-logical, as is the order of any created thing." As for classification,

> What makes most acts—of living and of writing—unsatisfactory, is that the person and/or the writer satisfy themselves that they can only make a form . . . by selecting from the full content some face of it, or plane, some part. And at just this point, by just this act, they fall back on the dodges of discourse, and immediately, they lose me, I am no longer engaged, this is not what I know is the going-on. . . . It comes out a demonstration, a separating out, an act of classification, and so, a stopping.

"Apollonius of Tyana"

In "Apollonius of Tyana, a Dance, with Some Words, for Two Actors," Olson addresses the reader through the medium of a contemporary of Christ, Apollonius, and the play's one other character, Tyana, the place of his origin, as well as through himself, as narrator/commentator. This last tells how Apollonius "knows . . . that *his* job, at least, is to find out how to inform all people how best they can stick to the instant, which is both temporal and intense, which is both shape and law." Apollonius makes his way through the Mediterranean world of the first century C.E., which "is already the dispersed thing the West has been since," conducting "a wide investigation into the local, the occasional, what you might even call the ceremonial, but without . . . any assurance that he knows how to make objects firm, or how firm he is."

Apollonius, readers are told, learned from his journeyings

> that two ills were coming on man: (1) unity was crowding out diversity (man was getting too multiplied to stay clear by way of the old vision of himself, the humanist one, was getting too distracted to abide in his own knowing with any of his old confidence); and (2) unity as a goal (making Rome an empire, say) had, as its intellectual pole an equally mischievous concept, that of the universal—of the "universals" as Socrates and Christ equally had laid them down. Form . . . was suddenly swollen, was being taken as a thing larger a thing outside a thing above any particular, even any given man.

These descriptions of the confusions which beset Apollonius clearly apply to those Olson himself was encountering, and therefore readers look to find, in Apollonius's solutions, those of Olson. This part of the work, however, rings less convincingly: Olson makes some rhetorical flourishes, but in the end the reader is simply told that Apollonius has learned that he must "commit himself"; he has also learned that Tyana (surely a figure for Olson's Gloucester) is intimately connected with his endeavor.

Problems of discourse

Olson's brilliance when specifying the major ills and his vagueness when speaking to their cure, as well as his inability to resolve the inherent contradictions between the latter and the former (how shall individuals make themselves responsible for many of the elements in a society in whose false unity and swollen forms they themselves are caught and of which they are a part?), all so clearly to be seen in this piece, persist throughout his canon. It is the problem he recognizes in Melville, who finds splendid embodiment for his society's evils in Ahab but who can never create a convincing hero. Large answers, the sweeping solution, evade Olson by the very nature of his method, which is to focus on particulars, even on "the blessing/ that difficulties are once more."

These difficulties include the obvious truth that Olson is trammeled at the outset by the very tricks of discourse he would overthrow: Witness, for example, his sweeping generalization, near the beginning of his essay "Human Universe": "We have lived long in a generalizing time, at least since 450 B.C.E." Again, and on the other hand, given that he is urgent about reeducating his contemporaries to eradicate society's evils before it is too late, his refusal to write in received forms was bound to delay dissemination of his message. Moreover, while he was embodying the difficulties and the particularities in highly difficult and particular forms, and thereby rendering these virtually inaccessible except by the slow "trickle-down" process which accompanies aesthetically responsible art, he was given, in both poem and essay, to assertion without supporting evidence—such is the nature of the intuitive perception he espoused, as against a stupefied insistence on proof—and thereby to alienating many more conventionally trained readers.

Open verse

That Olson could not accomplish his project was a result of its inherent impossibility; this failure, however, in no way erases the spellbinding body of his poetry. His magnificent embodiment and evocation of the dilemma in which he found himself remains as both consolation and exhortation. He gave a rationale for free (or, to use his own term, Open) verse, of which his own work is the most telling demonstration; he gave a scale and a scope to poetry which inspired and continue to inspire other poets and which make his own poems among the most compelling of all time. If his more general prescriptions regarding society—true as they still ring, particularly in their diagnostics—have been largely ineffectual against the momentum of social change (surely, from Olson's point of view, for the worse), his speculations, conjecture, and assertions concerning the practice of poetry stay valid, viable, and vital. Moreover, his insistence that the poet (as Percy Bysshe Shelley thought, a century and more before) be lawgiver to those of his day must be a salutary thorn in the side of any practitioner of the art.

"The Kingfishers"

The power of Olson's finest poems stems from a double movement: The poet strives to fill his poem with the greatest variety of subject matter that he can, while at the same time, the poet strives to empty his poem of everything he has brought into it. The plethora of subject matter (information, often conflicting) is there to say that the world is absolutely fascinating—its details are fit matter for anyone's attention; the act of emptying these out is to say nothing is as important, as worthy of attention, as the moment about to come into being.

"The Kingfishers" is a case in point: A quick topic sentence ("What does not change/ is the will to change"; "As the dead prey upon us,/ they are the dead in ourselves"), broad enough in application, allows Olson to bring in all manner of materials by logical or intuitive association that somehow fit under its rubric: Meditation upon change leads, first, to a recalled cocktail party conversation that touched upon the passing of the fashion for kingfishers' feathers; this soon leads Olson to recall Mao Zedong's speech upon the success of his revolution. A dialectic having now been set up between West (tyrannized by its markets—"fashion"—and associated with a dying civilization) and East (Mao's revolution, source of the rising sun), the poem proceeds to "dance" (one of Olson's favorite terms, used to denote the poetic act), its details representing East/novelty/uprising in among those representing West/stagnation/descent, in a vocabulary variously encyclopedic, colloquial, hortatory, cybernetic, lyrical, prosaic. It is a collage, then, but one filled with movement, bearing out Olson's dictum "ONE PERCEPTION MUST IMMEDIATELY AND DIRECTLY LEAD TO A FURTHER PERCEPTION." However, the poem ends: "shall you uncover honey/ where maggots are?// I hunt among stones," and while to one reader, this may suggest that the poet's weight is thrown on the side of those details that belong to the "East/novelty/uprising" sequence, to a reader who bears in mind that all these details now are of the past, it suggests that the poet opts for the present/future, which, being as yet all potential, is blank—as a stony landscape.

Projective verse

Ends, however, are only tiny portions of their poems and cannot cancel the keen pleasure a reader may take in tracing meaning among such enigmatically juxtaposed blocks of constantly altering language, while being carried along at such various velocities. There are many striking formulations—often evidently stumbled on in the compositional process, which appears to unfold before the reader's very eyes (and ears); these often appear as good counsel ("In the midst of plenty, walk/ as close to/ bare// In the face of sweetness,/ piss"; "The nets of being/ are only eternal if you sleep as your hands/ ought to be busy"). Syntax—at times so filled with baffles and circumlocutions as to be more properly parataxis—brilliantly evokes the difficulties Olson would name, even court; nouns carry much of the freight, whereas adjectives are scarce (description Olson thought not projective, not able to break the circle of representation); verbs tend to be those of concealment and discovery and of social acts—talking, urging, hearing, permitting, obtaining, and the like. Because his notation favors the phrase over the sentence, in Olson's poetry, words can appear to leap from the page, freed significantly of their usual subjections. Although on occasion Olson (an accomplished orator) segues into a Roman kind of rhetoric, for the most part, he stays true to his aim, namely, to attack a universe of discourse with a poetry not only of particulars but also particulate in its construction. As indicated earlier, each of these elements helps constitute an intense dialectic whose synthesis occurs only as the abolition of its components: "It is undone business/ I speak of, this morning,/ with the sea/ stretching out/ from my feet."

THE MAXIMUS POEMS AND ARCHAEOLOGIST OF MORNING

While Olson's poetry appeared as a number of volumes during his lifetime, these are now contained in two texts: *The Maximus Poems* and *Archaeologist of Morning* (containing all his non-Maximus poems). Maximus is the poetic figure Olson created to "speak" poems (sometimes called letters) to the people of Gloucester and, by extension, to any who would be people of "a coherence not even yet new"—persons of that vivid and imminent future which is the Grail to Olson's search and labor. Maximus knows the history of the geography of this seaport and, by extension, of both pre- and post-settlement New England; of the migratory movements of Europe and the ancient world; and of other civilizations which, at some (usually early) stage, discovered the will to cohere, which Olson praised. He is to some degree based upon Maximus of Tyre, a second century C.E. maverick sage akin to Apollonius of Tyana, although Olson appears not to have investigated this historical personage with much thoroughness, preferring, no doubt, not to disturb the introjected Maximus he was finding so fruitful.

The significance of the city of Gloucester in these poems is complex but has to do with a place loved so well that it repays its lover with a battery of guarantees and tokens, enabling him to withstand the greased slide of present culture, the suck of absentee ownership and built-in obsolescence. It is for Olson the place where, in William Wordsworth's terms, he first received those "intimations of immortality" that even in the beleaguered present can solace and hearten. In his attachment to its particulars, his heat for its physical reality, the reader is invited to discover feelings for some actual place or entity akin to that of the poet, thereby to be led to the commitment essential to an awakened sense of life and a practice of person equal "to the real itself."

OTHER MAJOR WORKS

SHORT FICTION: *Stocking Cap: A Story*, 1966.

PLAYS: *The Fiery Hunt, and Other Plays*, 1977.

NONFICTION: *Call Me Ishmael: A Study of Melville*, 1947; "Projective Verse," 1950; *Mayan Letters*, 1953; *Human Universe, and Other Essays*, 1965; *Proprioception*, 1965; *Selected Writings of Charles Olson*, 1966; *Pleistocene Man*, 1968; *Causal Mythology*, 1969; *Letters for "Origin," 1950-1956*, 1969 (Albert Glover, editor); *The Special View of History*, 1970; *On Black Mountain*, 1971; *Additional Prose: A Bibliography on America, Proprioception, and Other Notes and Essays*, 1974; *Charles Olson and Ezra Pound: An Encounter at St. Elizabeths*, 1975; *The Post Office*, 1975; *Muthologos: The Collected Lectures and Interviews*, 1978-1979 (2 volumes); *Charles Olson and Robert Creeley: The Complete Correspondence*, 1980-1996 (10 volumes; George F. Butterick, editor); *Charles Olson and Cid Corman: Complete Correspondence, 1950-1964*, 1987-1991 (2 volumes; George Evans, editor); *In Love, in Sorrow: The Complete Correspondence of Charles Olson and Edward Dahlberg*, 1990 (Paul Christensen, editor); *Charles Olson and Frances Boldereff: A Modern Correspondence*, 1999 (Ralph Maud and Sharon Thesen, editors); *Selected Letters*, 2000 (Maud, editor); *Poet to Publisher: Charles Olson's Correspondence with Donald Allen*, 2003 (Maud, editor).

MISCELLANEOUS: *Selected Writings of Charles Olson*, 1966; *Poetry and Truth: The Beloit Lectures and Poems*, 1971; *Collected Prose*, 1997 (Donald Allen and Benjamin Friedlander, editors); *A Charles Olson Reader*, 2005 (Maud, editor).

BIBLIOGRAPHY

Billitteri, Carla. *Language and the Renewal of Society in Walt Whitman, Laura (Riding) Jackson, and Charles Olson: The American Cratylus*. New York: Palgrave Macmillan, 2009. Examines Cratylism, the utopian desire for a perfect language that directly expresses what is real, and its relationship to the writings of Olson, Walt Whitman, and Laura (Riding) Jackson.

Bollobás, Eniko. *Charles Olson*. New York: Twayne, 1992. An introductory biography and critical study of selected works by Olson. Includes bibliographical references and index.

Clark, Tom. *Charles Olson: The Allegory of a Poet's Life*. 1991. Reprint. Berkeley, Calif.: North Atlantic Books, 2000. The first biography of Olson. Clark reveals that Olson was likely gay, was a very dominant personality, and took hallucinogens. Bibliography.

Grieve-Carlson, Gary, ed. *Olson's Prose*. Newcastle, England: Cambridge Scholars, 2007. This collection of essays looks at Olson's prose, which covered topics such as poetry and language.

Kim, Joon-Hwan. *Out of the "Western Box": Towards a Multicultural Poetics in the Poetry of Ezra Pound and Charles Olson*. New York: Peter Lang, 2003. Kim notes the blending of East and West in the poems of Olson and Ezra Pound.

Maud, Ralph. *Charles Olson at the Harbor*. Vancouver, B.C.: Talonbooks, 2008. Examines Olson's creativity and experimentation, touching on topics such as how his projective verse influenced other poets.

_______. *Charles Olson's Reading: A Biography*. Carbondale: Southern Illinois University Press, 1996. A narrative account of the life and work of Olson, focusing on the poet's lifelong reading material as a basis for understanding his work.

Pekar, Harvey, et al. *The Beats: A Graphic History*. Art by Ed Piskor et al. New York: Hill and Wang, 2009. Comic legend Harvey Pekar provides a history of the Beat poets in this graphic book. Contains an entry on and references to Olson.

Rifkin, Libbie. *Career Moves: Olson, Creeley, Zukofsky, Berrigan, and the American Avant-Garde*. Madison: University of Wisconsin Press, 2000. Argues that anti-establishment poets of the 1950's and 1960's, including Olson, were just as bent on building their careers, reputations, and audiences as were mainstream poets.

Sławek, Tadeusz. *Revelations of Gloucester: Charles Olson, Fitz Hugh Lane, and Writing of the Place*. New York: Peter Lang, 2003. Examines how two artists, poet Olson and painter Fitz Hugh Lane, treat Gloucester, Massachusetts, in their creations.

David Bromige

KENNETH PATCHEN

Born: Niles, Ohio; December 13, 1911
Died: Palo Alto, California; January 8, 1972

PRINCIPAL POETRY

Before the Brave, 1936
First Will and Testament, 1939
The Dark Kingdom, 1942
The Teeth of the Lion, 1942
Cloth of the Tempest, 1943
An Astonished Eye Looks Out of the Air, 1945
Outlaw of the Lowest Planet, 1946
Panels for the Walls of Heaven, 1946
Selected Poems of Kenneth Patchen, 1946, 1958, 1964
Pictures of Life and Death, 1947
They Keep Riding Down All the Time, 1947
To Say If You Love Someone, 1948
Red Wine and Yellow Hair, 1949
Orchards, Thrones and Caravans, 1952
The Famous Boating Party, and Other Poems in Prose, 1954
Poems of Humor and Protest, 1954
Glory Never Guesses, 1955
A Surprise for the Bagpipe Player, 1956
Hurrah for Anything, 1957
When We Were Here Together, 1957
Doubleheader, 1958
Poemscapes, 1958
Because It Is, 1960
The Love Poems of Kenneth Patchen, 1960
Hallelujah Anyway, 1966
But Even So, 1968
The Collected Poems of Kenneth Patchen, 1968
Love and War Poems, 1968
There's Love All Day, 1970
Wonderings, 1971
In Quest of Candlelighters, 1972
The Walking-Away World, 2008
We Meet, 2008

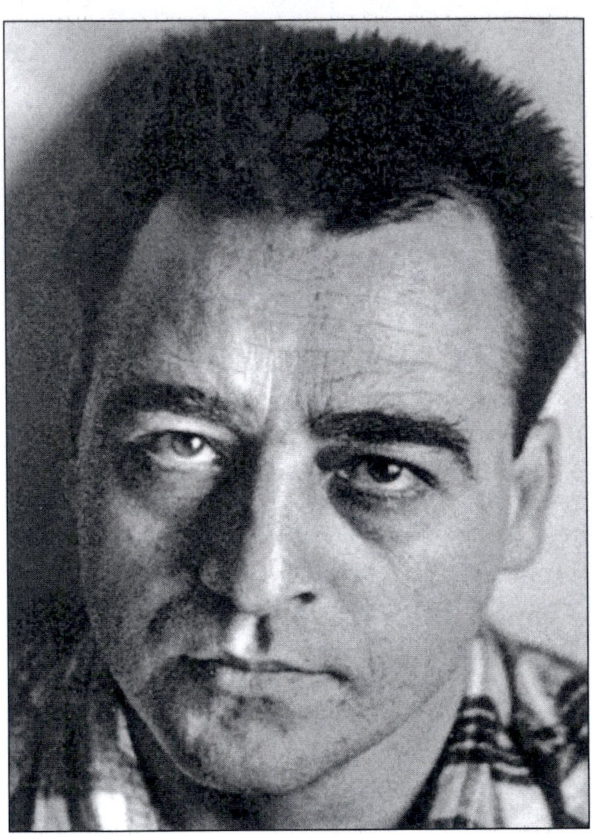

Kenneth Patchen

Other literary forms

Although mainly known as a poet, Kenneth Patchen (PAHT-chehn), a dedicated experimentalist, rejected normal genre distinctions, participating in radical new forms of prose, concrete poetry, poetry and jazz, picture poems, and surrealistic tales and fables, as well as other innovations. His first published prose work, a short story titled "Bury Them in God," appeared in a 1939 collection by New Directions. Two years later, in 1941, he published his most celebrated prose work, a pacifist antinovel titled *The Journal of Albion Moonlight*. After that, his prose work began to appear irregularly between the publication of his numerous books of poetry.

Achievements

An extremely prolific writer, Kenneth Patchen published roughly a book a year during his thirty-six-year writing career from 1936 to his death in 1972. Besides poetry, his artistic works consisted of prose and drama, silkscreen prints, paintings and drawings, hand-painted books, and even papier-mâché animal sculptures. Holding strongly to his belief in the "total artist," Patchen experimented with a wide variety of artistic forms, influencing a generation of poets with his creative energy.

Patchen also played a role in initiating the Poetry-and-Jazz movement in San Francisco during the 1950's. With Kenneth Rexroth and Lawrence Ferlinghetti, Patchen began reading his poetry to jazz accompaniment at the Cellar, a small club in San Francisco, in 1957. Patchen's own innovations in this area had begun six years earlier when he read and recorded his *Fables and Other Little Tales* (1953) to a jazz background. As early as 1945, in his novel *The Memoirs of a Shy Pornographer*, Patchen had presented a two-page list of "the disks you'll have to get if you want a basic jazz library."

In addition to the Poetry-and-Jazz movement, Patchen made important contributions to at least three other areas of poetic experimentation. First, in the 1950's, Patchen began to work with surrealistic fable and verse forms in such works as *Fables and Other Little Tales*, *Hurrah for Anything*, and *Because It Is*. Second, as an early experimenter in concrete poetry—particularly in *Cloth of the Tempest*, *Sleepers Awake* (1946), and *Panels for the Walls of Heaven*—Patchen provided American poetry with a uniquely visual poetic form in which the poet is concerned with making an object to be perceived rather than merely read. Patchen's third contribution, also involving visual expression, is his fusion of painting and writing forms. Many of Patchen's books include self-painted covers, drawings printed with poems, and picture-poem posters. Such "painted books" as *The Dark Kingdom*, *Panels for the Walls of Heaven*, *Red Wine and Yellow Hair*, and *Poemscapes* illustrate Patchen's impressive skill as a painter. Although he usually refused to exhibit his paintings, claiming that he preferred bookstores to art galleries, in 1969, a few years before his death, he finally conducted a one-man art show at the Corcoran Gallery in Washington, D.C.

Patchen received a Guggenheim Fellowship in 1936, the Ohioana Book Award for Poetry in 1946, the Shelley Memorial Award in 1954, and a cash award of ten thousand dollars in 1967 from the National Foundation of Arts and Humanities for his lifelong contribution to American letters. A small but moving volume titled *Tribute to Kenneth Patchen* (1977), published after the poet's death, attests the great respect in which he was held by contemporaries, publishers, critics, and friends.

BIOGRAPHY

Kenneth Patchen was born into a working-class milieu in Ohio's industrial and mining area, an environment that helped to forge his reputation in the late 1930's and 1940's as a significant proletarian poet. His father, Wayne Patchen, had spent more than twenty-five years working in the steel mills, where both Patchen and his brother also worked for a time. As Larry R. Smith writes in his biography *Kenneth Patchen* (1978), "much like D. H. Lawrence's mining background in England, Patchen's roots in a hard working yet culturally wasted community of poor and semi-poor gave him an early sense of strength and violation." In his early childhood, the family moved to nearby

Warren, Ohio, where Patchen received most of his schooling. The town is located a few miles from Garretsville, the birthplace of Hart Crane.

In Warren, Patchen began writing poetry. He also spent two summers working in the steel mills with his brother and father to earn tuition money for his brief attendance at the University of Wisconsin in 1929. Following this successful year at the university, Patchen wandered around the United States and Canada, working at odd jobs, writing poetry, attending Columbia University for a while, and eventually meeting Miriam Oidemus, the daughter of Finnish immigrants, whom he was to marry in June, 1934, and with whom he would spend the rest of his life.

With the exception of a brief period in Santa Fe, New Mexico, and a short stay in Hollywood in 1937, the Patchens lived in and around Greenwich Village from 1934 to 1950. Although his marriage was happy, Patchen spent a good part of his life in intense physical pain caused by a serious back disability that began in 1937 when Patchen tried to separate the locked bumpers of two cars that had collided. In 1950, a writer's committee, consisting of such notables as T. S. Eliot, W. H. Auden, E. E. Cummings, Thornton Wilder, and William Carlos Williams, gave a series of readings to earn money for Patchen to have corrective surgery.

Finding a renewed sense of mobility after the surgery, Patchen and his wife moved to San Francisco, where, in 1954, he befriended Kenneth Rexroth and Lawrence Ferlinghetti, with whom he collaborated in 1957, after a second spinal fusion, to create the Poetry-and-Jazz movement. By 1956, the Patchens were living in Palo Alto, at the southern end of San Francisco Bay, which was to become an important artistic center. In 1959, following a surgical mishap after prescribed exploratory surgery, further surgery was canceled and Patchen returned to Palo Alto to a bedridden life of almost constant pain. The 1960's, despite his disability, were productive years for Patchen, resulting in such books as *Because It Is*, *Hallelujah Anyway*, *But Even So*, and *The Collected Poems of Kenneth Patchen*, as well as several recordings of his works and an exhibition of his art in Washington, D.C.

By the time of his death in January, 1972, Patchen had gained a sound reputation as one of America's most influential avant-garde poets and "painters of poems." His experimentation with new forms, whether poetic or painterly, as well as his insistence on living the life of the "total artist," despite excruciating pain and deteriorating health, points unmistakably toward a quality that made him the greatly respected artist he was: action even in the face of chaos and pain. "The one thing which Patchen cannot understand, will not tolerate, indeed," wrote Henry Miller, "is the refusal to act. . . . Confronted with excuses and explanations, he becomes a raging lion."

Analysis

One way to trace the development of Kenneth Patchen's vast poetic output is to posit a shift from the emphasis on class-consciousness and protest in the poetry of the 1930's to 1940's to a later concern with a sense of wonder and with the spiritual and irrational side of existence. Another and perhaps more compelling approach is to view the entire body of Patchen's work as both spiritual and revolutionary, marked by the antiestablishment anger of the Old Testament prophets, who condemned the greed of the secular world while celebrating the coming of a just and sacred Kingdom of God.

BEFORE THE BRAVE

In his first book of poetry, *Before the Brave*, Patchen combines a vision of revolution with the wonder of the spiritual world. While lashing out angrily at the "sightless old men in cathedrals of decay" ("Letter to the Old Men") and the police with "their heavy boots grinding into our faces . . ." ("A Letter to a Policeman in Kansas City"), he still confirms, in Whitmanesque terms, the ability of humanity to seize control of events:

> O be willing to wait no longer.
> Build men, not creeds, seed not soil—
> O raise the standards out of reach.
>
> new men new world new life.

In contrast to the world of the "culture-snob" and the emptiness of "civic pride," Patchen's prophetic voice calls out for a world of unity and wonder, for a "jangling eternity/ Of fellowship and spring where good and law/ Is thicker love and every day shall spawn a god."

FIRST WILL AND TESTAMENT

In another of his so-called protest books of the 1930's, *First Will and Testament*, Patchen again combines or synthesizes the dual impulses of spiritual wonder and revolutionary zeal. In a poem called "A Revolutionary Prayer," he cries: "O great good God/ I do not know that this fistful of warm dirt/ Has any mineral that wills that the young die. . . ." Here the miner's son, Patchen, looks to the lesson of the ore that he, his father, and his brother had mined to confirm the injustice of war. Similarly, in "The Soldier and the Star," Patchen contrasts the grace, wonder, and wholeness of nature with the destruction of warfare. In the opening four lines, he writes: "Rifle goes up:/ Does what a rifle does/ Star is very beautiful:/ Doing what a star does."

ANTIWAR POETRY

In all Patchen's poetry, life's energy and fruitfulness is contrasted with the mechanical, dead, and often violent world of the war makers and the ruling elite. Throughout his work runs a triple vision that serves to direct his approach to the world. First is the painful reality of alienation and corruption, of a brutal, ruling monolith that forces people to move toward violence and control rather than growth and human fulfillment. In his earlier poetry, this force often takes the form of an actual ruling class in the language of Marxist ideology, while in later works, it appears as the nebulous darker side of human nature depicted by Mark Twain in his later works. Second is the need for humankind to become engaged in or committed to the fullness of life, unity, and social solidarity. Third is the sense of wonder and imaginative power that opposes the brutal side of human nature.

The corruption and alienation that Patchen sees running rampant in society are characterized largely by capitalist greed and human violence. Although the first evil is emphasized in his earlier works, the second emerges and is stressed throughout his entire poetic career. "War is the lifeblood of capitalism; it is the body and soul of fascism," wrote Patchen in his novel *The Journal of Albion Moonlight*, and it is mainly in his poetry that Patchen vividly depicts the bloody force of war. In such poems as "I DON'T WANT TO STARTLE YOU" and "Harrowed by These Apprehensions" (*First Will and Testament*), as well as in the later, more subtle antiwar works such as "In the Courtyard of Secret Life," from his 1957 book, *When We Were Here Together*, Patchen's pacifist sentiments, which he held his entire life, are powerfully expressed.

Love as redemption

Faced with chaos, alienation, and violence, Patchen believed that the poet must not fall into apathy or bitterness but rather must adopt a worldview in which belief, love, and action are possible. In the face of nothingness, Patchen offers the richness of being; in the face of chaos, he offers unity and order; and in the face of despair and confusion, he offers belief. In the poem "No One Ever Works Alone," from *Panels for the Walls of Heaven*, Patchen further pursues his prophetic faith that a new order will soon sweep away the injustice and evil of the outmoded system. "O Speak Out!," urges Patchen, "Against the dead trash of their 'reality'/ Against 'the world as we see it.'/ Against 'what it is reasonable to believe.'"

Ultimately, for Patchen, the path that leads from destruction to unity is the path of love. "There is only one power that can save the world," writes Patchen in "The Way Men Live Is a Lie" (*An Astonished Eye Looks Out of the Air*), "and that is the power of love for all men everywhere." Though it is a rather prosaic statement, this affirmation illustrates the poet's unswerving belief in the need for commitment to and engagement in the energy of life as opposed to the forces of death that always threaten to engulf humanity. Love, both sexual and spiritual, is an important weapon in that struggle.

A sense of wonder

Apart from love, another element that maintains unity in life, and one that is particularly evident in Patchen's later books, is a sense of wonder, or, one might say, childlike amazement toward life. In a 1968 interview with Gene Detro, Patchen speakes of the absolute necessity of childlike wonder. Losing this sense, for Patchen, would be equivalent to death. In "O Fiery River" (*Cloth of the Tempest*), Patchen warns that "men have destroyed the roads of wonder,/ And their cities squat like black roads/ In the orchards of life."

For Patchen, as for such Romantic poets as William Blake and William Wordsworth, the most perfect paradigm for wonder is to be found in the innocence of the child. In describing the wonder that exists between two people in sexual union, for example, Patchen speaks of how coming to his beloved Miriam's "wonder" ("For Miriam") is "Like a boy finding a star in a haymow" (*The Teeth of the Lion*). Like Blake in his *Songs of Innocence* (1789), Patchen finds a kind of salvation from injustice and pain in the world of childlike wonder. "Children don't want to know," writes Patchen in "O What a Revolution," a prose poem from *The Famous Boating Party, and Other Poems in Prose*, "They want to increase their enjoyment of not knowing." In "This Summer Day" (*An Astonished Eye Looks Out of the Air*), the child serves as a metaphor for both life and death. "O Death," writes Patchen, "must be this little girl/ Pushing her blue cart into the water," while "All Life must be this crowd of kids/ watching a hummingbird fly around itself."

As vividly as tanks and the "rustless gun" represent, for Patchen, the horror of history and the blind destructiveness of patriotism, the image of the child and childlike wonder (depicted often in collections of tales and verse such as *Fables and Other Little Tales*, *Hurrah for Anything*, and *But Even So*) represents the innocence, energy, and potential of life's richness. The critics who accuse Patchen of being a poet of dreary negativism ignore the fact that, throughout his poetry, Patchen offers a continuous prophecy of a world of wonder and delight that will inevitably shine through the universal darkness. As a revolutionary and a prophet, Patchen was never far removed from the vision of humanity's enormous potential.

Other major works

LONG FICTION: *The Journal of Albion Moonlight*, 1941; *The Memoirs of a Shy Pornographer*, 1945; *Sleepers Awake*, 1946; *See You in the Morning*, 1948.

SHORT FICTION: *Fables and Other Little Tales*, 1953 (revised as *Aflame and Afun of Walking Faces*, 1970).

PLAYS: *Don't Look Now*, pr. 1959; *Patchen's Lost Plays*, 1977.

RADIO PLAY: *The City Wears a Slouch Hat*, 1942 (music by John Cage).

Bibliography

Morgan, Richard G. *Kenneth Patchen: A Collection of Essays*. New York: AMS Press, 1977. A comprehensive and diverse collection of articles and essays on Patchen, with a foreword by Miriam Patchen. From reviews and radio interviews to critical analyses, this is a must for all who are interested in this poet.

_______. *Kenneth Patchen: A Comprehensive Bibliography*. New York: Paul Appel,

1978. A comprehensive, annotated, descriptive bibliography of primary and secondary works. Essential for the Patchen scholar.

Nelson, Raymond. *Kenneth Patchen and American Mysticism.* Chapel Hill: University of North Carolina Press, 1984. A full-length and important literary criticism of Patchen that attempts to secure him a place among contemporary poets without the stigma of "cultist following." Discusses his major works and his leanings toward the mystical in his poetry. An appreciative study of Patchen that concedes, however, that his work is uneven.

Nin, Anais. *The Diary of Anais Nin, 1939-1944*. Vol. 3. New York: Harcourt Brace Jovanovich, 1969. Contains a short biographical sketch of Patchen during his New York days. Favorably analyzes his work *The Journal of Albion Moonlight.*

Pekar, Harvey, et al. *The Beats: A Graphic History.* Art by Ed Piskor et al. New York: Hill and Wang, 2009. Comics legend Harvey Pekar provides a history of the Beat poets in this graphic book. Contains an entry on and references to Patchen.

Smith, Larry R. *Kenneth Patchen.* Boston: Twayne, 1978. This study attempts to correct misunderstandings about Patchen by placing him in the context of his independence. Notes that his love poetry combines "hard realism with a visionary idealism." Discusses also his "poetry-jazz" form, which was one of his highest achievements.

_______. *Kenneth Patchen: Rebel Poet in America.* Huron, Ohio: Bottom Dog Press, 2000. An authorized biography of Patchen by Smith, who completed an earlier critical study of Patchen's works published by Twayne, and a video docudrama *Kenneth Patchen: An Art of Engagement* in 1989. Here this American rebel artist stands exposed as a person of great strength and perseverance. His and wife Miriam's story is one of the great love stories in American literature.

Donald E. Winters, Jr.

MARIE PONSOT

Born: New York, New York; 1921

Principal poetry

True Minds, 1956
Admit Impediment, 1981
The Green Dark, 1988
The Bird Catcher, 1998
Springing: New and Selected Poems, 2002
Easy, 2009

Other literary forms

In addition to her poetry, Marie Ponsot (PAHN-saht) has also gained recognition for her translations of children's books from the French. She has translated numerous books, focusing primarily on fairy tales.

Achievements

Marie Ponsot's poetry has won several honors, including a creative writing grant from the National Endowment for the Arts, the Delmore Schwartz Memorial Prize, the Eunice Tietjens Prize from *Poetry* magazine, and the Modern Language Association's Mina P. Shaughnessy Medal. *The Bird Catcher* received the 1998 National Book Critics Circle Award and was a finalist for the 1999 Lenore Marshall Poetry Prize. She won the Shelley Memorial Award (2002) and the Frost Medal (2005) from the Poetry Society of America, and the Academy Award in Literature from the American Academy of Arts and Letters (2009). She became a chancellor of the Academy of American Poets in 2010.

Biography

Marie Ponsot was born Marie Birmingham in Queens, New York. Her father, William Birmingham, was a partner in a wine importing company. Her mother, Marie (Candee) Birmingham, was a schoolteacher. Marie began publishing her writing as a child, in *The Brooklyn Eagle*. She received a bachelor of arts degree from St. Joseph's College for Women in Brooklyn, then earned a master's degree with a concentration in seventeenth century literature from Columbia University. She has often spoken of how her parents stimulated her love of literature.

After World War II, Marie Birmingham went to Paris for postgraduate studies, where she met artist and painter Claude Ponsot. They were married in 1948. Together they had seven children, one daughter and six sons. They divorced in 1970. Marie

Ponsot met Beat poet and publisher Lawrence Ferlinghetti while they were fellow passengers on a boat. He published her first collection, *True Minds*, through City Lights Books in San Francisco in 1956.

Ponsot has had an extensive teaching career. When her second collection was published, she was an English professor at Queens College, from which she retired in 1991. She has also taught in graduate programs at Beijing United University, New York's YMHA Poetry Center, New York University, the New School, and Columbia University.

ANALYSIS

Marie Ponsot's use of her personal experiences never degenerates into the maudlin, nor does she invoke the circumstances of her life simply for dramatic effect. In *Strange Good Fortune: Essays on Contemporary Poets* (2000), poet David Wojahn suggests that such writing is misleading and dishonest, warning against writing talk-show poetry that aches for attention and headlines:

> For a poem of invective to work as it should, a writer must in most cases be especially careful to counterbalance the development of his/her argument with structural or formal devices which sharpen and underscore the writer's conviction and rage.

The strength of Ponsot's work is in how carefully she weaves her poems, using formal structural and sonic devices to sustain her argument. For example, when Ponsot speaks with anger about her divorce, her poems use traditional forms and fixed rhyme schemes to give the impression of a struggle between restraint and strong emotion. The emotion never sweeps away the poem, nor does the structure ever seem merely incidental or decorative. Both form and sense work together to create an organic whole.

TRUE MINDS

Lawrence Ferlinghetti published *True Minds*, Ponsot's first collection, just after he published Allen Ginsberg's *Howl* (1956). Based on Ferlinghetti's choice, the public expected that Ponsot's work would follow in Ginsberg's Beat style and therefore greeted Ponsot's measured, formal verses with a profound silence. Although she continued to publish individual poems in magazines and journals, twenty-five years would pass before the publication of her second book.

A slim collection, *True Minds* presents a metaphysical meditation within the context of her life experiences. The sonnet form underscores the spiritual stance that characterizes much of Ponsot's work. "Espousal" echoes the vibrance of Gerard Manley Hopkins's ecstatic poems. This sonnet uses four stanzas of three lines, employing an *abc* rhyme scheme in each stanza. The sonnet ends with a couplet using *bc*. This interlocking echoes the images, which also repeat, describing a link between the spiritual and physical worlds:

> And the cut-out sun-circle plunges, down it dives;
> And fire blazes at the earth's jewel-runneled core.

Ponsot takes liberties with the basic requirements of the form—the five-stress line with its regular rhyme scheme. The resulting poem celebrates the freshness of love as well as its connection to the natural world. This is a poem of young love that seems indestructible.

"The Given Grave Grown Green," a poem of foreboding, questions the assumption that love can endure, as if the poet foresees her future divorce. This is a poem of change. The poet experiences change occurring all around her. Wondering where she finds herself in the midst of such change, addressing the person who has been the agent of such turmoil, she finally says:

> You can watch from your closed window
> How true false love has grown.

These lines mirror the contradiction inherent in the title. A grave is green only because of growth above it, not life within it. Likewise, what is true about love in this poem is that the love has become false.

ADMIT IMPEDIMENT

Ponsot's second collection, *Admit Impediment*, provides a fuller exploration of the themes found in *True Minds*. Both collections take their titles from William Shakespeare's Sonnet 116, which begins, "Let me not to the marriage of true minds/ Admit impediments. . . ." Divided into four sections, the second collection opens with "For a Divorce," one of the longer poems gathered here. It is a dark poem, whose irregular stanzaic patterns lead the reader through the emotional intricacies that attend a divorce. This poem catalogs the pain of the divorce and the specific areas of brokenness, recalling the various images of the marriage itself. The short, strong lines emphasize the full-stop of the relationship, the sounds within the lines almost jarring at times. The poet concludes:

> Deaths except for amoeba articulate
> life into lives, separate, named, new.
> Not all sworn faith dies. Ours did.

This is an angry poem whose emotion is carefully controlled for vivid effect. While the poet attempts to avoid blame (the lines previously quoted are as close as she comes to specific details about the cause of the break), she achieves a level of clarity for the reader's consideration by beginning her poem with nearly all of Shakespeare's Sonnet 116. Although she does not quote Shakespeare's final two lines, their sense is implied throughout this collection:

If this be error, and upon me prov'd
I never writ, nor no man ever lov'd.

The Green Dark

Ponsot's third collection, *The Green Dark*, weaves mythic elements into the fabric of her poems, along with her accustomed biographical references, resulting in poems in which dream and reality share space. "Take Time, Take Place" is a long meditation in several parts. In part 1, the poet longs for the fantasy of passionate love but realizes that such love is inaccessible, saying, "Sleep take it. Awake I like a drier wine." Part 2 takes a different turn. Even the use of language becomes more grounded in day-to-day expression.

The poems in parts 1 and 2 use irregular line lengths and slant rhymes, which give the poem an exploratory, testing sense of experience, as if the poet would invite the reader on a journey whose end is uncertain. Part 3, however, is quite different. Comprising seven sonnets and ending with a five-line stanza, this section questions the assumptions of the first two parts. Beginning with "Fantasies dampen the pang of cherishing/ goods and chances lost or left behind," these poems challenge the easy redemption that fantasy alone can bring.

Each sonnet ends with a line that is repeated as the first line of the next sonnet, albeit sometimes slightly altered. The poet searches for signs, for the "hard sun of memory," which would enable her to enter the world of her fancy, but then realizes:

Such grace. It names the saving world I might seize
but am too locked in time to see: unless
we are what our imagination frees.

What the imagination frees is the human capacity to feel joy, even after a great pain has occurred. The bird that has flown throughout this poem becomes the unifying symbol of "thick experience." The poems that Ponsot crafts with such precision emphasize the idea that, as a poet, she is free to construct a world that encourages her selfhood and to leave any world that denies her the right to grow.

The Bird Catcher

Winner of the National Book Critics Circle Award, *The Bird Catcher* continues to probe Ponsot's fascination with poetic forms, using them to shape the expression of the emotive thrust in each poem. Likewise, the poet reviews the concerns that preoccupied her earlier work. Crafted in four sections, the book begins with "To the Muse of Doorways Edges Verges," which sets the creative tone. The "gentle visitor" in the doorway is someone whose visits are "irregular," as the poet makes her welcome. These visits, however, contain a nervy edge of warning:

She smiles. She speaks up, some.
Each word ravishes,
bright with the sciences
she practices
in the music business.

"One day, when you're not dumb,
you must come
to my place," she says,
and vanishes.

Twenty-five years elapsed between the publication of Ponsot's first and second books; meanwhile, she experienced marriage, the birth of her children, and her subsequent divorce. Tillie Olsen's *Silences* (1978) elaborates on the lives of female writers who fall silent for significant periods of their career, as did Ponsot. It would perhaps be accurate to read "dumb" as "mute," not as a reference to intelligence. The poet shows herself at the edge of an awakening, a rebirth into the world of her own words. This is the "place" to which the muse calls her.

The first section, "For My Old Self," contains poems that focus on her life as a wife and mother. The poet's use of forms becomes, at times, playful, as if concealing a more serious tone that is pervasive. "Trois Petits Tours et Puis . . ." speaks of conflicting ways in which the husband and wife interpret the world. Each seems unable to recognize the gift that is present in the spouse, until, finally, the inevitable break occurs. The sonnet uses a varied rhyme scheme and an irregular stanzaic pattern. The first stanza contains five lines, the second, seven, and the third, two. The final stanza summarizes the outcome:

His map omits her. His snapshots go to friends.
A fresh music fills her house, a fresh air.

For both, the end of this relationship is the beginning of another life. In each poem in which Ponsot discusses the breakdown of her marriage, she avoids a self-pitying stance that could undermine the vitality of her work. Instead, the poet affirms her own ability to continue—not merely to endure, but to flourish.

In the second section, "Separate, in the Swim," the poem "The Border" begins with a young girl's idealized vision of what marriage is. A flower girl for Dorothea's wedding, the girl practices walking so that she can gracefully present herself holding the flowers. Her grandmother tells her that she should not worry, as everyone will be looking at the bride. She then starts to blow bubbles, allowing them to float over the pansies into the bridal-wreath bush before they vanish. Her understanding is at once naïve and chilling:

Getting married is like that.
Getting married is not like that.

The poem is both an affirmation and a warning, as if the poet were speaking to herself as a young, newly married woman.

Other sections explore mythology, women who find themselves in situations that are conflicting, almost dream states. In "Persephone, Packing," the poet wonders whether the duality of Persephone's life—and by extension the poet's life—is actually a dream. She ponders whether life above or below is real. Again, the poet examines the institution of marriage, especially in Persephone's case, in which she has been taken against her will. How much of a woman's will must be sacrificed for the sake of the union is a question that Ponsot asks in her poetry, with no easy answers.

The final poem, "Even," uses jagged lines and enjambment to follow the story of Adam and Eve, as Eve finally comes to understand her position in the world. The poem refers to Noah and his wife, suddenly freed from danger. The poet then draws a parallel between modern women, including herself, and the need for a new way of being.

Springing

Springing culls selected work from Ponsot's previous collections and includes new poems and uncollected work from Ponsot's early career. The new work, which opens the text, is similar to that found in *The Bird Catcher*, in its dry wit, pared-down lines, and playful use of traditional forms, rhyme, and meter. These are intellectually savvy poems, philosophical in their intent but grounded in earthly realities; gardens and gardening, for example, are Ponost's most prevalent metaphors. "Pathetic Fallacies Are Bad Science But" suggests a desire to find human equivalency in nature, despite understanding, intellectually, the inevitable distance between the human world and the natural world. Ponsot writes, "I read this drenched in bird-panic,/ its spine-fusing loss all song, all loss; that loss mine." This tug-of-war between a desire for comfort in natural cycles and a reluctance to speak for the natural world pervades Ponsot's work, particularly her later poems. This tension gives the poems their energy. These are poems whose speakers are conscious of aging and time passing, and yet they refuse to give in to despair. With poems such as "Old Jokes Appreciate" and "What Would You Like to Be When You Grow Up," one gets the sense Ponsot is grappling with her increasing age with humor. In "Antepenultimate," the speaker positions herself as a poetic alternative to overly rational scientific time keeping: "He earns his living learning/ history & likelihood/ by reading trees, sliced dead ones./ Me too but/ with live ones." Again, the poems engage with difficult truths but with a decidedly Dickinsonian "slant." Formally speaking, the poems are also reminiscent of Emily Dickinson's sometimes elliptical lines and imagined dialogues, but Ponsot never seems old-fashioned. In the section "Uncollected Poems, 1946-1971," the poet's progression from a denser, iambic line and a more overtly narrative sensibility to quick, honed lyrics is evident. The humor, too, in "Private and Profane" (1950) is broader, as is the rhyme ("From loss of the old and lack of the new/ From failure to make the right thing do/ Save us, Lady Mary Wortley

Montagu") than the last poem in the section, "Out of the North: Two Views." In this poem, Ponsot begins to display two of the hallmark characteristics of her later work, indented stanzas and quotations: "I am a giant really and you therefore/ should love me since you/ claim you are a falcon, believe me,/ you are a giant, too." Here Ponsot creates a single landscape but from two views, that of the more powerful hawk and that of the lesser falcon. She writes from an animal's perspective but, in this earlier poem, with less anxiety.

Other major works

NONFICTION: *Beat Not the Poor Desk*, 1982 (with Rosemary Deen); *The Common Sense: What to Write, How to Write It, and Why*, 1985 (with Deen).

TRANSLATIONS: *Cinderella, and Other Stories of Charles Perrault*, 1957; *Fables of La Fontaine*, 1957; *The Fairy Tale Book*, 1958; *My First Picture Encyclopedia*, 1959; *Old One Toe*, 1959; *Once Upon a Time Stories*, 1959; *Mick and the AP-105*, 1961; *Russian Fairy Tales*, 1961; *Tales of India*, 1961; *Bemba*, 1962; *Pour toi*, 1966; *Chinese Fairy Tales*, 1973; *Golden Book of Fairy Tales*, 1999; *Love and Folly: Selected Fables and Tales of La Fontaine*, 2001; *The Snow Queen, and Other Tales*, 2001.

Bibliography

Burt, Stephen. "The Wonder Years." Review of *Easy. The New York Times Book Review*, December 20, 2009, p. 6L. Notes how this collection deals with themes of aging and critiques her style, finding her best when dealing with down-to-earth topics.

Gilbert, Sandra M. "The Last Wilderness of the Wild Old: On Marie Ponsot's *The Bird Catcher* and Rajzel Zychlinsky's *God Hid His Face*." In *On Burning Ground: Thirty Years of Thinking About Poetry*. Ann Arbor: University of Michigan Press, 2009. Compares the works of these two poets, who, she says, share a poetic intensity. However, Ponsot's poetry is more positive and life affirming than that of Zuchlinsky.

Hacht, Anne Marie, and David Kelly, eds. *Poetry for Students*. Vol. 24. Detroit: Thomson/Gale, 2006. Contains an in-depth analysis of Ponsot's "One Is One."

Krivak, Andrew. "The Language of Redemption." *Commonweal* 130, no. 9 (May, 2003): 12-16. Krivak discusses Ponsot in conjunction with two other Catholic poets, Adam Zagajewski and Lawrence Joseph.

Parini, Jay, ed. *The Oxford Encyclopedia of American Literature*. New York: Oxford University Press, 2004. Contains a biographical essay on Ponsot that examines her place in poetry.

Seaman, Donna. Review of *The Bird Catcher*. *Booklist* 94, no. 11 (February 1, 1998): 894. The reviewer celebrates the poet's use of homonyms and varied rhyme schemes, as well as linguistic and philosophical paradoxes.

Smith, Dinitia. "Recognition at Last for Poet of Elegant Complexity." Review of *The Bird Catcher*. *The New York Times*, April 13, 1999, p. E1. Provides an extensive analysis of the precision of word choice and the complexity of syntax that Ponsot employs in her poetry. The reviewer finds that the rhetorical patterns are well thought out and that Ponsot pays particular attention to the fixed forms such as the villanelle, the sestina, and the tritina.

Willis, Mary-Sherman. "Diving into It." Review of *The Bird Catcher. Poet Lore* 94, no. 4 (Winter, 2000). Discusses the poet's use of biographical elements in her work. The reviewer shows how the full life that Ponsot led has shaped these poems, which are ultimately life affirming. The reviewer finds that the general theme is one of movement, of buoyancy and danger, of leaving the shore and returning.

Martha Modena Vertreace-Doody
Updated by Lesley Jenike

KENNETH REXROTH

Born: South Bend, Indiana; December 22, 1905
Died: Montecito, California; June 6, 1982

PRINCIPAL POETRY

A Prolegomenon to a Theodicy, 1932
In What Hour, 1940
The Phoenix and the Tortoise, 1944
The Signature of All Things, 1949
The Dragon and the Unicorn, 1952
The Art of Worldly Wisdom, 1953
A Bestiary, 1955
Thou Shalt Not Kill, 1955
In Defense of the Earth, 1956
The Homestead Called Damascus, 1963
Natural Numbers, 1963
The Collected Shorter Poems, 1966
The Collected Longer Poems, 1967
The Heart's Garden, the Garden's Heart, 1967
The Spark in the Tinder of Knowing, 1968
Sky Sea Birds Trees Earth House Beasts Flowers, 1971
New Poems, 1974
On Flower Wreath Hill, 1976
The Silver Swan, 1976
The Love Poems of Marichiko, 1978
The Morning Star, 1979
Selected Poems, 1984
Sacramental Acts: The Love Poems of Kenneth Rexroth, 1997
Swords That Shall Not Strike: Poems of Protest and Rebellion, 1999 (Geoffrey Gardner, editor)
The Complete Poems of Kenneth Rexroth, 2003

OTHER LITERARY FORMS

In addition to more than thirty books of poetry, of which nearly half are translations from six languages, Kenneth Rexroth philosophically developed his erotic mysticism in verse drama, autobiographies, and critical essays. His four ritual plays of ecstatic transcendence in the midst of collapsing classical Greek civilization, influenced by Japanese Nō and Greek tragedy, were collected in 1951 as *Beyond the Mountains*, premiered by the Living Theater in New York. Praised as one of Rexroth's most enduring achievements by poet William Carlos Williams, the classical scholar George Woodcock, and Japanese scholars Kodama Sanehide and Sakurai Emiko, *Beyond the Mountains* is distinguished by its faithfulness to both the Eastern and Western traditions that fed its subtle form, by its passionate characters who dramatize modern as well as ancient spiritual crises, and by its sensuously intellectual style.

In *An Autobiographical Novel* (1966, 1978) and *Excerpts from a Life* (1981), Rexroth's adventures are boldly narrated just as he spoke—with the uncanny power of epigrammatically characterizing everyone he met. Moreover, his religious, philosophical, and literary ideas are amplified in his wide-ranging essays, which have served to expand the audience for modern poetry. Most of his essays have been collected, and he also provided important introductory essays to his editions of other writers.

ACHIEVEMENTS

Kenneth Rexroth's contributions to diverse literary and intellectual movements are suggested by Louis Zukofsky's inclusion of *A Prolegomenon to a Theodicy*, a long, cubist, philosophical revery, in *An "Objectivists Anthology"* (1932) and by Rexroth's membership in the Industrial Workers of the World, the John Reed Clubs, and the San Francisco "Libertarian Circle," among other revolutionary organizations, in which nonviolent, communitarian anarchism set an independent line in opposition to totalitarian communism and fascism as well as to the injustices of capitalistic democracy. His leadership in the Libertarian Circle was indispensable to the San Francisco Poetry Renaissance years before the Beat poets emerged in 1956, when Rexroth introduced poet Allen Ginsberg and others at the famous debut of Ginsberg's "Howl." He helped to advance the work of such poets as Denise Levertov, Gary Snyder, Jerome Rothenberg, Shiraishi Kazuko, and many others, and his translations of women poets of China and Japan were deliberately feminist contributions.

Rexroth's work is read widely in Asia and Europe as well as in the United States. His international reputation has been aided by the popularity of his translations, his extensive travels and publication abroad, his collaboration with many writers in Europe and Asia, and the steady support of James Laughlin, whose New Directions published many of Rexroth's books. Rexroth's anthologies and editions of other writers extended his influence in England, and his reputation in Europe is reflected in his Akademische Austauschdienst Award from West Berlin, which, with a Rockefeller grant, allowed him to travel around the world in 1967 on a poetry tour. Several tours of Asia, some of them sponsored by the United States Agency of International Communication, indicate the esteem with which he is held in that part of the world.

Rexroth received other honors as well: three Silver Medals from the Commonwealth Club of California (1940, 1944, 1979), two Guggenheim Fellowships (1948-1949), a Chapelbrook Award and a Eunice Teitjens Award from *Poetry* magazine (1957), a

Shelley Memorial Award from the Poetry Society of America (1958), an Amy Lowell Fellowship (1958), a Longview Award (1963), the National Institute of Arts and Letters Award (1964), a W. C. Williams Award from *Contact* magazine (1965), and the Copernicus Award (1975). He contributed to many prestigious magazines and newspapers, conducted a program of poetry and comment on KPFA in San Francisco, and, despite his aversion to academic restrictions and his lack of any degrees, taught at San Francisco State College, the University of Wisconsin at Milwaukee, and the University of California, Santa Barbara, besides giving lectures and readings at many other universities around the world.

BIOGRAPHY

Born in South Bend in 1905, Kenneth Charles Marion Rexroth grew up in Indiana, Michigan, Ohio, and Illinois. His ancestors were scholars, peasants, and religious and political dissenters from Germany and Ireland, along with native and black Americans, and pioneers, all of whom enriched his unique personality. His parents were sophisticated travelers who took him on his first European tour when he was seven. After they died a few years later, he became independently active in Chicago as a precocious and revolutionary painter, poet, actor, and journalist—appearing as a character inJames T. Farrell's *Studs Lonigan* (1934). After exploring Europe, Mexico, and the West Coast, he moved to San Francisco in 1927, where he made his home until moving to Santa Barbara in the late 1960's. Eastern and Western contemplative practices affected the visionary orientation of his poetry, painting, and philosophy. During World War II, he was a conscientious objector, working in a psychiatric hospital where he was severely injured by a patient. He also assisted interned and otherwise harassed Japanese Americans, and his friendships with Asians deepened his lifelong interest in Asian culture, especially Buddhism, which harmonizes in his work with an ecologically based sense of universal community.

Rexroth was married to Andrée Dutcher, an anarchist painter, from 1927 until her death in 1940; to Marie Kass, a nurse, from 1940 until their divorce in 1948; and to Marthe Larsen, a member of the Libertarian Circle, from 1949 until their divorce in 1961. Two daughters, Mary and Katherine, were born to them in 1950 and 1954 respectively. In 1974, he married the poet Carol Tinker, and they spent a year in Kyoto before returning to their home in Montecito. Rexroth also toured Asia in 1967, 1972, 1978, and 1980. He died on June 6, 1982.

ANALYSIS

Kenneth Rexroth wrote in the tradition of contemplative, mystical, visionary, philosophical, and prophetic poets such as William Butler Yeats, D. H. Lawrence, Walt Whitman, William Blake, Dante, Du Fu, Zeami Motokiyo, and Sappho, all of whom influenced him. Rextroth was an eclectic student of many traditions from many cultures:

Judeo-Christian, classical Greek and Roman, Chinese, and Japanese. He was a modernist poet with a passionate commitment to tradition—to that which has lasted for centuries and is worth saving. His work as a whole, expository and autobiographical prose as well as passionate love lyrics, heartrending elegies, ferocious satires, and richly intellectual epic-reveries and dramas, must be read in the context of these diverse traditions. His style ranged from cubist innovations that ally him with Ezra Pound, Gertrude Stein, T. S. Eliot, and other revolutionists of the word, to the limpid simplicity he learned from Chinese and Japanese masters. This stylistic variety, however, is informed by an unwavering central vision of mystical love, universal responsibility, and spiritual realization.

THE COLLECTED SHORTER POEMS

The Collected Shorter Poems offers a brilliant diversity of styles and forms drawn from Rexroth's work over four decades. "Andromeda Chained to the Rock the Great Nebula in Her Heart" and other cubist poems share affinities with Gertrude Stein and Louis Zukofsky, as well as with African and Native American song. In a more direct style are exquisite lyrics of love and nature, such as "We Come Back"; fierce intellectual satires such as "Last Visit to the Swimming Pool Soviets" (with aspersions on the so-called chic Hollywood leftists); prophetic poems of revolutionary heroism and defeat, such as "From the Paris Commune to the Kronstadt Rebellion"; and Chinese translations.

"Yin and Yang," Rexroth's most liturgical poem of natural cycles, is an Easter vision of resurrecting birds, flowers, and constellations in which imagery and rhythms are perfectly balanced. In it, the moon, moving through constellations from Leo to Virgo, fertilizes the Virgin, and the ear of wheat symbolizes the creative process of nature as it did in the Eleusinian mysteries. As moonlight proclaims the climactic coming of spring, under the world the sun swims in Pisces, the double fish and the Chinese symbol of Yin and Yang, the harmonious interactions of darkness and light, coldness and heat, female and male. The regular prosody, supporting the orderly revelation of mythology, is a combination of accentual and syllabic patterns. All but three lines have nine syllables each, and most lines have three accents each, with a fundamentally dactyllic movement supporting the prophetic tone of this memorable poem.

"When We with Sappho," perhaps Rexroth's greatest love poem, begins with his first translation, done as a teenager and convincing him that he was a creative artist; there follows his sacramental lyric of erotic bliss, in which he and the woman he loves—also his muse—merge in a summer meadow into the immortal world of Sappho. As he speaks intimately, hypnotically repeating "summer," each body becomes a "nimbus" over the world, as they unite in thunder, before separating toward death.

"A Letter to William Carlos Williams" centers on the sacramental value of poetry as living speech, person to person (rather than as a text analyzed as an object). The style echoes the intimate ebb and flow of conversation with an old friend, whom he compares with Saint Francis (whose flesh united with all lovers, including birds and animals) and Brother Juniper (a wise fool who laughed at indignities). Citing the quiet imagery of daily life in Williams's poetry, Rexroth praises Williams's stillness (like that of the Quaker George Fox and the peace of Jesus), and the poem concludes with a utopian vision of a beautiful Williams River, as a young woman of the future tells her children how it used to be the filthy Passaic, and how the poet Williams had embodied in his poetry a creative community of sacramental relationships.

Rexroth's most famous protest poem, "Thou Shalt Not Kill," has been recorded with jazz accompaniment. An elegy for Dylan Thomas, it mourns the destruction of many poets in this depersonalizing, violent century. Young men, Rexroth proclaims, are being murdered all over the world—such as Saints Stephen, Lawrence, and Sebastian—by the superego in uniform. The second section is reminiscent of "Lament for the Makaris," the elegy by the sixteenth century Scottish poet William Dunbar; in it Rexroth laments the impoverishment and deaths of many poets from Edwin Arlington Robinson through Elinor Wylie and Countée Cullen to Ezra Pound. The third section, in a deepening tone, tells of many others struck down by the Moloch of the modern world. Accusations become lyrical in the last section, as nearly everyone is blamed for having a hand in the destruction of poetic vision—even writers such as T. S. Eliot and Ernest Hemingway who have enjoyed fame and power. The poem has been condemned by some critics but praised by others as a passionate call for prophetic vision.

THE COLLECTED LONGER POEMS

The Collected Longer Poems, which should be read as a whole work, reveals Rexroth's spiritual and artistic development as summarized in the introduction to the original publication of *The Phoenix and the Tortoise* in 1944—from despair and abandon in the face of the violent collapse of civilization, through erotic mysticism and sacramental marriage, to a sense of universal responsibility. *The Homestead Called Damascus*, the first of five long philosophical reveries in the collection, is a richly allusive work reminiscent of Marcel Proust and Wallace Stevens. The loose syllabic verse—generally nine syllables per line—allows Rexroth considerable freedom for discursive, philosophical reflections. In part 1, the Damascan brothers, Thomas and Sebastian, whose names suggest the themes of skepticism and martyrdom that are interwoven throughout the poem, seek some kind of erotic-mystical escape from the decaying civilization symbolized by the mansion, the landscape, and the dreamy Renaissance girl, Leslie. In part 2, Sebastian yearns for an earth goddess envisioned as a black stripper named Maxine, whereas Thomas seeks faith in the black wounds of Jesus. Part 3 elaborates the dilemma between erotic/heroic mysteries and the decadence of domestic bliss. Both alternatives paralyze the brothers, although they speculate about the "ambivalent vicarity" of each person symbolizing others. In the final part, Thomas settles for this philosophical notion, while Sebastian sinks into sterility. Although the poem suffers from some obscurity of characterization and theme, it is a work of serious speculation, resplendent with hallucinatory images, mythological puns, and metaphysical questioning.

A Prolegomenon to a Theodicy and The Phoenix and the Tortoise

A Prolegomenon to a Theodicy, Rexroth's second long poem, is a search for transcendent perfection within the flux of experience, a search conducted by means of a cubist aesthetic in which he analyzes and recombines the elements of experience and language. He passes through a Dantean Hell before envisioning the Apocalypse in the most explicitly Christian imagery to be found in any of his poems. In his third long poem, *The Phoenix and the Tortoise*, whose title and theme of mystical love are derived from William Shakespeare's *The Phoenix and the Turtle*, Rexroth develops a religious, ecological viewpoint in which World War II and the injustices of all governments are anarchistically denounced, while value painfully emerges out of personal love. The style is clear, direct, often epigrammatically conveying a deeper faith in life than the previous two long poems.

The Dragon and the Unicorn and The Heart's Garden, the Garden's Heart

The fourth long poem, *The Dragon and the Unicorn*, is a postwar travel narrative in which Rexroth searches for the meaning of responsibility and its source in love as he proceeds across the United States and Europe. Witnessing the physical and spiritual effects of war and historical depersonalization, he condemns the collectivities of church, state, political parties, armies, and corporations for suppressing and destroying personality, and he celebrates the community of lovers that actually, miraculously, continues to exist. The last long poem in the collection, *The Heart's Garden, the Garden's Heart*, extends this celebration of actuality. It is a masterpiece of poetic communion with the *dao* in Japan, rich in allusions to Asian poetry and Buddhist wisdom, and culminating, in a musical style that shines with the sensuous imagery of rural and urban Japan, in the most fully realized passages of illumination in all his poetry. Hearing the music of waterfalls, he listens deep in his mind to transcendent music, overcoming the gap between actuality and Otherness. He does not seek visions, but rests in the innocent vision of actuality, which is also ultimate. Professor Kodama Sanehide of Doshisha Women's College in Kyoto has traced intricate allusions to Japanese poetry in this poem and others, leading him to conclude that of all American poets, Rexroth best understands Japanese culture. Certainly *The Heart's Garden, the Garden's Heart* is the most delightfully and wisely realized of his long poems.

Asian influences

Asian influences, apparent from the beginning of Rexroth's career, intensify in his later work, which includes several volumes of Chinese and Japanese translations, with women poets being singled out in three of them. Buddhist allusions radiate from *New*

Poems, *On Flower Wreath Hill* (his sixth long reverie), *The Silver Swan*, and, most of all, *The Love Poems of Marichiko*, a long sequence of Tantric ecstasy.

Rexroth has sometimes been criticized for being more concerned with philosophical speculation than with the subtleties of language, but these charges seem as superficial as the categorization of his work, by some early reviewers, as merely West Coast nature poetry; there is a vast range of linguistic and prosodic technique in his work. At one extreme is the cubist free verse of *A Prolegomenon to a Theodicy*, at the other extreme is the syllabic versification of much of his poetry of direct statement, influenced by Greek, Chinese, and Japanese traditions. Often nine syllables are a norm around which lines ranging from seven to ten syllables are skillfully arranged, the sounds falling into remarkable melodic patterns rare in modern poetry. Rexroth's vowel-patterns are especially distinctive, a technique absorbed from Japanese poetry. Sometimes jazz rhythms ("Travelers in Ere whom," for example), and ballad stanzas ("Songs for Marie's Lute-Book"), as well as a host of other styles, forms, and techniques are employed.

Finally, the many translations are of enormous value. They not only have introduced many readers to poetry in Chinese, Japanese, and European languages, but also deserve to be read as enduring works of art in their own right. The translations are organically inseparable from Rexroth's other work, bringing to life voices that harmonize with his own, in a complex but coherent vision of worldwide community.

OTHER MAJOR WORKS

PLAYS: *Beyond the Mountains*, 1951 (4 plays).

NONFICTION: *Bird in the Bush: Obvious Essays*, 1959; *Assays*, 1961; *An Autobiographical Novel*, 1966, 1978; *Classics Revisited*, 1968; *The Alternative Society: Essays from the Other World*, 1970; *With Eye and Ear*, 1970; *American Poetry in the Twentieth Century*, 1971; *The Elastic Retort*, 1973; *Communalism, from the Neolithic to 1900*, 1975; *Excerpts from a Life*, 1981; *World Outside the Window: The Selected Essays of Kenneth Rexroth*, 1987; *More Classics Revisited*, 1989; *Kenneth Rexroth and James Laughlin: Selected Letters*, 1991.

TRANSLATIONS: *Fourteen Poems by O. V. de L. Milosz*, 1952, 1982; *One Hundred Poems from the Japanese*, 1955, 1957, 1964; *One Hundred Poems from the French*, 1955, 1972; *Thirty Spanish Poems of Love and Exile*, 1956; *One Hundred Poems from the Chinese*, 1956, 1965; *Poems from the Greek Anthology*, 1962; *Pierre Reverdy Selected Poems*, 1969; *Love in the Turning Year: One Hundred More Poems from the Chinese*, 1970; *The Orchid Boat: Women Poets of China*, 1972 (with Ling Chung); *One Hundred More Poems from the Japanese*, 1974; *The Burning Heart: Women Poets of Japan*, 1977 (with Atsumi Ikuko); *Seasons of Sacred Lust: Selected Poems of Kazuko Shiraishi*, 1978 (with Carol Tinker, Atsumi, John Solt, and Morita Yasuyo); *Li Ch'ing Chao: Complete Poems*, 1979 (with Chung).

MISCELLANEOUS: *The Kenneth Rexroth Reader*, 1972 (Eric Mottram, editor).

BIBLIOGRAPHY

Gibson, Morgan. *Kenneth Rexroth*. New York: Twayne, 1972. The first book-length study of Rexroth and a good introduction to his life and work. Chronological in approach, the book traces Rexroth's career. Includes chronology, notes, select bibliography (including an annotated list of secondary sources), and index.

_______. *Revolutionary Rexroth: Poet of East-West Wisdom*. Hamden, Conn.: Archon Books, 1986. This book expands Gibson's *Kenneth Rexroth* (1972) in order to assess the poet's entire career. Benefiting from the close friendship with Rexroth, Gibson traces the evolution of themes and styles and analyzes the poems, plays, translations, and essays. Contains notes, bibliography, and index.

Grisby, Gordon K. "The Presence of Reality: The Poetry of Kenneth Rexroth." *Antioch Review* 31 (Fall, 1971): 405-422. Grisby links the directness and clarity of Rexroth's style to the nature of his vision. Many well-chosen examples from the poems illustrate the main themes of Rexroth's poetry.

Gutierrez, Donald. *The Holiness of the Real: The Short Verse of Kenneth Rexroth*. Madison, N.J.: Fairleigh Dickinson University Press, 1996. A critical study of selected poems by Rexroth. Includes bibliographical references and indexes.

_______. "Rexroth's 'Incarnation.'" *Explicator* 53, no. 4 (Summer, 1995): 236. Gutierrez explores how Rexroth renders sexual love in a context of nature so that nature ceases to be context in "Incarnation."

Hamalian, Linda. *A Life of Kenneth Rexroth*. New York: W. W. Norton, 1991. This biography of Rexroth relies on extensive interviews with Rexroth and other key individuals. Illustrating both positive and negative qualities, this book corrects Rexroth's account in *An Autobiographical Novel* (1966).

Houghlum, Brook. "Kenneth Rexroth and Radio Reading." *English Studies in Canada* 33, no. 4 (December, 2007): 55-67. Examines a 1957 broadcast on KPFA, a socially and politically active radio station in Berkeley, California, in which Rexroth read his poetry, and discusses how this reading demonstrates Rexroth's beliefs about what poetry is.

Pekar, Harvey. "Between Rexroth and Gary Snyder in the Bay Area." In *The Beats: A Graphic History*, by Harvey Pekar et al. Art by Ed Piskor et al. New York: Hill and Wang, 2009. Comic legend Pekar looks at Rexroth and Gary Snyder, two poets influenced by Asian philosophy and relation, in this graphic book on the Beat poets.

Rexroth, Kenneth. "An Interview with Kenneth Rexroth." Interview by Cyrena N. Pondrom. In *The Contemporary Writer: Interviews with Sixteen Writers and Poets*, edited by L. S. Dembo and Cyrena N. Pondrom. Madison: University of Wisconsin Press, 1972. Focuses on the mystical and philosophical ideas underlying Rexroth's poetry. Rexroth explains in detail the effects he tries to achieve in a poem. The influence of Asian culture, especially that of Buddhism, is abundantly illustrated.

Morgan Gibson

GARY SNYDER

Born: San Francisco, California; May 8, 1930

Principal poetry

Riprap, 1959
Myths and Texts, 1960
The Firing, 1964
Hop, Skip, and Jump, 1964
Nanao Knows, 1964
Riprap, and Cold Mountain Poems, 1965
Six Sections from Mountains and Rivers Without End, 1965
A Range of Poems, 1966
Three Worlds, Three Realms, Six Roads, 1966
The Back Country, 1967
The Blue Sky, 1969
Sours of the Hills, 1969
Regarding Wave, 1969, enlarged 1970
Manzanita, 1972
The Fudo Trilogy: Spel Against Demons, Smokey the Bear Sutra, The California Water Plan, 1973
Turtle Island, 1974
All in the Family, 1975
Axe Handles, 1983
Left Out in the Rain: New Poems, 1947-1986, 1986
No Nature: New and Selected Poems, 1992
Mountains and Rivers Without End, 1996
Danger on Peaks, 2004

Other literary forms

Gary Snyder's pioneering journal of personal environmental discovery, *Earth House Hold: Technical Notes and Queries to Fellow Dharma Revolutionaries* (1969), was an invitation to examine the treasures of the planet and to consider how it might be employed for the benefit of all living species. It represents the culmination of the work Snyder began nearly two decades before when he conceived of a major in literature and anthropology at Reed College, and its somewhat tentative, propositional format expresses the spirit of a movement that recognized the destructive aspects of modern industrial society and sought alternative approaches to the questions of planetary survival. Although Snyder was sometimes referred to disparagingly as "a kind of patron saint of ecology" by critics trapped in more conventional social arrangements, his interest in the environment has proved to be as perceptive and enduring as his best poetry, and the publication of *The Practice of the Wild* (1990) has deepened the context of his interests, offering the wisdom and experience of a lifetime spent living in and thinking about the natural world. The book is a linked series of reflective essays, and its amiable, reasonable tone—similar to Snyder's conversational voice in his interviews, most notably those collected in *The Real Work: Interviews and Talks, 1964-1979* (1980)—permits the power of his intellectual insights, his scholarly investigations, and his political theories to reach an audience beyond the experts he hopes to equal in his argument. Combining energetic conviction and poetic eloquence, Snyder's essays are intended to be a "genuine teaching text" and "a mediation on what it means to be human." They demonstrate his philosophy of composition as it reveals a poetics of existence and have been written to stimulate "a broad range of people and provide them with historical, ecological and personal vision." *A Place in Space: Ethics, Aesthetics, and Watersheds* (1995) continues his exploration of these concerns, which are summarized and extended in *Back on the Fire: Essays* (2007).

ACHIEVEMENTS

Before "ecology" had become a password of political correctness, Gary Snyder was devising a program of study designed to create a language of environmental advocacy; after many trendy Westerners had long since recoiled from the rigors of Eastern thought, Snyder completed a curriculum of apprenticeship in Japan and went on to develop an American version of Zen applicable to his locality. As Native American life and lore gradually seeped into the area of academic interest, Snyder continued his examinations of the primal tribal communities that lived in harmony with the North American land mass for pre-Columbian millennia and worked to apply their successes to contemporary life. While hippies and dropouts returned to the button-down corporate culture after a brief dalliance with a counterculture, Snyder built his own home at the center of a small community that endures as an example of a philosophical position in action. Most of all, while some of the other voices that arose during the post-"Howl" renaissance of the new American poetry have become stale or quaint, Snyder's use of a clear, direct, colloquial but literature-responsive language made it possible for his concerns to reach, touch, and move a substantial audience through his poetry.

Snyder's varied interests have given him extensive material for his poems, but the appeal of his work does not depend on a program calculated to educate or persuade. Much more than argument, the poetry is an outgrowth of the processes of Snyder's life—his work, his family, his intellectual and athletic interests, his cultural convictions, and his rapport with the landscape. He has been able to illustrate effectively how art and life can be intertwined in a reciprocal interchange that does not depend on academic procedures or traditional schools (while not denying their usefulness), an interchange that enriches and expands both realms, and in this he joins Herman Melville (the sailor),

Henry David Thoreau (the naturalist), Ralph Waldo Emerson (the philosopher and teacher), and Walt Whitman (the celebrator) in a line of American artists whose work was, in a profound sense, the spiritual and aesthetic expression of their life's focus.

Snyder won the Pulitzer Prize in 1975 for *Turtle Island*. He has received numerous other awards, including the Bess Hokin Prize (1964), an Academy Award from the National Institute of Arts and Letters (1966), the Levinson Prize (1968), the Shelley Memorial Award (1986), the American Book Award from the Before Columbus Foundation (1984), Silver Medals from the Commonwealth Club of California (1986, 2002), the Fred Cody Award for lifetime achievement (1989), the Robert Kirsch Award from the *Los Angeles Times* (1996), the Bollingen Prize (1997), the John Hay Award for Nature Writing (1997), the Lila Wallace-*Reader's Digest* Writers' Award (1998), the Masaoka Shiki International Haiku Grand Prize (2004), and the Ruth Lilly Poetry Prize (2008). He served as chancellor for the Academy of American Poets from 2003 to 2009.

BIOGRAPHY

Gary Sherman Snyder was born in San Francisco in 1930, the son of Harold Alton Snyder and Lois Wilkie Snyder. His parents moved back to their native Pacific Northwest in 1932, where they settled on a dairy farm near Puget Sound in Washington. Snyder's mother moved to Portland, Oregon, to work as a newspaper-woman when Snyder was twelve, and she reared Snyder and his younger sister Anthea as a single parent, insisting that Snyder commute downtown to attend Lincoln High, the most intellectually demanding school in the Portland system.

In 1947, he received a scholarship to Reed College, where he devised a unique major in anthropology and literature. Early in his college years, he joined the Mazamas and the Wilderness Society, both outdoors groups, and took up backcountry hiking and skiing and snow-peak mountaineering. His first poems were published in the Reed College literary magazine. He lived in an old house shared by a dozen other students similarly interested in art and politics, including the poets Philip Whalen and Lew Welch, who became his close friends. Snyder wrote for *The Oregonian* newspaper at night and spent the summer of 1950 on an archaeological dig at old Fort Vancouver in Washington. At about that time, he was briefly married to Allison Gass, a fellow student.

Upon graduation from Reed, Snyder completed one semester of graduate studies in linguistics at Indiana University before transferring to the University of California, Berkeley, to study Asian languages. During the summers of the years he pursued graduate work, he took a job first as a fire-watcher in the Cascade mountains and later, after he was fired in the McCarthy-era hysteria of 1954, as a choker-setter for the Warm Springs Lumber Company. Utilizing skills in woodcutting he had learned from his family and neighbors, Snyder "was often supporting himself" in his student years, and his first accomplished poems were related to these experiences as well as to his work on a trail crew in Yosemite in 1955.

That fall, Snyder met Allen Ginsberg and Jack Kerouac and became involved in the exploding art scene in San Francisco, where he took part in the historic Six Gallery reading where Ginsberg read "Howl" in public for the first time. Snyder followed this extraordinary performance with his own poetry in a very different vein and was also successful in capturing the attention of the audience. He and Kerouac shared a cabin in Mill Valley, California, through that winter and spring, and then Snyder traveled to Kyoto, Japan, to take up residence in a Zen temple, beginning a twelve-year sojourn in Japan that was broken by a nine-month hitch as a crewman on the tanker *Sappa Creek* and a brief return to San Francisco in 1958. His translations from the Chinese poet Han-shan, who lived in the seventh century, were published in the *Evergreen Review* in 1958 as "Cold Mountain Poems," and his first collection, *Riprap*, was published by Cid Corman's Origin Press in Japan in 1959.

Working as a part-time translator and researcher of Buddhist texts, Snyder eventually became a student of Rinzai Zen under Oda Sesso, Roshi (master), and established contacts with activist groups concerned with ecology, women's issues, and world peace. His next collection, *Myths and Texts*, was published in 1960, the same year he married the poet Joanne Kyger. In 1962, he traveled to India with Ginsberg, Peter Orlovsky, and Kyger, and his association with the poet Nanao Sakaki drew him into artistic circles in Tokyo in 1964. He returned to the United States to teach at Berkeley in 1965, won a Bollingen grant, and returned to Japan. His marriage with Kyger was over when he met Masa Uehara, a graduate student in English, and they were married in 1967.

With his wife and his son, Kai, who was born in Kyoto, Snyder returned to the Western Hemisphere, settling in the northern Sierra Nevada mountains, where he built a home (called "Kitkitdizze," meaning "mountain misery" in a local dialect) in 1970 with a crew of friends. His first book of poems reflecting his commitment to his native country, *Turtle Island* (from an old Native American name for the continent), was published in 1974 and won the Pulitzer Prize. During this time, Snyder was traveling to universities three or four months a year to read poetry, working on the needs of his immediate mountain community, and serving the state of California as the chairman of its Arts Council. At the end of the decade, he published a collection called *The Real Work*, and in 1983, he published *Axe Handles*, poems written during the previous ten years. In 1985, he joined the English department at the University of California, Davis, where he taught literature and ecological matters until his retirement in 2002. He began to travel widely, visiting Hawaii, Alaska, China, and parts of Europe to speak "on the specifics of Buddhist meditation, ecological practice, language and poetics, and bioregional politics." The poems he had written but left uncollected were published in *Left Out in the Rain: New Poems, 1947-1986*. In 1988, he was divorced from Masa Uehara and married Carole Koda, and in 1990, he completed a book that presented a program for personal renewal and planetary conservation called *The Practice of the Wild*. That same year, a compilation of comments, reminiscences, poems, and assorted other statements was published by the Sierra Club under the title *Gary Snyder: Dimensions of a Life* in celebration of the poet's sixtieth birthday. Snyder completed his epic "poem of process" *Mountains and Rivers Without End* in 1996 and continued to train students at Davis to deal with environmental crises. In the first decade of the twenty-first century, Snyder traveled extensively, sharing his ideas about environmental advocacy to a worldwide audience that recognized him as one of the visionary founders of an increasingly widespread "deep ecology" movement. His good-natured, inspiring and enlightening comments about the ecosystems of the planet were gathered in the essays of *Back on the Fire*, while his first collection of poems in twenty years, *Danger on Peaks*, was both a recapitulation and reaffirmation of the themes and subjects of his life's work and a mature reflection and reassessment of his most personal concerns. The hero-figure Kerouac patterned after Snyder in *The Dharma Bums* (1958), "Japhy Ryder," has become the source of wisdom, as the poet Snyder has grown into an elder of the tribe.

Analysis

Among many evocative statements about his life and work, a particularly crucial one is Gary Snyder's claim that

> As a poet, I hold the most archaic values on earth. They go back to the late Paleolithic; the fertility of the soil, the magic of animals; the power-vision in solitude, the terrifying initiation and rebirth; the love and ecstasy of the dance, the common work of the tribe.

The social and philosophical principles he has expressed are the fundamental credo of his convictions as a man and an artist. He uses the word "archaic" to suggest "primal" or "original"—the archetype or first pattern from which others may evolve. His citation of the late Paleolithic era as source-ground stems from his belief that essential lessons concerning human consciousness have been learned and then lost. Thus Snyder devotes much time to the study of ancient (and primitive) cultures. The values he holds stand behind and direct his poetry, as it is drawn from his studies and experiences. His values include a respect for land as the source of life and the means of sustaining it; a respect for all sentient creatures and for the animalistic instincts of humans; a recognition of the necessity for the artist to resist social pressure in order to discover and develop power from within; an acknowledgment of the necessity for participation in both communal ritual and individual exploration of the depths of the subconscious to transcend the mundane and risk the extraordinary; an acceptance of the body and the senses—the physical capabilities, pleasures, and demands of the skin; and a feeling for the shared labor of the community, another version of "the real work" that unites the individual with a larger sense and source of meaning. Neither the poet as solitary singer nor as enlightened visionary is sufficient without the complex of relationships that joins the local, the bioregional, and ultimately the planetary in an interdependent chain of reliance, support, and enlightened use of resources. It is with these values in mind that Snyder defines an ethical life as one that "is mindful, mannerly and has style," an attitude that is crucial to the accomplishment of "the real work."

Each of these precepts has an important analogue in the technical execution of the poems themselves. As Jerome Rothenberg has observed, "where I continue to see him best is as he emerges from his poems." Poetically, then, "the fertility of the soil" is worthless without the labor that brings it to fruition, and as Snyder has commented, "the rhythms of my poems follow the rhythms of the physical work I'm doing and life I'm leading at any given time—which makes the music in my head which creates the line." The linkage between the rhythmic movement of the body, the larger rhythmic cycles of the natural world, and the structure of words in a particular poem follows the precepts that Charles Olson prescribed in the landmark essay "Projective Verse" (1950), and Snyder, like Ginsberg, Robert Creeley, and others, has always favored the creation of a particular shape or form to suit the purpose of the poem under attentive development. The rhythms of a particular poem are derived from an "energy-mind-field-dance" that, in turn, often results from labor designed to capitalize on the life of the earth.

Similarly, when Snyder speaks of "the magic of animals," he is identifying one of his central subjects, and the images of many of his poems are based on his observations of animals in the wild. The importance of wilderness and the manner in which animals seem to interact instinctively with their natural surroundings are, for Snyder, keys to his conception of freedom. The magic of their existence is part of a mystery that humans need to penetrate. Thus, as image and subject, animals and their ways are an important part of the "etiquette of freedom" that Snyder's work serves.

The concept of the "power vision in solitude" is derived from both the shamanistic practices that Snyder has studied in primitive societies and the varieties of meditation he has explored in his research into and expressions of Buddhist thought. Its immediate consequence in poetry is the necessity for developing a singular, distinct voice, a language with which one is comfortable, and a style that is true to the artist's entire life. For Snyder, this has meant learning to control the mood of a poem through tonal modulation, matching mood to subject and arranging sequences of poems that can sustain visionary power as well as intimate personal reflection. "The terrifying initiation and rebirth" is a corollary of the power vision. It implies that once a singular voice has been established, it must be followed according to the patterns of its impulsive organization—in other words, to its points of origin in the subconscious. Snyder speaks of the unconscious as "our inner wilderness areas," and sees in the "depths of the mind" the ultimate source of the imagination. The exploration of the wilderness within is vital to the image-making function of poetry.

The "love and ecstasy" Snyder speaks of stems from the revolt that Snyder and his colleagues led against the stiff, formal, distant academic poetry favored by critics in the 1950's, and its application has been to influence the colloquial nature of his language, to encourage the use of primitive techniques such as chant to alter perceptive states, to permit the inclusion of casual data from ordinary existence to inform the poem, and, most of all, to confront the most personal of subjects with honesty and self-awareness. There is a discernible narrative consciousness present in Snyder's poetry even when he avoids—as he generally does—personal pronouns and definite articles. However, his resistance to cultural authority is balanced by his praise for the "common work of the tribe," the artistic accomplishment that he treasures. As he has said, "I feel very strongly that poetry also exists as part of a tradition, and is not simply a matter of only private and personal vision." Explaining his interests in Ezra Pound, William Carlos Williams, Wallace Stevens, John Milton, and others, Snyder says he wants "to know *what* has been done, and to see *how* it has been done. That in a sense is true craft." Almost paradoxically, considering his emphasis on originality, he advocates (and practices) extensive examination of multidisciplinary learning, explaining that knowledge of the past saves one "the trouble of having to repeat things that others have done that need not be done again. And then also he knows when he writes a poem that has never been written before."

RIPRAP

Snyder's first collection, *Riprap*, is evidence of the writing and thinking that Snyder had been doing through the mid-1950's. *Riprap* took shape while Snyder was working on a backcountry trail crew in 1955, and its title is at first a description of "stone laid on steep, slick rock to make a trail for horses in the mountains," then a symbol of the interlinkage of objects in a region and a figure for the placement of words in a poetic structure. It serves to connect language and action, reflective thought and the work that generates it. The poems in the collection are dedicated to the men Snyder worked with, the "community" of cohesion and effort he joined, men who knew the requirements of the land and who transmitted their skills through demonstration. *Riprap* includes elements of the oral tradition Snyder intersected, and the title "celebrates the work of the hands" while some of the poems "run the risk of invisibility" since they tried "for surface simplicity set with unsettling depths." Poems such as "Above Pate Valley" and "Piute Creek" begin with direct description of landscape and move toward an almost cosmic perspective concerning the passage of time across the land over geological epochs. The specific and the eternal coalesce:

Hill beyond hill, folded and twisted
Tough trees crammed
In thin stone fractures
A huge moon on it all, is too much.
The mind wanders. A million
Summers, night air still and the rocks
Warm. Sky over endless mountains.

All the junk that goes with being human
Drops away, hard rock wavers.

Poetry, as Snyder put it in "Burning: No. 13" from *Myths and Texts*, is "a riprap on the slick road of metaphysics," helping one find meaning and explaining why one reads "Milton by Firelight" (the title of another poem) and finds new versions of hell and "the wheeling sky" in the Sierras.

MYTHS AND TEXTS

Myths and Texts is Snyder's first attempt to organize his ideas into an evolving, complex structural framework. In it, Snyder's wilderness experience is amplified by the use of Pacific Coast Indian texts, which are set as a kind of corrective for the exploitation and destruction of the environment that Snyder sees as the result of misguided American-European approaches to nature. The crux of the matter is the failure of Judeo-Christian culture to recognize the inherent sacredness of the land, and Snyder uses what he feels is a kind of Buddhist compassion and a Native American empathy as a corrective thrust. The three books of the collection are called "Logging," which uses the lumber industry as an example of "technological drivenness" that destroys resources and shows no respect for the symbolic or ritualistic aspect of the living wilderness; "Hunting," which explores the intricate relationship between the hunter and the quarry (and between mind and body) in primitive societies; and "Burning," which is somewhat less accessible in its intriguing attempt to find or chart a symbolic synthesis that integrates the mythic material Snyder has been presenting into a universal vision of timeless cycles of destruction and rebirth.

As Snyder defines the terms, in a preliminary fashion, the myths and texts are the "two sources of human knowledge—symbols and sense-impressions." The larger context at which he aims—the "one whole thing"—is built on the power of individual poems, and among the best are ones such as "Logging: No. 8," in which the logged ground is likened to a battlefield after a massacre; "Logging: No. 3," in which the lodgepole pine is treated as an emblem of nature's enduring vitality; "Logging: No. 13," in which a fire-watcher reports a fire ("T36N R16E S25/ Is burning. Far to the west") and seems more interested in the abstract beauty of the landscape than in any specific situation; and among several hunting songs, the exceptional "No. 6," which carries the dedication, "*this poem is for bear*."

Snyder read the original version of "The Woman Who Married a Bear" in an anthropology text in Reed College and was fascinated by the interaction of the human and animal cultures. He devotes a chapter to the story in *The Practice of the Wild*, lamenting that "the bears are being killed, the humans are everywhere, and the green world is being unraveled and shredded and burned by the spreading of a gray world that seems to have no end." His poem is placed at the convergence of several cultures and is structured by the different speaking "voices"—not specifically identified but clear from tone and context. First, in a quote from the anthropological text, the bear speaks: "As for me I am a child of the god of the mountains." Then, a field scientist, observing the data:

> You can see
> Huckleberries in bearshit if you
> Look, this time of year
> If I sneak up on the bear
> It will grunt and run.

This relatively matter-of-fact, outside position is replaced by a tale of the girl who married a bear: "In a house under the mountain/ She gave birth to slick dark children/ With sharp teeth, and lived in the hollow/ Mountain many years." A shift has been made to the Native American culture, and what follows is the burden of the legend, as the girl's tribe goes to reclaim her. The next voice is the hunter addressing the bear:

> honey-eater
> forest apple
> light-foot
> Old man in the fur coat, Bear! come out!
> Die of your own choice!

Now the poet enters, turning the tale (text) into poetry (myth): "Twelve species north of Mexico/ Sucking their paws in the long winter/ Tearing the high-strung caches down/ Whining, crying, jacking off." Then the tale continues, as the girl's brothers "cornered him in the rocks," and finally the "voice" of the bear-spirit speaks, as through a shaman perhaps, in the "Song of the snared bear":

> "Give me my belt.
> "I am near death.
> "I came from the mountain caves
> "At the headwaters,
> "The small streams there
> "Are all dried up.

In a deft conclusion, Snyder reduces the dramatic tension by the interposition of the disarmingly personal. As if inspired by the story, he begins to imagine himself a part of the Paleolithic hunter culture: "I think I'll go hunt bears." However, he is too solidly grounded in reality to go beyond a reading of the text: "Why s— Snyder,/ You couldn't hit a bear in the ass/ with a handful of rice." Although, of course, in the poem, he has hit the target squarely by assimilating the different voices (as different strands of culture) into his own modern version of the myth.

COLD MOUNTAIN POEMS

The *Cold Mountain Poems*, published together with *Riprap* as *Riprap and the Cold Mountain Poems*, are "translations" (in the Poundian sense) from Han-shan, a hermit and poet of the Tang dynasty, and they represent Snyder's identification with a kind of nature prophet at home in the wild as well as his inclination to isolate himself from those aspects of American (or Western) society he found abhorrent until he could fashion a program to combat the social ills he identified. As in most effective translations, there is a correspondence in sensibility between the two artists, and Snyder's comfort with the backcountry, as well as his growing sense of a cross-cultural and transepochal perspective, may be seen in lines like

> Thin grass does for a mattress,
> The blue sky makes a good quilt.
> Happy with a stone underhead
> Let heaven and earth go about their changes.

Calling Han-shan a "mountain madman" or "ragged hermit," Snyder expresses through the translations his admiration for a kind of independence, self-possession, and mindful alertness that he saw as a necessity for psychic survival in the Cold War era, a husbanding of strength to prepare for a return to the social struggle. "Mind solid and sharp," he says, he is gaining the vision to "honor this priceless natural treasure"—the world around him ("the whole clear cloudless sky")—and the insight ("sunk deep in the flesh") to understand the complementary wonder within.

REGARDING WAVE

With *Regarding Wave*, Snyder's work turned from the mythic and philosophical toward the intimate and immediately personal. He had begun a family (his son Kai was born in 1968) and returned to the United States, and the poems recall his last days in the Far East and his sense of how he had to proceed after returning to his native land at a time of strife and turmoil. The family poems are celebratory, written in wonder, open and exuberant in the first flush of parenthood, expressing his delight with his wife Masa and their infant son. There are poems that are like meditations on the sensual: "Song of the View," "Song of the Tangle," or "Song of the Taste," and poems that are drawn from the experience of rearing a child, like "The Bed in the Sky" or "Kai, Today," which is an awestruck reflection on the act of birth, or the supra-mundane "Not Leaving the House," in which Snyder admits "When Kai is born/ I quit going out," and justifies his inward angle of view by concluding "From dawn til late at night/ making a new world of ourselves/ around this life."

After returning to the United States, Snyder found that the political situation was troubling ("Off the coast of Oregon/ The radio is full of hate and anger"), and he was warned that "beards don't make money," so he began to plan a life as a poet and activist in the United States. The effects of his action become clearer in his next collection, but the cast of his mind is apparent in the transitional "What You Should Know to Be a Poet," which calls together what he had learned from his life to that point:

> all you can about animals as persons
> the names of trees and flowers and weeds
> names of stars, and the movements of the planets
> and the moon.
>
> your own six senses, with a watchful and elegant mind

and then blends it with a kind of resolution to confront the bestial nature of humans to prepare to engage the evil at large in the world, as expressed in the crucial central stanza beginning, "kiss the ass of the devil." From that point, the poem alternates positive aspects of existence ("& then love the human: wives husbands and friends") with an acceptance of the trials and burdens of life ("long dry hours of dull work swallowed and accepted/ and livd with and finally lovd") until it concludes with an unsettling sense of the future, "real danger. gambles. and the edge of death."

THE FUDO TRILOGY

Snyder's ambivalent feelings about living in the United States are again expressed in the hilarious "Smokey the Bear Sutra," in which the familiar symbol of the forest service is depicted as a kind of Asiatic avenging demon protecting the environment and resisting polluters. Published in 1973 as a part of *The Fudo Trilogy*—a pamphlet that included "The California Water Plan" (a section of *Mountains and Rivers Without End*) and "Spel Against Demons"—it combines Snyder's serious concerns about the environment and his continuing pursuit of Asiatic culture with his characteristically engaging high good humor. The chant, "Drown their butts; soak their butts" is presented in mock seriousness as a mantra of righteousness, while Smokey is depicted more as a lovable child's pet than the fierce scourge of evil that the archetype suggests. The comic conception works to keep Snyder's considerable anger under control, so that he does not turn his poetry into polemic.

TURTLE ISLAND

By the early 1970's, Snyder had become fully involved in the bioregional movement and committed to the local community of San Juan Ridge, where he had built a home. He began to follow a dual course in his poetry. The overarching theme of his work was to protect and preserve "Turtle Island—the old/new name for the continent, based on many creation myths," and it was expressed in poems that "speak of place, and the energy-pathways that sustain life" and in poems that decry the forces of destruction unleashed by the stupidity of "demonic killers" who perpetrate "aimless executions and slaughterings."

The poems were published under the title *Turtle Island*, sold more than 100,000 copies, and won the Pulitzer Prize. Among the most memorable poems Snyder has written, the ones that explore the "energy pathways" sustaining life include "The Bath"—a Whitmanesque rapture in appreciation of the body that challenges the latent Puritanism and fear of the skin in American society by describing in loving detail the physical wonder of his son, his wife, and himself in a bath. The sheer glory of the body glowing with health and the radiant reflection of the natural world around them build toward a feeling of immense physical satisfaction and then toward a complementary feeling of metaphysical well-being. The frankness of the language may be difficult for some readers, but Snyder's tasteful, delicate, and comfortable handling of it makes his declaration "this is our body," an echoing chorus, an assertion of religious appreciation. In an even more directly thankful mode, the translation of a Mohawk "Prayer for the Great Family" unites the basic elements of the cosmos in a linked series of gemlike depictions, concluding with one of Snyder's essential ideas: that there is an infinite space "beyond all powers and thoughts/ and yet is within us—/ Grandfather Space/ The Mind is his Wife." Other expressions of "eternal delight" include "By Frazier Creek Falls," "Source," and "The Dazzle," as well as many poems in the book's last section, a kind of basic history primer called "For the Children," that convey considerable emotion without lapsing into obvious emotional tugging.

The more overtly political poems and sketches tend to be somber, frequently employing a litany of statistics to convey grim information that needs little additional comment, but in "The Call of the Wild," Snyder's anger is projected in language purposefully charged with judgmental fervor. Avoiding easy partisanship, Snyder condemns, first, "ex acid-heads" who have opted for "forever blissful sexless highs" and hidden in fear from what is interesting about life. His image of people missing the point of everything by living in trendy "Geodesic domes, that/ Were stuck like warts/ In the woods" is as devastating as his cartoon conception of advanced technology declaring "a war against earth" waged by pilots with "their women beside them/ in bouffant hairdos/ putting nail-polish on the/ gunship cannon-buttons."

AXE HANDLES

The poems in *Axe Handles* have a reflective tone, moving inward toward the life Snyder has been leading in his local community, to which he dedicated the collection. His concerns do not change, but in a return to the more spare, lyrical poems of *Riprap*, Snyder condenses and focuses his ideas into "firm, clean lines of verse reminiscent of Ezra Pound's *Rock-Drill* cantos," according to critic Andrew Angyal. The title has a typically dual meaning, referring to language as an instrument for shaping meaning and to the entire meaning of tools in human life. The theme of "cultural continuity" is presented in terms of Snyder's passing his knowledge on to his family, friends, and readers and is explicitly explained in the parable of the title poem. The book evokes an ethos of harmony in cycles of renewal and restoration, rebirth and reconsideration. Snyder moves beyond his specific criticism of human social organizations in the late twentieth century and toward, in Angyal's words, his "own alternative set of values in communal cooperation, conservation, and a nonexploitative way of life that shows respect for the land." The compression and density of Snyder's thinking are evident in the poem "Removing the Plate of the Pump on the Hydraulic System of the Backhoe," which reads in entirety

> Through mud, fouled nuts, black grime
> it opens, a gleam of spotless steel
> machined-fit perfect
> swirl of intake and output
> relentless clarity
> at the heart
> of work.

The pursuit of "relentless clarity" in everything characterizes Snyder's life and art, but the pressures of the search are alleviated by his congenial nature and sense of humor. While emphasizing the importance of Zen "mindfulness," Snyder has also stressed that "a big part of life is just being playful." In accordance with this approach, Snyder has kept dogmatic or simplistic solutions out of his work and has cherished the wild and free nature of humankind. In "Off the Trail," which he wrote for his wife, Koda, he envisions a life in which "all paths are possible" and maintains that "the trial's not the way" to find wisdom or happiness. "We're off the trail,/ You and I," he declares, "and we chose it!" That choice—the decision to go against the grain "to be in line with the big flow"—has led to a poetry of "deeply human richness," as Charles Molesworth puts it in his perceptive study of Snyder's work, in which "a vision of plenitude" leads to a "liminal utopia, poised between fullness and yet more growth."

MOUNTAINS AND RIVERS WITHOUT END

On April 8, 1956, Snyder began to work on a "poem of process" somewhat akin to Pound's *Cantos* (1970) or Williams's *Paterson* (5 volumes, 1946-1956) that he called *Mountains and Rivers Without End*. Initially inspired by East Asian brush painting (*sumi*) on a series of screens and by his own experiences with what he viewed as "a chaotic universe where everything is in place," Snyder brought in elements of Native American styles of narration, his continuing study of Zen Buddhism, Asian art and drama, and the varied landscapes that he traversed on several continents during the next four decades as the primary features of the poem. "It all got more complicated than I predicted and the poems were evasive," Snyder remarked in retrospect about the project. A particular problem involved the central narrative consciousness, since the traditional idea of an epic hero as a focal perspective seemed outmoded. As an alternate center of coherence, Snyder devised an elaborate structural arrangement built on ways in which "walking the landscape can be both ritual and meditation" so that the evolving perceptual matrix of the artist provided a fundamental frame for the materials of the poem.

Drawing on the "yogic implications" of mountains as representations of "a tough spirit of willed self-discipline" and rivers as a projection of "generous and loving spirit of concern for all beings" (as Snyder explained in "The Making of *Mountains and Rivers Without End*," an afterword to the poem), the epic is energized by the interplay between these elemental forces. The essential things of the poet's life—his practice of Zen meditation and action, his abiding concern for the "ark of biodiversity," his love and care for friends and family, his investigative interest in the previous inhabitants of the North American continent, and his sense of himself as an artist whose poetry is an extension of the patterns of his working world—provide the distinct subjects and incidents for the separately composed poems that constitute individual sections, written (as he notes in his signatory final line) from "Marin-an 1956" to "Kitkitdizze 1996."

Like Pound, whom Snyder calls "my direct teacher in these matters," Snyder wanted to include what he considered the most important intellectual, mythological, and cultural aspects of his times, but he noted that "big sections of the *Cantos* aren't interesting." To avoid the kind of obscurity that requires endless emendations, Snyder provided several pages of explanation in endnotes and included a record of publication of the individual parts, which functions as an accompanying chronology. Nevertheless, the technical strategies Snyder employs to "sustain the reader through it" are fairly intricate and designed to maintain a discernible structure that contributes to the cohesion of the poem. The guiding principle behind the entire enterprise depends on Snyder's conviction that, as he stated in an afterword to a 1999 reprint of *Riprap*, the whole universe can be seen as "interconnected, interpenetrating, mutually reflecting and mutually embracing." Therefore, while some individual parts may contain names, ideas, and references that appear esoteric or strictly personal, "there will be enough reverberations and echoes from various sections so that it will be self-informing." Since the poem's progress is not chronological, arranged according to place rather than period, there is no ultimate sense of completion. For Snyder, the poem is not "closed up" but ideally should continue to maintain a "sense of usefulness and relevance" as it offers "stimulation and excitement and imagination" for the reader.

In addition to the widest patterns of intersection, Snyder uses several prominent technical devices to tie things together. Initially, he expected to have twenty-five sections, each centering on a key phrase. While this plan was not maintained for every part of the poem, there are some especially important key phrases, as in the seventh poem ("Bubbs Creek Haircut"), in which the third line from the last, "double mirror waver," is described by Snyder as a "structure point" conveying infinite reflection. Similarly, in "Night Highway 99," the third poem, the image of a "network womb" is described by Snyder as a reference to the Buddhist concept of "the great womb of time and space which intersects itself." The poem "The Blue Sky," which concludes part 1, contains what Snyder describes as a "healing" word, "sky/tent/curve," an image of an arc that connects the disparate horizons of isolated nations. This sense of joining is a crucial philosophical precept in the poem, since the original idea of landscape paintings on screens or scrolls is exemplified by Snyder's remark that he "would like to have the poem close in on itself but on some other level keep going."

The final form of the poem is clarified by the publication record, which indicates an unleashing of energy in the 1960's followed by an ingathering of strength during the mid-1970's to mid-1980's, when Snyder's travels took him to "most of the major collections of Chinese paintings in the United States." His sense of the poem was also "enlarged by walking/working visits to major urban centers," which became important social complements to the portrayals of the natural world. In the 1990's, Snyder says, "the entire cycle clicked for me" and he wrote sixteen of the poem's sections while revising the typography of some earlier parts and reorganizing the placement of the poems in the final version. While each individual poem can function as an independent entity, the completed poem has, as poet Robert Hass has commented, "the force and concentration of a very shaped work of art."

An overview of the poem reveals Snyder's shaping strategies. The first of the four parts deals with the origins of a voyage, the inner and outer landscapes to be traveled, and the ways in which the features of the terrain can be gathered into a personal vision. "Night Highway 99," for instance, is Snyder's *On the Road*, embracing the Pacific Coast route where Snyder hitchhiked south from his home ground and met people like Ginsberg ("A. G."), a road brother. The second part extends the journey to the concrete bleakness and compulsive energy of giant urban complexes. "Walking the New York Bedrock" revels in the sheer magnitude of a great city, which still recalls the "many-footed Manhatta" of Whitman's paean. The parallels Snyder draws here between geologic strata, canyons, and skyscrapers imply a commonality in disparate forms. The third part moves toward a reconciliation of forces and forms, while the fourth, containing poems written more recently, conveys the now mature poet's reflective estimate of enduring values. The poem for Snyder's wife, Koda, "Cross-Legg'd," is a kind of prayer of appreciation for the rewards of the journey, an expression of serenity and alertness. As a demonstration of the qualities he esteems, its conclusion, "we two be here what comes," celebrates the condition of mindful awareness Snyder sought when he began his study of Buddhist ways.

Toward the poem's conclusion, "The Mountain Spirit" reframes the conception of mountains and rivers that launched the journey. Its declaration, "Streams and mountains never stay the same," is like a motto for the poet's way of being, while its statement "All art is song/ is sacred to the real" reemphasizes his fundamental credo. His quote "nothingness is shapeliness" is at the core of Zen practice, also echoing Ginsberg's claim, "Mind is shapely/ Art is Shapely." The final poem, "Finding the Space in the Heart," explores the infinity of space, which Snyder sees as a symbol of freedom, ending the poem in an ethos of gratitude epitomized by the "quiet heart and distant eye," which he acknowledges as the supreme gift of "the mountain spirit." Even with all of the evocative, vividly descriptive passages illuminating the natural world, Snyder's poetry remains firmly grounded on the human values he sees as the fundamentals of existence. As he has said, "In a visionary way, what we would want poetry to do is guide lovers toward ecstasy, give witness to the dignity of old people, intensify human bonds, elevate the community and improve the public spirit."

Danger on Peaks

Danger on Peaks is both a reflective recollection of important incidents and moments from earlier years and a continuing demonstration of the kinds of energy and insight that have made Snyder's work as a poet and environmental visionary so impressive. The essays in *Back on the Fire*, which acts as a companion volume, explore some of the same subjects that have been Snyder's most enduring concerns and reveal some of the circumstances that shaped the poems. The essays recall and comment on earlier poems, and the poems often illuminate some of the situations that led toward the composition of the essays. Notably, at the close of *Back on the Fire*, Snyder bids farewell to his wife, to whom *Danger on Peaks* is dedicated:

> Carole Lynn Koda
>
> OCTOBER 3, 1947-JUNE 29, 2006
>
> gone, gone,   gone beyond
> gone beyond beyond
>
> bodhi
>
> *svāhā*

This deeply emotional statement, cast in direct, clear language imbued with the kind of personal philosophical perspective that has informed Snyder's work, exemplifies the tone and attitude that make the poems in *Danger on Peaks* so appealing for readers familiar with his work and an appropriate introduction for those reading him for the first time. The book is divided into six thematic sections, each one focused on a particular part of Snyder's life recalled and reconsidered for the pleasure of the memory and the revivified moment.

The first section, "Mount St. Helens," evokes the spirit of the landscape that drew Snyder into the wild when he was thirteen. Spirit Lake, when he first saw it, "was clear and still, faint wisps of fog on the smooth silvery surface," but the lake was obliterated when the volcano erupted, and the changes in the small span (in geologic terms) of time since then leads to a meditation on transformation and the value of what endures. The next section, "Yet Older Matters," is a gathering of short lyrics of appreciation for the infinite range and fundamental features of the natural world, followed by versions of haiku expressing the poet's psychological moods at a moment of awareness:

Clumsy at first
my legs, feet and eye learn again to leap
skip through the tumbled rocks

The third section, "Daily Life," is a series of short poetic accounts, mostly on one page, on subjects such as "reading the galley pages of [James] Laughlin's *Collected Poems*," "working on hosting Ko Un great Korean poet," visiting "Mariano Vallejo's Library," and in a high-spirited, rollicking song of pleasure and praise, building an addition to his home, "Old Kitkitdizze." The good-humored, energy-charged, inclusive communal atmosphere that has made Snyder's company as well as his writing so appealing is evident in his use of rhyming in short stanzas, listing, naming, and celebrating. The fourth section, "Steady, They Say," is a gallery of portraits, Snyder's friends from the recent (Seamus Heaney) and distant past ("To All the Girls Whose Ears I Pierced Back Then").

The last two sections take a turn toward the contemplative as Snyder offers brief narratives leading toward a poems that is both a commentary on an incident and a kind of concluding thought. The narrations are set as an unfolding present, each poem like a step toward a wider arc of apprehension. In "One Day in Late Summer," Snyder relates how he "had lunch with my old friend Jack Hogan," part of a group who "hung out in North Beach back in the fifties." Then, thinking about a half-century passing, he remarks:

This present moment
        that lives on

to become

long ago

The last section, "After Bamiyan" (the valley where the Taliban destroyed colossal statues of Buddha carved in caves in the sixth century) begins as an exchange with "A person who should know better" about the value of art and human life, leading Snyder to insist "Ah yes . . . impermanence. But this is never a reason to let compassion and focus slide, or to pass off the suffering of others." He supports this with Issa's great haiku about the "dew-drop world," in Japanese and then with his own translation, providing poetry and vivid prose in the service of the things Snyder regards as sacred. The volume, appropriately, does not close with a feeling of finality, as the last poem, "Envoy," is succeeded by one of Snyder's own photographs of Mount St. Helens in August, 1945, then two pages of explanatory notes, then "Thanks To" (another list as a poem), a page of acknowledgments, and lastly a photo of Snyder himself, smiling, a benediction and gift for the world to enjoy.

OTHER MAJOR WORKS

NONFICTION: *Earth House Hold: Technical Notes and Queries to Fellow Dharma Revolutionaries*, 1969; *The Old Ways*, 1977; *He Who Hunted Birds in His Father's Village: The Dimensions of a Haida Myth*, 1979; *The Real Work: Interviews and Talks, 1964-1979*, 1980; *Passage Through India*, 1983, expanded 2007; *The Practice of the Wild*, 1990; *A Place in Space: Ethics, Aesthetics, and Watersheds*, 1995; *Gary Snyder Papers*, 1995; *Back on the Fire: Essays*, 2007; *The Selected Letters of Allen Ginsberg and Gary Snyder*, 2009 (Bill Morgan, editor).

MISCELLANEOUS: *The Gary Snyder Reader: Prose, Poetry, and Translations, 1952-1998*, 2000.

BIBLIOGRAPHY

Gray, Timothy. *Gary Snyder and the Pacific Rim*. Iowa City: University of Iowa Press, 2006. An interesting study of the poet, his work, and his countercultural place in literary history.

Hunt, Anthony. *Genesis, Structure, and Meaning in Gary Snyder's "Mountains and Rivers Without End."* Las Vegas: University of Nevada Press, 2004. An intelligent interweaving of Snyder's aesthetic and environmental concerns and the development of his forty-year epic.

Murphy, Patrick. *A Place for Wayfaring: The Poetry and Prose of Gary Snyder*. Corvallis: Oregon State University Press, 2000. After three introductory chapters on themes in Snyder's work, especially mythological themes, Murphy offers close readings of a number of individual poems.

_______. *Understanding Gary Snyder*. Columbia: University of South Carolina Press, 1992. A useful overview, written for students and general readers, of Snyder's work and influences, with detailed explications of his work.

_______, ed. *Critical Essays on Gary Snyder*. Boston: G. K. Hall, 1990. A comprehensive, well-chosen collection of critical essays by one of Snyder's most intelligent critics. This book, which captures the earliest responses to the poet's work as well as the next three decades of criticism, is evidence of the variety of perspectives Snyder's work has brought forth.

Phillips, Rod. *"Forest Beatniks" and "Urban Thoreaus": Gary Snyder, Jack Kerouac, Lew Welch, and Michael McClure*. New York: P. Lang, 2000. Examines the attitudes toward nature, ecology, and conservation in the Beats' poetry, countering the notion that Beat poetry was a purely urban phenomenon.

Schuler, Robert Jordan. *Journeys Toward the Original Mind: The Long Poems of Gary Snyder*. New York: P. Lang, 1994. Close readings of *Myths and Texts* and *Mountains and Rivers Without End*, focusing on Snyder's concept of "original mind," in which the mind is purified of all its cultural baggage in order to comprehend the universe directly.

Scigaj, Leonard M. *Sustainable Poetry: Four American Ecopoets*. Lexington: University Press of Kentucky, 1999. Along with Snyder, discusses and compares A. R. Ammons, Wendell Berry, and W. S. Merwin and their treatment of nature and environmental concerns in their works. Bibliographical references, index.

Smith, Eric Todd. *Reading Gary Snyder's "Mountains and Rivers Without End."* Boise, Idaho: Boise State University Press, 2000. An extended close reading of Snyder's four-decades-long epic of individual environmental exploration and Asian aesthetic expression.

Suiter, John. *Poets on the Peaks: Gary Snyder, Philip Whalen, and Jack Kerouac in the North Cascades*. Washington, D.C.: Counterpoint, 2002. Examines the environmental influences on Snyder, Jack Kerouac, and Philip Whalen that occurred through living in the Pacific Northwest mountains. Includes thirty-five photographs of places where Snyder lived and worked.

Leon Lewis
Updated by Lewis

GILBERT SORRENTINO

Born: Brooklyn, New York; April 27, 1929
Died: New York, New York; May 18, 2006

PRINCIPAL POETRY

The Darkness Surrounds Us, 1960
Black and White, 1964
The Perfect Fiction, 1968
Corrosive Sublimate, 1971
A Dozen Oranges, 1976
White Sail, 1977
The Orangery, 1978
Selected Poems, 1958-1980, 1981
A Beehive Arranged on Humane Principles, 1986
New and Selected Poems, 1958-1998, 2004

OTHER LITERARY FORMS

Although Gilbert Sorrentino (saw-rehn-TEE-noh) started out writing poetry, his first novel, *The Sky Changes*, was published in 1966. *The Sky Changes* ignores time sequences and scrambles the past, present, and future. This was followed by a remarkable output of fiction: *Steelwork* in 1970, *Imaginative Qualities of Actual Things* the following year, *Red the Fiend* in 1995, and *The Abyss of Human Illusion* in 2009, among others.

Sorrentino's fiction was experimental and won praise from critics, but it was only with the 1979 publication of *Mulligan Stew* that Sorrentino earned popular success. The novel is considered Sorrentino's masterpiece and won rave reviews in almost every influential newspaper. *Mulligan Stew* attacked the conventions of traditional novels, with their linear plot lines, "real" characters, and language subordinated to story.

Sorrentino also published a play, *Flawless Play Restored: The Masque of Fungo* (pb. 1974), and a work of nonfiction, *Something Said*, in 1984.

ACHIEVEMENTS

The controversial Vietnam War and the social upheaval of the Civil Rights movement spurred an experimental writing movement that began in the 1950's and 1960's. Gilbert Sorrentino was among the literary avant-garde of the period, along with Thomas Pynchon, Robert Coover, John Barth, William H. Gass, and LeRoi Jones (Amiri Baraka). In 1956, while at Brooklyn College, he founded the magazine *Neon* with college friends. The issues that Sorrentino edited contained contributions from prominent writers, including William Carlos Williams, Jones, Hubert Selby, Jr., and Joel Oppenheimer. From 1961 to 1963, Sorrentino wrote for and edited *Kulchur*, a literary magazine publishing writers from the Black Mountain school, the Beats, and the New School.

In addition to many grants, including Guggenheim Fellowships in 1973 and 1987, Sorrentino won the John Dos Passos Prize for Literature in 1981, an Academy Award in Literature from the American Academy of Arts and Letters in 1985, the Lannan Literary Award for Fiction in 1992, and the Lannan Lifetime Achievement Award in 2005.

BIOGRAPHY

Gilbert Sorrentino was born in Brooklyn in 1929 to a Sicilian-born father and a third-generation Irish mother. He was raised in Roman Catholic milieus and blue-collar neighborhoods, which form the setting for two of his novels. When he was eighteen years old, he moved across the river to investigate the cultural centers of Manhattan and enrolled in Brooklyn College, but a stint in the U.S. Army Medical Corps in 1951 interrupted his education. He decided to become a writer after two years in the Army and started a novel that was eventually aborted. He returned to Brooklyn College in 1955 and founded the magazine *Neon* with, among others, Hubert Selby, Jr., with whom he formed a lifelong friendship based partly on their common background.

The Darkness Surrounds Us, his first book of poetry, appeared in 1960 and was followed by another collection, *Black and White*, in 1964. The following year, Sorrentino started what was to become a long and distinguished teaching career with a course at Columbia University, and he published his first novel, *The Sky Changes*, in 1966. He worked at Grove Press until 1970 as an assistant, then an editor; his first editing assignment was Alex Haley's *The Autobiography of Malcolm X* (1965). This was followed by teaching stints at the Aspen Writers' Workshop, Sarah Lawrence College, and the New School for Social Research. In 1979 he was appointed Edwin S. Quain Professor of Literature at the University of Scranton in Pennsylvania, and in 1982 he joined the faculty of Stanford University, where he taught creative writing until his retirement in 1999.

ANALYSIS

Although Gilbert Sorrentino is not usually identified with the Beat poets, he was contemporaneous with them and published many as the editor of *Kulchur* magazine from 1961 to 1963. Significantly, Sorrentino's first published book of poetry appeared in 1960. The term "Beat poets" is applied to a loosely knit group of American lyric poets identified more by their shared social attitudes, such as apolitical and anti-intellectual orientations and romantic nihilism, than by stylistic, thematic, or formal unity of expression. They were centered in San Francisco and New York. The term "Beat" expressed both exhaustion and beatification. The writers were tired and disgusted with what they saw as a corrupt, crass, commercial world ruled by materialism and believed that by disassociating with that world they would provide a sort of blissful illumination for it, aided by drugs and alcohol. In the best of the Beats, such as Allen Ginsberg, Gregory Corso, and Jack Kerouac, there is a personal statement and power that goes beyond the jargon and "hip" vocabulary many of them used.

Sorrentino's poetry owes much to the Beat movement, although as his poetry continued to develop it became difficult to classify. Sorrentino had faith in the power of the word and its multiple technical possibilities, which may be the subject of all his works. The only rules that he adhered to were a rigorous parsimony for his poetic diction and a luxurious inventiveness for his fictional language.

"Midnight Special" and "Nightpiece"

These two poems from Sorrentino's first book of poems, *The Darkness Surrounds Us*, use techniques that would be found again in his work. The title "Midnight Special" is taken from a song of that name and refers to a midnight special train ride, but in the poem it refers to a nightmare the poet has of his son in a snowy garden. In another ironic twist, the last line of the poem, "shine your everloving light on me," uses the last line of the song's chorus to address the child directly. The world of music would play an important part in Sorrentino's later poetry.

"Nightpiece" is a city poem ostensibly about rats that first are seen along a wall. One of the rats enters a house and is eventually trapped in a room and beset by fear and disorientation. The poem ends with a shocking comparison to men, who "have shot themselves// in the head/ for less reason." The poem uses images of bleak despair that are omnipresent in some of Sorrentino's later collections.

The Perfect Fiction

In an interview in 1994, Alexander Laurence asked Sorrentino about his interest in formalism. Sorrentino replied that he had always been interested in the formal, which, in his sense, is

> a structure or series of structures that can, if one is lucky enough, generate "content," or, if you please, the wholeness of the work itself. Almost all of my books are written under the influence of some sort of preconceived constraint or set of rules.

In *The Perfect Fiction*, dedicated to his mother, who died in 1960, Sorrentino presents his vision of the city through a series of untitled poems written in three-line verse units called triplets and populated with shadowy, anonymous, vaguely threatening figures. The tone is uniformly dismal, creating a metropolis inhabited by lonely, lost souls, such as this image: "an old woman maybe// was kind to her cats is dying/ of loneliness. Hers is that face/ in the window, how impossibly// remote." Other characters who populate this city are "a huge black man/ riding on a motorcycle," "The stupid painter," and "stinking" people who "know that they/ are garbage and this fact/ somehow consoles them."

The triplet form of the work occasionally admits slight variations, such as "(*pentagram*)," a poem constructed of ten triplets arranged with five down each side of the page. Each stanza is very brief, the lines consisting of only one or two syllables, or only punctuation, until the last stanza, which begins with the word "nostalgia." Another variation is found in the untitled poem that begins with "Such a long walk to get out/ of any pocket, any abstract/ one," in which the third line of each triplet consists of only one word, spaced to the right of the first two lines.

Although the triplet form has never been used as widely as the couplet or the quatrain, it was used in the collection *The Desert Music and Other Poems* (1954) by William Carlos Williams, a poet whom Sorrentino always admired and whom he published in his literary magazine *Neon*.

A Dozen Oranges

A slim paper volume, *A Dozen Oranges* contains twelve poems using the word "orange." It typifies the use of color in Sorrentino's poetry, which became increasingly important as he continued to write. All the poems published in *A Dozen Oranges* were reprinted in *The Orangery*, to which Sorrentino added another sixty poems.

White Sail

White Sail is a collection saturated with color. Although many of the poems feature other colors, such as "Drifting Blue Canoe" and "Navy Blue Room," there are also ten "Orange Sonnets" included here, each a fourteen-line poem using the color orange. One "Orange Sonnet" begins with the line "She was all in black" and expands the shade of black as symbol for the darkness of evil: "We know black here in America./ Why, it's a scream." By the third stanza the black becomes both color and metaphor: "Stick a point of orange in it/ just for fun. Just to see what comes of it." Another "Orange Sonnet" describes a town the poet sees or imagines "across the water," a town drenched in "lime-green haze" and filled with "Mothers and children in blue," where "the sky is blue." Yet the poem ends with a playful reference to orange in a direct address to the reader: "I forgot orange. There."

In a third "Orange Sonnet," subtitled "1939 World's Fair," the poet describes the fair with its "fake orange trees" and includes this image: "My mother was beautiful/ in the blue gloom." Yet by the end of the poem "She died ice-grey in Jersey City" after "Depression and loneliness/ dulled her soft bloom." Color is used here to signify emotional states, and the gentle rhyme of "gloom" with "bloom," echoed by "word" in the last line, gives the poem a certain poignancy.

The Orangery

The Orangery is one of Sorrentino's most memorable collections of poetry. Each poem includes the word "orange," the "preconceived constraint" upon which the poet planned this book. Orange appears and reappears as a color, a fruit, a memory, an intrusion, a word seeking a rhyme, or an unexpected presence. On first publication William Bronk wrote, "In *The Orangery* Sorrentino makes things which are hard, gaudy, and sometimes scary. They are stark artifacts of our world. . . . They are made to last."

The poem titled "King Cole" takes two lines from a song that Nat King Cole made popular—"Wham! Bam! Alla Kazam!/ out of an orange colored sky"—and focuses on the nonsense words. In two spare free-verse stanzas the poet brings the reader's attention to the way the words "Wham! Bam! Alla Kazam!" somehow achieve a meaning of their own within the "foolish song," a meaning wedded to the sound of the words even more powerfully than the image of "a sky colored orange." The poem is modern in its self-referential quality; it is basically about itself and the images contained within it. Yet the last word of the poem, "Fruitless," is ambiguous; the reader does not know if it refers to the "foolish song," to the analytic method of the poem itself, or to both. Sorrentino seems to be experimenting in this poem, trying out tricks to see how they work, such as the use of a parenthesis that is not closed.

Many of the poems in *The Orangery* experiment with form as well as meaning. There are sonnet variations, including the poems "Cento," "Fragments of an Old Song," and "One Negative Vote, "which keep the fourteen-line sonnet form but ignore the traditional iambic pentameter and rhyme scheme. One of the most charming poems in this collection is "Villanette," a word that does not exist yet and was presumably created by the poet to title this variation on the venerable villanelle, an Old French form derived from Italian folk song. The villanelle is composed of five tercets (rhyming triplets) in the rhyme scheme *aba*, followed by a closing quatrain in the scheme *abaa*.

Sorrentino's "Villanette" contains only four tercets, which maintain the rhyme scheme, and closes with a rhymed couplet. The subject of the poem is certain words denoting a northern winter, compared to the pleasures of winter in Florida. The form lends a certain dignity to the topic, adds importance, and renders it more memorable.

OTHER MAJOR WORKS

LONG FICTION: *The Sky Changes*, 1966; *Steelwork*, 1970; *Imaginative Qualities of Actual Things*, 1971; *Splendide-Hotel*, 1973; *Mulligan Stew*, 1979; *Aberration of Starlight*, 1980; *Crystal Vision*, 1981; *Blue Pastoral*, 1983; *Odd Number*, 1985; *Rose Theatre*, 1987; *Misterioso*, 1989; *Under the Shadow*, 1991; *Red the Fiend*, 1995; *Pack of Lies*, 1997; *Gold Fools*, 1999; *Little Casino*, 2002; *A Strange Commonplace*, 2006; *The Abyss of Human Illusion*, 2009.

SHORT FICTION: *The Moon in Its Flight*, 2004.

PLAY: *Flawless Play Restored: The Masque of Fungo*, pb. 1974.

NONFICTION: *Something Said*, 1984; *Lunar Follies*, 2005.

TRANSLATION: *Suspiciae Elegidia/Elegiacs of Sulpicia*, 1977.

Bibliography

Conte, Joseph. "Gilbert Sorrentino: A Crystal Vision." *Critique* 51 (2010): 140-146. Conte, a friend and colleague of Sorrentino, remembers the poet-novelist in this brief but informative article.

Howard, Gerald. "A View from the Ridge: Back in the Old Neighborhood with Postmodern Prole Gilbert Sorrentino." *Bookforum*, February/March, 2006. A detailed article on the life and work of Sorrentino.

Klinkowitz, Jerome. *The Life of Fiction*. Urbana: University of Illinois Press, 1977. Explores major developments in American fiction, with an emphasis on modernism and its nucleus in New York. Contains a chapter on Sorrentino.

Mottram, Eric. "The Black Polar Night: The Poetry of Gilbert Sorrentino." *Vort*, 1974, 43-59. This is an exhaustive discussion of Sorrentino's poetry, focusing on his color imagery, his humor, and his poetic techniques. Especially strong in documenting the poet's bleak vision.

O'Brien, John, ed. *Gilbert Sorrentino Number*. Elmwood Park, Ill.: Dalkey Archive, 1981. Contains critical writings on Sorrentino's work.

Sorrentino, Gilbert. "Shoveling Coal." Interview by Barry Alpert. *Jacket* 29 (April, 2006). Sorrentino discusses his life and his works.

Sheila Golburgh Johnson

JACK SPICER

Born: Los Angeles, California; January 30, 1925
Died: San Francisco, California; August 17, 1965

PRINCIPAL POETRY
After Lorca, 1957
Billy the Kid, 1959
The Heads of the Town up to the Aether, 1962
Lament for the Makers, 1962
The Holy Grail, 1964
Language, 1965
Book of Magazine Verse, 1966
A Book of Music, 1969
A Red Wheelbarrow, 1971
Admonitions, 1974
Fifteen False Propositions About God, 1974
An Ode and Arcadia, 1974 (with Robert Duncan)
The Collected Books of Jack Spicer, 1975 (Robin Blaser, editor)
One Night Stand, and Other Poems, 1980
The Tower of Babel, 1994
Golem, 1999
My Vocabulary Did This to Me: The Collected Poetry of Jack Spicer, 2008

OTHER LITERARY FORMS

Although Jack Spicer often employed prose in his works, the results were more poetic than otherwise, yielding short prose poems that he linked together in series. Spicer stretched literary boundaries by giving poems names normally reserved for prose works, as he did in calling one poem series a "novel." Spicer also employed letters, drawn from either imaginary or real correspondence, as a means of literary expression and included them in his first poetry book, *After Lorca*, as well as in other collections. He did publish some nonfiction, such as notes and reviews for the *Boston Public Library Quarterly*.

ACHIEVEMENTS

Jack Spicer exerted a major influence on West Coast Beat poetry in the late 1950's and early 1960's, initially as a teacher and workshop-leader and subsequently as a poet whose books influenced countless others, especially after his death. His interactions with other poets helped galvanize the poetry scene in San Francisco, especially from

1957 to 1964, while his poems reached their greatest audiences in two posthumous collections, *The Collected Books of Jack Spicer* and *My Vocabulary Did This to Me*. In 2009, Spicer was awarded the American Book Award by the Before Columbus Foundation for *My Vocabulary Did This to Me*.

BIOGRAPHY

Jack Spicer was born John Lester Spicer, in Los Angeles, in 1925 to John Lovely Spicer and Dorothy Clause Spicer, who ran a hotel in Hollywood. At the age of three, Spicer was sent to Minnesota to live with his grandparents while his mother was pregnant with his younger brother. This early separation caused Spicer to resent his sibling and to become estranged from his family.

Spicer attended the University of Redlands from 1943 to 1945, then left for the University of California, Berkeley, where he began working seriously on his poetry. During his time in Berkeley, from 1945 to 1955, he became friends with fellow poets Robert Duncan and Robin Blaser, among others. After a few weeks of exploring life in New York City in 1955, Spicer moved to Boston, where Blaser was living, and found work as editor and curator in the Rare Book Room of the Boston Public Library. He soon returned to the West, settling in San Francisco in 1956. Out of dissatisfaction with his own poetry, he began developing new ideas about its composition. Writing poetry, he came to believe, is a form of "dictation." He made his ideas public during his Poetry as Magic Workshop in 1957, held under the auspices of San Francisco State College. The workshop inspired a follow-up workshop directed by Duncan, as well as a long series of poetry events that enlivened San Francisco bars.

A period of intense creativity followed the 1957 publication of his first book, *After Lorca*. Spicer completed *Admonitions*, *A Book of Music*, *Billy the Kid*, and *Fifteen False Propositions Against God* in 1958. However, none of these poem-series, which he often called"books," saw immediate publication. From 1959 through 1961, Spicer continued producing works, including *Helen: A Revision* and *Lament of the Makers*. The latter saw publication in 1962, as did the collection *The Heads of the Town up to the Aether*, which included "A Fake Novel About the Life of Arthur Rimbaud" and "A Textbook of Poetry." In 1962, Spicer also wrote his ambitious *The Holy Grail*, composed of seven series of poems that drew on figures from the Holy Grail story. In 1964, he wrote *Language*.

After Spicer died from alcohol-induced liver failure in 1965, a number of his works were published posthumously. *Fifteen False Propositions Against God* was published as *Fifteen False Propositions About God*. Blaser edited *The Collected Books of Jack Spicer*, which presented Spicer's works in their original order of composition, based on their original texts, and was published by Black Sparrow Press a decade after the poet's death. A later collection, *My Vocabulary Did This to Me*, included some poems that had not been previously published, including *Helen: A Revision*.

Analysis

Jack Spicer wrote a poetry of imagistic and conceptual juxtaposition reminiscent, at times, of Dadaist randomness. He considered true poetry to be "dictated," and thus removed from the conscious control of the poet. Spicer's own poetry never completely lacks sense or meaning, however. Spicer believed that the "dictated" poem of necessity employs the materials present in the poet's mind. Since the poet's understanding of the world is part of that valid source-material, that understanding might be expected to appear in the dictated work. The poet's understanding does not shape that work, however. Spicer argued that personal experience provides the material or vocabulary for poetry even while the conscious mind provides a less than ideal means for transforming that material into poetry.

In a real sense, Spicer embraced the traditional notion of the Muse, without using the term and without arriving at traditional results in his poetry. He felt and expressed the sense of there being an "Other" who dictated his poems, whom he sometimes humorously identified as a Martian. Although Spicer is often viewed as a Surrealist, this attitude toward "dictation" sets his works apart from those of earlier Surrealist poets. To the degree that he was successfully receptive to such dictation, his poems could be regarded as objective but nonanalytical in nature, in common with Surrealists. His poems are also intentional, however, with their intent often arising from a strong impulse to teach.

After Lorca

Spicer wrote the poems in his first book using the ideas he introduced and developed during his 1957 workshop. In addition to dictation, he arrived at the idea of the poem-series, or "book," which is a larger form that incorporates and helps give meaning to the individual, component poems. His first such grouping, *After Lorca*, uses Federico García Lorca's poems as a jumping-off point. The book begins with a fictitious introduction that is presented as having been written by García Lorca himself, twenty years after his own death. Spicer then presents an extravaganza of erratically bold and freewheeling "translations," intermixed with a series of letters Spicer imagined writing to García Lorca.

The pseudo-translations give Spicer an opportunity to salute such varied figures as Paul Verlaine, Walt Whitman, and Buster Keaton, as well as García Lorca. A freshness of invention animates even the briefest of the poems, while the imaginary letters to García Lorca state some of the poet's ambitions: "I would like to make poems out of real objects. . . . The imagination pictures the real. I would like to point to the real, disclose it, to make a poem that has no sound in it but the pointing of a finger." In this "correspondence" with García Lorca, Spicer plays with the meanings of the word "correspond": "Things do not connect; they correspond. That is what makes it possible for a poet to translate real objects, to bring them across language as easily as he can bring them across time." He notes that his own letter, now an object, will inspire an act akin to his own:

"some future poet will write something which *corresponds* to them. That is how we dead men write to each other." Spicer's inclination to engage in verbal discovery, often through use of puns, would reappear in many later works.

"A TEXTBOOK OF POETRY"

"A Textbook of Poetry" was one of several "books" that appeared under a title that suggested a literary form other than what it actually was. Lacking the straightforward "how to" nature of a handbook, "The Textbook of Poetry" instead presents in imaginative terms Spicer's notions about poetry, its composition, and its meaning. The text is presented as prose, in paragraphs that are fully justified, rather than left-justified as is standard for poetry. All the same, the lines themselves have a character indistinguishable from Spicer's other poetry. After stating "Metaphors are not for humans," Spicer writes this short paragraph:

> The wires dance in the winds of the noise our poems make. The noise without an audience. Because the poems were written for ghosts.

In "The Textbook of Poetry," Spicer further develops his notion of the dictation of poems. The other voice that is within the poet, as well as the true poetry that is contained within the dictated poem, are elusive and perhaps are never completely within the grasp of understanding: "The ghosts the poems were written for are the ghosts of the poems. We have it second-hand. They cannot hear the noise they have been making." However, these inner voices, or "ghosts," are acting with purposeful intent, for they are "teaching an audience."

Spicer's lines approach the mystery of Daoist utterance in attempting to express these elusive notions or images: "I can write a poem about him a hundred times but he is not there. . . . I have not words for him." An element of Plato's concept of reality plays into the poem, with the inexpressible that Spicer "cannot proclaim" being akin to Plato's Ideal, in that it "descends to the real." Spicer even uses the Greek word *logos*, both in association with the name God ("I mean the real God") and, simultaneously, divorced from the notion ("I did not mean the real God").

The unreliable-title approach of "The Textbook of Poetry" was anticipated by his early "The Unvert Manifesto and Other Papers Found in the Rare Book Room of the Boston Public Library in the Handwriting of Oliver Charming," which Spicer wrote during his brief Boston period. Although he called it a "manifesto," it resembled poetry in parts, and, in others, fiction, in its use of narrative and dialog.

LANGUAGE

Spicer had been working on *Language* in the last two years of his life, and it includes several sequences of poems that show his further exploration of themes and approaches that already had characterized his works. Just as earlier poems had used the Orphic and

Holy Grail myths for springboards, "Baseball Predictions, April 1, 1964" uses for its central concern the death of President John F. Kennedy, an event that had already taken on mythic dimensions in American culture. Other poems, including the sequences "Love Poems," "Intermissions," "Transformations," "Phonemics," and "Graphemics," intertwine Spicer's idiosyncratic meditations on love and death, including again Kennedy's death, with his continuing exploration of the nature of poetry. In writing *Language*, Spicer was succumbing yet again to the heuristic impulse and talking about poetry as a way of teaching about poetry. He also, more unusually, seems to have given in to the need for self-explanation: Assertions appear among these lines, as if in self-defense, that what he is writing is, indeed, poetry.

After leading the workshop in San Francisco in 1957, Spicer never managed to depart completely from teaching about his chosen subject: what poetry is and is not, and how it is written, or rather dictated. Even the grail in *The Holy Grail* is presented in such a way as to give insight into poetry: "The grail is the opposite of poetry/ Fills us up instead of using us as a cup the dead drink from." Some of Spicer's continuing influence arises from the fact that he is so engaging and thought-provoking as a teacher, even when at his most enigmatic.

Other major works

NONFICTION: *Dear Ferlinghetti: The Spicer/Ferlinghetti Correspondence: Dear Jack*, 1964 (with Lawrence Ferlinghetti); *The House That Jack Built: The Collected Lectures of Jack Spicer*, 1998 (Peter Gizzi, editor).

Bibliography

Boyd, Nan Alamilla. *Wide-Open Town: A History of Queer San Francisco to 1965*. Berkeley: University of California Press, 2003. A history of the gay culture within which Spicer lived during his most productive years, covering events up through the time of his death.

Ellingham, Lewis, and Kevin Killian. *Poet Be Like God: Jack Spicer and the San Francisco Renaissance*. Hanover, N.H.: Wesleyan University Press, 1998. This biography emphasizes Spicer's position among the Beats, whose development in 1950's San Francisco he helped catalyze, with discussion of his feelings concerning his lack of success relative to other, higher-profile Beat generation writers.

Foster, Edward Halsey. *Jack Spicer*. Boise, Idaho: Boise State University Press, 1991. An early biography that recognizes Spicer's strengths as a poet of the 1950's and offers evidence of his significance beyond the San Francisco scene. Part of the Western Writers series.

Glaser, Robin. "The Practice of Outside." In *The Collected Books of Jack Spicer*, edited by Glaser. Los Angeles: Black Sparrow Press, 1975. This invaluable essay provides perspective on Spicer's work, with emphasis on his unusual understanding of composition, written by a man who was both longtime friend and fellow poet.

Mayhew, Jonathan. *Apocryphal Lorca: Translation, Parody, Kitsch.* Chicago: University of Chicago Press, 2009. An examination of García Lorca's influence in the United States, especially through translation, with discussions of Robert Duncan, Robert Creeley, and Spicer, among others.

Spicer, Jack. *The House That Jack Built: The Collected Lectures of Jack Spicer.* Edited by Peter Gizzi. Hanover, N.H.: Wesleyan University Press, 1998. Gizzi presents his essay "Jack Spicer and the Practice of Reading" along with his transcriptions of Spicer's lectures. An appendix includes previously uncollected prose by Spicer.

Mark Rich

DIANE WAKOSKI

Born: Whittier, California; August 3, 1937

PRINCIPAL POETRY

Coins and Coffins, 1962
Discrepancies and Apparitions, 1966
The George Washington Poems, 1967
Inside the Blood Factory, 1968
The Moon Has a Complicated Geography, 1969
The Magellanic Clouds, 1970
The Motorcycle Betrayal Poems, 1971
Smudging, 1972
Dancing on the Grave of a Son of a Bitch, 1973
Looking for the King of Spain, 1974
Virtuoso Literature for Two and Four Hands, 1975
Waiting for the King of Spain, 1976
The Man Who Shook Hands, 1978
Cap of Darkness, 1980
The Magician's Feastletters, 1982
The Collected Greed, Parts 1-13, 1984 (part 1 pb. in 1968)
The Rings of Saturn, 1986
Emerald Ice: Selected Poems, 1962-1987, 1988
Medea the Sorceress, 1991
Jason the Sailor, 1993
The Emerald City of Las Vegas, 1995
Argonaut Rose, 1998
The Butcher's Apron: New and Selected Poems, Including "Greed: Part 14," 2000

OTHER LITERARY FORMS

Diane Wakoski (wah-KAH-skee) wrote three critical essays that were published by Black Sparrow Press: *Form Is an Extension of Content* (1972), *Creating a Personal Mythology* (1975), and *Variations on a Theme* (1976). These essays, with other essays that had originally appeared in *American Poetry Review*, where she was a regular columnist between 1972 and 1974, and in her books of poetry, were reprinted in *Toward a New Poetry* (1980).

ACHIEVEMENTS

More popular with poetry readers than with poetry critics, Diane Wakoski has nevertheless carved a niche for herself in American poetry. A prolific writer (she has published some fifty books of poetry) and indefatigable reader of her own poetry, she has gained a following of readers who appreciate her intensely personal subject matter, her personal mythology, her structural use of digression and repetition, and her long narrative forms. Throughout her work, the subject is herself, and the themes of loss, betrayal, and identity recur as she probes her relationships with others, most often father figures and lovers. Though her poems are read sympathetically by feminists, she is herself not political and rejects the notion that she can be identified with a particular ideology or school of poetry. Her work has brought her several awards, among them the Bread Loaf Robert Frost Fellowship and the Cassandra Foundation Award, as well as grants from such sources as the Guggenheim Foundation and the National Endowment for the Arts. *Emerald Ice* won the Poetry Society of America's William Carlos Williams Award in 1989.

Her work, sometimes criticized for its perceived self-pity, actually uses loss or betrayal as the impetus for the speaker to work through different self-images and gender reversals to celebrate—usually with a trace of ironic self-awareness—beauty or the self and, in effect, to solve the problem posed at the beginning of the poem.

BIOGRAPHY

Diane Wakoski was born in Whittier, California, in 1937 to parents who shaped not only her life but also her poetry. Shortly after her birth, her father, John Joseph Wakoski, reenlisted in the U.S. Navy and made it his career. Her contact with the "Prince Charming" figure, as she describes him in an autobiographical account, was infrequent and unfulfilling, leaving her with a sense of loss she later explored in her poetry. Her relations with her mother were equally unsatisfying and stressful; by the time she left high school, Wakoski says, she found her mother, whom her father had divorced, a "burden." Speaking of her childhood, Wakoski claims that she was born into a "world of silence," that she was "surrounded by silent people." She was poor, emotionally isolated (she also had few friends), and—from her own point of view—physically unattractive. These factors surely relate to the fixation with male figures and subsequent betrayal in her poems and explain, to some extent, the compulsive need to analyze, to dissect, and to communicate at length in a prolific body of work.

The only positive reinforcement she received in high school was from sympathetic teachers who encouraged the development of her academic talents. She also discovered that she enjoyed performing for an audience. (This "exhibitionistic" tendency, as she has described it, is reflected in her poetry readings, which are very much "performances.") After graduation from high school, she passed up a scholarship to the University of California, Berkeley, and attended Fullerton Junior College because she expected her high school sweetheart to enroll there as well. When he attended a different college and responded dutifully, not supportively, to the news of her pregnancy, she experienced a "betrayal," rejected his marriage proposal, and subsequently gave up her baby for adoption.

In the fall of 1956, after attending a poetry class at Whittier College, she enrolled at Berkeley, where she began writing poetry in earnest, publishing some of it in *Occident*, the campus literary magazine. Wakoski believes that her career was launched when her student poetry reading at the San Francisco Poetry Center resulted in another reading there, this time as a "real" poet. Before she left Berkeley, she was pregnant again, this time by a fellow artist-musician with whom she later moved to New York; since marriage did not seem appropriate and both were career-minded, she again gave up her baby for adoption.

In New York, Wakoski continued to write poetry and give poetry readings, while she became acquainted with several established writers, one of whom, LeRoi Jones (later Amiri Baraka), published some of her poems in *Four Young Lady Poets* in 1962. *Coins and Coffins*, her first book of poems, was also published in 1962, but it was not until 1966, with the publication of *Discrepancies and Apparitions* by a major publishing house, Doubleday, that she became an established poet. In rapid succession, she published two of her most important books, *The George Washington Poems* and *Inside the Blood Factory*, as well as the first four parts of *Greed*. During the late 1960's, she also experienced a failed first marriage and a few failed romantic relationships, one of which produced the raw material for *The Motorcycle Betrayal Poems*, her most publicized collection of verse.

The 1970's were a productive decade for Wakoski, who published regularly, maintained an almost frenetic pace with poetry readings, and gained at the University of Virginia the first of many academic posts as writer-in-residence. She also began a long-standing association with Black Sparrow Press, which has published many of her books. Of particular interest in this decade is the appearance of two collections of poetry concerning yet another mythological figure, the King of Spain. During this period, she turned her attention to criticism, writing a regular column for *American Poetry Review* and publishing a collection of her criticism in *Toward a New Poetry*.

Wakoski's personal life continued to provide content for her verse: Her second marriage ended in divorce in 1975. The following year, she began teaching at Michigan State University, where she would remain. In 1977, she renewed her friendship with poet Robert Turney and was married to him in 1982. The 1980's also saw the completion of *Greed*, which she had begun in 1968, and other books of poetry, though her productivity decreased. Other significant publications included *The Rings of Saturn* and *Medea the Sorceress*, two volumes that rework old themes and myths but also extend Wakoski's "universe," which is at once personal and all-inclusive. *Medea the Sorceress* became the first of four books that make up her series *The Archaeology of Movies and Books*, her major endeavor of the 1990's.

Analysis

Since Diane Wakoski believes that "the poems in her published books give all the important information about her life," her life and her art are inextricably related. She states that the poem "must organically come out of the writer's life," that "all poems are letters," so personal in fact that she has been considered, though she rejects the term, a confessional poet. While most readers have been taught to distinguish between the author and the "speaker" of the poem, Wakoski is, and is not, author and speaker. She refers to real people and to real events in her life in detail that some critics find too personal as she works through a problem: "A poem is a way of solving a problem." For Wakoski, writing a poem is almost therapeutic; it is talking the problem out, not to a counselor or even to the reader, but to herself. She has said, "The purpose of the poem is to complete an act that can't be completed in real life"—a statement that does suggest that there are both reality and the poem, which is then the "completed" dream. As a pragmatist, she has learned to live with these two worlds.

Wakoski believes that once a poet has something to say, he or she finds the appropriate form in which to express this content. In her case, the narrative, rather than the lyric, mode is appropriate; free verse, digression, repetition, and oral music are other aspects of that form. She carves out a territory narrowly confined to self and then uses the universe (the moon, the rings of Saturn, Magellanic clouds), history (George Washington, the King of Spain), personal experience (the motorcycle betrayal poems), and literary feuds to create, in the manner of William Butler Yeats, her personal mythology. The mythology is, in turn, used to develop her themes: loss and acceptance, ugliness and beauty, loss of identity and the development of self. Her themes are dualistic and, significantly, susceptible to the resolution she achieves in the poem. For her, poetry is healing, not fragmenting.

Coins and Coffins

Coins and Coffins, Wakoski's first book of poetry, is dedicated to La Monte Young, the father of her second child and another in a series of lost loves. In this volume, she introduces the image of the lost lover, thereby creating her own personal mythology. "Justice Is Reason Enough" is a poem indebted to Yeats: "the great form and its beating wings" suggests "Leda and the Swan." The "form" in this poem, however, is that of her apocryphal twin brother, David, with whom she commits incest. She mourns her brother, "dead by his own hand," because of the justice that "balances the beauty in the world." Since beauty is mentioned in the last line of the poem, the final mood is one of acceptance and affirmation.

Discrepancies and Apparitions

The missing lover is also the central figure of *Discrepancies and Apparitions*, which contains "Follow That Stagecoach," a poem that Wakoski regards as one of her best and most representative. Though the setting is ostensibly the West, with the archetypal sheriff and Dry Gulch Hollow, the hollow quickly becomes a river; the speaker, a swimmer in a black rubber skin-diving suit; and the tough Western sheriff, a gay authority figure. The opening lines of the poem, "The sense of disguise is a/ rattlesnake," suggest the poses and masks, even the genders, she and the lover-sheriff put on and discard as he fails her: "oh yes you are putting on your skin-diving suit very fast running to the/ ocean and slipping away from this girl who carries a loaded gun." The roles are reversed as she assigns herself the potency he lacks: His gun "wanders into/ hand," while her phallic gun is constantly with her. The poem ends with characteristic confidence: "So I'll write you a love poem if I want to. I'm a Westerner and/ not afraid/ of my shadow." The cliché cleverly alludes to the "shadow" as the alter ego, her second, masculine self; the lover, it is implied, rejects his own wholeness.

THE GEORGE WASHINGTON POEMS

In *The George Washington Poems*, dedicated to her father and her husband, Wakoski continues to debunk the American hero, this time taking on "the father of my country" (a title that is given to one of the poems), the patriarchal political and militaristic establishment. In the twenty-three poems in the volume, "George Washington" appears in his historical roles as surveyor, tree chopper, general politician, and slave owner; however, he also anachronistically appears as the speaker's confidant, absentee father, and (sometimes absentee) lover. When the first poem, "George Washington and the Loss of His Teeth," begins with the image of "George's" (Wakoski refers irreverently to "George" throughout the poems) false teeth, Wakoski wittily and facetiously undercuts the historical image of male leadership in the United States.

In "The Father of My Country," Wakoski demonstrates both the extraordinary versatility of the "George Washington" figure and the way repetition, music, and digression provide structure. The first verse-paragraph develops the idea that "all fathers in Western civilization must have/ a military origin," that all authority figures have been the "general at one time or other," and concludes with Washington, "the rough military man," winning the hearts of his country. Often equating militancy and fatherhood and suggesting that it is the military that elicits American admiration, the speaker abruptly begins a digression about her father; yet the lengthy digression actually develops the father motif of the first verse-paragraph and examines the influence he has had on her life. Although his is a name she does not cherish because he early abandoned her, he has provided her with "military,/ militant" origins, made her a "maverick," and caused her failed relationships. Having thought her father handsome and having wondered why he left her, she is left with the idea of a Prince Charming at once desirable and unattainable. When she speaks of "Father who makes me know all men will leave me/ if I love them," she implies that all her relationships are fated reenactments of childhood love betrayed.

At the end of the poem she declares that "George" has become her "father,/ in his

20th. century naval uniform" and concludes with a chant, with repetitions and parallels, that expresses both her happiness and her uncertainty: "And I say the name to chant it. To sing it. To lace it around/ me like weaving cloth. Like a happy child on that shining afternoon/ in the palmtree sunset her mother's trunk yielding treasures,/ I cry and/ cry,/ Father,/ Father,/ Father,/ have you really come home?"

Inside the Blood Factory

Inside the Blood Factory, Wakoski's next major poetic work, also concerns George Washington and her absentee father, but in this volume, her range of subject matter is much wider. There is Ludwig van Beethoven, who appears in later poems; a sequence concerning the Tarot deck; a man in a silver Ferrari; and images of Egypt—but pervading all is the sense of loss. In this volume, the focus, as the title implies, is on physiological responses as these are expressed in visceral imagery. The speaker wants to think with the body, to accept and work with the dualities she finds in life and within herself.

Inside the Blood Factory also introduces another of Wakoski's recurring images, the moon, developed more extensively later in *The Moon Has a Complicated Geography* and *The Magellanic Clouds*. For Wakoski, the moon is the stereotypical image of the unfaithful woman, but it is also concrete woman breast-feeding her children, bathing, communicating with lovers, and menstruating. Wakoski insists on the physicality of the moon-woman who is related to the sun-lover, but who is also fiercely independent. She loves her lover but wants to be alone, desires intimacy ("wants to be in your wrist, a pulse") but does not want to be "in your house," a possession. (Possession becomes the focus for the ongoing thirteen parts of *Greed.*) When the question of infidelity arises, the speaker is more concerned with being faithful to herself than to her lover(s). In this poem ("3 of Swords—for dark men under the white moon" in the Tarot sequence) the moon-woman can be both submissive and independent, while the sun-lover both gives her love and indulges in his militaristic-phallic "sword play."

As is often the case in Wakoski's poetry, an image appears in one volume and then is developed in later volumes. Isis, a central figure in *The Magellanic Clouds*, is introduced in "The Ice Eagle" of *Inside the Blood Factory*. The Egyptian goddess-creator, who is simultaneously mother and virgin, appears as the symbolic object of male fear: "the veiled woman, Isis mother, whom they fear to be greater than all else." Men prefer the surface, whether it be a woman's body or the eagle ice sculpture that melts in the punch bowl at a cocktail party; men fear what lies beneath the surface—the woman, the anima—in their nature.

The Magellanic Clouds

The Magellanic Clouds looks back at earlier volumes in its reworking of George Washington and the moon figures, but it also looks ahead to the motorcycle betrayal figure and the King of Spain. Of Wakoski's many volumes of poetry, *The Magellanic*

Clouds is perhaps the most violent as the speaker plumbs the depth of her pain. Nowhere is the imaging more violent than in the "Poems from the Impossible," a series of prose poems that contain references to gouged-out eyes, bleeding hands, and cut lips.

Isis, the Queen of the Night speaker, figures prominently in *The Magellanic Clouds*. In "Reaching Out with the Hands of the Sun," the speaker first describes the creative power of the masculine sun, cataloging a cornucopia of sweetmeats that ironically create "fat thighs" and a "puffy face" in a woman. The catalog then switches to the speaker's physical liabilities, ones that render her unbeautiful and unloved; with the "mask of a falcon," she has roamed the earth and observed the universal effect that beauty has on men. At the end of the poem, the speaker reaches out to touch the "men/ with fire/ direct from the solar disk," but they betray their gifts by "brooding" and rejecting the hands proffered them.

In "The Queen of Night Walks Her Thin Dog," the speaker uses poetry, the "singing" that recurs in Whitmanesque lines, to penetrate the various veils that would separate her from "houses," perhaps bodies, in the night. The poem itself may be the key in the locked door that is either an entrance or an exit—at the end of the poem, "Entrance./ Exit./ The lips" suggests a sexual and poetic act. In the third poem, "The Prince of Darkness Passing Through This House," the speaker refers to the "Queen of Night's running barking dog" and to "this house," but the Prince of Darkness and the Queen of Night are merged like elemental fire and water. Like a Metaphysical poet, Wakoski suggests that the universe can be coalesced into their bodies ("our earlobes and eyelids") as they hold "live coals/ of commitment,/ of purpose,/ of love." This positive image, however, is undercut by the final image, "the power of fish/ living in strange waters," which implies that such a union may be possible only in a different world.

The last poem in the volume, "A Poem for My Thirty-second Birthday," provides a capsule summary of the speaker's images, themes, and relationships. In the course of the poem, she associates a mechanic with a Doberman that bites, and then she becomes, in her anger, the Doberman as she seeks revenge on a lover who makes her happy while he destroys her with possessive eyes that penetrate the "fences" she has erected. After mentioning her father and her relatives, who have achieved "sound measure/ of love" ("sound measure" suggests substance but also a prosaic doling out of love), she turns to her mother, who threatens her with a long rifle that becomes a fishing pole with hooks that ensnare her. The speaker reverts to her "doberman" behavior, and, though she persists in maintaining "distance," she uses her poems and songs to achieve acceptance: "I felt alive./ I was glad for my jade memories."

The Motorcycle Betrayal Poems

In *The Motorcycle Betrayal Poems*, betrayal, always a theme in Wakoski's poetry, becomes the central focus; the motorcycle mechanic represents all the men who have betrayed her. The tone is at times humorous, so much so that the poems may not be taken seriously enough, but there is also a sense of desperation. These poems explore the different roles and images available to define identity, and the roles are not gender-bound. The speaker, who expresses her condition in images of isolation and entrapment, is fascinated with aggressive male roles, embodied in the motorcyclist. While she wryly admits that she is the "pink dress," she at times would like to reverse the roles; she is also aware, however, that the male roles do not satisfy her needs, do not mesh with her sexual identity. In this collection her identity is again developed in terms of lunar imagery, this time with reference to Diana, associated with the moon and the huntress, here of the sexual variety, and with the desert: both are lifeless, and both reflect the sterility of her life. The speaker does suggest, through the water imagery that pervades her poems, that this condition is not permanent, that her life can be sustained, but only through a man's love. Ultimately, the speaker is plagued with another duality: She desires what has persistently destroyed her.

SMUDGING

The same contradictory feelings about men are reflected in the title poem of *Smudging*, a collection of verse that includes King of Spain poems, prose poems, two parts of *Greed*, and miscellaneous poems touching on recurrent themes, motifs, and myths. "Smudging," another of Wakoski's favorite poems, encapsulates many of the themes as it probes the divided self. There are two "parts" of the speaker, the part that searches "for the warmth of the smudge pot" and the "part of me that takes your hand confidently." That is, the speaker both believes that she has the warmth and fears that she lacks it. Like her mother, she must fear the "husband who left her alone for the salty ocean" (with associations of sterility and isolation); yet she, like the orange she metaphorically becomes, transcends this fear through "visions" and the roles she plays in her head—these make her "the golden orange every prince will fight/ to own."

With Wakoski, transcendence seems always transitory; each poem must solve a problem, often the same one, so that the speaker is often on a tightrope, performing a balancing act between fear and fulfillment. As the poem moves to its solution, the speaker continues to waver, as is the case in "Smudging." At the beginning of the poem, the speaker revels in warmth and luxuriance; she refers to amber, honey, music, and gold as she equates gold with "your house," perhaps also her lover's body, and affirms her love for him. Even before the change signaled by "but" occurs in the next line, she tempers the image: "the honeysuckle of an island" is not their world but "in my head," and the repetition of "your" rather than "our" suggests the nagging doubts that lead to memories of her childhood in Orange County, California. The fear of the laborers outside the house, the memory of the absentee father—she has left these behind as she finds love and warmth with her mechanic lover, whose warmth is suspect, however, because he "threw me out once/ for a whole year." Mechanically expert, he does not understand or appreciate her "running parts" and remains, despite their reunion, "the voices in those dark nights" of her childhood. She, on the other hand, has become the "hot metal," "the golden orange" that exists independently of him.

Dancing on the Grave of a Son of a Bitch

Dancing on the Grave of a Son of a Bitch is a bit of a departure from Wakoski's earlier poetry, although it is consistent in mythology and themes with the rest of her work. The title poem, dedicated to her motorcycle betrayer, the mechanic of "Smudging," reiterates past injustices and betrayals, but the speaker is more assured than vengeful. Despite the opening curse, "God damn it," and her acknowledgment that his leaving made her "as miserable/ as an earthworm with no earth," she not only has "crawled out of the ground," resurrecting herself, but also has learned to "sing new songs," to write new poems. She denies that hers is an angry statement, affirming instead that it is joyful, and her tone at the end of the poem is playful as she evokes the country singer's "for every time/ you done me wrong."

There is similar progression in the "Astronomer Poems" of the volume. As in earlier poems, she uses the moon/sun dichotomy, but there is more acceptance, assurance, and assertiveness as she explores these myths. In "Sun Gods Have Sun Spots," she not only suggests male-sun blemishes but also affirms her own divinity in a clever role reversal: "I am/ also a ruler of the sun." While "the sun has an angry face," the speaker in "The Mirror of a Day Chiming Marigold" still yearns for the poet or astronomer to study "my moon." Wakoski thus at least tentatively resolves two earlier themes, but she continues to develop the King of Spain figure, to refer to the "rings of Saturn," to include some Buddha poems and some prose fables, and to use chants as a means of conveying meaning and music. In her introduction to the book, she explains that she wishes readers to read the poems aloud, being "cognizant" of the chanted parts. Since Wakoski is a performing poet, the notion of chants, developed by Jerome Rothenberg, was almost inevitable, considering her interest in the piano (another theme for future development) and music. In fact, Wakoski uses chants, as in "Chants/Chance," to allow for different speakers within the poem.

Virtuoso Literature for Two and Four Hands

Virtuoso Literature for Two and Four Hands, a relatively slender volume of poetry, not only alludes to Wakoski's fifteen years of piano study but also plays upon the keyboard-typewriter analogy to explore past relationships and her visionary life. Two of Wakoski's favorite poems, "The Story of Richard Maxfield" and "Driving Gloves," which are included in this volume, involve people she resembles, one a dead composer and artist and one a Greek scholar with a failed father, but the poems conclude with affirmations about the future. It is not Maxfield's suicide that disturbs the speaker; she is concerned with his "falling apart," the antithesis of his "well-organized" composing. The poem, despite the repetition of "fall apart," ends with her certainty "that just as I would never fall apart,/ I would also never jump out of a window." In the other poem, the speaker begins with familiar lamentations about her sad childhood and turns to genes and the idea of repeating a parent's failures. Noting that she, like her mother, wears driving gloves, she is terrified that she will be like her boring, unimaginative mother; Anne, like her unpublished novelist/father, is a bad driver. Despite Anne's belief that "we're all like some parent/ or ancestor," the speaker tells Anne that "you learned to drive because you are not your father" and states that she wears gloves "because I like to wear them." Asserting that their lives are their own, she dismisses the past as "only something/ we have all lived/ through." This attitude seems a marked departure from earlier poems in which her life and behavior are attributed to her father's influence.

WAITING FOR THE KING OF SPAIN

While *Waiting for the King of Spain* features staple Wakoski figures (George Washington, the motorcycle mechanic, the King of Spain), lunar imagery (one section consists of fifteen poems about an unseen lunar eclipse, and one is titled "Daughter Moon"), and the use of chants and prose poems, it also includes a number of short poems—a startling departure for Wakoski, who has often stated a preference for long narrative poems. As a whole, the poems continue the affirmative mood of *Virtuoso Literature for Two and Four Hands*. The King of Spain, the idealized lover who loves her "as you do not./ And as no man ever has," appears and reappears, the wearer of the "cap of darkness" (the title of a later collection), in stark contrast to the betrayers and the George Washington persona. Here, too, there is less emphasis on the masculine sun imagery, though it appears, and more of a celebration of the moon imagery.

The two poems in the collection that Wakoski considers most illustrative of her critical principles are warm, accepting, flippant, and amusing. In "Ode to a Lebanese Crock of Olives" the speaker again refers to the body she regards as physically unattractive, but she accepts her "failed beach girl" status and stacks the deck metaphorically in favor of abundance ("the richness of burgundy,/ dark brown gravies") over the bland ("their tan fashionable body"). In fact, the "fashionable" (always a negative word for Wakoski) body provides the point of contrast to affirm Wakoski's own beauty: "Beauty is everywhere/ in contrasts and unities." This condemnation of thinness is extended to art and poetry in "To the Thin and Elegant Woman Who Resides Inside of Alix Nelson." For Wakoski, fullness is all: "Now is the time to love flesh." Renouncing the Weight Watchers and *Vogue* models of life and poetry, she argues for the unfettered fullness of "American drama" and the "substantial narrative." Wakoski declares, "My body is full of the juice of poetry," and concludes the poem with an amusing parody of the Lord's Prayer, ending with "Ah, men" (surely the source of the false doctrine of beauty).

THE MAN WHO SHOOK HANDS

The Man Who Shook Hands represents a point of departure for Wakoski, who seems in this volume to return to the anger, hostility, and bitterness of her earlier poems. The feelings of betrayal, here embodied in the figure of a man who merely shakes hands the morning after a one-night relationship, resurface as the speaker's quest for love is again unsuccessful. The speaker in "Running Men" is left with the "lesson" the departing lover "so gently taught in your kind final gesture,/ that stiff embrace." The sarcasm in "gently" and "kind" is not redeemed by her concluding statement that she lives "in her head" and that the only perfect bodies are in museums and in art. This realization prepares the reader for the last line of the volume: "How I hate my destiny."

Greed

Although the temporally complete *Greed*, all thirteen parts, was published in 1984, parts of it were printed as early as 1968, and Wakoski has often included the parts in other collections of her poetry. It is bound by a single theme, even if greed is defined in such general terms that it can encompass almost everything. It is the failure to choose, the unwillingness to "give up one thing/ for another." Because the early parts were often published with other poems, they tend to reflect the same themes—concerns with parents, lovers, poetry—and to be written in a similar style. Of particular interest, however, given Wakoski's preference for narrative, is part 12, "The Greed to Be Fulfilled," which tends to be dramatic in form. What begins as a conversation between the speaker and George becomes a masque, "The Moon Loses Her Shoes," in which the actors are the stock figures of Wakoski mythology. The resolution of the poem for the speaker is the movement from emotional concerns to intellectual ones, a movement reflected in the poetry-music analogy developed in part 13.

Later poetry

Wakoski's other later poetry suggests that she is reworking older themes while she incorporates new ones, which also relate to her own life. In *Cap of Darkness* and *The Magician's Feastletters* she explores the problem of aging in a culture that worships youth and consumption; this concern is consistent with the themes of *Virtuoso Literature for Two and Four Hands*.

The Rings of Saturn, with the symbolic piano and ring, and *Medea the Sorceress*, with its focus on mythology and woman as poet-visionary, reflect earlier poetry but also reflect the changing emphasis, the movement from emotion to intellect, while retaining the subjectivity, as well as the desire for fulfillment, beauty, and truth, that characterize the entire body of her work. The latter volume became the first part of a major Wakowski endeavor with the collective title *The Archaeology of Movies and Books*. *Jason the Sailor*, *The Emerald City of Las Vegas*, and *Argonaut Rose* are the other three parts.

The best introduction to Wakoski's art—her themes and methods—is *The Butcher's Apron: New and Selected Poems, Including "Greed: Part 14,"* published in 2000. In fashioning this collection, Wakoski decided to cut across a wide body of work by selecting those poems that concern food and drink. Moreover, as she writes in the introduction, "All of the poems in this collection . . . focus on the on-going process of discovering beauty and claiming it for myself." At the same time, she has built a structure that outlines her personal mythology as it is revealed by or rooted in geographical and cultural landscapes. Part 1, "A California Girl," concerns her self-projection "as a daughter of the Golden State," while later parts elaborate and complicate Wakoski's shifting personae. Thus, her arrangement of older and newer poems is made in the service of a mythic map of her inner terrain.

Though often compared to Sylvia Plath, a comparison she destroys in part 9 of *Greed*, and often seen as squarely in the feminist mainstream, Wakoski remains a unique and intensely personal voice in American poetry. She is constantly inventive, rarely predictable, and, in a way that somehow seems healthy and unthreatening, enormously ambitious.

OTHER MAJOR WORKS

NONFICTION: *Form Is an Extension of Content*, 1972; *Creating a Personal Mythology*, 1975; *Variations on a Theme*, 1976; *Toward a New Poetry*, 1980.

BIBLIOGRAPHY

Brown, David M. "Wakoski's 'The Fear of Fat Children.'" *Explicator* 48, no. 4 (Summer, 1990): 292-294. Brown observes how the poem's common diction and grotesque imagery work to create a successful postmodern confessional in which the speaker expresses not only guilt but also the urge for self-reformation.

Gannon, Catherine, and Clayton Lein. "Diane Wakoski and the Language of Self." *San Jose Studies* 5 (Spring, 1979): 84-98. Focusing on *The Motorcycle Betrayal Poems*, Gannon and Lein discuss the betrayal motif in terms of the speaker's struggle for identity. The poems' speaker uses the moon image to consider possible alternative images for herself, and in the last poem of the book she achieves a "richer comprehension of her being."

Hughes, Gertrude Reif. "Readers Digest." *Women's Review of Books* 18, no. 7 (April, 2001): 14-16. Treats *The Butcher's Apron* along with collected works by Carolyn Kizer and Kathleen Raine. Gives high praise to "Greed, Part 14," which is granted the status of a major long poem that redeems much else in the collection.

Lauter, Estella. *Women as Mythmakers: Poetry and Visual Art by Twentieth-Century Women*. Bloomington: Indiana University Press, 1984. Lauter devotes one chapter to Wakoski's handling of moon imagery in several of the poet's books. There is also a related discussion of Isis and Diana as aspects of the speaker's personality.

Martin, Taffy Wynne. "Diane Wakoski's Personal Mythology: Dionysian Music, Created Presence." *Boundary 2: A Journal of Postmodern Literature* 10 (Fall, 1982): 155-172. According to Martin, Wakoski's sense of absence and lost love prompts desire, which in turn animates the poetry, giving it life. Martin also discusses

Wakoski's mythmaking, her use of digression as a structural device, and her use of musical repetition.

Newton, Robert. *Diane Wakoski: A Descriptive Bibliography*. Jefferson, N.C.: McFarland, 1987. Newton unravels Wakoski's career in print through its first quarter century.

Ostriker, Alicia Luskin. *Stealing the Language: The Emergence of Women's Poetry in America*. Boston: Beacon Press, 1986. An outstanding history of women's poetry, Ostriker's book includes extended readings of some of Wakoski's works, especially *The George Washington Poems*. For the most part, Ostriker focuses on the divided self (the all-nothing and the strong-weak) in Wakoski's poetry and discusses the ways in which the poet's masks and disguises become flesh. There is an extensive bibliography concerning women's poetry.

Wakoski, Diane. "An Interview with Diane Wakoski." Interview by Deborah Gillespie. *South Carolina Review* 38, no. 1 (Fall, 2005): 14-21. Wakoski discusses her childhood and her life as a writer. She describes what and who influenced her.

_______. *Toward a New Poetry*. Ann Arbor: University of Michigan Press, 1980. The book includes not only Wakoski's criticism, much of which is commentary to her own poetry, but also five revealing interviews, only two of which had previously been published in major journals. In the introduction, Wakoski lists her "best" poems, the ones she believes illustrate her personal mythology, her use of image and digression, and the kind of music she thinks is important to contemporary poetry.

Thomas L. Erskine
Updated by Philip K. Jason

PHILIP WHALEN

Born: Portland, Oregon; October 20, 1923
Died: San Francisco, California; June 26, 2002

PRINCIPAL POETRY

Three Satires, 1951 (privately printed)
Self Portrait from Another Direction, 1959
Like I Say, 1960
Memoirs of an Interglacial Age, 1960
Monday in the Evening, 1964 (privately printed)
Three Mornings, 1964
Every Day, 1965
The Invention of the Letter: A Beastly Morality, 1967
T/O, 1967
On Bear's Head, 1969
Scenes of Life at the Capital, 1970
Severance Pay, 1970
The Kindness of Strangers: Poems, 1969-1974, 1976
Prolegomena to a Study of the Universe, 1976
Zenshinji, 1977
Decompressions: Selected Poems, 1978
Enough Said: Fluctuat Nec Mergitur—Poems, 1974-1979, 1980
Tara, 1981
Heavy Breathing: Poems, 1967-1980, 1983
Two Variations: All About Love, 1983
A Vision of the Bodhisattvas, 1984
For C., 1984
The Elizabethan Phrase, 1985
Window Peak, 1986
Driving Immediately Past, 1989
Canoeing Up Cabarga Creek: Buddhist Poems, 1955-1986, 1996
Mark Other Place, 1997
Overtime: Selected Poems, 1999
Some of These Days, 1999
The Collected Poems of Philp Whalen, 2007 (Michael Rothenberg, editor)

Other literary forms

Although he gave priority to his poetry, Philip Whalen (WAY-lehn) enjoyed success as a novelist. His first novel, *You Didn't Even Try* (1967), drew upon his experiences in San Francisco in the years 1959-1964. In the year it was published, he began work on his second novel, *Imaginary Speeches for a Brazen Head* (1972), while in Kyoto, Japan. His third, *The Diamond Noodle* (1980), likewise had its origins in the 1960's. Whalen also wrote nonfiction and journals, and he produced short volumes of calligraphic and "doodle" works, including *Highgrade: Doodles, Poems*, published in 1966.

Achievements

Numerous literary organizations have recognized Philip Whalen's importance in the American poetry scene. His awards include the Poets Foundation Award (1962) and V. K. Ratcliff Award (1964). A grant-in-aid award from the American Academy of Arts and Letters assisted Whalen in his move to Japan. In 1968, 1970, and 1971, he received grants from the Committee on Poetry. The American Academy of Arts and Letters further honored him with the 1985 Morton Dauwen Zabel Award, and in 2001, he received a Lifetime Achievement Award from the Before Columbus Foundation.

Biography

Philip Whalen grew up in the small town of The Dalles on the Columbia River, where he attended public school. In his high school years, he contributed to his high school literary magazine and commenced his readings in Asian literature and philosophy. Since his family was unable to send him to college, after his graduation in 1941, Whalen took minor jobs before being drafted into the U.S. Army Air Corps. He received training in radio operation and maintenance and was given stateside military posting during the war. His military service left him adequate free time to continue pursuing his writing.

Receiving his military discharge in 1946, Whalen returned to Oregon, where he enrolled at Reed College on the G.I. Bill. He pursued a course in creative writing and developed several important friendships, including with fellow students Lew Welch and Gary Snyder. The trio shared lodgings in a rooming house in 1950, the year they also met and received encouragement from William Carlos Williams, who spent a week at Reed on a reading tour. The encounter marked the point when Whalen began taking himself seriously as a writer. After leaving Reed, Whalen supported himself with a string of odd jobs along the West Coast that ended with summer employment as a fire spotter in Mount Baker National Forest, in 1955. This experience is reflected in his poem "Sourdough Mountain Lookout." That fall, he moved to San Francisco, and at Snyder's invitation took part in the historic Six Gallery reading of October 13 at which Allen Ginsberg presented his ground-breaking "Howl" for the first time. The event was pivotal, marking the beginning of the West Coast Beat movement. Whalen's circle of literary friends expanded rapidly, growing to include Ginsberg, Jack Kerouac, and Gregory Corso, among others. Ginsberg and Kerouac were expecially influential in freeing Whalen's poetic sensibility from earlier conventions.

The maturing of Whalen's poetic voice during the mid-1950's saw fruition in 1960, when two major Whalen collections, *Like I Say* and *Memoirs of an Interglacial Age*, were published. In the same year, he was included in Donald Allen's influential anthology, *The New American Poetry, 1945-1960*. In the mid-1960's, he joined Snyder in Kyoto, Japan. Kyoto would serve as his primary residence until the early 1970's, although he spent time in the United States in 1969 overseeing the publication of his first major volume of collected poems, *On Boar's Head*. After his final return to the United States, he moved to the San Francisco Zen Center, where he was ordained as a Zen monk in 1973. Several volumes of Whalen's poetry appeared in the 1970's, subsequently collected in *Heavy Breathing*. In 1991, he was made abbot of San Francisco's Hartford Street Zen Center. At the end of the decade, in 1999, his major collection *Overtime* was published. He died in 2002, after a long illness.

Analysis

Although often considered experimental and sometimes obscure, the poetry of Philip Whalen is marked by a directness of expression that matches his concern with directness of experience. The seemingly oblique or broken sentences reflect the movements of mind, in its perceptions and thoughts.

"For C."

The poem "For C.," written in 1957, presents one of the clearest expressions of a mode characteristic of Whalen's work. Perhaps tellingly for a man who became ordained as a Zen monk, a note of retrospective longing comes to the fore in many poems, with the object of longing often being, or being represented by, a woman in his life. "For C." begins with a moment of vulnerability: "I wanted to bring you this Jap iris/ Orchid-white with yellow blazons/ But I couldn't face carrying it down the street/ Afraid everyone would laugh/ And now they're dying of my cowardice." His embarrassment arises from the idea of the "yellow blazons" announcing to the world his sexual desire, which ironically he displays to the world in the poem itself. His awkward yearning for bodily satisfaction finds its counterpoint in his other embarrassments, including the recurring worry over being overweight. The poem itself is expression of frustration: "After all this fuss about flowers I walked out/ Just to walk, not going to see you (I had nothing to bring—/ This poem wasn't finished, didn't say/ What was on my mind; I'd given up)."

The directness of "For C." recalls the 1956 poem "Invocation and Dark Sayings in the Tibetan Style," another expression of sexual longing and loneliness, which identifies "the biggest problem in the world" as the question, "Where are you?" The young poet presents his sexual feelings for his absent lover unabashedly, while offering a parallel presentation of his feelings, in lines he is "not saying." What he is not saying, Whalen tells the reader, are lines such as, "This is a picture of a man./ The man is hiding something./ Try to guess what it is." Although Whalen rarely points directly to the fact that in his poems he is passing along direct experience of the moment, by offering the reader what he might have written, had he been trying to transform the moment poetically, he effectively does so.

"Small Tantric Sermon"

Similarly another 1956 poem, "Small Tantric Sermon," treats the sexual act itself as seriously as poets of a previous century might have treated the purely emotional quality of romantic love. In this poem, he finds that the effort to talk directly about sex ". . . breaks down,/ Here, on paper," although the effort to do so has its own rewards, as he notes by continuing, "although I am free/ To spread these words, putting them/ Where I want them (something of a release/ In itself)."

"Delights of Winter at the Shore"

Other frustrations provide Whalen with the galvanizing impulse toward poetic expression, including problems relating to simple existence. In one poem that vacillates between emotional distress and objective acceptance of his situation in the world, 1958's "Delights of Winter at the Shore," Whalen engages in a series of self-searching reflections as he recalls an editor asking him "Why don't you just sit down & write a novel?" The question is voiced at a time when the poet's mortgage is nearly foreclosed and his power is threatened with being shut off. Downturns of fortune likewise affect the worldly achievements others have expected of him—"It goes like that, all the 'talent,' the 'promise'"—which provokes him to a moment of personal crisis: "How loyal have I been to myself?/ How far do I trust . . . anything?/ I wonder 'self-confidence' *vs.* years of self-indulgence/ (am I feeling guilty?)/ How would anything get done if I quit? Stopped/ whatever it is you choose to call it?" The crisis forces him to look both inward and outward, as he assesses the achievement of being one who has spent his life working at "whatever it is."

Highgrade

Made up of quite short poems, or individual pages of calligraphy and pen drawings that may be regarded as poems, *Highgrade* gives insight into Whalen's compositional process. Whalen had used calligraphy in his work since his Reed College days and had grown used to using the India-ink pen for writing drafts of his poem. *Highgrade* provides examples of how Whalen "sees" his poems. In the printed versions of his poems, for example, words often appear in all capitals, which some readers might take as "shouting" or overemphasis. In these poems the upper-case words appear with naturalness on the page, where they can be seen as elements of graphic design.

Whalen's calligraphic work aims not for the elegant perfection of typical calligraphy, but rather for the emulation of font types, in a variety of styles and sizes. The impulsive and sometimes whimsically humorous character of Whalen's writing becomes more pronounced in this format. The posthumously published calligraphic work, *The Unidentified Accomplice: Or, The Transmissions of C. W. Moss* (2005), is revealing for the same reason.

"THE GARDEN"

"The Garden" brings Whalen's talent for expressing the immediate into the foreground. His tendency to focus on minutiae overlooked by others finds itself mirrored in scenes around his Japanese lodgings, as he observes the landlady. While she is sweeping leaves off the moss, she is joined in her sweeping by her husband. Whalen intermixes direct observation with commentary on Japanese life, then arrives at a moment of deep concentration: "They sweep the shrubs and bushes, too,/ Old man has an elegant whiskbroom, a giant shaving brush/ Gets rid of dust and spiders, leaf by leaf." This 1966 poem represents Whalen's achievement of what he attributed to an ancient Greek poet, in 1952's "Homage to Lucretius": for he is presenting to the reader "A world not entirely new/ but realized."

Similarly, in his 1957 poem written in Berkeley, "The Same Old Jazz," Whalen points to the direct relation between inner and outer worlds: "And it all snaps into focus/ The world inside my head & the cat outside the window/ A one-to-one relationship." Although the lines address perception, both inner and outer, the breakthrough they describe also has to do with poetry, since the two lines immediately beforehand are these: "She wants to sleep & I get up naked at the table/ Writing."

Simultaneous reflections on the self and on the outer world animate many of the writings of Whalen. As in "Delights of Winter at the Shore," the question of self-indulgence may arise, just as they arise with the work of most poets associated with the Beat movement. In Whalen's case, the self-awareness is not self-absorption, and the "one-to-one relationship" between inner and outer worlds in Whalen's poetry makes it perhaps the most balanced of Beat-influenced work, even when his poetry is at its most intimately revealing.

OTHER MAJOR WORKS

LONG FICTION: *You Didn't Even Try*, 1967; *Imaginary Speeches for a Brazen Head*, 1972; *The Diamond Noodle*, 1980; *Two Novels* (*You Didn't Even Try* and *Imaginary Speeches for a Brazen Head*), 1985.

NONFICTION: *Intransit: The Education Continues Along Including Voyages, a TransPacific Journal*, 1967; *Prose [Out]Takes*, 2002.

MISCELLANEOUS: *Highgrade: Doodles, Poems*, 1966; *The Unidentified Accomplice: Or, The Transmissions of C. W. Moss*, 2005.

BIBLIOGRAPHY

Kherdian, David. *Six Poets of the San Francisco Renaissance: Portraits and Checklists*. Fresno, Calif.: Giligia Press, 1965. Provides valuable source material on the San Francisco Beat movement and Whalen.

Rothenberg, Michael, and Suzi, Winson, eds. *Continuous Flame: A Tribute to Philip Whalen*. New York: Fish Drum, 2005. A collection of tributes to Whalen, demonstrating the degree to which he served as an example and inspiration to other writers.

Snyder, Gary, Lew Welch, and Philip Whalen. *On Bread and Poetry: A Panel Discussion with Gary Snyder, Lew Welch, and Philip Whalen*. Edited by Donald Allen. Berkeley, Calif.: Grey Fox Press, 1973. A wide-ranging reunion discussion between three poet friends.

Suiter, John. *Poets on the Peaks: Gary Snyder, Philip Whalen, and Jack Kerouac in the Cascades*. Berkeley, Calif.: Counterpoint, 2002. An illustrated exploration of the years the three Beat writers spent as fire spotters in the Cascades, including an interview with Whalen covering topics including his ordination as a Zen monk.

Whalen, Philip. Interview by Donald Allen. In *Off the Wall: Interviews with Philip Whalen*. Edited by Allen. Bolinas, Calif.: Grey Fox Press, 1978. An exploration of the attitudes and ideas of the poet in his early years of being a Zen monk.

_______. "Philip Whalen." Interview by David Meltzer. In *San Francisco Beat: Talking with the Poets*, edited by Meltzer. San Francisco: City Lights, 2001. Whalen discusses his involvement in the San Francisco scene, his interest in Japan, and his training in Buddhism, along with his poetry.

Mark Rich

CHECKLIST FOR EXPLICATING A POEM

I. The Initial Readings

A. Before reading the poem, the reader should:

1. Notice its form and length.
2. Consider the title, determining, if possible, whether it might function as an allusion, symbol, or poetic image.
3. Notice the date of composition or publication, and identify the general era of the poet.

B. The poem should be read intuitively and emotionally and be allowed to "happen" as much as possible.

C. In order to establish the rhythmic flow, the poem should be reread. A note should be made as to where the irregular spots (if any) are located.

II. Explicating the Poem

A. *Dramatic situation*. Studying the poem line by line helps the reader discover the dramatic situation. All elements of the dramatic situation are interrelated and should be viewed as reflecting and affecting one another. The dramatic situation serves a particular function in the poem, adding realism, surrealism, or absurdity; drawing attention to certain parts of the poem; and changing to reinforce other aspects of the poem. All points should be considered. The following questions are particularly helpful to ask in determining dramatic situation:

1. What, if any, is the narrative action in the poem?
2. How many personae appear in the poem? What part do they take in the action?
3. What is the relationship between characters?
4. What is the setting (time and location) of the poem?

B. *Point of view*. An understanding of the poem's point of view is a major step toward comprehending the poet's intended meaning. The reader should ask:

1. Who is the speaker? Is he or she addressing someone else or the reader?
2. Is the narrator able to understand or see everything happening to him or her, or does the reader know things that the narrator does not?
3. Is the narrator reliable?
4. Do point of view and dramatic situation seem consistent? If not, the inconsistencies may provide clues to the poem's meaning.

C. *Images and metaphors*. Images and metaphors are often the most intricately crafted vehicles of the poem for relaying the poet's message. Realizing that the images and metaphors work in harmony with the dramatic situation and point of view will help the reader to see the poem as a whole, rather than as disassociated elements.

1. The reader should identify the concrete images (that is, those that are formed from objects that can be touched, smelled, seen, felt, or tasted). Is the image projected by the poet consistent with the physical object?
2. If the image is abstract, or so different from natural imagery that it cannot be associated with a real object, then what are the properties of the image?
3. To what extent is the reader asked to form his or her own images?
4. Is any image repeated in the poem? If so, how has it been changed? Is there a controlling image?
5. Are any images compared to each other? Do they reinforce one another?
6. Is there any difference between the way the reader perceives the image and the way the narrator sees it?
7. What seems to be the narrator's or persona's attitude toward the image?

D. *Words*. Every substantial word in a poem may have more than one intended meaning, as used by the author. Because of this, the reader should look up many of these words in the dictionary and:

1. Note all definitions that have the slightest connection with the poem.
2. Note any changes in syntactical patterns in the poem.
3. In particular, note those words that could possibly function as symbols or allusions, and refer to any appropriate sources for further information.

E. *Meter, rhyme, structure, and tone*. In scanning the poem, all elements of prosody should be noted by the reader. These elements are often used by a poet to manipulate the reader's emotions, and therefore they should be examined closely to arrive at the poet's specific intention.

1. Does the basic meter follow a traditional pattern such as those found in nursery rhymes or folk songs?
2. Are there any variations in the base meter? Such changes or substitutions are important thematically and should be identified.
3. Are the rhyme schemes traditional or innovative, and what might their form mean to the poem?
4. What devices has the poet used to create sound patterns (such as assonance and alliteration)?
5. Is the stanza form a traditional or innovative one?
6. If the poem is composed of verse paragraphs rather than stanzas, how do they affect the progression of the poem?

7. After examining the above elements, is the resultant tone of the poem casual or formal, pleasant, harsh, emotional, authoritative?

F. *Historical context.* The reader should attempt to place the poem into historical context, checking on events at the time of composition. Archaic language, expressions, images, or symbols should also be looked up.

G. *Themes and motifs.* By seeing the poem as a composite of emotion, intellect, craftsmanship, and tradition, the reader should be able to determine the themes and motifs (smaller recurring ideas) presented in the work. He or she should ask the following questions to help pinpoint these main ideas:

1. Is the poet trying to advocate social, moral, or religious change?
2. Does the poet seem sure of his or her position?
3. Does the poem appeal primarily to the emotions, to the intellect, or to both?
4. Is the poem relying on any particular devices for effect (such as imagery, allusion, paradox, hyperbole, or irony)?

BIBLIOGRAPHY

Biographical sources

Baughman, Ronald, ed. *American Poets*. Vol. 3 in *Contemporary Authors: Bibliographical Series*. Detroit: Gale Research, 1986.

Bold, Alan. *Longman Dictionary of Poets: The Lives and Works of 1001 Poets in the English Language*. Harlow, Essex: Longman, 1985.

Conte, Joseph, ed. *American Poets Since World War II: Fourth Series*. Dictionary of Literary Biography 165. Detroit: Gale Research, 1996.

_______. *American Poets Since World War II: Fifth Series*. Dictionary of Literary Biography 169. Detroit: Gale Research, 1996.

_______. *American Poets Since World War II: Sixth Series*. Dictionary of Literary Biography 193. Detroit: Gale Research, 1998.

Cyclopedia of World Authors. 4th rev. ed. 5 vols. Pasadena, Calif.: Salem Press, 2003.

Greiner, Donald J., ed. *American Poets Since World War II*. Dictionary of Literary Biography 5. Detroit: Gale Research, 1980.

Gwynn, R. S., ed. *American Poets Since World War II: Second Series*. Dictionary of Literary Biography 105. Detroit: Gale Research, 1991.

_______. *American Poets Since World War II: Third Series*. Dictionary of Literary Biography 120. Detroit: Gale Research, 1992.

International Who's Who in Poetry and Poets' Encyclopaedia. Cambridge, England: International Biographical Centre, 1993.

Riggs, Thomas, ed. *Contemporary Poets*. Contemporary Writers Series. 7th ed. Detroit: St. James Press, 2001.

Wakeman, John, ed. *World Authors, 1950-1970*. New York: H. W. Wilson, 1975.

_______. *World Authors, 1970-1975*. Wilson Authors Series. New York: H. W. Wilson, 1991.

Willhardt, Mark, and Alan Michael Parker, eds. *Who's Who in Twentieth Century World Poetry*. New York: Routledge, 2000.

Criticism

Alexander, Harriet Semmes, comp. *American and British Poetry: A Guide to the Criticism, 1925-1978*. Manchester, England: Manchester University Press, 1984.

Annual Bibliography of English Language and Literature. Cambridge, England: Modern Humanities Research Association, 1920- .

Brooks, Cleanth, and Robert Penn Warren. *Understanding Poetry*. 4th ed. Reprint. Fort Worth, Tex.: Heinle & Heinle, 2003.

Childs, Peter. *The Twentieth Century in Poetry: A Critical Survey*. New York: Routledge, 1999.

Cline, Gloria Stark, and Jeffrey A. Baker. *An Index to Criticism of British and American Poetry*. Metuchen, N.J.: Scarecrow Press, 1973.

Contemporary Literary Criticism. Detroit: Gale Research, 1973- .

Day, Gary. *Literary Criticism: A New History*. Edinburgh, Scotland: Edinburgh University Press, 2008.

Guide to American Poetry Explication. Reference Publication in Literature. 2 vols. Boston: G. K. Hall, 1989.

Kuntz, Joseph M., and Nancy C. Martinez. *Poetry Explication: A Checklist of Interpretation Since 1925 of British and American Poems Past and Present*. 3d ed. Boston: Hall, 1980.

Lodge, David, and Nigel Wood. *Modern Criticism and Theory*. 3d ed. New York: Longman, 2008.

Magill, Frank N., ed. *Magill's Bibliography of Literary Criticism*. 4 vols. Englewood Cliffs, N.J.: Salem Press, 1979.

MLA International Bibliography. New York: Modern Language Association of America, 1922- .

Roberts, Neil, ed. A Companion to Twentieth-Century Poetry. Malden, Mass.: Blackwell Publishers, 2001.

Twentieth-Century Literary Criticism. Detroit: Gale Research, 1978- .

Walcutt, Charles Child, and J. Edwin Whitesell, eds. *Modern Poetry*. Vol. 1 in *The Explicator Cyclopedia*. Chicago: Quadrangle Books, 1968.

The Year's Work in English Studies. 1921- .

DICTIONARIES, HISTORIES, AND HANDBOOKS

Carey, Gary, and Mary Ellen Snodgrass. *A Multicultural Dictionary of Literary Terms*. Jefferson, N.C.: McFarland, 1999.

Deutsch, Babette. *Poetry Handbook: A Dictionary of Terms*. 4th ed. New York: Funk & Wagnalls, 1974.

Draper, Ronald P. *An Introduction to Twentieth-Century Poetry in English*. New York: St. Martin's Press, 1999.

Drury, John. *The Poetry Dictionary*. Cincinnati, Ohio: Story Press, 1995.

Hamilton, Ian, ed. *The Oxford Companion to Twentieth-Century Poetry in English*. New York: Oxford University Press, 1994.

Kamp, Jim, ed. *Reference Guide to American Literature*. 3d ed. Detroit: St. James Press, 1994.

Kinzie, Mary. *A Poet's Guide to Poetry*. Chicago: University of Chicago Press, 1999.

Lennard, John. *The Poetry Handbook: A Guide to Reading Poetry for Pleasure and Practical Criticism*. New York: Oxford University Press, 1996.

Matterson, Stephen, and Darryl Jones. *Studying Poetry*. New York: Oxford University Press, 2000.

Packard, William. *The Poet's Dictionary: A Handbook of Prosody and Poetic Devices.* New York: Harper & Row, 1989.

Parini, Jay, ed. *The Columbia History of American Poetry.* New York: Columbia University Press, 1993.

Perkins, David. *Modernism and After.* Vol. 2 in *A History of Modern Poetry.* 2 vols. Cambridge, Mass.: Belknap-Harvard University Press, 1987.

Perkins, George, Barbara Perkins, and Phillip Leininger, eds. *Benét's Reader's Encyclopedia of American Literature.* New York: HarperCollins, 1991.

Preminger, Alex, et al., eds. *The New Princeton Encyclopedia of Poetry and Poetics.* 3d rev. ed. Princeton, N.J.: Princeton University Press, 1993.

INDEXES OF PRIMARY WORKS

American Poetry Index: An Author, Title, and Subject Guide to Poetry by Americans in Single-Author Collections. Great Neck, N.Y.: Granger, 1983-1988.

Annual Index to Poetry in Periodicals. Great Neck, N.Y.: Poetry Index Press, 1985-1988.

Caskey, Jefferson D., comp. *Index to Poetry in Popular Periodicals, 1955-1959.* Westport, Conn.: Greenwood Press, 1984.

Frankovich, Nicholas, ed. *The Columbia Granger's Index to Poetry in Anthologies.* 11th ed. New York: Columbia University Press, 1997.

_______. *The Columbia Granger's Index to Poetry in Collected and Selected Works.* New York: Columbia University Press, 1997.

Guy, Patricia. *A Women's Poetry Index.* Phoenix, Ariz.: Oryx Press, 1985.

Hazen, Edith P., ed. *Columbia Granger's Index to Poetry.* 10th ed. New York: Columbia University Press, 1994.

Hoffman, Herbert H., and Rita Ludwig Hoffman, comps. *International Index to Recorded Poetry.* New York: H. W. Wilson, 1983.

Index of American Periodical Verse. Lanham, Md.: Scarecrow, 1971.

Index to Poetry in Periodicals, 1925-1992: An Index of Poets and Poems Published in American Magazines and Newspapers. Great Neck, N.Y.: Granger, 1984.

Poem Finder. Great Neck, N.Y.: Roth, 2000.

Poetry Index Annual: A Title, Author, First Line, Keyword, and Subject Index to Poetry in Anthologies. Great Neck, N.Y.: Poetry Index, 1982- .

POETICS, POETIC FORMS, AND GENRES

Attridge, Derek. *Poetic Rhythm: An Introduction.* New York: Cambridge University Press, 1995.

Brogan, T. V. F. *English Versification, 1570-1980: A Reference Guide with a Global Appendix.* Baltimore: Johns Hopkins University Press, 1981.

_______. *Verseform: A Comparative Bibliography.* Baltimore: Johns Hopkins University Press, 1989.

Fussell, Paul. *Poetic Meter and Poetic Form*. Rev. ed. New York: McGraw-Hill, 1979.

Hollander, John. *Rhyme's Reason*. 3d ed. New Haven, Conn.: Yale University Press, 2001.

Malof, Joseph. *A Manual of English Meters*. Bloomington: Indiana University Press, 1970.

Padgett, Ron, ed. *The Teachers and Writers Handbook of Poetic Forms*. 2d ed. New York: Teachers & Writers Collaborative, 2000.

Pinsky, Robert. *The Sounds of Poetry: A Brief Guide*. New York: Farrar, Straus and Giroux, 1998.

Preminger, Alex, and T. V. F. Brogan, eds. *New Princeton Encyclopedia of Poetry and Poetics*. 3d ed. Princeton, N.J.: Princeton University Press, 1993.

Shapiro, Karl, and Robert Beum. *A Prosody Handbook*. New York: Harper, 1965.

Turco, Lewis. *The New Book of Forms: A Handbook of Poetics*. Hanover, N.H.: University Press of New England, 1986.

Williams, Miller. *Patterns of Poetry: An Encyclopedia of Forms*. Baton Rouge: Louisiana State University Press, 1986.

TWENTIETH CENTURY AND CONTEMPORARY

Altieri, Charles. *The Art of Twentieth-Century American Poetry: Modernism and After*. Malden, Mass.: Blackwell, 2006.

Axelrod, Steven Gould, and Camille Roman, eds. *Modernisms, 1900-1950*. Vol. 2 in *The New Anthology of American Poetry*. New Brunswick, N.J.: Rutgers University Press, 2005.

Beach, Christopher. *The Cambridge Introduction to Twentieth-Century American Poetry*. New York: Cambridge University Press, 2003.

Davis, Lloyd, and Robert Irwin. *Contemporary American Poetry: A Checklist*. Metuchen, N.J.: Scarecrow Press, 1975.

Gioia, Dana, David Mason, and Meg Schoerke, eds. *Twentieth-Century American Poetics: Poets on the Art of Poetry*. Boston: McGraw-Hill, 2004.

_______. *Twentieth-Century American Poetry*. Boston: McGraw-Hill, 2003.

Haralson, Eric L., ed. *Encyclopedia of American Poetry: The Twentieth Century*. Chicago: Fitzroy Dearborn, 2001.

Kane, Daniel. *All Poets Welcome: The Lower East Side Poetry Scene in the 1960's*. Berkeley: University of California Press, 2003.

Kirsch, Adam. *The Wounded Surgeon: Confession and Transformation in Six American Poets*. New York: W. W. Norton, 2005.

Leo, John R. *Modern and Contemporary*. Vol. 2 in *Guide to American Poetry Explication*. Boston: G. K. Hall, 1989.

McPheron, William. *The Bibliography of Contemporary American Poetry, 1945-1985: An Annotated Checklist*. Westport, Conn.: Meckler, 1986.

Moramarco, Fred, and William Sullivan. *Containing Multitudes: Poetry in the United States Since 1950*. Critical History of Poetry Series. New York: Twayne, 1998.

Rasula, Jed. *This Compost: Ecological Imperatives in American Poetry*. Athens: University of Georgia Press, 2002.

Shucard, Alan, Fred Moramarco, and William Sullivan. *Modern American Poetry, 1865-1950*. Boston: Twayne, 1989.

Ward, Geoffrey. *Statutes of Liberty: The New York School of Poets*. New York: Palgrave Macmillan, 2001.

Maura Ives
Updated by Tracy Irons-Georges

GUIDE TO ONLINE RESOURCES

Web Sites

The following sites were visited by the editors of Salem Press in 2010. Because URLs frequently change, the accuracy of these addresses cannot be guaranteed; however, long-standing sites, such as those of colleges and universities, national organizations, and government agencies, generally maintain links when their sites are moved.

Academy of American Poets
http://www.poets.org

The mission of the Academy of American Poets is to "support American poets at all stages of their careers and to foster the appreciation of contemporary poetry." The academy's comprehensive Web site features information on poetic schools and movements; a Poetic Forms Database; an Online Poetry Classroom, with educator and teaching resources; an index of poets and poems; essays and interviews; general Web resources; links for further study; and more.

Contemporary British Writers
http://www.contemporarywriters.com/authors

Created by the British Council, this site offers profiles of living writers of the United Kingdom, the Republic of Ireland, and the Commonwealth. Information includes biographies, bibliographies, critical reviews, and news about literary prizes. Photographs are also featured. Users can search the site by author, genre, nationality, gender, publisher, book title, date of publication, and prize name and date.

LiteraryHistory.com
http://www.literaryhistory.com

This site is an excellent source of academic, scholarly, and critical literature about eighteenth, nineteenth, and twentieth century American and English writers. It provides individual pages for twentieth century literature and alphabetical lists of authors that link to articles, reviews, overviews, excerpts of works, teaching guides, podcasts, and other materials.

Literary Resources on the Net
http://andromeda.rutgers.edu/~jlynch/Lit

Jack Lynch of Rutgers University maintains this extensive collection of links to Web sites that are useful to researchers, including numerous sites about American and English literature. This collection is a good place to begin online research about poetry, as it links to other sites with broad ranges of literary topics. The site is organized chronologically, with separate pages about twentieth century British and Irish literature. It also has separate pages providing links to Web sites about American literature and to women's literature and feminism.

LitWeb
http://litweb.net

LitWeb provides biographies of hundreds of world authors throughout history that can be accessed through an alphabetical listing. The pages about each writer contain a list of his or her works, suggestions for further reading, and illustrations. The site also offers information about past and present winners of major literary prizes.

The Modern Word: Authors of the Libyrinth
http://www.themodernword.com/authors.html

The Modern Word site, although somewhat haphazard in its organization, provides a great deal of critical information about writers. The "Authors of the Libyrinth" page is very useful, linking author names to essays about them and other resources. The section of the page headed "The Scriptorium" presents "an index of pages featuring writers who have pushed the edges of their medium, combining literary talent with a sense of experimentation to produce some remarkable works of modern literature."

Outline of American Literature
http://www.america.gov/publications/books/outline
-of-american-literature.html

This page of the America.gov site provides access to an electronic version of the ten-chapter volume *Outline of American Literature*, a historical overview of poetry and prose from colonial times to the present published by the Bureau of International Information Programs of the U.S. Department of State.

Poetry Foundation
http://www.poetryfoundation.org

The Poetry Foundation, publisher of *Poetry* magazine, is an independent literary organization. Its Web site offers links to essays; news; events; online poetry resources, such as blogs, organizations, publications, and references and research; a glossary of literary terms; and a Learning Lab that includes poem guides and essays on poetics.

Poet's Corner
http://theotherpages.org/poems

The Poet's Corner, one of the oldest text resources on the Web, provides access to about seven thousand works of poetry by several hundred different poets from around the world. Indexes are arranged and searchable by title, name of poet, or subject. The site also offers its own resources, including "Faces of the Poets"—a gallery of portraits—and "Lives of the Poets"—a growing collection of biographies.

Representative Poetry Online
http://rpo.library.utoronto.ca

This award-winning resource site, maintained by Ian Lancashire of the Department of English at the University of Toronto in Canada, has several thousand English-language poems by hundreds of poets. The collection is searchable by poet's name, title of work, first line of a poem, and keyword. The site also includes a time line, a glossary, essays, an extensive bibliography, and countless links organized by country and by subject.

Voice of the Shuttle
http://vos.ucsb.edu

One of the most complete and authoritative places for online information about literature, Voice of the Shuttle is maintained by professors and students in the English Department at the University of California, Santa Barbara. The site provides countless links to electronic books, academic journals, literary association Web sites, sites created by university professors, and many other resources.

Voices from the Gaps
http://voices.cla.umn.edu/

Voices from the Gaps is a site of the English Department at the University of Minnesota, dedicated to providing resources on the study of women artists of color, including writers. The site features a comprehensive index searchable by name, and it provides biographical information on each writer or artist and other resources for further study.

ELECTRONIC DATABASES

Electronic databases usually do not have their own URLs. Instead, public, college, and university libraries subscribe to these databases, provide links to them on their Web sites, and make them available to library card holders or other specified patrons. Readers can visit library Web sites or ask reference librarians to check on availability.

Canadian Literary Centre

Produced by EBSCO, the Canadian Literary Centre database contains full-text content from ECW Press, a Toronto-based publisher, including the titles in the publisher's Canadian fiction studies, Canadian biography, and Canadian writers and their works series; *ECW's Biographical Guide to Canadian Novelists*; and *George Woodcock's Introduction to Canadian Fiction*. Author biographies, essays and literary criticism, and book reviews are among the database's offerings.

Literary Reference Center

EBSCO's Literary Reference Center (LRC) is a comprehensive full-text database designed primarily to help high school and undergraduate students in English and the humanities with homework and research assignments about literature. The database contains massive amounts of information from reference works, books, literary journals, and other materials, including more than 31,000 plot summaries, synopses, and overviews of literary works; almost 100,000 essays and articles of literary criticism; about 140,000 author biographies; more than 605,000 book reviews; and more than 5,200 author interviews. It contains the entire contents of Salem Press's MagillOnLiterature Plus. Users can retrieve information by browsing a list of authors' names or titles of literary works; they can also use an advanced search engine to access information by numerous categories, including author name, gender, cultural identity, national identity, and the years in which he or she lived, or by literary title, character, locale, genre, and publication date. The Literary Reference Center also features a literary-historical time line, an encyclopedia of literature, and a glossary of literary terms.

MagillOnLiterature Plus

MagillOnLiterature Plus is a comprehensive, integrated literature database produced by Salem Press and available on the EBSCOhost platform. The database contains the full text of essays in Salem's many literature-related reference works, including *Masterplots*, *Cyclopedia of World Authors*, *Cyclopedia of Literary Characters*, *Cyclopedia of Literary Places*, *Critical Survey of Poetry*, *Critical Survey of Long Fiction*, *Critical Survey of Short Fiction*, *World Philosophers and Their Works*, *Magill's Literary Annual*, and *Magill's Book Reviews*. Among its contents are articles on more than 35,000 literary works and more than 8,500 poets, writers, dramatists, essayists, and philosophers; more than 1,000 images; and a glossary of more than 1,300 literary terms. The biographical essays include lists of authors' works and secondary bibliographies, and hundreds of overview essays examine and discuss literary genres, time periods, and national literatures.

Rebecca Kuzins; updated by Desiree Dreeuws

GEOGRAPHICAL INDEX

FINLAND
Hollo, Anselm, 136

GREAT BRITAIN
Gunn, Thom, 123
Larkin, Philip, 152

UNITED STATES
Beat Poets, 1
Blackburn, Paul, 9
Brautigan, Richard, 21
Bukowski, Charles, 27
Corso, Gregory, 42
Di Prima, Diane, 51
Duncan, Robert, 61
Everson, William, 73
Ferlinghetti, Lawrence, 89
Gilbert, Jack, 101
Ginsberg, Allen, 106
Gunn, Thom, 123
Hollo, Anselm, 136
Kaufman, Bob, 146
McClure, Michael, 165
Olson, Charles, 172
Patchen, Kenneth, 183
Ponsot, Marie, 191
Rexroth, Kenneth, 199
Snyder, Gary, 207
Sorrentino, Gilbert, 226
Spicer, Jack, 232
Wakoski, Diane, 238
Whalen, Philip, 251

CATEGORY INDEX

BLACK MOUNTAIN POETS
Blackburn, Paul, 9
Duncan, Robert, 61
McClure, Michael, 165
Olson, Charles, 172
Snyder, Gary, 207

CONCRETE POETRY
Patchen, Kenneth, 183
CONFESSIONAL POETS
Ginsberg, Allen, 106
CUBISM
Rexroth, Kenneth, 199

DEEP IMAGE POETS
Wakoski, Diane, 238
DRAMATIC MONOLOGUES
Blackburn, Paul, 9
Gunn, Thom, 123

ECOPOETRY
McClure, Michael, 165
Snyder, Gary, 207
EKPHRASTIC POETRY
Gunn, Thom, 123
ELEGIES
Gilbert, Jack, 101
Rexroth, Kenneth, 199
EPICS
Ferlinghetti, Lawrence, 89
Snyder, Gary, 207
EXPERIMENTAL POETS
Hollo, Anselm, 136
Patchen, Kenneth, 183
Whalen, Philip, 251

FEMINIST POETS
Di Prima, Diane, 51

GAY AND LESBIAN CULTURE
Duncan, Robert, 61
Ginsberg, Allen, 106
Gunn, Thom, 123
Spicer, Jack, 232

HAIKU
Blackburn, Paul, 9
Di Prima, Diane, 51
Ginsberg, Allen, 106
McClure, Michael, 165
Snyder, Gary, 207
HYMNS
McClure, Michael, 165

IMAGISM
Wakoski, Diane, 238

JAZZ POETS
Kaufman, Bob, 146
Patchen, Kenneth, 183
JEWISH CULTURE
Ginsberg, Allen, 106

LANGUAGE POETRY
Hollo, Anselm, 136
LOVE POETRY
Brautigan, Richard, 21
Gilbert, Jack, 101
Patchen, Kenneth, 183
Rexroth, Kenneth, 199

LYRIC POETRY
Blackburn, Paul, 9
Duncan, Robert, 61
Ferlinghetti, Lawrence, 89

MINIMALIST POETRY
Brautigan, Richard, 21
Bukowski, Charles, 27
MOVEMENT POETS
Gunn, Thom, 123
Larkin, Philip, 152

NARRATIVE POETRY
Rexroth, Kenneth, 199
Wakoski, Diane, 238
NATURE POETRY
Rexroth, Kenneth, 199

OBJECTIVISM
Rexroth, Kenneth, 199
ODES
McClure, Michael, 165
ORAL TRADITION
Kaufman, Bob, 146

POLITICAL POETS
Ferlinghetti, Lawrence, 89
Olson, Charles, 172
Rexroth, Kenneth, 199
POSTCONFESSIONAL POETS
Bukowski, Charles, 27
Ponsot, Marie, 191
POSTMODERNISM
Blackburn, Paul, 9
Brautigan, Richard, 21
Corso, Gregory, 42
Duncan, Robert, 61
Everson, William, 73
Ferlinghetti, Lawrence, 89
Gilbert, Jack, 101
Ginsberg, Allen, 106
Gunn, Thom, 123
Larkin, Philip, 152
McClure, Michael, 165
Olson, Charles, 172
Patchen, Kenneth, 183
Snyder, Gary, 207
Sorrentino, Gilbert, 226
Spicer, Jack, 232
Wakoski, Diane, 238
PROSE POETRY
Brautigan, Richard, 21
Ferlinghetti, Lawrence, 89
Kaufman, Bob, 146
Patchen, Kenneth, 183
Spicer, Jack, 232

RELIGIOUS POETRY
Everson, William, 73

SATIRIC POETRY
Rexroth, Kenneth, 199
SONNETS
Ponsot, Marie, 191
Sorrentino, Gilbert, 226
SURREALIST POETS
Kaufman, Bob, 146

VISIONARY POETRY
Ginsberg, Allen, 106
McClure, Michael, 165

WOMEN POETS
Di Prima, Diane, 51
Ponsot, Marie, 191
Wakoski, Diane, 238

SUBJECT INDEX

"Abrasive" (Everson), 79
Admit Impediment (Ponsot), 193
After Lorca (Spicer), 234
Against the Silences (Blackburn), 18
American Way, The" (Corso), 46
Americus, Book I (Ferlinghetti), 97
Ancient Rain, The (Kaufman), 150
"Apollonius of Tyana" (Olson), 177
"Apprehensions" (Duncan), 68
Archaeologist of Morning (Olsen), 180
At Terror Street and Agony Way (Bukowski), 34
Axe Handles (Snyder), 218

Bagel Shop Jazz (Kaufman), 149
Beat generation, 1-8
Beatnik, definition of, 6
Before the Brave (Patchen), 187
Bending the Bow (Duncan), 68
Bird Catcher, The (Ponsot), 194
"Birdbrain" (Ginsberg), 117
Blackburn, Paul, 9-20
- *Against the Silences*, 18
- *Brooklyn-Manhattan Transit*, 17
- "Call It the Net," 16
- "December Journal: 1968," 19
- *Early Selected y Mas*, 13
- "How to Get Through Reality," 14
- "Lines, Trees, and Words," 16
- "Mestrović and the Trees," 14
- "The Net of Moon," 16
- "The Purse Seine," 16
- *The Reardon Poems*, 19
- "Ritual I," 15
- "Ritual IV," 15

Blake, William, 2
Blowing of the Seed, The (Everson), 82
Bone Pallace Ballet (Bukowski), 39
"Born Yesterday" (Larkin), 157
Boss Cupid (Gunn), 134
"Bouzouki music" (Hollo), 140
Brautigan, Richard, 21-26
- *Loading Mercury with a Pitchfork*, 25
- *The Pill Versus the Springhill Mine Disaster*, 24
- *Rommel Drives on Deep into Egypt*, 24

Brooklyn-Manhattan Transit (Blackburn), 17
Brother Antoninus. *See* Everson, William
"Building, The" (Larkin), 161
Bukowski, Charles, 27-41
- *At Terror Street and Agony Way*, 34
- *Bone Pallace Ballet*, 39
- *A Bukowski Sampler*, 34
- *Burning in Water, Drowning in Flame*, 36
- *Cold Dogs in the Courtyard*, 33
- *Crucifix in a Deathhand*, 33
- *Dangling in the Tournefortia*, 38
- *The Days Run Away Like Wild Horses over the Hills*, 35
- *Flower, Fist, and Bestial Wail*, 31
- *The Genius of the Crowd*, 33
- *It Catches My Heart in Its Hand*, 32
- *The Last Generation*, 39
- *Last Night of the Earth Poems*, 39
- *Longshot Poems for Broke Players*, 32
- *Love Is a Dog from Hell*, 37
- *Mockingbird Wish Me Luck*, 35
- *Open All Night*, 39
- *Play the Piano Drunk Like a Percussion Instrument Until the Fingers Begin to Bleed a Bit*, 37

Poems Written Before Jumping out of an Eight Story Window, 34
Run with the Hunted, 32
"The Twins," 31
Bukowski Sampler, A (Bukowski), 34
Burning in Water, Drowning in Flame (Bukowski), 36

"Call It the Net" (Blackburn), 16
"Chainsaw" (Everson), 86
"Chronicle of Division, The" (Everson), 81
"Church Going" (Larkin), 158
Coins and Coffins (Wakoski), 241
Cold Dogs in the Courtyard (Bukowski), 33
Cold Mountain Poems (Snyder), 216
Collected Longer Poems, The (Rexroth), 203
Collected Poems (Larkin), 162
Collected Poems, 1947-1997 (Ginsberg), 119
Collected Shorter Poems, The (Rexroth), 202
Coney Island of the Mind, A (Ferlinghetti), 94
"Continent, The" (Duncan), 68
Corso, Gregory, 42-50
"The American Way," 46
Elegiac Feelings American, 46
"Field Report," 48
Gasoline, 45
The Happy Birthday of Death, 45
Herald of the Autochthonic Spirit, 47
Long Live Man, 46
"Marriage," 46
Mindfield, 47
"Window," 47
Cosmopolitan Greetings (Ginsberg), 117
Crooked Lines of God, The (Everson), 83
Crucifix in a Deathhand (Bukowski), 33

Dance Most of All, The (Gilbert), 104
Dancing on the Grave of a Son of a Bitch (Wakoski), 246
Danger on Peaks (Snyder), 222
Dangling in the Tournefortia (Bukowski), 38
Days Run Away Like Wild Horses over the Hills, The (Bukowski), 35
"December Journal: 1968" (Blackburn), 19
"Delights of Winter at the Shore" (Whalen), 254
Di Prima, Diane, 51-60
Dinners and Nightmares, 54
Earthsong, 55
Loba, 56
"Notes Toward a Poem of Revolution," 58
Revolutionary Letters, 57
Dinners and Nightmares (Di Prima), 54
Discrepancies and Apparitions (Wakoski), 241
"Dockery and Son" (Larkin), 159
"Dog" (Ferlinghetti), 95
Dozen Oranges, A (Sorrentino), 229
Dragon and the Unicorn, The (Rexroth), 204
Duncan, Robert, 61-72
"Apprehensions," 68
Bending the Bow, 68
"The Continent," 68
"Food for Fire, Food for Thought," 67
Ground Work: Before the War, 70
The Opening of the Field, 66
"Passages Poems," 69
"A Poem Beginning with a Line by Pindar," 67
Roots and Branches, 67
"Sage Architect," 68

Early Selected y Mas (Blackburn), 13
Earthsong (Di Prima), 55
Eberhart, Richard, 5
Elegiac Feelings American (Corso), 46
Everson, William, 73-88
"Abrasive," 79
The Blowing of the Seed, 82

"Chainsaw," 86
"The Chronicle of Division," 81
The Crooked Lines of God, 83
"The Fictive Wish," 82
"First Winter Storm," 78
The Hazards of Holiness, 83
"I Know It as the Sorrow," 78
"The Illusion," 80
The Integral Years, 87
"The Kiss of the Cross," 84
Man-Fate, 85
The Masculine Dead, 80
The Masks of Drought, 85
"Moongate," 86
"The Presence," 81
The Rose of Solitude, 84
"Saints," 83
"The Screed of the Flesh," 83
"The Sides of a Mind," 80
These Are the Ravens, 78
"Who Sees Through the Lens," 79
The Year's Declension, 83

Fall of America, The (Ginsberg), 116
Far Rockaway of the Heart, A (Ferlinghetti), 96
Ferlinghetti, Lawrence, 5, 89-100
Americus, Book I, 97
A Coney Island of the Mind, 94
"Dog," 95
A Far Rockaway of the Heart, 96
How to Paint Sunlight, 96
"Fictive Wish, The" (Everson), 82
"Field Report" (Corso), 48
Fighting Terms (Gunn), 126
First Will and Testament (Patchen), 187
"First Winter Storm" (Everson), 78
Flower, Fist, and Bestial Wail (Bukowski), 31
"Food for Fire, Food for Thought" (Duncan), 67
"For Artaud" (McClure), 169
"For C." (Whalen), 253
Fudo Trilogy, The (Snyder), 217

"Garden, The" (Whalen), 255
Gasoline (Corso), 45
Genius of the Crowd, The (Bukowski), 33
George Washington Poems, The (Wakoski), 242
Gilbert, Jack, 101-105
The Dance Most of All, 104
The Great Fires, 104
Monolithos, 103
Refusing Heaven, 104
Views of Jeopardy, 103
Ginsberg, Allen, 3, 106-122
"Birdbrain," 117
Collected Poems, 1947-1997, 119
Cosmopolitan Greetings, 117
The Fall of America, 116
"Howl," 4, 111
"Kaddish," 112
"Kral Majales," 114
Mind Breaths, 116
Plutonian Ode, 116
White Shroud, 117
"Witchita Vortex Sutra," 114
"Going, Going" (Larkin), 160
Great Fires, The (Gilbert), 104
Greed (Wakoski), 248
Green Dark, The (Ponsot), 194
Ground Work: Before the War (Duncan), 70
Guests of Space (Hollo), 143
Gunn, Thom, 123-135
Boss Cupid, 134
Fighting Terms, 126
Jack Straw's Castle, and Other Poems, 131
The Man with Night Sweats, 133
Moly, 130

My Sad Captains, and Other Poems, 127
The Passages of Joy, 131
Positives, 129
The Sense of Movement, 127
Touch, 129
Undesirables, 132

Happy Birthday of Death, The (Corso), 45
Hazards of Holiness, The (Everson), 83
Heart's Garden, the Garden's Heart, The (Rexroth), 204
Herald of the Autochthonic Spirit (Corso), 47
High Windows (Larkin), 160
Highgrade (Whalen), 254
Hollo, Anselm, 136-145
"Bouzouki music," 140
Guests of Space, 143
"Manifest destiny," 139
Notes on the Possibilities and Attractions of Existence, 142
"Old space cadet speaking," 140
Rue Wilson Monday, 141
"How to Get Through Reality" (Blackburn), 14
How to Paint Sunlight (Ferlinghetti), 96
"Howl" (Ginsberg), 4, 111
"Hymn to St. Geryon, I" (McClure), 168

"I Know It as the Sorrow" (Everson), 78
"I Remember, I Remember" (Larkin), 157
"Illusion, The" (Everson), 80
Inside the Blood Factory (Wakoski), 243
Integral Years, The (Everson), 87
It Catches My Heart in Its Hand (Bukowski), 32

Jack Straw's Castle, and Other Poems (Gunn), 131
Jeffers, Robinson, 74

"Kaddish" (Ginsberg), 112
Kaufman, Bob, 146-151
The Ancient Rain, 150
Bagel Shop Jazz, 149
Kerouac, Jack, 1; *Mexico City Blues*, 6
"Kingfishers, The" (Olson), 179
"Kiss of the Cross, The" (Everson), 84
"Kral Majales" (Ginsberg), 114

Language (Spicer), 235
Larkin, Philip, 152-164
"Born Yesterday," 157
"The Building," 161
"Church Going," 158
Collected Poems, 162
"Dockery and Son," 159
"Going, Going," 160
High Windows, 160
"I Remember, I Remember," 157
The Less Deceived, 157
"The Mower," 162
The North Ship, 156
The Whitsun Weddings, 159
Last Generation, The (Bukowski), 39
Last Night of the Earth Poems (Bukowski), 39
Less Deceived, The (Larkin), 157
"Lines, Trees, and Words" (Blackburn), 16
Loading Mercury with a Pitchfork (Brautigan), 25
Loba (Di Prima), 56
Long Live Man (Corso), 46
Longshot Poems for Broke Players (Bukowski), 32
Love Is a Dog from Hell (Bukowski), 37

McClure, Michael, 165-171
"For Artaud," 169
"Hymn to St. Geryon, I," 168
"Peyote Poem, Part I," 169

"The Robe," 168
"The Rug," 168
Selected Poems, 169
Magellanic Clouds, The (Wakoski), 243
Man-Fate (Everson), 85
Man Who Shook Hands, The (Wakoski), 247
Man with Night Sweats, The (Gunn), 133
"Manifest destiny" (Hollo), 139
"Marriage" (Corso), 46
Masculine Dead, The (Everson), 80
Masks of Drought, The (Everson), 85
Maximus Poems, The (Olson), 180
"Mestrović and the Trees" (Blackburn), 14
Mexico City Blues (Kerouac), 6
"Midnight Special" (Sorrentino), 228
Mind Breaths (Ginsberg), 116
Mindfield (Corso), 47
Mockingbird Wish Me Luck (Bukowski), 35
Moly (Gunn), 130
Monolithos (Gilbert), 103
"Moongate" (Everson), 86
Motorcycle Betrayal Poems, The (Wakoski), 244
Mountains and Rivers Without End (Snyder), 219
"Mower, The" (Larkin), 162
My Sad Captains, and Other Poems (Gunn), 127
Myths and Texts (Snyder), 214

"Net of Moon, The" (Blackburn), 16
"Nightpiece" (Sorrentino), 228
North Ship, The (Larkin), 156
"Notes Toward a Poem of Revolution" (Di Prima), 58
Notes on the Possibilities and Attractions of Existence (Hollo), 142

"Old space cadet speaking" (Hollo), 140
Olson, Charles, 172-182
"Apollonius of Tyana," 177
Archaeologist of Morning, 180
"The Kingfishers," 179
The Maximus Poems, 180
Open All Night (Bukowski), 39
Opening of the Field, The (Duncan), 66
Orangery, The (Sorrentino), 229
"Passages Poems" (Duncan), 69

Passages of Joy, The (Gunn), 131
Patchen, Kenneth, 183-190
Before the Brave, 187
First Will and Testament, 187
Perfect Fiction, The (Sorrentino), 228
"Peyote Poem, Part I" (McClure), 169
Phoenix and the Tortoise, The (Rexroth), 204
Pill Versus the Springhill Mine Disaster, The (Brautigan), 24
Play the Piano Drunk Like a Percussion Instrument Until the Fingers Begin to Bleed a Bit (Bukowski), 37
Plutonian Ode (Ginsberg), 116
"Poem Beginning with a Line by Pindar, A" (Duncan), 67
Poems Written Before Jumping out of an Eight Story Window (Bukowski), 34
Ponsot, Marie, 191-198
Admit Impediment, 193
The Bird Catcher, 194
The Green Dark, 194
Springing, 196
True Minds, 192
Positives (Gunn), 129
"Presence, The" (Everson), 81
Prolegomenon to a Theodicy, A (Rexroth), 204
"Purse Seine, The" (Blackburn), 16

Reardon Poems, The (Blackburn), 19
Refusing Heaven (Gilbert), 104
Regarding Wave (Snyder), 216

Revolutionary Letters (Di Prima), 57
Rexroth, Kenneth, 4, 199-206
The Collected Longer Poems, 203
The Collected Shorter Poems, 202
The Dragon and the Unicorn, 204
The Heart's Garden, the Garden's Heart, 204
The Phoenix and the Tortoise, 204
A Prolegomenon to a Theodicy, 204
Riprap (Snyder), 213
"Ritual I" (Blackburn), 15
"Ritual IV" (Blackburn), 15
"Robe, The" (McClure), 168
Rommel Drives on Deep into Egypt (Brautigan), 24
Roots and Branches (Duncan), 67
Rose of Solitude, The (Everson), 84
Rue Wilson Monday (Hollo), 141
"Rug, The" (McClure), 168
Run with the Hunted (Bukowski), 32

"Sage Architect" (Duncan), 68
"Saints" (Everson), 83
San Francisco Renaissance, 3
"Screed of the Flesh, The" (Everson), 83
Selected Poems (McClure), 169
Sense of Movement, The (Gunn), 127
"Sides of a Mind, The" (Everson), 80
"Small Tantric Sermon" (Whalen), 254
Smudging (Wakoski), 245
Snyder, Gary, 207-225
Axe Handles, 218
Cold Mountain Poems, 216
Danger on Peaks, 222
The Fudo Trilogy, 217
Mountains and Rivers Without End, 219
Myths and Texts, 214
Regarding Wave, 216
Riprap, 213
Turtle Island, 217
Sorrentino, Gilbert, 226-231
A Dozen Oranges, 229
"Midnight Special," 228
"Nightpiece," 228
The Orangery, 229
The Perfect Fiction, 228
White Sail, 229
Spicer, Jack, 232-237
After Lorca, 234
Language, 235
"A Textbook of Poetry," 235
Springing (Ponsot), 196
Symmes, Robert Edward. *See* Duncan, Robert

"Textbook of Poetry, A" (Spicer), 235
These Are the Ravens (Everson), 78
Touch (Gunn), 129
True Minds (Ponsot), 192
Turtle Island (Snyder), 217
"Twins, The" (Bukowski), 31

Undesirables (Gunn), 132

Views of Jeopardy (Gilbert), 103
Virtuoso Literature for Two and Four Hands (Wakoski), 246

Waiting for the King of Spain (Wakoski), 247
Wakoski, Diane, 238-250
Coins and Coffins, 241
Dancing on the Grave of a Son of a Bitch, 246
Discrepancies and Apparitions, 241
The George Washington Poems, 242
Greed, 248
Inside the Blood Factory, 243
The Magellanic Clouds, 243
The Man Who Shook Hands, 247
The Motorcycle Betrayal Poems, 244
Smudging, 245

Virtuoso Literature for Two and Four Hands, 246
Waiting for the King of Spain, 247
Whalen, Philip, 251-256
"Delights of Winter at the Shore," 254
"For C.," 253
"The Garden," 255
Highgrade, 254
"Small Tantric Sermon," 254
White Sail (Sorrentino), 229
White Shroud (Ginsberg), 117
Whitsun Weddings, The (Larkin), 159
"Who Sees Through the Lens" (Everson), 79
"Window" (Corso), 47
"Witchita Vortex Sutra" (Ginsberg), 114

Year's Declension, The (Everson), 83